KANT AND THE
SUBJECT OF CRITIQUE

T0338940

KANT
AND THE
SUBJECT OF
CRITIQUE

ON THE REGULATIVE ROLE
OF THE PSYCHOLOGICAL IDEA

AVERY GOLDMAN

Indiana University Press
Bloomington and Indianapolis

This book is a publication of

Indiana University Press
601 North Morton Street
Bloomington, Indiana 47404-3797 USA

iupress.indiana.edu

Telephone orders   800-842-6796
Fax orders   812-855-7931

⊛ The paper used in this publication meets the minimum require-
ments of the American National Standard for Information Sciences—
Permanence of Paper for Printed Library Materials, ANSI Z39.48-1992.

Manufactured in the United States of America

Library of Congress Cataloging-in-Publication Data

Goldman, Avery, [date]
    Kant and the subject of critique : on the regulative role of
the psychological idea / Avery Goldman.
        p.   cm. — (Studies in Continental thought)
    Includes bibliographical references (p.   ) and index.
      ISBN 978-0-253-35711-3 (cloth : alk. paper) —
ISBN 978-0-253-22366-1 (pbk. : alk. paper) — ISBN 978-0-253-00540-3
(electronic book) 1. Kant, Immanuel, 1724–1804. Kritik der reinen
Vernunft. 2. Subject (Philosophy) I. Title.
B2779.G65   2012
193—dc23
                                                        2011034869

1 2 3 4 5   17 16 15 14 13 12

For Theo, Noa, and Pippa

CONTENTS

ACKNOWLEDGMENTS

This book developed over many years out of the research I undertook for my doctoral dissertation in the Philosophy Department at The Pennsylvania State University. I have benefited greatly from the involvement of both John Sallis, who directed my dissertation, and Pierre Kerszberg, with whom this research began. They offered not only important direction for my research, but also examples of the kind of scholarship that I have tried to undertake. I am indebted to them both. Special thanks go to David Farrell Krell and Rick Lee, my colleagues in DePaul University's Philosophy Department, both of whom read through drafts of the manuscript as it neared completion, and offered extremely helpful comments. Michael Baur, Andrew Cutrofello, and John Russon have all offered important assistance for my research. I have also benefited greatly from the many undergraduate and graduate students at DePaul University who have engaged with these issues in my seminars. The anonymous reviewers for Indiana University Press offered very helpful recommendations.

I would like to thank the College of Liberal Arts and Sciences and the University Research Council at DePaul University for supporting my research through grants and paid leaves. The Philosophy Department at DePaul has been an extremely hospitable environment for bringing this research to fruition. I am also grateful for the support that I received in the Philosophy Departments at Fordham University and The Pennsylvania State University. Dee Mortensen, Angela Burton, and Marvin Keenan at Indiana University Press patiently moved this project along, and Merryl Sloane offered her fine editorial eye. All are to be thanked.

Finally, I am grateful to the editors of the following journals and collections who have given me permission to include material from my previously published articles: "Kant, Heidegger, and the Circularity of Transcendental Inquiry." *Epoché* 15.1 (2010): 107–20; "What Is Orientation in Critique?" In *Recht und Frieden in der Philosophie Kants: Akten des X. Internationalen Kant-Kongresses,* ed. V. Rohden, R. Terra, G. de Almeida, and M. Ruffing, vol. 2, 245–54. Berlin: de Gruyter, 2008; "Critique and the Mind: Towards a Defense of Kant's Transcendental Method." *Kant-Studien* 98.4 (2007): 403–17; "The Metaphysics of Kantian Epistemology." In *Philosophy at the Boundary of Reason: Proceedings of the American Catholic Philosophical Association,* ed. Michael Baur, 239–52. New York: American Catholic Philosophical Association, 2003; and "Transcendental Reflection and the Boundary of Possible Experience." In *Kant und die Berliner Aufklärung: Akten des IX. Internationalen Kant-Kongresses,* ed. V. Gerhardt, R. Horstmann, and R. Schumacher, vol. 2, 289–97. Berlin: de Gruyter, 2001.

KANT AND THE
SUBJECT OF CRITIQUE

Introduction:
The Circularity of Critique

This book opens with a dilemma: Kant's *Critique of Pure Reason* (*Kritik der reinen Vernunft*) begins by rejecting the possibility of knowledge of things in themselves (noumena), restricting itself to investigating appearances (phenomena). In this way Kant is able to uncover the conditions of the possibility of experience, deducing the faculties of cognition from this limited field of appearances. But in so distinguishing the faculties of sensibility and understanding, Kant would appear to have transcended the very limits that he has set for himself, making some sort of metaphysical claim about our cognitive faculties. And so, while Kant repeatedly claims that we "know even ourselves only through inner sense, thus as appearance" (A278/B334),[1] as phenomena and not noumena, the account that he offers of the cognitive faculties would seem to be asserting something about what the self is like apart from its appearance to itself. The question with which this book begins is thus: What can be said on behalf of these faculties, namely, sensibility, with its *a priori* forms of space and time; the understanding, with its twelve *a priori* concepts; and the transcendental unity of apperception that they imply? Such a question requires that we investigate the underlying methodology of Kantian critique. Kant is clearly arguing for more than merely inductive certainty when he defines the *a priori* conditions of experience, but what claim is being made on behalf of these faculties that appear to fit comfortably within the realms of neither appearances nor things in themselves?[2] And further, what does Kant claim on behalf of such human experience, the limited, spatiotemporal field of appearances within which the analysis of the cognitive faculties takes place?

Kant admits the complexity of the relation that binds experience and the *a priori* rules that are deduced from it when, in the Transcendental Doctrine of Method, he describes "the special property [*die besondere Eigenschaft*]" of his method of proof (A737/B765). Kant explains that the principles (*Grundsätze*), the rules governing empirical objects that follow from the *a priori* concepts of the understanding, both depend upon experience in order to be proven and are themselves shown to be necessary for the designation of the realm of experience, inasmuch as already prior to their analysis these principles distinguish its confines. In the case of the modal principle of possibility (*Möglichkeit*) such circularity is especially clear: possibility is distinguished by Kant as an *a priori* condition of experience; and yet experience is itself defined by this conception of possibility, which limits experience to what can be sensibly given to a perceiving consciousness. In short, the Kantian conception of experience both permits the analysis of such *a priori* rules and follows from them.

But how can we understand such circularity? It would appear difficult to interpret Kant as naïve about his own presuppositions when he so clearly admits the dependence of his analysis of the cognitive faculties on the conception of experience from which they are deduced.[3] Martin Heidegger has emphasized such circularity in his interpretation of Kantian critique, arguing that it helps to clarify the limits of the analysis.[4] The circularity of critique points Heidegger to all that lies between the subject and the thing, the complexity of an entanglement that surpasses the attempt to designate its ground.[5] What this means for Heidegger is that we must now set aside such cognitive analysis, emphasizing instead that which precedes it.[6] But must we? Clearly an investigation of the circularity of transcendental inquiry will change the way that we view the *a priori* claims about the cognitive faculties that this method affords. But it is not so obvious that uncovering such circularity must lead us to set aside the faculties altogether, as it does for Heidegger, as if the circularity of critique marked a deficiency in the inquiry and so pointed beyond, which is to say away from, the analysis of the cognitive faculties. The present goal is to follow Heidegger in emphasizing such circularity, but rather than being led beyond the critical system I will instead investigate whether such an interpretation of Kantian circularity might not, in fact, be the key to understanding Kant's elusive transcendental method. The question then is: What can be claimed on behalf of the cognitive faculties once the circularity of their elucidation has been distinguished?

Kant offers further discussion of such circularity in his analysis of the role played by the transcendental subject, the I of the Transcendental Deduction, that brings unity to our empirical apperception and is itself but a logical inference. Such a subject, Kant explains, can be conceived only through the thoughts that it permits, offering in this way a "perpetual circle [*beständigen Zirkel*]" (B404/ A346).[7] We can say something about this underlying I only by referring to the very appearances that it is meant to explain. When we attempt to transform this transcendental subject into an object of knowledge apart from the appearances that it permits, we fall into the errors that Kant examines in the Paralogisms chapter of the *Critique of Pure Reason*: no such knowledge of the thinking self apart from the appearances it permits is attainable. The goal of such rational psychology is illusory.

However, in the appendix to the Transcendental Dialectic of the first *Critique*, which is to say, following the critique of the pursuit of metaphysical knowledge,

Kant explains that the three ideas of metaphysical pursuit—the soul, the world, and God—continue to work as regulative goals for our thinking (A671/B699). While they do not offer us knowledge of the objects of speculative metaphysics, the regulative pursuit of such ideas allows our empirical cognition to be "cultivated and corrected" (ibid.). How this is so, how each of the three ideas of reason stand as regulative goals, is not made entirely clear in this provocative section.[8] In relation to the psychological idea Kant explains that while the goal of such a rational psychology remains elusive, "nothing but advantage can arise from such a psychological idea, if only one guards against letting it hold as something more than a mere idea, i.e., if one lets it hold merely relative to the systematic use of reason in respect of the appearances of the soul" (A683/B711). In its regulative role the psychological idea directs us to look upon the subject of philosophical inquiry as unified, simple, persistent, and distinct from the spatial appearances that constitute experience, even though the psychological idea evades cognition (ibid.). We can continue to be directed by the idea of such a subject as long as we refrain from attempting to attain knowledge of it. Such direction would appear to address the initial presupposition of Kant's analysis of experience, that of a subject distinct from the objects it perceives. The goal of my inquiry will be to work out the details of this relation, connecting the metaphysical idea of the subject taken as a regulative principle and the analysis of the cognitive faculties that such a regulative principle directs.[9] Could it be that Kant's critique of metaphysics, in directing us to those uses of rational psychology that avoid proclaiming knowledge of the subject of critique, offers the key that unlocks the presuppositions of his celebrated analysis of the cognitive faculties?[10]

But even before such an analysis is undertaken it should be evident that this relation, and the use of the psychological idea in such a regulative fashion, embraces a circularity reminiscent of the circularity Kant describes for both the principles of the understanding and the transcendental subject. The idea of the subject that the psychological idea directs permits the analysis of our cognitive faculties, and yet the analysis of the cognitive faculties is what permits Kant's critique of metaphysics. Thus, Kant's analysis of the cognitive faculties both permits the critique of the metaphysical idea of the subject *and* follows from it. Kant does not explicitly describe such a regulative relation as circular, and yet he does distinguish the regulative use of the ideas of reason from the "vicious circle [*fehlerhafter Zirkel*]" into which we enter when we take a metaphysical idea, the example he uses is that of God, the "highest order being," not as distinguishing the systematic unity toward which we regulatively strive, but instead as offering the "ground" of what is to be investigated (A693/B721). To do so assumes knowledge of the object of metaphysical speculation and so subverts all regulative accomplishment.[11] The regulative use of the ideas of reason does not presuppose knowledge of such ideas; they are not the "ground" of the analysis, but the regulative goals for which we strive. So while Kant rejects such "vicious" circularity, the regulative pursuit of these ideas, which avoids claiming knowledge of their objects, would appear to offer entry into the "perpetual circle" (B404/A346) of transcendental philosophy. Kant will be seen to embrace rather than reject the circularity of his undertaking as long as such analysis avoids proclaiming metaphysical knowledge beyond our finite faculties.

Chapter 1 begins with an introduction to the problem of the subject or self of Kantian critique. Kant's three *Critiques* attempt to offer a unified picture of human reason, distinguishing both its theoretical and its practical pursuits, and yet it remains unclear what can be said of the subject that has such robust cognitive faculties. The two most obvious solutions to such a problem, the empirical and the rational self, are both ruled out by Kant. He explains that the self of critique cannot be the empirical self as it experiences itself in inner sense or empirical consciousness, because such a self, Kant repeatedly reminds us, is but an appearance and says nothing about what the self is in itself. The subject of critique also cannot be the rational self of metaphysical speculation, as we can neither prove nor disprove the truth of metaphysical speculation concerning the self. But where does this leave the investigation of the subject of critique if the empirical self is but appearance and the rational self remains elusive? Kant does appear to offer a positive account of the self in his analysis of the cognitive faculties. In Kant's account, the experience of objects requires the dual faculties of sensibility, which permits the reception of objects, and of understanding, which provides for their cognition. The Kantian self would seem to be constituted by the faculties so determined. And yet such faculties, and the subject they thus entail, are conceived only in relation to the conception of our experience of spatiotemporal objects with which critical inquiry begins. These faculties are but the conditions of the possibility of experience so conceived. If the subject of critique is that which underlies such faculties, then we must ask about the designation of the realm of experience within which these faculties have been deduced.

With such a question chapter 1 is drawn into the demand for a critique of the very terms of Kant's analysis. I will address Johann Georg Hamann's rhetorical demand for a metacritique of the Kantian critical system in order to investigate how Kant justifies the analysis of the self of experience.[12] Hamann challenges Kant's designation of the two sources of cognition, sensibility and understanding, arguing that their division distorts the very experience that it wishes to explain. Hamann concludes that any such attempt fails, inasmuch as experience surpasses any reductive analysis. In this way Hamann challenges the transcendental project, Kant's attempt to deduce the synthetic *a priori* structures of cognition. But must Kant's analysis be accepted as such a naïve reduction? Chapter 1 ends with a brief account of how Kant can be read contra Hamann. The guiding question is whether Kant's critical system offers a justification of the tools on which his analysis of the conditions of the possibility of experience depends.

Chapter 2 begins with an investigation of the self of critique insofar as it is distinguished through an analysis of spatiotemporal experience. The question that guides this chapter is whether Kant's analysis of the cognitive faculties might be related to the metaphysical conception of the unified thinking self that he investigates in the Paralogisms of Pure Reason chapter of the first *Critique*. There Kant argues that we cannot have knowledge of such a subject, but he later raises the possibility that such an idea can be used as a regulative principle, in some way guiding the investigation of our subjectivity.[13] Such a regulative role for the metaphysical idea of the subject is most provocatively addressed in the suggestive §76 of Kant's *Critique of Judgment* (*Kritik der Urteilskraft*).[14] Chapter 2 investigates this section in order to raise the possibility of such a role for the metaphysical idea of the subject in the analysis of the finite faculties. The chapter examines the ways that all three of the ideas of metaphysics that Kant addresses in the *Critique of Pure Reason*, ideas that surpass our finite faculties, are described in §76 of the *Critique of Judgment* as offering regulative accomplishment. This is most clearly demonstrated in relation to the theological idea which offers the regulative principle of the "purposiveness [*Zweckmäßigkeit*]" of nature, directing both aesthetic and teleological judgment, the topics of the *Critique of Judgment*.[15] Kant explains that in a similar way the cosmological idea can be seen to offer a regulative principle, guiding both mechanistic analysis and the pursuit of freedom. Such a regulative use of the cosmological idea reiterates the solution to the third antinomy in the *Critique of Pure Reason*, that of the contradiction between mechanism and freedom. Kant goes on to write in §76 that the analysis of our finite faculties depends upon a regulative principle; but how this is so is not easily explained. In the *Critique of Pure Reason*, Kant argues against the possibility of knowledge of the three ideas of reason—the soul, the world, and God—explaining, however, that all three metaphysical ideas can be used hypothetically, directing our inquiries in ways that avoid error.[16] It is clear that two of these ideas of reason, the theological (God) and the cosmological (the world), are being addressed in §76, and it would appear that the third, the psychological (the soul), is here being raised by Kant as the regulative principle governing the designation of our finite faculties. This section in the *Critique of Judgment* is suggestive, but its claims remain elusive. To address the role that a regulative principle, following from the metaphysical investigation of the rational subject, plays in the analysis of the cognitive faculties and so what claim it offers on behalf of the subject of critique, we will first need to investigate how a regulative principle could be thought to play *any* role in the designation of the *a priori* structures of cognition.

Chapter 3 returns to look at the *Critique of Pure Reason* with the regulative insights of the *Critique of Judgment*. The question that guides this chapter concerns whether Kant's analysis of finite cognition can be said to depend upon a regulative principle born of our metaphysical inquiries into the soul. At first glance this would appear surprising, since Kant offers the analysis of the *a priori* elements of cognition without discussion of the dependence of this analysis on any such presupposition. For this reason interpreters have attempted either to naturalize Kant's epistemology, which is to say claim that the cognitive faculties so described are self-evident, or else, against Kant's own claims, to proclaim him a realist, transforming the analysis of appearances into one of things in themselves.[17] Neither approach takes the metacritical demand seriously, because neither questions the conception of experience with which Kant's analysis begins. Kant deduces the dualism of sensibility and understanding from the initial presupposition that experience, which for Kant means spatiotemporal perception, is that with which our philosophical inquiries should begin, and yet one could, and perhaps must, still ask about the presuppositions of this starting point.

Such a presupposition is most clearly evident in the Analytic of Principles (*Grundsätze*) of the first *Critique*. Chapter 3 continues with an analysis focusing on the chapter of the Principles titled the Postulates of Empirical Thought, emphasizing the role that the postulates of possibility and actuality play in Kant's account of experience. These modal rules designate all the previously distinguished characteristics of objects as conforming to the distinction between the possible and the actual. As mentioned above, in the Transcendental Doctrine of Method that closes the first *Critique* Kant describes this need to presuppose the conception of experience in order to elucidate apodictic principles (*Grundsätze*) as the "special property" of his method of proof (A737/B765). The *a priori* concepts of the understanding and the principles that follow from them are deduced from the conception of experience, and yet this conception of experience has itself been distinguished by means of just these principles. Heidegger, in his 1935–1936 lecture course, published under the title *What Is a Thing?* (*Die Frage nach dem Ding*), develops an interpretation that emphasizes the dual role of the modal principles: they designate the terrain of Kantian critique and are themselves a product of it.[18] Heidegger interprets such circularity, implicit in the Kantian analysis of objects, as drawing us beyond the subject-object divide or, rather, into this divide, emphasizing that such circularity points toward that which lies between the things and us, that which precedes such a division.[19] In this way, Heidegger continues the emphasis of his earlier *Kant and the Problem of Metaphysics* (*Kant und das Problem der Metaphysik*) on that toward which Kant's analysis points: to the elusive transcendental imagination that Heidegger speculatively raises as the "common root" of the cognitive faculties.[20] While following Heidegger's emphasis on the circularity of the Kantian undertaking, I will proceed by following Kant in "shrinking back

[*Zuruckweichen*],"[21] as Heidegger charges, from the nether reaches of critique, but rather than remaining quiet about the presuppositions of the critical system, as Kant mainly does, I will instead investigate the method that permits him such range. The question then concerns what it is that allows Kant to point beyond critique; in this way I will not be rejecting the ontological inquiry that Heidegger undertakes but instead will investigate the circular system that permits Kant to describe what Heidegger calls "the between—between us and the thing [*das Zwischen—zwischen uns und dem Ding*]."[22]

To this end chapter 3 concludes with a discussion of Kant's Refutation of Idealism, which he inserted into the Postulates, directly after the discussions of the principles of possibility and actuality, in the second edition of the *Critique of Pure Reason*. The goal of this section is to interpret Kant's notoriously difficult refutation in light of the circularity announced by the section within which it was placed. Kant argues that any analysis of the temporal nature of conscious-ness presupposes "something **persistent** [*etwas Beharrliches*]" (B275) apart from consciousness. Kant explains that such a "thing outside me [*Ding außer mir*]" is not merely a representation but is in some way beyond the realm of appearances (ibid.). Interpreters have struggled with the question of what Kant means by the reference to something "outside me" that is not an appearance. How could Kant be inferring knowledge of a metaphysical object when he so persuasively argues that such knowledge is beyond our finite faculties? The suggestion that I will make in this chapter is that such a "thing outside me" can be understood to be referring to all that is juxtaposed with the regulative principle of the subject: we can describe our temporal consciousness, and so examine our cognitive faculties, only in relation to the idea of the thinking subject that distinguishes itself from objects outside of it; the subject of critique must be presupposed in order to examine the qualities of just such a subject. The chapter will offer the beginning of such an interpretation of Kant's Refutation of Idealism in line with that of the circularity of Kantian critique, an interpretation that will be fully developed in this book's concluding chapter.

Chapter 4 continues the investigation of the Kantian conception of experi-ence, focusing on the account of transcendental reflection raised by Kant in an appendix to the Transcendental Analytic of the *Critique of Pure Reason*. In so doing I once again follow Heidegger's lead, this time in connecting the elusive discussion of possibility and actuality in §76 of the *Critique of Judgment* to the reflective parsing of the field of representations that Kant introduces as a "duty" (A263/B319) that is necessary in order to discover anything about the *a priori* conditions of experience.[23]

Kant argues that in order to pursue cognition in the limited phenomenal realm of possible experience we must already have distinguished those represen-tations that can be sensibly compared from those that can only be intellectually compared. We must distinguish those representations that offer objects that permit the differentiation of possibility and actuality from those whose objects could be conceived as existing without any connection of their actuality to possibility. This is to say that we must distinguish those representations that are merely temporal, those of inner sense, from those that conform to both temporal and spatial forms of intuition, those of outer sense, for those representations that offer themselves only to our intellectual faculties, those thoughts that have no empirical determination, are still temporal. They are thought, or represented, in a manner that necessitates their temporal ordering, and yet they offer no spatial appearance that would allow our finite faculties to be analyzed.

In Heidegger's late essay "Kant's Thesis about Being [*Kants These über das Sein*]," he interprets Kant's account of transcendental reflection as a reflection on the relation of the knowing subject to the objects known, explaining it as the mark of the "double role" that thought must be conceived as playing: thought designates both the reflective positing of the existence of objects and the "situating" of such positing, a reflection on this reflective designation of being that Kant calls "transcendental reflection."[24] Transcendental reflection thus explains how critical philosophy determines the boundary within which the analysis of cognition takes place. This designation is itself described by Kant as a reflective act, and yet in this appendix Kant does not explain how this act, announced as fundamental to the critical enterprise, can be justified. The question then is: Can this second-order reflection be explained within the conceptual system that its use affords? Heidegger holds out no hope for such a thematization of the method of Kantian inquiry, directing us instead beyond critique to that which precedes the Kantian reflection, and from out of which Kant so designated being. What this chapter will investigate is whether transcendental reflection, like other reflective accomplishments in the Kantian system, is dependent upon a regulative principle for its parsing of representations. This is to ask whether transcendental reflection can be conceived, in the manner of all other Kantian acts of reflection, as depending upon a regulative principle. I will attempt to interpret the methodology of Kant's inquiry from the seeming paradox of his circular inquiry. Such an investigation will bring us back to the analysis of chapter 2 where, in examining §76 of the *Critique of Judgment*, I ask whether the psychological idea could be understood as offering a regulative principle for the designation of our cognitive faculties as finite. This can now be understood as asking whether the psychological idea offers the regulative principle of transcendental reflection. Such a question will make it clear that we are no longer asking, with Hamann, for a metacritique of the tools of the analysis of finite cognition; rather, we are asking, contra Hegel's interpretation of Kant, whether there might not be a justifiable role for Kant's metaphysics in his analysis of finite cognition.[25]

Chapter 5 offers a discussion of the critique of rational psychology in the Paralogisms of Pure Reason chapter as it is set forth in both the first and the second editions of the *Critique of Pure Reason*. While in both versions this chapter argues that knowledge of the subject, the rational self, resists our finite faculties, this does not make such a critique merely negative. Kant's argument is that such knowledge is unattainable, that we cannot infer anything determinate about the merely logical I that stands as the basis of all claims about our faculties; but these arguments do not rule out the possibility of continuing to speak about the self in ways that avoid such cognitive claims. The chapter follows the path of these arguments, the four routes offered in the first edition as well as the single overarching version that is the focus of the second edition, in order to elucidate what is left of such inquiries into the subject of critique when these errors are avoided. The issue relevant for the current investigation concerns what can be said of the rational self, the subject of critique, when all hope of determinate knowledge has been dashed.

While no metaphysical knowledge concerning the thinking subject is possible, the critique of rational psychology distinguishes the conception of subjectivity that is required for the analysis of the experience of objects and that, while uncognizable, does not lead to contradiction. In the first edition's Paralogisms chapter Kant explains that such a conception of the self must bring to these inquiries the division of inner and outer sense, the designation of the field of the inquiry into finite cognition, even though such a division cannot be determined (A385). The task that remains is to show that when such an inquiry can be directed away from all determinate claims, it can function as a regulative principle, directing the division of the unknown subject from the objects it perceives, and so permitting the analysis of the subject's cognitive faculties. In this way, the illusory metaphysical idea of a rational subject, demanded like all ideas of reason, "with every right [*mit allem Recht*]" (Bxx), will be shown to explain the presuppositions implicit in the orienting act of transcendental reflection and thus in the analysis of cognition that it affords.

Chapter 6 begins with a discussion of Kant's 1786 "What Does It Mean to Orient Oneself in Thinking? [Was heißt: sich im Denken orientieren?]."[26] In this essay, Kant raises a conception of orientation that extends beyond the spatial to the sort of orientation in thought that appears relevant for questions concerning the presuppositions of critique. Kant argues that our orientation in thought depends upon ideas of reason that help to guide our thinking by offering it direction without proclaiming determinate cognition. In this concluding chapter, I investigate both the origins of Kant's essay, namely, the pantheism controversy that led to its writing, and the way in which the orienting role of the ideas of reason can be conceived in terms of regulative principles.[27]

Chapter 6 then goes on to investigate the account of "the hypothetical use of reason [*der hypothetische Gebrauche der Vernunft*]" (A647/B675) that Kant offers in the appendix to the Transcendental Dialectic of the first *Critique*. Kant here describes the regulative use of each of the three ideas of reason: the soul, the world, and God. It is the first idea, the soul, the object of rational psychology, that can now be understood to play a vital role in the designation of the region of experience within which the analysis of finite cognition takes place. Kant explains that the regulative use of the psychological idea permits the representation of "all **appearances** in space as entirely distinct from the actions of **thinking** [*den Handlungen des Denkens*]" (A683/B711). It is such a division, the subject of critique as distinct from the objects it perceives, that is accomplished by the act of transcendental reflection. And such an act, I will argue, is dependent upon a regulative principle born of the psychological idea.

The unknowable idea of the rational subject is used to designate the field of the inquiry into the cognitive faculties of just such a subject. The critical analysis of experience is therefore a regulative and not a constitutive project. The unified faculties of the thinking subject are pursued within the field of appearances, and this relation is itself directed by the psychological idea. Kant has begun his analysis of the conditions of the possibility of objects of experience with an implicit adherence to a conception of the relation of objects to the subjects for whom they appear, for the objects constitutive of the experience of this subject are limited to those that spatially appear.

The chapter then investigates the implications associated with finding such a regulative principle at the heart of the critical analysis of cognition. Kant's elusive claim in the Refutation of Idealism, examined in chapter 3, is that any examination of temporal consciousness depends upon "something **persistent** [*Beharrliches*]" (B275) apart from consciousness. Such a persisting thing, Kant explains, is not merely a representation, implying that it is outside us in some way that is not merely that of the spatiality of appearances. What I argue is that the idea of objects apart from the perceiving subject, the regulative principle born of the psychological idea, offers just such a persisting thing for our analysis. Beyond the help that this analysis of the regulative role of the psychological idea offers for solving particular textual difficulties, it will more generally allow for an explanation of the overarching method of transcendental inquiry.

The Kantian conception of orientation will help to bring together both the regulative role of the psychological idea announced in the appendix to the Transcendental Dialectic of the *Critique of Pure Reason,* and the elusive reference in §76 of the *Critique of Judgment* to the role that a regulative principle plays in the designation of finite cognition. After the critique of the cognitive pretensions of rational psychology in the Paralogisms, the idea of the rational subject continues to direct Kant's analysis of the cognitive faculties. What this idea offers is the regulative principle of the subject distinct from the objects that it thinks, the guiding idea of Kantian transcendental reflection in which the field of critical inquiry is designated. And the dependence of the analysis of cognition on a regulative principle, on an idea of reason that is itself dependent for its elucidation on the very analysis of cognition that it permits, announces the circularity of the critical enterprise. What I will argue is that such circularity is not merely a narrowly circumscribed account of the analysis of transcendental subjectivity but is more generally the method of Kant's undertaking, describing the designation of the realm of experience by means of the regulative principle emanating from the psychological idea. Such a regulative principle will be shown to both permit the analysis of cognition and follow from it. The question of the subject of critique will not yield the sort of answer that Hamann rhetorically demanded and that Kant interpreters have often literally pursued,[28] but it will also not be able to avoid all such suppositions by following Heidegger back to the ontological source of cognition. What the question of the subject of critique offers is a way to elucidate the methodology of Kantian critique by means of an investigation of the presuppositions with which Kant's analysis begins.

ONE

The Ideas of Reason

I. The Subject of Critique

What, in the end, does Kant have to say about the self, the subject as the locus of both cognition and action, the I whose reason tends toward both theoretical and practical pursuits? Such a question is more elusive than one might expect from a writer who so carefully addresses the intricacies of our cognitive faculties. The difficulty of such a task, as well as Kant's ambivalence toward it, is summed up in the opening pages of his *Anthropology from a Pragmatic Point of View (Anthropologie in pragmatischer Hinsicht)*, where he explains:

> He who ponders natural phenomena, for example, what the causes of the faculty of memory [*Erinnerungsvermögen*] rest on, can speculate back and forth (like Descartes) over the traces of impressions remaining in the brain, but in doing so he must admit that in this play of his representations he is a mere spectator [*bloßer Zuschauer*] and must let nature run its course, for he does not know the cranial nerves and fibers, nor does he understand how to put them to use for his purposes.[1]

Even after the exhaustive analysis of the cognitive faculties undertaken in the three critiques, the workings of the mind remain elusive. Kant explains that we cannot trace our sensory experience to its source, offering the example of the faculty of memory, but his point is intended more generally: the attempt to examine our thought is confounded by the problem that we can only speculate on the sources of that which appears, and doing so, Kant concludes, is a "pure waste of time."[2]

More than two hundred years after Kant offered this criticism of what he calls "physiological anthropology" in his *Anthropology*, corresponding to empirical psychology in the *Critique of Pure Reason*,[3] there has no doubt been progress made in the way that we are able to investigate the mind and so map its varied powers.[4] Yet Kant's criticism of empirical psychology is not that he found himself in the unfortunate position of lacking some data or tool that could at some later point be found, offering a solution for the vexing difficulties concerning self-knowledge; rather, Kant addresses self-knowledge in the same way that he addresses knowledge of objects outside us. What philosophy lacks is any criteria that could offer us proof that our claims about the world, however seemingly well founded, however much progress they may appear to offer, actually correspond to the truth of the world. And the truths that transcendental philosophy calls into question include that of the self.

Kant's Copernican turn famously begins his transcendental undertaking by setting aside all question of things in themselves, as they would exist apart from us, and investigates instead the way that objects appear (Bxvi). Like Copernicus, who conceived of the motion of the earth from the apparent motion of the solar system, Kant distinguishes the cognitive faculties that are required for the manner in which objects appear. In this way Kant can be seen to have embraced rather than responded to Hume's skepticism, accepting that causal necessity is not to be found apart from human thought. Hume famously describes the mind as a theater, offering ever more discrete impressions.[5] Kant, in his *Anthropology*, calls us, in a like way, "mere spectator[s]" when we attempt to offer an account of the mind solely from our representations. This is a Humean insight: we are but spectators in the theater of the mind, forever removed from not only the truth of that which appears, but also from the manner of its presentation.

The *Critique of Pure Reason* is written from such a theoretically skeptical perspective, from, that is to say, the recognition that we cannot conceive of the mind in its actual workings, and that if we are to avoid limiting ourselves to a Humean investigation of our habits, which is to say to a "pragmatic anthropology," if we are to say something about our faculties, including the elusive imagination, in an *a priori* fashion, then we must embrace the experiment of transcendental inquiry.[6] And yet, within the "turn" that initiates Kant's transcendental inquiry, he retains the distinction between the perceiving subject and the objects such a subject perceives, importing into this inside the very confidence in the distinction between subject and object that the Copernican turn would have us reject. To explain that such a distinction now holds only for appearances, and so the rationalist certainty that Hume challenged has been overturned, does not explain why this reinstated distinction is valid even for appearances.

One need only look at the first edition's preface, where Kant explains that his analysis offers the completion of metaphysics, describing it as "the **inventory** of all that we possess through pure reason" (Axx), to see Kant's confidence in his analysis from his newfound perspective. Such confidence is particularly surprising when one takes into consideration the first edition's Third Paralogism, where Kant proposes a skepticism much more radical than that of the Humean/Cartesian variety. Kant raises the possibility that the self, rather than being the unity of the temporal moments that consciousness offers, might in fact be an unconnected succession, a series of discrete moments in the manner of balls striking one another, with no stable identity for the whole of this temporal chain

(A363–64n); and so the appearance of temporal unity, the subject of inner sense, the Cartesian *cogito*, or even, one could say, the Humean "theater" or "bundle," might in fact be illusory.[7] Kant was clearly aware that the self as conceived in inner sense could be challenged, that its temporal unity could be illusory, and yet he maintained the identity of such an inside, even going so far as marking off within this inner temporal continuity a region of outer appearances. While one might be tempted to explain away Kant's first-edition confidence in reason as his initial enthusiasm for his undertaking, which was tempered in the second edition, even the second edition maintains the distinction between inner and outer within the Copernican-inspired self. The question then is twofold: What justifies this continued commitment to the distinction between the thinking subject and the appearances it perceives, between an inside and an outside that, because of the Copernican turn, is no longer conceived as properly outside us but is now merely a property of that which appears within us? And further, what can be said about the self that is so conceived?

In the second edition of the *Critique of Pure Reason*, among other changes and additions offered six years after this work's initial publication, Kant returns repeatedly to the question concerning the sort of claim that he has offered on behalf of the self, the subject of critique. Kant finds it necessary to include three reminders to the reader that the self that this work offers is but appearance and so offers no cognition of what it is in itself. This is to say that the phenomenal appearance of the subject to itself in inner sense, the temporal self-affection of the subject, does not offer the cognition of subjectivity as it is in itself, as it would appear if its faculty of intuition were intellectual. In this way, the second edition confirms the claims made in the first edition, where Kant, in the Transcendental Aesthetic, briefly remarks that the self, the object of inner sense, is but appearance (A36/B53); and such a claim is made as well in the Paralogisms of Pure Reason chapter of the Transcendental Dialectic, where Kant explains that we can no more infer the "actuality [*Wirklichkeit*] of external objects" than we can the self or soul, "the objects of my inner sense" (A371).[8] In the second edition Kant returns to these issues concerning the limits of our self-knowledge, doing so in a way that highlights the importance of this question for the overall project of his transcendental system.

In the Transcendental Aesthetic of the second edition, in concluding his discussion of inner sense, Kant explains that it must be understood as "the way in which the mind is affected by its own activity" (B68), and such a self-representation remains but appearance and cannot be thought to offer the self as it is in itself, as it would if our intuition were intellectual. Kant repeats this claim in the second edition's rewritten Transcendental Deduction, describing such temporal self-affection as the empirical consciousness that offers "no cognition of myself as I am, but only as I appear to myself" (B158). And even earlier in the rewritten

Transcendental Deduction, Kant adds a much lengthier warning against misconceiving the nature of the empirical claim about the self, and he does so in a way that hints at the importance of this question for his critical project.

Kant describes the issue concerning how inner sense "presents [*darstelle*]" us to ourselves only as appearance as a "paradox" (B152). The "paradox" concerns the way that we affect ourselves. If, as Kant explains, we "intuit ourselves only as we are internally **affected**" then we "would have to relate passively to ourselves" (B153).[9] This is to say that if we accept the critical limits on our cognition, then we need to understand ourselves as both affecting and affected, as the active agent through which we are given to ourselves and as the passive recipient of the self. This dilemma might lead us to conflate these two roles. To do so, Kant writes, would be "to treat **inner sense** as the same as the faculty of **apperception**" (ibid.), and so to proclaim the possibility of an intellectual intuition by means of which we would know ourselves, not as we appear, but as we are in ourselves. To avoid such metaphysical speculation, Kant carefully maintains the distinction between the passivity of inner sense and the activity of the understanding and its transcendental apperception through which sensibility is affected by the self. Transcendental apperception brings unity to the sensible manifold, unifying the given that is offered through the categories (A108).[10] Our inner sense is affected by means of this cognitive act of unification, but such a cognitive activity occurs only in relation to outer sense and its spatial appearances, which are determined by the categories, while inner sense and its merely temporal appearances offer no such possibility of cognition, so evading the determination of the categories. Kant explains that this is clear to us when we attempt to think about the temporal intuition of our inner sense, for time, as a succession, can only be represented through the image of a line, the spatial determination that permits us any representation of temporal unity (B156).[11] This is the case, Kant implies, for all determinations of inner sense: they can be determined only in relation to spatial appearances through which inner sense is affected by the understanding, and so by outer sense; the I is determined in this relation of inner to outer sense. In this way we are offered the appearance of the self insofar as inner sense is passively affected by the unity of apperception.[12] Our self-affection is thus constituted in relation to the spatial objects of experience.

Kant explains that the apparent contradiction that surrounds inner sense, which relates to the question of how we can be passively affected by ourselves, is answered by conceiving of space as "a mere pure form of the appearances of outer sense" through which objects of both inner and outer sense remain but appearances (B156). Our empirical apperception thus includes both passive and active elements: the passive reception of inner sense and the active affection of this sense, performed by the transcendental unity of apperception in relation to spatial appearances. It is thus clear why Kant explains that the answer to the question of how we can be an object for ourselves is just as difficult as the question of "how the I that I think is to differ from the I that intuits itself . . . and yet be identical with the latter as the same subject" (B155). Kant answers the question of how we can be an object for ourselves, that is to say, how it is that passivity and activity can coexist not only in a single self but in a single act, by distinguishing between our inner sense and the cognition that determines it. While describing the self in this dualistic manner allows Kant to argue that passivity and activity need not contradict, the self or subject that is so distinguished remains elusive. This is to say that the contradiction of passive and active elements is only apparent, but the paradox that they entail, a disparate self that is in some sense unified, is real.[13]

Perhaps one could say that such an emphasis on our empirical self-awareness in the search for the nature of the subject of critique yields only appearance, and points toward the self's paradoxical nature, but one would be overlooking Kant's true accomplishment. To begin such an inquiry with the conception of the self as empirically self-affected may in this way exaggerate the importance for Kant of the empirical self, and in this way minimize the transcendental analysis of the subjective faculties that is grounded in the deduction of the categories of the understanding as the conditions of the possibility of objects of experience. Is not the faculty of understanding, constituted by the categories, the twelve *a priori* concepts of the understanding, the true self of the Kantian system? And yet, Kant explains, in themselves these categories are empty, requiring sensible givenness in order to offer determinate cognition; their universality must be paired with particularity if they are to avoid being empty abstractions.[14] These categories comprise the faculty of understanding insofar as they afford us the cognition of "objects [*Gegenstände*]." This is to say that their authority follows from the initial presupposition that such objects constitute the limited terrain of cognition.[15] While it is clear that such a faculty dictates the subjective sources of the cognition of objects, it is not nearly so clear, even after Kant's meticulous analysis, what can be said of the subject that is composed of such faculties. Kant has analyzed the cognitive faculties that are needed for the experience of objects—the faculties of sensibility and understanding, and the imagination that connects them—and yet we are no nearer to the elucidation of the subject, or self, of critique, for the self of such categories is dependent upon the distinction of inner and outer sense, and the analysis of its faculties in relation to the spatial objects deemed external to it. In pursuing the structure of phenomenal experience, while avoiding all claim to noumenal reality, it is not obvious what sort of assertion Kant is making on behalf of these faculties, the *a priori* conditions of phenomenal appearances.[16]

And if such an inquiry into the subject of critique turns to the transcendental unity of apperception that underlies all cognitive synthesis as the thinking self, the I that Kant recognizes must be presupposed in all thinking, what we find is that this unifying "I think" of self-consciousness has no attendant intuition and is thus utterly empty of all cognitive content (A401–402). Kant explains that this "I think" cannot be an object for itself and thus cannot be known phenomenally because it is the presupposition of all cognition.[17] In order to analyze the conditions of the possibility of experience we must presuppose the unity of apperception. Nothing more can be said of the thinking self, "this I, or He, or It (the thing) [*dieses Ich, oder Er, oder Es (das Ding)*], which thinks," than that it is the "transcendental subject of thoughts = x";[18] and such a subject, as the unity of apperception, can be conceived only through the thoughts that it permits (B404/A346). Kant explains that our philosophical inquiries uncover in this way a "perpetual circle [*beständigen Zirkel*]" (ibid.):[19] in order to say something about this subject, the transcendental unity of apperception, to make an empirical judgment about it which would synthetically fill out our merely analytic claim, we would need to make use of the very unity that we want to explain. And for this reason, Kant explains, "the subject of the categories cannot, by thinking them, obtain a concept of itself as an object [*Objekt*] of the categories" (B422).[20]

And we cannot avoid the limitations implied by such circularity by attempting to transform the subject as a logical unity into a metaphysical claim about this self. Any attempt to attain such non-sensible knowledge fails, as Kant shows in the Paralogisms chapter of the first *Critique*. Kant rejects the attempt to transform the "I think" of apperception into an object of rational cognition; and yet, it is the "powers [*Kräfte*]" (A683/B711) of just such an idea of a rational subject that, in the second part of the appendix to the Transcendental Dialectic of the *Critique of Pure Reason,* titled On the Final Aim of the Natural Dialectic of Human Reason, Kant tells us to pursue in the examination of our representations. Kant writes that reason's principles of systematic unity direct us to pursue the unity of the self

> by considering all determinations as in one subject, all powers [*Kräfte*], as far as possible, as derived from one unique fundamental power [*Grundkraft*], all change as belonging to the states of one and the same persistent being, and by representing all **appearances** in space as entirely distinct from the actions of **thinking** [*den Handlungen des Denkens*]. (A682–83/B710–11)

Even after the paralogistic failure to attain knowledge of the simple subject, reason continues to direct us to pursue its fourfold unity, and so to look upon the subject of philosophical inquiry as unified, simple, persistent, and distinct from spatial appearances.[21] To do so goes further than the mere logical unity offered by transcendental apperception, since what Kant calls for is not merely the condition of the unity of perceptual experience, but a commitment to the idea of such a rational subject in the context of a discussion of the uses of metaphysics after the rejection of its cognitive pretensions.[22]

Kant's announcement of the need for a continued commitment to the idea of the rational subject does not represent a return to the metaphysical pursuit of knowledge in the three areas of reason that surpass our finite faculties, those corresponding to the psychological, cosmological, and theological ideas. On the contrary, rather than dragging us back into these illusions, reason makes use of the critique of metaphysics to develop our finite faculties of thinking in ways that are *not* premised on the attainment of metaphysical knowledge. By designating the objects of metaphysical thought as illusory and the arguments used to determine them as flawed, Kant's Transcendental Dialectic has distinguished the limitations of metaphysical thought;[23] and in so doing, in identifying the errors that follow from our attempts to treat metaphysical ideas as finite objects, Kant has sketched a map that directs our metaphysical thought away from such illusory claims. Rather than ending all metaphysical inquiry, this critique directs our safe passage through the dangers of metaphysics, permitting the development of our finite modes of thinking in ways that avoid such errors.

Reason, when thoroughly critiqued, does not neuter itself. However, its progeny are not the purified truths of metaphysical dreams. By avoiding all claim to metaphysical knowledge, reason is able to make use of the metaphysical ideas it pursues in order to further develop our finite faculties. The critique of the pursuit of metaphysics initiated by Kant uncovers the illusory nature of these goals, and rather than merely marking the territory beyond which we should not advance, and so retreating into the safety of our finite faculties, this critique provides a way to advance into the territory of metaphysics without being enticed by its illusory offerings. Through the use of the ideas of reason as goals to be pursued and not as objects to be cognized we can develop our finite faculties in diverse ways that avoid all claims to metaphysical knowledge. But how can such a development say something about the subject of critique, the self of these finite faculties, which appears to be not a product of this critique of metaphysics, but in fact its presupposition?

In the appendix to the Transcendental Dialectic of the first *Critique*, Kant makes use of the threefold goal of metaphysical knowledge in the pursuit of what he calls "the hypothetical use of reason" (A647/B675). Such regulative pursuit of the psychological, cosmological, and theological ideas of metaphysics directs the development of our finite faculties in ways that avoid the errors that are usually associated with such metaphysical interests. The clearest explanation of the regulative appropriation of the ideas of metaphysics within critical philosophy is to be found in Kant's examination of teleology in the *Critique of Judgment*. In this work, Kant proceeds beyond the mechanistic explanation of nature and explains the further possibility of a teleological account of the systematic unity of nature's mechanistic laws. This teleological investigation is directed by the idea of the systematic order of the world, what Kant calls the "purposiveness" of nature, a regulative idea that corresponds to the unknowable theological idea in Kant's critique of metaphysics in the first *Critique*.[24] Such a pursuit avoids all attempts to hypostatize this idea, to transform the thought of a super-sensible being into an object to be known, and yet affords the development of our account of nature, combining mechanistic laws into ever more developed systems.

The account of teleology offers an example of the Kantian use of regulative ideas: an idea of reason, after its critique, is shown to offer regulative guidance in the post-critical region of metaphysics, offering a way to proceed beyond what is afforded by the understanding. In this way, with teleological inquiry following mechanistic analysis, it would appear that the regulative use of metaphysics follows the use of the *a priori* concepts of the understanding to determine experience; and yet, the division of judgment insofar as it can both determine and reflect, of judgment in relation to understanding and reason, respectively, is not so clear. Kant explains that mechanistic analysis is itself driven by the cosmological idea, the idea of reason that posits the completion of the chain of causal nature, and so directs the examination of ever-further causal laws.[25] But is this all that can be said for the regulative use of metaphysics in the Kantian system? Does it direct only mechanistic and teleological pursuits, leaving no regulative role for the psychological idea? If there is no hypothetical role to be found for the idea of rational psychology, if the regulative use of metaphysical ideas can only be understood to follow from the analysis of cognition and not to direct it, then this analysis of cognition, the Kantian epistemology and the conception of the thinking subject that is implied in it, must be understood to claim that it is free of all metaphysical presuppositions.[26] And yet, does not the analysis of the conditions of the possibility of experience, the designation of the cognitive faculties of the finite subject, depend upon the critique of metaphysics insofar as it is able to avoid the illusory goals of metaphysics in beginning its inquiries within the limited field of phenomenal objects? Such a question directs this investigation to the problems that surround the general orientation of Kant's critical system.

Kant begins the *Critique of Pure Reason* with an analysis of both the sensible and the intellectual preconditions of synthetic cognition, building from this start the conceptual apparatus that permits the critique of metaphysics. But we must still wonder about the metaphysical presuppositions of this starting point, of the examination of experience, and hence of spatial appearances as the limited font of our *a priori* cognition and so our cognitive faculties. Such a beginning point presupposes that metaphysical knowledge is beyond our grasp, and that human knowledge is limited to, which is also to say attainable in, the sphere of the spatial appearances of empirical objects; and it is such a conception of the subject of finite cognition that Kant would appear to be addressing when, in the above-quoted passage from the appendix to the Transcendental Dialectic, he directs us to continue to conceive of the subject of thought in opposition to the objects that it thinks, even as such a division remains elusive (A682–83/B710–11). Kant is even clearer about the role of the subject, or soul, in the Transcendental Doctrine of Method that closes the first *Critique:*

> It is entirely permissible to **think** the soul as simple in order, in accordance with this **idea**, to make a complete and necessary unity of all powers of the mind [*Gemütskräfte*], even though one cannot have insight into it *in concreto*, into the principle [*Prinzip*] of our judgment of its inner appearances [*inneren Erscheinungen*]. (A771–72/B799–800)

But how exactly does the idea of the soul permit us to bring unity to the "powers of the mind" without leading us into metaphysical speculation? Kant does not say, reminding us merely that we must not "assume" that such a simple soul exists even as its thought directs the examination of our powers. The task of this inquiry is to work out what role is played by a regulative principle related to the psychological idea, the soul, in Kant's analysis of *a priori* cognition. This is to ask: What role does the Kantian critique of metaphysics play in the celebrated epistemology that, at least in its presentation in the *Critique of Pure Reason,* precedes it?

With such questions we have returned to the issue of the circularity of transcendental inquiry. In the passage quoted above Kant describes the transcendental subject, that which brings unity to cognition but which does not offer itself as an object of cognition, as initiating a "perpetual circle" (B404/A346). Any cognitive claim about such an underlying subject already presupposes just such subjectivity. And in the Transcendental Doctrine of Method of the first *Critique,* in discussing the "principles [*Grundsätze*]" of the understanding, Kant describes such circularity, or "self-referentiality," as the "special property [*besondere Eigenschaft*]" of this method of proof (A737/B765).[27] Transcendental inquiry is marked by such circularity, and what I am arguing is that this is not merely a feature of this or that argument, of transcendental subjectivity or the principles of the understanding, but instead that such circularity can be seen to describe the overarching methodology of Kant's transcendental inquiry. The regulative role of the psychological idea will be shown to be required for the designation of the terrain of the analysis of cognition; and such a use of the metaphysical idea of the subject can avoid the errors of metaphysical speculation only by means of the analysis of cognition that permits the uncovering of such illusions. What this means is that the metaphysical idea of the subject, taken as a regulative principle, will be shown to depend upon the very analysis of cognition that it permits, demonstrating the "special property" of Kant's inquiry.

If we return with the question concerning the basic orientation of the critical system to Kant's claim that we need to continue pursuing the elusive subject of metaphysical speculation (A671–72 / B699–700), we will be able to develop the critical response to the apparent naïveté of his epistemological analysis. In telling us to regard the subject of philosophical inquiry as unified, simple, persistent, and distinct from spatial appearances, Kant has directed the regulative use of the psychological idea, the soul as the object of our metaphysical concerns.[28] By pursuing the analysis of cognition guided by the idea of the subject of metaphysics, even though it does not offer itself for cognition, we are able to investigate the subjective structure of the experience of objects. Without such a presupposition, without pursuing an analysis of cognition under the direction of the idea of the nature of the subject, which is to say a subject that is distinct from the objects it perceives, our philosophical investigation would be unable to escape the radical incoherence of the representational manifold. Why should philosophical reflection begin its task with an unflagging confidence in the objects that it purports to investigate? And further, what directs its certainty that such an analysis offers the systematic structure of our cognitive faculties? The investigation called for by such questions has two parts: first, we must connect the intricacies of Kant's analysis of cognition to the underlying subject of critique; and second, if this justification of the philosophical orientation of the critical project is to be found in the regulative use of the fourfold paralogistic failure to attain knowledge of the rational subject, then this metaphysical presupposition must be shown to avoid restoring the very metaphysical illusion that it is meant to correct.

To pursue such questions is to enter into an investigation of the subject of the reflective project of critical inquiry. Kant has begun his analysis of the conditions of the possibility of objects of experience with an implicit adherence to a conception of the relation of objects to the subject for whom they appear, since the objects constitutive of the experience of this subject are limited to their spatial appearances; and yet the cognition that we have of ourselves is, as has been discussed above, merely appearance (B157–59). The conception of the subject, the self of thought with which the first *Critique* proceeds, remains elusive.

Could the regulative pursuit of this metaphysical subject explain the underlying conception of subjectivity that directs Kant's epistemological analysis? Such a question leads us to an interpretation of the critical account of the conditions of the possibility of experience that designates them as accomplishments that follow from the regulative pursuit of the goals distinguished by rational psychology. If we are to say that the subject of critique is in some sense a regulative claim, that its pursuit is directed by an unknowable and yet non-contradictory metaphysical idea, which is precisely what I will argue, then we will have to investigate what this means for such an inquiry's epistemological claims; for if there is a metaphysical conception of subjectivity embedded in Kant's designation of experience, but one pursued regulatively and not as an object of cognition, then what will be required is a reinterpretation of the transcendental method that it demonstrates. Kant's insistence that we continue to conceive of the unity of the "fundamental power [*Grundkraft*]" of our perceptual experience, and so maintain the metaphysical conception of the subject even as attempts to gain knowledge of it fail, will thus be seen to refer to the presuppositions of the critical account of cognition. We cannot deny all interest in the metaphysical conception of the subject, for doing so would be unfaithful to the beginnings of the critique in which we have been directed by just such an idea; and yet it is also true that it is by means of beginning his epistemological analysis without reference to its metaphysical presuppositions that Kant is able to distinguish a conceptual language that permits both the critique of metaphysics and the designation of the conception of subjectivity that underlies his epistemological achievement. Integrating these two approaches, the metaphysical and the epistemological, both of which appear to claim a certain priority, is the challenge of interpreting the circularity of the Kantian philosophical system.

Concerns about the presuppositions of Kant's epistemological accomplishments will direct this inquiry to the question of the underlying methodology of the critical system: How has Kant oriented his critique, directed his examination of human cognition to the sensible representations of things as distinguished from all non-sensible metaphysical thoughts, without presupposing a conception of the subject for whom such sensible objects are given? What I will investigate is the conception of subjectivity that allows Kant to deduce the *a priori* conditions of experience, which appears to follow from the concern that was directed at Kant from the earliest reception of the *Critique of Pure Reason:* the demand for a metacritique of the critical apparatus.[29] Does Kant's critical system offer a justification of the tools on which his analysis of the conditions of the possibility of experience depends? And can any attempt to deduce the division of our human faculties do so without presupposing metaphysically dogmatic conceptions of both the self and the objects it perceives?

II. The Metacritical Challenge to the Critical Project

Investigating the dependence of Kant's analysis of finite cognition on the pursuit of metaphysical knowledge of the rational subject literally follows the questions that Johann Georg Hamann raises as rhetorical criticisms of Kant's project in his "Metacritique of the Purism of Reason [Metakritik über den Purismum der Vernunft]."[30] In this essay Hamann challenges Kant's designation of the two sources of cognition—sensibility and understanding—arguing that their division distorts the very experience that he wishes to explain. He writes: "But if sensibility and understanding spring as two stems of human cognition [*Erkenntnis*] from one common root . . . to what end such a violent, unwarranted, obstinate divorce [*Scheidung*] of what nature had joined together!"[31] In Hamann's account, the Kantian dualism of sensibility and understanding is accomplished by separating the cognitive faculty of the understanding from its sensible embodiment in culture. Understanding is thus torn from the sensible, offering the possibility of distinguishing not only its *a priori* concepts, but also the pure forms of sensibility: space as the form of outer sense and time as the form of inner sense. Kant thus reduces experience beyond all empirical givenness, and what Hamann claims is that the Kantian reduction reaches its apex in the accounts of space and time, for which there is not even the possibility of a deduction from experience; they are, rather, merely asserted "with neither an object nor a sign of the same from the pure and empty property [*Eigenschaft*] of our outer and inner mind."[32]

Hamann's demand for a metacritique that could explain how the terms of the analysis of cognition in the critical project are themselves known is a rhetorical demand intent on directing the inquiry beyond critique to the unity of reason in culture and language from which, he claims, this critical dualism has been violently torn.[33] What is needed is a questioning of what lies behind the Kantian reduction, the "natural" state that has been inductively partitioned, turning the complexity of experience into a dualism of barren stems. To reduce experience to the cognitive dualism of sensibility and understanding separates what is implicitly unified; rather than distinguishing the forms of sensibility from the concepts of the understanding, Hamann traces their unity back to their origin in the irreducible ground of language, and attempts to demonstrate the unity of sensible form and rational structure in what he describes as the oldest means of communication. All temporal measurement has its roots in music, "the oldest language," and in painting and drawing can be seen the original "system of space." Hamann's claim is that "sounds and letters [*Laute und Buchstaben*]"[34] are the "pure forms *a priori*" of all thought, the hidden preconditions of all systems of reason. The Kantian *a priori* forms of sensibility—space and time—are in this way replaced by what Hamann terms the pure forms of all thought, the precondition of all language and hence of all thinking, in which temporal and spatial determinations are expressed in a manner that is indistinguishable from the cognition that they permit. Hamann is not offering the building blocks of a new system; rather, his claim is that Kant's analysis of the *a priori* structures of cognition—the categories of understanding and the forms of sensibility—does not go back far enough. When one traces the genesis of our thought back to its origins, what one finds is not rules with which to build a system, but the atomistic beginnings of language, reason in its original state, undifferentiated from its sensible manifestations.

In so doing Hamann has challenged not merely the dual poles of Kant's analysis of cognition—sensibility and understanding—and the conception of experience that they distinguish, but also the transcendental project itself, the attempt to deduce the synthetic *a priori* structures of cognition from the unity of such cognitive faculties in the intersection of language and reason. Clearly, the manner in which Hamann raises such a challenge cannot justify its designation of the linguistic origin of thinking.[35] His claim is that language cannot be contrasted with reason in a way that language could be examined by such a fundamental power; for Hamann, the two are inseparable, and any attempt to investigate language cannot escape reason's grasp. The demand for a metacritique of Kant's analysis of cognition is a rhetorical tool meant to show the indefensibility of not only the Kantian construct but any attempt to reduce experience to its *a priori* elements.

Kant himself can be seen to recognize the difficulty of investigating the origin of the *a priori* structure of cognition that he defends, explaining that his analysis of cognition makes no claim about the genesis of the structures that are deduced. In the *Prolegomena to Any Future Metaphysics* (*Prolegomena zu einer jeden künftigen Metaphysik*), directly after the presentation of the transcendental "Table of Concepts of the Understanding," he explains that "it is first of all necessary to remind the reader that the discussion here is not about the genesis [*Entstehen*] of experience, but about that which lies in experience."[36] We find ourselves with certain cognitive accomplishments, and we go on to deduce the conditions of their possibility. Rather than attempting to examine the development of human reason, Kant has elucidated the faculties of understanding and sensibility as the conditions of the possibility, not of thinking in general and so not of reason in general, but of the objects that experience affords us.

In the preface to the first edition of the *Critique of Pure Reason*, Kant explains that he will set aside the question "how is the **faculty of thinking** [*das Vermögen zu Denken*] itself possible?" a question that deals with the subjective sources of thought, and address instead the objective validity of our cognition. The relevant question for Kant is thus: "What and how much can understanding and reason cognize free of all experience?" (Axvii).[37] Kant calls this inquiry the "chief question [*Hauptfrage*]," which is to say the one that affords us the deduction of the *a priori* concepts. Hamann reverses such a priority, arguing that "if a chief question does remain," it is the more primordial one, concerning thinking in general. To ask such a question, Hamann adds, does not demand a deduction of the cognitive faculties; rather, the question immediately bespeaks "the genealogical priority of language" over the deduced cognitive faculties.[38] In this way Hamann is pointing to the linguistic origins of thought from which the narrowly defined faculties are deduced. Kant sets aside an initial inquiry into thinking in general, into reason in its broadest sense, emphasizing instead an analysis of *a priori* cognition in the limited realm of objects of experience, and so of the understanding. Only with the latter inquiry are the criteria for the investigation of the conditions of the possibility of objects of experience determined. Only by investigating our cognitive accomplishments can the question of the possibility of thought be fruitfully approached. Without such an investigation, thought—and hence language and reason—remains necessarily opaque. And it is to this opacity that Hamann directs us.[39]

Kant's turning from the opacity of the **"faculty of thinking"** to the structure of the faculties of cognition is, in the most general sense, a shift from the illusions engendered by reason's pursuit of metaphysical ideas to the investigations made possible by the regulative employment of such ideas. This limiting of our philosophical goals, which is to say the response to our metaphysical failures when such limits are not guarded, will be shown to be responsible for the division of understanding and reason. Only by turning from the failure of rationalist endeavors, from reason's metaphysical pursuits, to the limited region of thought associated with sensible appearances, that is to say, to the territory of understanding, can we avoid the path of Hamann's skeptical arguments; and yet, such a turning from reason's failure to attain metaphysical knowledge, a turning to understanding and finite cognition, must be able to explain the thread that guides this search for a unified account of *a priori* concepts if it is to claim to be thoroughly critical. Such is the challenge offered by Hamann's demand for a metacritique: What presuppositions are embedded in this reflective classification of the endless flux of thought, what metaphysical conception of subjects and objects is retained in this epistemological endeavor to produce, from out of the metaphysically indecipherable manifold, the faculty of understanding?

For Hamann, no such reappraisal of our cognitive faculties follows the skeptical rejection of reason's pretensions. Hamann portrays the opacity of reason's pursuits when he describes the indistinguishability of language and reason in a letter to Herder on August 8, 1784:

> If I were as eloquent as Demosthenes I would yet have to do nothing more than repeat a single word three times: reason is language [*Vernunft ist Sprache*], logos. I gnaw at this marrow-bone and will gnaw myself to death over it. There still remains a darkness, always, over this depth for me; I am still waiting for an apocalyptic angel with a key to this abyss [*Abgrund*].[40]

Reason offers no coherent explanation, no systematic account that could distinguish it from the language within which it exists; any attempt to do so will fall into the abyss of language, the ever-shifting process of linguistic sedimentation. Yet, is there a way to avoid such an abyss in the examination of reason? Can human reason be investigated without presupposing its transparent explanation in a manner that avoids the failings that provoke Hamann's ire? It is just such an approach that Kant can be seen to have undertaken: the inquiry into metaphysics in the Transcendental Dialectic, in marking out the limits of our cognition, elucidates how Kant has been able to offer an explanation of our finite accomplishment.

Hamann's conception of Kant's critical philosophy as destructive of the language and culture of actual human experience in its all-consuming reduction will serve as a foil for my attempt to investigate the systematic examination of the understanding as an achievement produced by reason insofar as it has been brought to recognize its cognitive limits. To interpret Kant by way of Hamann's criticism is clearly to read the metacritique against itself. Doing so, however, is not without historical justification. In a letter to Kant dated July 27, 1759, Hamann answered Kant's attempt to reclaim him for the Enlightenment with the response that it is Hume who recognized the need for faith.[41] Hume as the standard-bearer of anti-rationalist faith sounds as odd as does Hamann as the key to understanding transcendental philosophy. And yet Hamann's reference to Hume appears to be Kant's earliest introduction to his skeptical interlocutor.[42] Could it be that it was on Hamann's prodding that Kant was awakened by Hume from his "dogmatic slumber"? This speculative question must be set aside as we investigate the manner in which Kant has constructed his system of cognition from the foundation of such a skeptical insight. The designation of the understanding through the analysis of cognition, launched in the Transcendental Analytic, and juxtaposed against the other stem of human cognition, sensibility, will come to demarcate an accomplishment in the "abyss of language." Distinguishing the boundary of the region of experience within which Kant has successfully launched his analysis of the conditions of the possibility of objects must itself come to be seen as an accomplishment that follows from reason's pursuit of the illusory ideas of metaphysics. But how can these ideas, after their critique, direct the designation of the territory of experience without drawing critical thought back into the illusory pursuit of their objects? How can reason, after the critique of its metaphysical pretensions, permit us the analysis of the faculty of understanding?

III. The Boundary of Experience

If Kant's critical project is understood as beginning its investigation of "how synthetic *a priori* knowledge is possible" with an inquiry into the conditions of the possibility of objects of experience, then it would have distinguished the cognitive dualism of sensibility and understanding in a thoroughly unjustifiable manner, for the transcendental investigation of synthetic cognition that affords these designations would then begin with the presupposition that experience is composed of spatially appearing objects. The question is then: How is Kant able to justify this beginning point, this acceptance of the pre-philosophical conception of empirical objects as constitutive of human experience? Kant's critical accomplishment depends upon the designation of the terrain of spatial objects in order to begin from this point the transcendental investigation of the subjective sources of such experience; only by means of the designation of the difference between spatial objects and ourselves, only by beginning philosophical investigation with the everyday certainty that spatial appearances have a reality that evades all non-spatially determined representations—the certainty of an empirical realist—does the flux of thought yield itself to critical analysis. And only through such a distinction, which is to say insofar as we do not doubt the empirical reality of objects, can a transcendental inquiry be pursued that analyzes spatial appearances in a manner that both generates the conceptual framework of the understanding and permits the critique of metaphysics.

For Kant, transcendental idealism does not deny empirical realism. The empirical conception of objects existing apart from a perceiving subject, the pre-philosophical confidence in a world of existing objects, does not contradict the transcendental investigation of such objects as subjective phenomena, as transcendentally ideal, and thus as unknowable in themselves. Kant writes that the transcendental idealist is, therefore, an empirical realist and concedes to matter as appearance an actuality that does not need to be inferred but is directly perceived (A371). The transcendental idealist investigates only the subjective representation of objects, but in so doing, in accepting that what appears can be deemed an object even though it cannot be known as such apart from its appearance, Kant's transcendental idealism accepts the actuality of such spatial objects with the caveat that "space itself is in us" (A370). Kant's transcendental accomplishment does not merely permit a return to such empirical realism within the confines of the analysis of experience, but begins its analysis from this starting point. The conception of objects with which Kant approaches the analysis of the flux of representations is that of the empirical realist. Thus, transcendental philosophy must defend itself against the claim that it has imported the conception of objects as empirically real into its analysis, beginning the examination of cognition by presupposing that spatially appearing objects are those which must be examined. For if Kant begins his critical philosophy with an unchallenged, and seemingly uncritical, conception of objects and the limits of cognition, and from this beginning investigates the subjective conditions that make them possible, can he then justify the presuppositions with which his critical epistemology has begun? Such an inquiry is needed if we are to stave off the fear that although Kant has produced an elegant system, its starting point is philosophically unjustified.

What must be examined is how in the philosophical investigation of the whole range of our thought, in the reflection on all our "actions of thinking" (A683/B711), we are able to mark off the boundary of possible experience prior to the critique of metaphysics that is itself made possible by the analysis of this region of experience. Kant describes this designation of the realm of possible experience as "**setting the boundary** to the field of experience through something that is otherwise unknown to it,"[43] and he distinguishes "boundaries [*Grenzen*]" from mere "limits [*Schranken*]." While for Kant a *limit* is a purely negative distinction marking completion, a *boundary* is part of that which it distinguishes. Boundaries mark out and take part in what is bounded. Kant explains that a point is the boundary and not the limit of the line, for the point both distinguishes the confines of the line and is itself part of it.[44] Transposing this idea into the complex discussion of the realm of possible experience, Kant writes:

> But **setting the boundary** to the field of experience through something that is otherwise unknown to it is indeed a cognition that is still left to reason from this standpoint, whereby reason is neither confined [*beschlossen*] within the sensible world nor raving [*schwärmend*] outside it, but, as befits knowledge of a boundary, restricts itself solely to the relation of what lies outside the boundary to what is contained within.[45]

The setting of the boundary between the realm of experience and what is unknown to reason must offer something positive to that for which it is the boundary. This boundary separates what is sensibly given, and hence knowable, from what can be thought but never known, as it must be able to distinguish the region of experience within which the analysis of finite cognition takes place. Spatially appearing objects are distinguished as the field of analysis of synthetic cognition by means of this designation of the boundary of what is to count as experience. Yet how can we distinguish that which offers cognition from that which can *merely* be thought prior to the investigation of what is to stand as cognition, such that we can begin our analysis of this limited realm of "possible experience"? This question is particularly vexing, as not only do we need to make use of this metaphysical beyond in order to distinguish what is to count as "experience," but the analysis of this empirical region also provides the tools that allow Kant to dismantle the illusions of metaphysics.

In the appendix to the Transcendental Analytic, titled On the Amphiboly of the Concepts of Reflection, Kant describes the need for a reflective act prior to the critical analysis of cognition. This act that readies the ground for critique is called by Kant transcendental reflection (A261/B317). Coming at the end of the Transcendental Analytic, and thus after the analysis of the subjective conditions that permit the experience of objects, it is not surprising that this discussion of a preparatory reflective act to be accomplished prior to the reflective achievements of the first *Critique* has been overlooked;[46] and yet Kant describes it as "a duty from which no one can escape if he would judge anything about things *a priori*" (A263/B319). In order to "judge anything about things *a priori*," we must fulfill a prior "duty." We must, Kant writes, step back from the comparison of representations that is needed for all empirical concept formation, and distinguish whether the given representations being compared are sensible or whether they are purely intellectual (A261/B317). Prior to any attempt to pursue *a priori* judgment, we must reflect upon the varied comparisons of representations that constitute our thought in the attempt to differentiate those that concern what is offered sensibly from those that belong to "pure understanding." This parsing of our representations, which is necessary prior to the accomplishments of the Transcendental Analytic, distinguishes those of our representations that refer to spatial appearances from those that have no sensible content and do not offer themselves for sensible intuition. The boundary of possible experience is thus first demarcated by the act of transcendental reflection even though this act itself is only described by Kant after the epistemological exploits of the Transcendental Analytic.

Finally, after elucidating the *a priori* conditions of the possibility of objects of experience, Kant addresses the conception of experience with which this investigation has begun. He explains that we must distinguish those representations that have a sensible source from those that have an intellectual source in order to investigate the subjective conditions of phenomenal objects. Doing so allows us to avoid the errors of both Locke and Leibniz: the error of the former was that he **"sensualized [sensifiziert]"**[47] the intellectual, while that of the latter was that he **"intellectualized [intellektuierte]"** the sensible (A271/B327). The *Critique of Pure Reason* depends upon a conception of experience that prioritizes neither the sensible nor the intellectual, designating the field of their interaction as its terrain; and yet, such a seemingly fundamental issue is only addressed in the appendix to the Transcendental Analytic, and there in a rather cursory manner. Unfortunately, Kant does not explain how this method of transcendental reflection, which secures *a priori* judgment, can itself be justified. The task ahead of me is to explain both why such a reflective act is necessary prior to the reflective systemization of experience, and how such a philosophical reflection can be understood in relation to the critical edifice that, ultimately, it supports. What conception of reflection, and of the subject who both reflects and is reflected upon, who is thus both the subject and object of this reflection, is presupposed in this seemingly foundational act of Kant's transcendental philosophy, an act that must be accomplished prior to the critical examination of cognition?[48]

To investigate such issues is to delve into the core of Kant's Copernican revolution. Why should Kant's philosophical consciousness, newly awakened by Hume from its dogmatic slumber,[49] begin its analysis of experience with the confidence that the realm of spatially represented appearances can be distinguished from that of metaphysical illusions, especially when Hume denies precisely such a distinction in his refutation of the knowledge of both empirical and metaphysical things (i.e., both gold and souls)?[50] To answer that what Kant was interested in was precisely the manner in which we experience those objects that are given spatially, how they can appear to us even when no knowledge of them as they exist apart from our perception is forthcoming, is, as Hume might have argued, to beg the question. Why should we limit our philosophical investigation to spatial appearances, setting aside that which offers no spatial element for examination and eventual rejection, only after and by means of the analysis of such spatial appearances?

One might be tempted to look for an answer to this question in the alternative explanation offered by Kant for his awakening from dogmatism. In the *Prolegomena*, he mentions not only Hume, but also the discovery of reason's antinomies, its conflicts with itself, as the path out of dogmatism.[51] The recognition of the incompatibility of mechanism and freedom, the famous third antinomy of the first *Critique*,[52] might appear to answer the question concerning the direction of the critical project beyond that which "the remembrance [*Erinnerung*] of David Hume"[53] could offer. While Hume's skeptical critique cannot explain why transcendental philosophy should differentiate between spatial appearances and metaphysical ideas, the antinomy directs just such a division: between appearances, which are governed by causal law, and the realm of ideas, in which freedom from such causal law is possible. The solution to the antinomy offered by Kant would seem to mark the boundary between phenomena and noumena, abolishing the need to investigate both its designation and the presuppositions its accomplishments bespeak. And yet, if this is all there is to Kantian critique, if it does not turn its critical apparatus toward its own presuppositions, then it would appear to offer merely the production of a new dogmatism. At the very least, must we not demand of Kant a justification of these presuppositions within the conceptual language that his system has produced in order to avoid Hamann's charge that the analysis of cognition within the phenomenal realm, with its dualism of sensibility and understanding, distorts the essential unity of the experience that it wishes to explain?[54] Such an investigation denies the importance of neither Hume nor the antinomies for the development of Kant's "critique of reason."[55] The issue, however, is not what awakened Kant, be it the antinomies or reading Hume;[56] rather, it concerns that to which he was awakened. The critical system to which Kant was directed must investigate the presuppositions of its claims if it is not to reinstate the very dogmatism it intended to overthrow.

V. Conclusion:
The "Metaphysics of Thinking Nature" (A846/B874)

In what follows, I will pursue Hamann's metacritical demand within the confines of the critical enterprise itself. This is to say that I will follow Hamann's demand for a justification of the terms of Kant's analysis, but rather than searching for the elusive foundation of critique, I will investigate whether the completed

Kantian system offers a way to justify the conceptual structure with which the critical undertaking has begun; and so I will attempt to piece together the metaphysical claims of the completed system. Kant's critique of metaphysics appears to offer little room for such positive claims about the presuppositions of critique, and yet, beyond even the above-cited command of reason that we continue to pursue its goal of the unified thinking subject (A683/B711), Kant explains that after the critique of metaphysics, a metaphysics of the subject, of our "thinking nature," is still to be found (A846/B874).[57] Investigating this post-critical idea of the metaphysics of the self, raised by Kant in the Transcendental Doctrine of Method that ends the first *Critique*, will go a long way toward showing that the account of the metaphysical presuppositions of critique that is here being unraveled, and the conception of the transcendental method that follows from it, is not a revision of the Kantian system aimed to save it from its early critics, but rather an integral part of the system itself.

In the chapter of the Transcendental Doctrine of Method, titled the Architectonic of Pure Reason, Kant addresses metaphysics as it can be conceived after the critique of its illusory goals. Metaphysics after its critique, after, as Kant writes in the preface to the second edition of the first *Critique*, it has been "purified by critique" (Bxxiv), permits not only moral freedom but also the possibility of faith in the territory beyond that of empirical cognition. And yet, how could this offer us any sort of positive metaphysical content when neither of these areas of post-metaphysical accomplishment offers determinate claims? Kant explains that the post-critical field of metaphysics, insofar as it can be said "to present [*darstellen*]" the "systematic unity" of *a priori* cognition, can be said to consist of both transcendental philosophy and what he calls "the **physiology** of pure reason" (A845/B873). The former comprises the accomplishments of the first *Critique*, offering the study of the faculties of understanding and reason as a "system of all concepts and principles [*Grundsätze*]" that refer to objects without assuming their noumenal reality. In this sense, metaphysics includes the critical analysis of the subjective conditions of the possibility of objects, the *ontologia* of the Transcendental Analytic (ibid.). The latter portion of metaphysics that proceeds beyond critical epistemology is the "**physiology** of pure reason." This elusive conception refers to the study of nature, but not nature merely as it is demarcated by the conditions of the possibility of experience, as it is distinguished within transcendental philosophy, but rather nature itself as "the sum total **of given** objects [*Gegenstände*] (whether they are given by the senses or, if one will, by another kind of intuition)" (ibid.). It is this latter portion of metaphysics that must be investigated, for the question with which we are concerned is: What conception of nature, of objects, and particularly of ourselves as thinking subjects can be distinguished within the territory of the critique of metaphysics; and thus, how does such a metaphysical conception avoid surpassing the very limits on knowledge that direct the critical system?

Kant explains that the "**physiology** of pure reason" includes both the transcendent and the immanent uses of reason. The "transcendent" use of reason refers to the pursuit of illusory metaphysical knowledge, the inquiries into the metaphysical objects of the soul, the world, and God that the Transcendental Dialectic has shown to be, at best, inconclusive. The "immanent" use of reason, on the other hand, offers accomplishment even after the critique of the illusions of transcendent metaphysics. Such an immanent physiology, Kant explains, "considers nature as the sum total of all objects of the senses" (A846/B874), designating not an empirical pursuit, but an attempt to illuminate the sum, or unity, of all of nature. Immanent physiology has two divisions: corporeal nature, the object of outer sense, and the soul or thinking nature, the object of inner sense. The physiological metaphysics of corporeal nature is called *rational physics;* that of thinking nature is called *rational psychology.*

In the *Metaphysical Foundations of Natural Science (Metaphysiche Anfangsgründe der Naturwissenschaft)*, Kant offers just such a conception of a rational physics, while arguing that psychology offers but a limited empirical account of inner sense.[58] And so too, in the *Critique of Pure Reason* itself Kant twice rejects physiological inquiry into the thinking subject. In the first edition's preface he describes the initial optimism for but eventual failure of Locke's "**physiology** of the human understanding" (Aix). While Locke purported to produce an account of the understanding from out of sensible experience, he continued to embrace the dogmatic metaphysics that he had meant to overcome. Kant again rejects the possibility of such a physiology at the end of the introduction to the Paralogisms of Pure Reason of the first *Critique;* Kant describes the goal of a "**physiology** of inner sense," an "empirical psychology" in which we make use of "more than the *cogito,*" relying on "observations about the play of our thoughts and the natural laws of the thinking self created from them" (B405/A347). Such a physiology would neither "serve to teach **apodictically**" about our natures, nor provide a "rational psychology" (A347/B406). It would, rather, observe the workings of thought and search for "natural laws" that could describe them. Kant explains that such a physiology of inner sense examines only the way that inner sense appears to us, and so it too cannot offer the "metaphysics of thinking nature" described by him at the end of the first *Critique* when he distinguishes the "**rational cognition**" of psychology (A846/B874).[59] Kant describes the latter inquiry as concerned not with the thinking subject insofar as it conceives of objects of experience, but with such a self taken as an "object [*Gegenstand*]" for itself (ibid.). But where does this leave us? Kant has claimed that we are not known to ourselves, that we remain but an appearance, that of inner sense, to our faculties of cognition.[60] The workings of these faculties point to the analytic unity of apperception, but any attempt to pursue knowledge of such unity, to turn this logical point into knowledge of the soul, fails, as Kant argues in the Paralogisms. So what could Kant mean by a "metaphysics of thinking nature" (ibid.), and how could it fit into the methodological discussions that close the *Critique of Pure Reason?* [61]

The post-critical conception of metaphysics, introduced by Kant in the Transcendental Doctrine of Method of the first *Critique* under the rubric of an "immanent physiology," obviously does not revert to the dogmatic goals of rational psychology; and yet Kant does not explain how this metaphysical investigation of psychology as a "**physiology** of thinking nature" can be achieved. If it comprises neither the empirical investigation of psychological appearance, nor the goal of the rational cognition of the soul, then what sort of pursuit is this "physiology of thinking nature"? This is to ask how the Kantian physiology of our thinking natures can be located between the opposing poles of Locke's "**physiology** of the human understanding" (Aix), on one side, and the rationalist attempt to produce a "**physiology** of inner sense" (B405/A347), on the other.

The question then is: How can a "rational cognition" of the thinking subject avoid the illusions that, Kant has argued, are the fate of all traditional metaphysical inquiries? The possibility that will here be developed is that the regulative pursuit of the psychological idea, announced by Kant in the appendix to the Transcendental Dialectic as the "hypothetical use of reason" (A647/B675), offers a way to conceive of this metaphysics of the self. This is to say that the self as the unity of inner sense, the rational cognition of the thinking subject, can be conceived as the idea of the self that the Paralogisms have shown avoids contradiction, even as it is beyond our cognitive reach. Rather than taking the judgment of this whole as a teleological task, and thus as concerned with the systematic unity of empirical laws, this unity would be seen as the "principle [*Prinzip*]" that regulates the pursuit of an analysis of the faculties of our ultimately unknowable thinking natures. The psychological idea would thus offer the regulating principle of our self-analysis, a physiology of our thinking nature constituted by the critical investigation of our cognitive faculties.

If this can be shown to be the case, then Kant's "metaphysics of thinking nature" (A846/B874) would refer to the critical analysis of the faculties of *a priori* cognition, an analysis that relies upon a conception of the sum of all appearances of inner sense, the metaphysical subject of the psychological idea. Such an analysis must begin with an idea of what pertains to its investigation—the bounded confines of possible experience, and thus the accomplishments of transcendental reflection—such that it can then proceed to distinguish the workings of the cognitive faculties.

But how is the idea of the self that directs such a physiology itself justified? If, as I propose, this self follows from the critique of metaphysics as a regulative principle born of the critique of our metaphysical interest in rational psychology, then critical philosophy must admit a unified thinking nature that both directs the critique of metaphysics and follows from it. For only if this physiology of the soul is construed as the product of a regulative principle, following from a post-critical idea of reason, can such an analysis be understood to represent a transcendental accomplishment rather than a dogmatic epistemology. Such a conception of the Kantian system, in addressing the metacritical demand for a justification of the tools of its own analysis, leads Kant to the seemingly paradoxical position that he describes as the "perpetual circle" (B404/A346) of his approach. The question with which we are now left is: How can the analysis of finite cognition that opens the *Critique of Pure Reason* be seen both to depend upon *and* permit the critique of metaphysics with which this work concludes?

TWO

The Boundary of
Phenomena and Noumena

I. On the Relation of Understanding and Reason

At the end of the *Prolegomena to Any Future Metaphysics,* Kant claims that the

unavoidable dialectic of pure reason deserves, in a metaphysics
considered as a natural predisposition [*Naturanlage*], not only to
be explained as an illusion that needs to be resolved, but also (if
one can) as a **natural institution** [*Naturanstalt*] in accordance
with its purpose—although this endeavor, as super-meritorious
[*überverdienstlich*], cannot rightly be required of metaphysics
proper.[1]

To explain the human tendency toward metaphysics as a "natural institution"
that permits us to perform a task that "cannot rightly be required of metaphysics proper" would appear to point to the moral use of metaphysical inquiry that
follows from the critique of the cosmological antinomies in the Transcendental
Dialectic of the *Critique of Pure Reason*. However, since Kant terms the above
provision "super-meritorious," and so a task that stands beyond merit and duty,
it would appear to point not to the inquiry into moral duty, but to the account
of teleological judgment, and therefore to the pursuit of the systematic organization of scientific laws that Kant describes seven years later in the *Critique of
Judgment*. Yet, in the above section, Kant goes on to imply that the question of
reason's "natural predisposition" for metaphysics lies not merely with morality and teleology, areas in which Kant has developed the use of metaphysical
inquiry after its critique, but with the dependence of the understanding itself
on "principles of reason [*Vernunftprinzipien*]" in its examination of experience.
But in what sense can the understanding, the faculty of *a priori* cognition, be said
to depend on "principles of reason," on metaphysical inquiry, even after Kant
has shown that metaphysics does not afford us cognition? Investigating such a
role for the ideas of reason is the task at hand. The question can be stated thus:
Is there a way to elucidate the dependence of the understanding on reason in a
manner that responds to the metacritical charge that the structure of the critical
inquiry cannot be justified?

Kant describes the ideas of reason as offering principles that afford insight into the critical examination of experience. Such principles are obviously not constitutive of experience, since reason's interests carry it beyond all possible experience, achieving no object in its metaphysical pursuit, but Kant does call the relation of understanding and reason that such principles (*Prinzipien*) afford an "agreement [*Übereinstimmung*],"[2] one, it would seem, that directs the critical examination of finite cognition.[3] Kant compares the relation in which understanding and reason rest to that between sensibility and understanding; just as nature does not inhere in sensibility, but only in sensibility's relation to the understanding, so too "a unified possible experience"[4] can belong to the understanding only when the understanding is viewed in relation to reason. In this way, just as the laws of nature can be determined only in terms of the relation of sensibility and understanding, so too the unity of the understanding that explains the entirety of possible experience must be viewed in its relation to reason. What this appears to mean is that just as nature, within critical philosophy, cannot be viewed as merely sensible, since it is subordinate to the legislation of the understanding, so too the realm of the totality of possible experience that comprises nature must itself be viewed as the province of the understanding only when it is subordinate to the legislation of reason.

The influence that reason exerts over the understanding, an influence, Kant writes, that "seems to be constitutive and law-giving with respect to experience,"[5] but cannot be, would appear to raise the possibility of a positive function within the *Critique of Pure Reason* for the transcendental dialectic. What such an account offers is the possibility of an answer to the question of how Kant is able to mark out the boundary of possible experience such that the categories of the understanding can be exhibited prior to the critique of metaphysics that these categories make possible. Or, as Kant writes earlier in the *Prolegomena*, in describing the relation of phenomena and noumena: "Both are considered together in our reason, and the question arises: how does reason proceed in setting boundaries for the understanding with respect to both fields?"[6] Could it be that through an examination of the dependence of the account of the unity of the understanding on reason, we will be able to approach the metacritical questions that have shadowed the critical enterprise, offering a literal response to the rhetorical demands of those, beginning with Hamann, who have asked how Kant is able to designate the criteria through which possible experience is examined? Unfortunately, Kant does not develop the account of the dependence of the understanding on reason in the *Prolegomena*, consigning the task to those who would investigate "the nature of reason beyond its use in metaphysics."[7] Kant does refer the reader to the *Critique of Pure Reason* and the first section of the appendix to the Transcendental Dialectic, titled On the Regulative Use of the Ideas of Pure Reason, for a treatment of such a question; but when we turn to this appendix, we find only a reaffirmation of the general issue, and not an examination of the precise manner in which reason's ideas, when in relation to the understanding, can be seen to be legislative over experience.[8] In this section Kant describes the pursuit of reason's ideas after their designation as illusory as the "hypothetical use of reason" (A647/B675). To pursue reason's ideas hypothetically is to transform the illusory ideas into the means through which regulative progress is possible in fields that do not permit direct cognition. To pursue hypothetically that which cannot be an object of cognition is to proceed in accordance with a problematic concept when no rational concept can be distinguished. While such a furthering of reason's interests is comprehensible in terms of the pursuit of ever more mechanistic explanation, Kant is here expressing a use of the ideas of reason, after their critique, that proceeds beyond what has been thematized in the analysis of the cosmological idea.

In the Antinomy of Pure Reason Kant explains that even though the totality of the series of causes cannot be uncovered, we can proceed to uncover further causal laws governing nature without presupposing that the idea of the causally explained world will offer itself to our cognition (A509/B537). To pursue the cosmological idea regulatively, we must proceed as if the series of causal connections in the natural world were unending. To do so is to treat the cosmological idea "only as a rule, prescribing a regress in the series of conditions for given appearances, in which regress is never allowed to stop with an absolutely unconditioned" (A508–509/B536–37). And yet, this does not preclude our proceeding as if there were, outside of this series of mechanistic causes, a causality by means of freedom. The antinomy following from the cosmological idea leads to both the regulative pursuit of ever further empirical analysis of causal relations and the designation of transcendental freedom that makes possible the pursuit of human freedom.[9] But how, we must ask, could such a regulative use of the ideas of reason explain Kant's claim in the *Prolegomena* that reason legislates human experience in general? Could it be that the "thoroughgoing unity [*durchgängige Einheit*]" that reason is said to offer "in the use of this understanding, for the sake of a unified possible experience,"[10] concerns merely the empirical extension of the understanding in its determination of experience and not the conceptual examination of the understanding itself? If this were the case, then it would certainly be difficult to interpret Kant's reference to the interest "experts" might have in transcendental philosophy, which he describes in the *Prolegomena* as directed to the relation of the faculties of understanding and reason, when all that would appear to be implied is the empirical extension of the former by means of the latter, since the regulative use of the cosmological idea offers only a further empirical extension of our use of the understanding and not the basic designation of the conditions that comprise a "unified possible experience."

In developing the account of the accomplishments of the "hypothetical use of reason" in the second section of the appendix to the Transcendental Dialectic, titled On the Final Aim of the Natural Dialectic of Human Reason,

Kant describes three regulative principles (A671–72 / B699–700): each of the ideas of reason that the Transcendental Dialectic investigates offers a regulative principle (*Prinzip*) when the unattainable goal of its cognition is taken as the schema, or rule, that directs our striving, even though the objects of these metaphysical pursuits do not offer themselves for cognition. And yet, how can the psychological and the theological ideas offer themselves for regulative pursuit? Could it be that one of these ideas of reason, which, unlike the cosmological idea, end not in antinomy but merely in incomprehension, explains the relation of understanding and reason in Kant's transcendental philosophy?

What we will see, as my investigation turns to the *Critique of Judgment*, is that the theological idea offers the regulative principle for the teleological investigation of nature. I will then proceed to investigate whether the unity of the understanding that is elucidated in the Transcendental Analytic can be said to follow from the remaining idea of reason, the psychological idea. This is to claim that the first of the three ideas of reason, the psychological idea, performs its regulative function by directing the analysis of the unified structure of the understanding's *a priori* concepts insofar as it has been followed as a merely regulative principle and not pursued as an object of cognition. Such a possibility will offer a way to examine the presuppositions of critique. However, prior to such an interpretation of the psychological idea, what must be established is why the analysis of the understanding undertaken in the Transcendental Analytic of the *Critique of Pure Reason* depends upon a prior metaphysical accomplishment. How can the analysis of the categories of the understanding be said to depend upon an accomplishment that follows from the pursuit of the ideas of reason? Could it be that the pursuit of the problematic concept of the idea of a rational subject brings unity to the examination of the understanding and makes reason and its illusory ideas "the **touchstone of the truth** for its [the understanding's] rules [*der Probierstein der Wahrheit der Regeln*]" (A647 / B675)? These questions are most directly addressed in the much-celebrated §76 of Kant's *Critique of Judgment*, about which Schelling wrote, "Perhaps there have never been so many deep thoughts compressed [*zusammengedrängt*] into so few pages."[11]

II. §76 of the *Critique of Judgment*

Kant begins §76 by remarking that the following "consideration [*Betrachtung*]" should be viewed not as a rigorous proof but merely as an attempt to raise certain issues for further examination. These issues, while not fundamental to the investigation of teleological judgment, Kant writes, "certainly deserve to be elaborated in detail in transcendental philosophy."[12] The "digression" that follows appears to raise issues that have not been addressed directly in Kant's transcendental philosophy, but "deserve" to be further examined, as they will be seen to begin to address the question concerning the relation of understanding and reason within the critical system.

Kant begins this complex discussion with the claim that reason is "a faculty of principles [*ein Vermögen der Prinzipien*]."[13] In interpreting this claim we must be careful to distinguish Kant's use of the term *Prinzip* from that of *Grundsatz*.[14] Kant describes the rules that order the unity of appearances for the understanding as *Grundsätze*, while reason provides "the unity of the rules of the understanding" under the rubric of *Prinzipien*. Principles, in the sense of *Grundsätze*, which is to say principles related to the *a priori* concepts of the understanding, "bear this name not merely because they contain in themselves the grounds [*Gründe*] of other judgments, but also because they are not themselves grounded on higher and more general cognitions" (B188/A148). And yet these principles (*Grundsätze*) cannot furnish synthetic cognition from concepts, needing the sensibly given to produce cognition. Principles (*Prinzipien*), in the full meaning of the term, are, like *Grundsätze*, not based on higher, more universal concepts, but they must also offer the grounds of synthetic cognition through concepts alone. Thus, while the Transcendental Analytic uncovers universal rules of synthetic cognition, rules that govern determinate judgment, they are not principles (*Prinzipien*), Kant writes, "[f]or they would not even be possible *a priori* if we did not bring in pure intuition (in mathematics) or the conditions of a possible experience in general" (B357/A301); these rules are *Grundsätze* and not *Prinzipien* as they cannot provide cognition merely from themselves, but do so only when accompanied by sensible content.[15] A principle in the sense of a *Prinzip* would provide for cognition from concepts alone; it would allow for cognition of the ideas of reason that would not be beholden to sensible givenness.

Yet, it is precisely the attempt to attain such metaphysical cognition, that which is not dependent on the sensibly given, that Kant proves is illusory in the Transcendental Dialectic. Obviously, Kant has not returned in §76 of the *Critique of Judgment* to a pre-critical conception of reason (*Vernunft*) in his designation of reason as a faculty of principles (*Prinzipien*); however, Kant is also not invoking the faculty of reason merely to distinguish our finite intellects from an intuitive intellect that could attain such knowledge. These ideas of reason are now broached as principles (*Prinzipien*) that are subjectively binding even when no objective justification can be provided. The accomplishments that reason affords, those discussed in §76, are born of the regulative uses of the principles (*Prinzipien*) of reason. Such regulative uses follow from our metaphysical tendencies but do so when reason no longer strives for objective cognition in the metaphysical realm.

Reason aims beyond the limits of possible experience, striving not for the principles (*Grundsätze*) of the objects of experience, but for the unconditioned itself. Reason, as a faculty of principles (*Prinzipien*), does not admit of the sort of proof that Kant pursues for the *a priori* concepts of the understanding. This is because reason never attains the cognition that it pursues, and thus never offers a law for objective justification.[16] In the *Prolegomena* Kant suggestively implies that it might be reason that promises for the understanding "a unified possible experience."[17] Such a possibility is not explicitly developed in the *Critique of Pure Reason*, where Kant begins his analysis of the conditions of the possibility of experience without an attempt to justify his starting point. For this reason, my inquiry must turn to the *Critique of Judgment* in order to investigate the role that a regulative principle can be said to play in the analysis of the understanding, for it is in this later work that Kant hints at some such dependence of our examination of phenomenal experience on a regulative principle. The question that guides this investigation is: Could the regulative use of a principle (*Prinzip*) of reason permit the designation of the realm of possible experience within which the categories of the understanding are deduced?[18]

Kant begins the inquiry into regulative principles in §76 by restating the illusory nature of the ideas of reason. To pursue a principle beyond possible experience leads to the pursuit of transcendent ideas, where understanding, as the cognitive faculty of objectivity, cannot follow reason's demands. So far, Kant has merely repeated the general conclusions of the Transcendental Dialectic. Yet Kant goes on to address more directly the relation of understanding and reason. In explaining how reason can be a principle for the understanding, one that is regulative rather than constitutive, Kant appears to venture beyond the use of regulative principles in both the teleology of the *Critique of Judgment* and the mechanism of the *Critique of Pure Reason*, gesturing toward an explanation of how an account of the unity of the understanding is itself dependent upon a regulative principle.

Kant writes that the understanding is unable to follow reason in its pursuit of the ideas, because it is limited in its application to the sensibly given; yet, without the involvement of the understanding, reason's ideas cannot even pretend to offer objective validity:

> The understanding . . . restricts the validity of those ideas of reason solely to the subject, although still universally for all members of this species, i.e., understanding restricts the validity of these ideas to the condition which, given the nature of our (human) cognitive faculty . . . we cannot and must not think otherwise [*nicht anders als so könne und müsse gedacht werden*], but without asserting that the basis for such a judgment lies in the object.[19]

Kant argues that the understanding limits the "ideas of reason" to the claim that while they offer no objective cognition they are valid for the cognitive faculties of all finite rational beings. Such a restriction permits the teleological use of the ideal of reason to secure the systematic unity of nature, and both the pursuit of the mechanistic elaboration of experience and the practical pursuit of moral freedom as distinguished in the third antinomy of the cosmological idea, yet this only raises further questions. Does Kant dogmatically presuppose that "we cannot and must not think otherwise," designating the region of finite cognition without the influence of reason and its pursuit of the absolute? And further, does this regulative use of the ideas of reason limit itself to the cosmological and the theological ideas, offering no regulative role for the psychological?

In restricting the ideas of reason to the subjective universality of human thought, Kant has distinguished the ideas as regulative principles, propositions that guide the development of human thought without claiming for themselves objective validity. Could it be that what makes this section "deserve to be elaborated in detail in transcendental philosophy," and yet also deems it not to be fundamental to an account of teleological judgment, is that one such regulative principle does not concern the empirical laws of nature but can actually be said to explain the claim that our thinking cannot be otherwise?

Kant follows these provocative introductory remarks with an account of three "examples," describing different areas in which reason affords us accomplishments even after we have come to recognize the illusory nature of its ideas. These areas appear to correspond to the three ideas of reason (psychological, cosmological, and theological). Kant explains the cosmological idea in terms of the pursuit of freedom, while the ideal of reason, the theological idea, is explained in terms of the purposiveness of nature, the explicit explanatory project of the Critique of Teleological Judgment in the third *Critique*. What is particularly striking about this section is that Kant appears to associate the psychological idea with his analysis of finite cognition and the dual faculties of sensibility and understanding that are needed for cognition. Kant explains that for our finite cognition the faculty of understanding must be able to distinguish between the possibility and the actuality of things, which is to say that cognition always depends upon sensibility, on the ability to transform what is thought into something that is actually given. At first glance this does not appear to add much to our comprehension of the Kantian account of finite cognition. We must distinguish our finite cognition from that of an intuitive intellect, whose cognition does not depend upon sensibility and for whom the actual cannot be distinguished from the possible; and yet, Kant introduces this description of the dualism of our finite cognition in the context of a description of the regulative principles that follow from our metaphysical inquiries, and this discussion of the nature of our finite faculties, following Kant's architectonic, appears to designate an accomplishment associated with the first idea of reason, the psychological.

Obviously, one must be careful when interpreting this section, concerning which Kant writes: "We will adduce examples, which are certainly too important as well as too difficult for them to be immediately pressed upon the reader as proven propositions, but will still provide material to think over, material that can serve to elucidate what our proper concern [*eigentliches Geschäft*] is here."[20] Yet it does appear that Kant is distinguishing a tripartite use of reason after the critique of metaphysics. The three examples that he describes offer discussions of the three ideas of reason: the soul, the world, and God. It is the first of these ideas, the soul, the unattainable object of rational psychology, that is most relevant for the present inquiry, for it appears that what Kant is arguing is that the ability to distinguish possibility from actuality, which he claims is fundamental for our finite faculties, corresponds in some manner to the psychological idea. But how do the principles (*Grundsätze*) of possibility and actuality, the empirical rules following from the modal categories, depend upon reason's ideas such that they could be a topic of a discussion parallel to the topics of practical reason and teleological judgment in §76? Unfortunately, such a question is not explicitly answered by Kant, but it would seem to lead us to an explanation of the enigmatic opening section of this paragraph. Does Kant claim that the investigation of the regulative use of reason is relevant for transcendental philosophy but is a digression in the discussion of teleological judgment because it elucidates the regulative underpinnings of the examination of finite cognition that transcendental philosophy accomplishes? What must be investigated is whether §76 is claiming that the account of experience according to the categorical designations of possibility and actuality, the modal categories, depends upon a principle (*Prinzip*) emanating from the critique of metaphysics, and hence whether the account of finite cognition depends in some way upon a regulative principle stemming from the psychological idea.[21]

In undertaking a detailed examination of the three sections of §76, which appear to correspond to the three ideas of reason as they function as regulative principles, I will proceed by reversing the order of both the text of §76 and the Transcendental Dialectic of the first *Critique*. Thus, I will begin by investigating teleological judgment, which corresponds to the theological idea; then proceed to practical freedom, with its dependence on the cosmological idea; and finally turn to finite cognition, which, in keeping with Kant's architectonic, appears to relate to the psychological idea. In reversing the order of the section, as well as the order of the ideas in the Transcendental Dialectic, I will be able to progress from what is more obvious in the context of the Critique of Teleological Judgment to that which presents a considerably more complex interpretive problem.

Reversing the order of the ideas of reason can also be justified through Kant's own classification of the order of these ideas as either analytic or synthetic. In a footnote to the introduction to the Transcendental Dialectic added in the second edition of the first *Critique*, Kant claims that a systematic representation of the metaphysical ideas would begin with the idea of God, proceed to that of freedom, and finally take up the idea of the soul's immortality, as if it were the conclusion of an argument in which the other two ideas were premises (B395n). Such an order would express the metaphysical ideas synthetically. In the *Prolegomena* Kant describes a *synthetic approach* as one that expresses "the structural organization of a quite peculiar faculty of cognition, in its natural connection."[22] As is well known, Kant's investigation of the ideas in the Transcendental Dialectic never produces such a comprehensive account. What Kant does provide is an explanation of why the three ideas of reason will never offer us determinate cognition, and he himself follows the reverse order, beginning with the psychological idea (immortality) and proceeding to the cosmological (freedom) and then the theological (God). In the footnote added in the second edition, Kant calls this reversal of the synthetic order the *analytic order*, explaining that such an investigation begins with what "experience makes immediately available" (ibid.) and then proceeds to what is further from common experience in order to direct the investigation of that which we might otherwise overlook (in this case, freedom and God). An analytic order can thus be understood as one in which the main points of a particular science are raised without attempting to express them in the fullness of their "natural connection." In this footnote Kant explains that the analytic order, which he follows in the Transcendental Dialectic, must precede the synthetic order; yet the synthetic order, which would make "the highest ends of our existence, dependent solely on the faculty of speculative reason [*spekulativen Vernunftvermögen*]" (ibid.), is never directly addressed by Kant after the critique of metaphysical cognition that is launched successfully in the Transcendental Dialectic. Kant writes that the analytic order "is more suitable to the end of completing our great project [*unseren großen Entwurf*]" (ibid.), and what is readily assumed is that no synthetic account of the ideas is possible once the Transcendental Dialectic has shown that none of them lead to the kind of speculative cognition that metaphysics has traditionally pursued. Such an assumption is reinforced by the absence of an account by Kant of the reversal of the ideas that would be needed for their synthetic account, a reversal that is not required for natural science but that instead hopes "to get beyond nature" (ibid.).

However, such an analytic investigation of the ideas of reason, the merely negative critique of metaphysics, would seem to be surpassed in an investigation of the regulative use of these ideas that evade cognition. To investigate the accomplishments born of the ideas of reason even after they have proven themselves cognitively elusive is not to return to the ideas with "what experience makes immediately available to us" (B395n); rather, it is to approach the regulative accomplishments that such ideas afford, beginning with the most obvious of these accomplishments (teleology) and proceeding, finally, to the most ambiguous (psychology). In this sense, while Kant writes that his "great project" (ibid.) calls for the analytic order in its investigation of the ideas, this does not deny the possibility of a synthetic, although not metaphysically dogmatic, approach to these ideas. Such an approach would follow the synthetic path, which, to recall what Kant writes in the *Prolegomena* regarding another complex issue concerning reason, because of its dryness will recommend itself only to "experts [*Kenner*]" in transcendental philosophy.[23]

In quoting once again from §60 of the *Prolegomena*, I am taking the liberty of connecting the question concerning the relation of understanding and reason that Kant there raises to the reversal of the ideas of reason that their regulative use affords. This connection is precisely what I must develop in what follows, but at this point it is enough, I think, to remark that we need not assume that in his refraining from offering a synthetic account of the ideas Kant has ruled out such a possibility. For, as can be seen in the *Prolegomena*, Kant is willing to leave out important questions related to his project of transcendental philosophy if they are not necessary for its basic elucidation, leaving "future additions" to others.[24] What must be asked is: In §76 of the *Critique of Judgment*, has Kant elaborated the synthetic thematization of the ideas for which the *Critique of Pure Reason* has readied us but finally omitted?

III. The Theological Idea as a Regulative Principle

If we are to investigate the varied uses of reason in the regulative sense that Kant raises in §76, we must begin by examining the discussion of regulative principles that unites the seemingly disparate divisions of the *Critique of Judgment* in the account of reflective judgment (*reflektierende Urteilskraft*) in relation to both beauty and teleology. In the original introduction to this work, Kant defines as *reflective* those judgments that search for the universal corresponding to a given particular. Reflective judgments can therefore be distinguished from determinative judgments in that the latter offer the subsumption of a particular under a preordained universal, while the former direct the search for a universal from the perspective of particularity.[25] In both types of judgments a sensible representation must be given. In determinative judgments, a sensible representation is brought under the *a priori* concepts of the understanding. In reflective judgment, where no such concept precedes the judgment, an empirical concept is inductively produced of which the sensibly given object is an example. Such a reflective accomplishment is not a spontaneous act of the understanding, and therefore does not constitute a furthering of the mechanistic analysis of possible experience; rather, it is the production of an empirical concept that, instead of constituting possible experience, expands the systematic account of the empirical laws that govern objects of experience.[26]

Kant describes two varieties of reflective judgment, relating to beauty and teleology. These seemingly distinct areas of inquiry are conjoined in the *Critique of Judgment* insofar as both exemplify the reflective search for a universal that is not given to cognition. In aesthetic reflective judgment, a representation that is still connected to an object is judged insofar as it provokes a feeling in the subject and not as it concerns an object that is determined by the categories of the understanding. While such aesthetic judgment does not afford the designation of a rule that governs the beauty that is judged, it does exemplify a similar parsing of particulars in the pursuit of a general rule that could explain how that which is deemed beautiful can be differentiated from that which merely pleases the senses. While the current account is focused on teleological reflective judgment in order to examine the role of regulative principles described by Kant in §76 of the *Critique of Judgment*, it is worth reminding ourselves that these disparate areas, beauty and teleology, are both examples of reflective judgment, and that both, in Kant's account, exemplify a dependence on regulative principles.[27] Such a shared dependence is what unites the two divisions of the *Critique of Judgment*.

To reflect is to compare representations in the search for a unifying concept.[28] Kant explains that reflective judgment needs a principle to direct this comparison of representations.[29] Such a principle will not determine the constitution of the objects that are reflected upon, a role played by the *a priori* concepts of the understanding when judgment determines the objects of possible experience; rather, the principle of reflective judgment must direct the comparison of representations, dictating what questions are to be asked, and thus how a rule is to be distinguished for diverse representations.

The principle (*Prinzip*) that directs reflection on objects of nature through which teleology establishes the systematic unity of empirical laws is that "for all things in nature empirically determinate **concepts** can be found."[30] This principle is no mere tautology, for why should the manifold of natural objects offer itself in such a way that we can establish laws pertaining to its systematic coherence when reason, in its pursuit of metaphysical knowledge, is unable to distinguish such systematic unity? In order to reflectively judge the system of nature's empirical laws, nature must be viewed as purposive (*zweckmäßig*) for our examination. This is not to claim that nature in its diversity is purposive, or even that such purposiveness follows from the investigation of nature as the totality of possible experience; rather, what is presupposed is the purposiveness of nature for our reflection, that nature must be viewed as pursuing comprehensible purposes. The presupposition of the systematicity of nature is the regulative principle that the reflective power of judgment must give to itself in order to permit the reflective judgment of the diversity of phenomenal nature.[31] In giving itself the principle (*Prinzip*) of the purposiveness of nature, reflective judgment is directed by an idea that reason has been unable to cognize. In the pursuit of the material condition of all that exists, reason finds itself unable to attain any determinate cognition, yet it is precisely such an idea that stands as the principle (*Prinzip*) that is presupposed in all reflective judgment.[32]

In the appendix to the Transcendental Dialectic of the *Critique of Pure Reason*, Kant writes:

> The third idea of pure reason, which contains a merely relative supposition of a being as the sole and all-sufficient cause of all cosmological series, is the rational concept of **God**. . . . the idea of that being, like all speculative ideas, means nothing more than that reason bids us consider every connection in the world according to principles [*Prinzipien*] of a systematic unity, hence **as if** they had all arisen from one single all-encompassing being, as supreme and all-sufficient cause. (A686/B714)

The transcendental ideal provides the idea of the unity of all causal laws, and it is this purposive unity which reflective judgment must presuppose.[33] What is presupposed is not the cognition of the "all-sufficient cause" but the systematic explanation of the variety of "connection[s]" that the understanding has determined. Reason's ideal offers the regulative principle of the system of nature through which reflective judgment organizes the diversity of nature while avoiding the metaphysical illusions to which all claims for the cognition of such a system succumb.

In the *Critique of Judgment*, Kant explains that in order to judge reflectively the systematic unity of nature, reflective judgment must

> further assume for this purpose that nature in its boundless multiplicity [*grenzenlosen Mannigfaltigkeit*] has hit upon a division of itself into genera and species that makes it possible for our judgment to find consensus in the comparison of natural forms and to arrive at empirical concepts . . . i.e., judgment presupposes a system of nature which is also in accordance with empirical laws and does so *a priori*, consequently by means of a transcendental principle [*Prinzip*].[34]

Our reflective investigation of the systematic unity of the empirical laws of nature presupposes that nature offers laws to be discovered. This regulative principle directs reflective judgment, implicitly furnishing it with the direction to reflectively judge the systematic unity of nature's laws. The transcendental principle of reflective judgment deems that reflection can distill empirical laws of nature when it presupposes that nature, the totality of the objects of possible experience, in its diversity, is "qualified for a **logical system** of its multiplicity under empirical laws."[35] Such a principle is transcendental, for it distinguishes the conditions of the possibility of reflective judgment without which we would not be able to judge the empirical unity of such laws. This is not to say that such empirical, reflectively distilled concepts offer universal laws; rather, that if in our examination of the multiplicity of nature we are to make use of empirical laws of the systematic coherence of this diversity, then we need to recognize that we are presupposing a principle that regulates the reflective power of judgment.

Kant begins the final paragraph of §76—the third "example" of reason's regulative use, corresponding with the theological idea (the ideal of reason), which in accordance with a synthetic account of the ideas of reason should begin a discussion of reason—by stating that the following concerns "the case before us."[36] This is to say that the following examination of reason's regulative use concerns teleological judgment, the subject of the second division of the *Critique of Judgment*. My investigation of reason's regulative uses will begin with this section as a prelude to those that in not regarding teleological judgment fall outside the bounds of the *Critique of Judgment* and raise further complications. From the explicit dependence of teleological judgment on a regulative principle (*Prinzip*), I will attempt to examine the more elusive claims that Kant makes concerning reason's varied regulative uses, particularly in relation to the psychological idea and its relevance for the analysis of our finite faculties.

Concerning teleology, Kant writes in §76: "we would find no distinction between a natural mechanism and a technique of nature, i.e., a connection to purposes [*Zweckverknüpfung*] in it, if our understanding were not of the sort that went from the universal to the particular."[37] As we have seen, Kant's account of teleological judgment in the *Critique of Judgment* does not overturn the mechanistic account of nature that the *Critique of Pure Reason* puts forward; rather, it follows from the examination of the understanding that validates a mechanistic view of nature. Kant's account of causality, as one of the twelve *a priori* concepts of the understanding that together with the pure forms of sensibility (space and time) explain the conditions that make possible our experience, distinguishes a mechanistic examination of causes as an empirical project that has its justification not, as Hume claimed, merely in the habits formed by the succession of events, but rather as the condition of the possibility of objects of experience. Kant claims in §76 that we are able to distinguish the "natural mechanism and the technique of nature" only because our understanding proceeds from the universal to the particular. This can be understood in relation to the account of causal explanation as one of the conditions of our experience, one of the *a priori* rules through which the world is made objective. This is to say that particulars are not merely translated into universal forms. The particular, a representation that can be known as an object only by means of the universal concepts that the understanding brings to it, is marked by the contingency of its sensible givenness; while this particular is subsumed under the understanding's universal concepts, it retains its particularity in the spatial determination that distinguishes it as this particular and not another, even if this other manifests the same conceptual determination. Only because understanding proceeds in such a fashion, from the universal to the particular, branding all determination with the mark of contingency, can we distinguish the teleological pursuit of the systematic unity of nature's laws from the mechanistic pursuit of ever-further causal explanation in accordance with the conceptual determination of objects.

The accomplishments stemming from the teleological investigation of nature, "unity, hence lawfulness, in the connection of particular laws of nature,"[38] follow from the contingency of the particular that retains the possibility of further empirical unification. Kant calls the lawfulness that the teleological power of judgment brings to its inquiries the purposiveness of nature; this lawfulness is what judgment must offer its inquiries in order to bring unity to the empirical laws governing either organized beings or nature in general, for what such a principle (*Prinzip*) unites is precisely the contingency that does not give itself over to the conceptual determination of the categories of the understanding. Such particularity does not offer itself to the power of judgment as objectively lawful or purposive; rather, hidden in our judgment of the systematic unity of empirical laws must be the rational idea of the purposiveness of nature, the principle of unity that directs the systematic combination into law of what is otherwise distinct.

To summarize, one could not distinguish a mechanistic account of nature from a teleological one, Kant writes in §76 of the *Critique of Judgment*, if it were not for the account of objectivity in which the understanding proceeds from the universal to the particular, to that which is subsumed under the universal but forever marks the conceptually determined object with its particularity. Teleological judgment depends on this excess, this conceptually indeterminate particularity, for the sphere of its endeavors, but its investigation of this excess to conceptuality cannot presume to attain objective cognition inasmuch as it begins where conceptual determination ends, pursuing the systematic unity of the empirical laws of nature that the mechanistic examination of nature uncovers.

In the account of teleological judgment in §76, Kant argues that the ability to distinguish mechanism from teleology follows from his explication of the conditions of the possibility of objects. Teleology ventures beyond the mechanistic inquiry of determinate cognition, but can do so only when regulated by a rational principle.[39] The possibility of distinguishing mechanism and teleology depends upon the differentiation of the account of the understanding (i.e., finite cognition), in its dependence on sensible particularity, from an intuitive intellect that would not depend on sensible givenness. It is in this sense that we must understand Kant's answer to the antinomy of teleological judgment.[40] Teleology does not contradict mechanism because the former proceeds where the latter leaves off, with the particularity that evades determinate judgment, permitting further examination of what has been determinately judged a law of empirical nature. This is not to claim that teleological judgment furthers the objective constitution of experience, for teleological judgment elucidates the systematicity of the empirical laws of nature only by means of its dependence on the idea of nature's purposiveness. Only through the regulative idea of nature as in itself purposive, through the theological idea of an intelligent world cause, are we able to examine nature teleologically. This is not to claim that there is an actual being that corresponds with this idea of an *intellectus archetypus;* rather, the claim is that teleology and mechanism can be distinguished without contradiction if we are able to contrast "our discursive, image-dependent understanding [*Bilder bedürftigen Verstandes*] (*intellectus ectypus*)"[41] with the thought of an intellect that would not depend on sensible images for its cognition.[42] Kant's claim is that as long as the idea of such an intellect can be thought without contradiction, it can validate the distinction between mechanism and teleology. The conception of such an intellect thus plays a dual role in the case of teleological inquiry: on the one hand, it offers a contrast with our finite faculties, allowing us to distinguish mechanistic from teleological nature without contradiction; on the other hand, the idea of the systematicity that such an intuitive intellect could provide—the purposiveness of nature—offers the regulative principle of teleological reflective judgment, promising the unity that we find in nature.[43]

Kant concludes this section by stating that the subjective principle that reason supplies for teleological judgment is a regulative principle that is "just as necessarily valid for our human power of judgment as if it were an objective principle [*Prinzip*]."[44] This does not mean that such a subjective principle (*Prinzip*) should be conflated with the categories of the understanding that are constitutive of our experience of objects; rather, it states that we can no more deny our dependence on teleological judgment than we can deny our dependence on determinate judgment in the examination of our finite understanding. The *a priori* laws of the understanding are tied to the subjective principle of teleological judgment in a manner that avoids contradiction without denying their difference.

In §77 Kant goes on to explain that both mechanistic and teleological investigations of nature depend upon the presupposition of "the idea of a possible understanding other than the human one."[45] Such an archetypal intellect must be presupposed in teleological judgment as the intentional cause of nature's unity, "just as in the *Critique of Pure Reason* we had to have in mind [*in Gedanken*] another possible intuition if we were to hold our own to be a special kind, namely one that is valid of objects merely as appearances."[46] Yet why is the thought of such a foil to our finite cognition necessary for Kant's analysis of the understanding such that he would write that teleological judgment, which demands a regulative principle, is dependent upon the *intellectus archetypus* in the same way that the analysis of finite cognition has been shown to be so dependent in the *Critique of Pure Reason*?

In the *Critique of Pure Reason,* Kant comes closest to directly addressing a positive role for the *intellectus archetypus* in the analysis of the understanding found in the final chapter of the Analytic of Principles (*Grundsätze*), titled On the Basis of the Distinction of All Objects [*Gegenstände*] as Such into *Phenomena* and *Noumena*. Kant writes of the noumenon, the object that would be given "intuitively in a non-sensible intuition," that through it "our understanding acquires a negative expansion, i.e., it is not limited [*eingeschränkt*] by sensibility, but rather limits [*schränkt*] it by calling things in themselves (things not considered as appearances) noumena" (A256/B312). The negative expansion that the thought of the object of the *intellectus archetypus* provides the understanding designates the ability to limit sensibility to the spatial and temporal forms of experience, marking the boundary of possible experience within the confines of sensible intuition.[47] Kant explains that the thing in itself is deserving of the label noumenon precisely because of such a positive function.[48] And yet, how the noumenon offers more than a mere contrast with our finite intellect is not easy to specify. The question then is: How can the understanding, through the thought of the object of the *intellectus archetypus,* come to be able to limit possible experience to that which is sensibly intuitable?[49]

This complex issue—distinguishing the boundary of possible experience in relation to a regulative principle—is raised in §76 in the course of Kant's investigation of the regulative use of reason's principles. In this section Kant appears to imply that a regulative principle is at work in the distinction of possibility and actuality that underlies the Kantian designation of the realm of experience. But such an inquiry into the regulative principle emanating from the psychological idea must be set aside for a short while longer so that we can continue the synthetic investigation of the regulative uses of the ideas of reason. Having completed an inquiry into the theological idea, the ideal of reason that regulates teleological inquiry, we must now address the cosmological idea and its role as a regulative principle in both mechanistic inquiry and the pursuit of practical freedom. Once this has been done, we will be ready to address the psychological idea and so complete our analysis of §76 by returning to the question of how the understanding, in marking out the boundary of possible experience, can be viewed as dependent upon the thought of a non-sensible object of the sort that can only be known by an *intellectus archetypus.* In so doing we will have returned to the question with which this discussion began: How can the relationship between reason and understanding be conceived? This question can now be viewed as asking whether it is a regulative principle emanating from reason's metaphysical pursuits that directs the understanding's elucidation of the boundary that distinguishes the phenomena of possible experience.

IV. The Cosmological Idea as a Regulative Principle

In describing the second regulative use of the ideas of reason, Kant writes that the concept of "freedom . . . can serve us as a universal **regulative principle**."[50] As we know from Kant's argument in the third antinomy of the first *Critique,* a mechanistic account of nature does not rule out the possibility of human freedom; this is because the mechanistic explanation of causation does not negate the possibility of freedom. The mechanistic account of experience that the first *Critique* offers does not claim that the causality of the natural world governs nature in itself; rather, as the Copernican revolution that Kant initiated in philosophy makes clear, mechanism offers an explanation of the material world as we, human subjects, are affected by it. Since mechanism does not profess to offer a theory of nature, in itself, it makes possible a very different causal principle: the unconditioned causality of human freedom.

Kant writes that when we approach nature theoretically, we "must assume the idea of an unconditioned necessity of its primordial ground [*Urgrundes*]."[51] This is to say that we must approach the mechanistic explanation of nature as if it could explain nature in its entirety. This, Kant claims, is the regulative use of the cosmological idea. Even though we cannot complete such an account, we pursue ever-further mechanistic explanation, ever-further causal explanation of the objects of experience. While the *a priori* concepts of the understanding explain the determinate judgments that mark the conditions of the possibility of objects of experience, causal explanation must be pursued regulatively. In describing the cosmological idea in section 8 of the Antinomy of Pure Reason, Kant writes:

> thus it is a *principium* of reason [*Principium der Vernunft*] which, as a **rule**, postulates what should be effected by us in the regress, but **does not anticipate** what is given in itself **in the object** [*Objekte*] prior to any regress. Hence I call it a **regulative** principle [*Prinzip*] of reason. (A509/B537)[52]

The cosmological idea can be understood to offer a regulative principle that directs the striving of mechanistic explanation even though no completed nature can be thought.[53] Alongside such a regulative conception of mechanistic causality, there is still the possibility of human freedom. Since nature is to be explained in a manner that is so limited, one can posit human freedom as a further causal structure that does not conflict with mechanism and that describes actions unconditioned by mechanistic causes.

Kant describes this sense of the transcendental condition of freedom in the *Critique of Pure Reason*:

> By freedom in the cosmological sense, on the contrary, I understand the faculty of beginning a state **from itself**. . . . Freedom in this signification is a pure transcendental idea, which, first, contains nothing borrowed from experience, and second, the object [*Gegenstand*] of which also cannot be given determinately in any experience. (A533/B561)

The conception of freedom that is thus regulated is the idea of "a spontaneity, which could start to act [*zu handeln*] from itself" (ibid.); it is freedom from the mechanistic causality of nature, a conception of freedom that is not itself taken from experience. It is not because we experience the pull of moral duty that we claim that the transcendental principle of freedom must exist. Although Kant's devotion to such a moral commitment can be said to have given rise to the critical project, freedom is not here justified experientially. Rather, Kant's justification of the transcendental idea of freedom is limited to the avoidance of a contradiction between it and mechanism. Mechanism cannot uncover the unconditioned that is the basis of its conditions; understanding proceeds regulatively toward the goal of the unconditioned, but in its essential limitation such a pursuit leaves open the possibility that there could be a mode of causality apart from the mechanistic chain. This idea that reason "creates" (ibid.) what Kant calls "the transcendental idea of freedom" does not follow from any empirical accomplishment; rather, it offers the possibility of the empirical accomplishment of practical freedom. The development of this account of practical freedom is made possible within critical philosophy by the designation of the transcendental condition of such freedom in opposition to that of mechanism.

Such a transcendental principle of freedom, however, does not depend upon "an intelligible world, corresponding completely with the moral law."[54] Reason offers the possibility of freedom to a being that cannot attain knowledge of the intelligible world and that, if it is to avoid dialectical illusion, can pursue such freedom only in the practical realm; moral duty is thus understood as the regulative attempt to live in accordance with the universal moral law, to purify the maxims of our actions in the pursuit of this universal order without presupposing that the world as it appears conforms to such a posited order. What is morally necessary is empirically contingent, as what ought to happen does not always happen, and yet this does not negate the possibility of morality, but merely highlights the relation of freedom and mechanistic causality that the third antinomy has shown avoids contradiction. The idea of freedom is the condition that underlies the critical justification of the attempt to live according to a universal moral order, even though such an order is not only beyond our reach but would be possible only for a rational being for whom "everything would be actual merely because it is (as something good) possible."[55]

Kant completes this section on the transcendental principle (*Prinzip*) of freedom in its regulative function by stating that this principle does not "determine the character of freedom, as a form of causality, objectively."[56] The antinomy that follows from the cosmological idea does not determine the causal structure of freedom as if freedom were merely a continuation of the mechanism of phenomenal nature or, on the contrary, as if freedom could be objectively determined.[57] What it does offer is a conception of transcendental freedom as a regulative principle that "makes the rules of action in accordance with that idea into commands [*Geboten*] for everyone"[58] without contradicting the mechanistic account of nature.

Kant develops the account of the universal command of morality in the *Critique of Practical Reason*, elucidating the "postulates of practical reason" which produce the admiration for, and commitment to, the moral law that the transcendental principle of freedom has deemed possible, as well as the categorical imperative which directs the choosing between possible maxims of actions.[59] In this account Kant can be understood to be developing the regulative possibility raised in the third antinomy of the first *Critique*, for it is the cosmological idea that directs all finite rational beings to the transcendental idea of freedom as a way to develop their moral feeling systematically. The deliberation that follows from the categorical imperative can be said to proceed regulatively; the attempt to purify maxims draws us closer to the universal law that cannot be determined.[60]

V. The Regulative Foundation of Critique

We can now return to Kant's enigmatic discussion of finite cognition in §76 of the *Critique of Judgment*. In the midst of a discussion of the regulative roles played by the ideas of reason, Kant explains that our finite cognition, in its differentiation of the possibility and the actuality of things, is in some way dependent upon a regulative principle. Regulative principles have been shown to be at work in those areas in which cognition is unattainable. In both aesthetic and teleological judgment, regulative principles following from the theological idea are presupposed in their respective reflective acts, and in terms of the cosmological idea, regulative inquiry directs further causal explanation while permitting alongside of it the regulative pursuit of freedom. Yet how does a regulative principle (*Prinzip*) find its way into Kant's account of determinate judgment, into the differentiation of possibility and actuality, when unlike the other areas of regulative inquiry, such judgment *does* offer the chance for cognitive accomplishment?

In the Postulates of Empirical Thought chapter of the first *Critique*, Kant explains that the modal principles (*Grundsätze*)—possibility, actuality (the category of existence [*Dasein*]), and necessity—are not additions to the constitution of the phenomenal object, "but rather express only the relation to the faculty of cognition" (A219/B266). An object can be either possible or actual depending on whether the sensible determination corresponding to the conceptual representation is given. Such modal judgments determine the subject's relation to the object. The object as sensibly given is actual, a sensible thing that can be said to exist; yet even if such an object is not given to the senses, if it can be thought as conforming to the structure of human sensibility, if the object thought is potentially sensible, then it can be judged as an object of possible experience.

The critical classification of objects according to their relation to the perceiving subject follows from the Copernican revolution that the first *Critique* initiates. By examining the human faculties that permit phenomenal experience, Kant avoids the dilemma that follows from the attempt to justify our claims about how things exist apart from our perception of them. He does so by divesting the historical investigation of cognition of the need to claim such authority for its judgment. By distinguishing human finite cognition from the absolute cognition that has been the elusive goal of metaphysical inquiry, that is to say, by separating the faculties of understanding and reason, Kant distinguishes the sensibly given as the criterion of objective cognition. For Kant, only by recognizing the interconnection of the two sources of human cognition, sensibility and understanding, can we "judge about things with objective validity" (A271/ B327); in this way, sensibility designates the basic criterion of human cognition but does so without negating the understanding's role in cognition, for not only does cognition demand that the sensibly given be subsumed under the understanding's categories, but so too while an object of experience must offer the possibility of being sensibly given, it need not be sensibly given for its possibility to be cognized. The limits of sensibility mark out the region of finite cognition, a territory that Kant has famously designated as possible experience.

Since the modal principles of possibility and actuality follow from the investigation of finite cognition that prioritizes neither sensibility nor understanding, if we are to look for an explanation of how it is that the possible-actual distinction depends upon a regulative principle, and hence how the realm of possible experience does as well, then we will need to rethink the very beginnings of the critical project. The question then is: How does Kant justify the claim that both understanding and sensibility are required for cognition (ibid.)? This question returns us to the demand for a metacritique that Hamann launched, the rhetorical criticism of the Kantian system that claims that its divisions destroy what they are meant to explain. While the above examination of teleology proves why one need not deem Kant's metaphysical inquiries merely negative, as they permit the coexistence of not only mechanism and freedom, but also mechanism and teleology, this proliferation of non-contradictory approaches to the manifold of human representations still appears arbitrary. How can Kant justify the dualistic account of finite cognition that distinguishes possibility from actuality and hence mechanism from both freedom *and* teleology?

In §76 of the *Critique of Judgment*, Kant writes that for the exercise of our cognitive faculties it is indispensable that the possibility and actuality of objects be distinguished, and that this follows from the "nature" of our faculties.[61] Kant would appear to have justified the phenomenal distinction of possibility and actuality with a dogmatic claim about our faculties, yet he goes on to imply that the account of the "nature" of the human cognitive faculties is, itself, dependent upon a regulative principle that affords the designation of the modal principles (*Grundsätze*) of possibility and actuality. In the Postulates, Kant explains that the distinction of possibility and actuality (as well as necessity) restricts the use of the understanding to empirical and not transcendental use (A219/B266). By means of the examination of the use of the understanding merely in relation to that for which the possible-actual distinction is valid, Kant has been able to account for the categories as an *a priori* component of empirical cognition, for only by means of such categories is the experience of objects possible. Yet, how is Kant able to justify the confinement of the examination of cognition to the empirical use of the understanding prior to the critique of metaphysics, as it is by means of the examination of the understanding that Kant is able to show the futility of the transcendent use of this faculty? The answer that is here being developed is that it is a regulative principle emanating from reason's pursuit of the ideas that provides the boundary of possible experience and limits the investigation of cognition to that which can be empirically given.

The differentiation of possible and actual objects rests upon the exercise of the two components of human cognition. An object is possible when it can be thought, represented not merely according to the *a priori* concepts of the understanding, but also according to the formal conditions of sensibility; but such a thought, conceptually determined, can be designated as actual only when a sensible representation can be subsumed under it. If our human understanding were intuitive, rather than discursive, if it could provide the intuition of all that it thought conceptually, it would have only actual objects, for it would never lack the intuition that distinguishes the possible from the actual. Since human understanding is not intuitive, it cannot infer the actuality of an object that it thinks without such an object being sensibly given.

Kant writes in §76 that we cannot presuppose that thought and intuition are the two distinct elements of cognition for all possible cognition. Cognition could occur in such a way that there would be no distinction between the sensible and the intellectual, and therefore none between possibility and actuality. The designation of objects of experience as defined by the distinction of possibility and actuality is thus merely a claim about our finite faculties and not one that "lies in the things themselves [*in den Dingen selbst liege*]."[62] Kant explains that we know this to be so

> [f]rom the unremitting [*unablässlichen*] demand of reason to assume some sort of thing (the original ground) as existing absolutely necessarily, in which possibility and actuality can no longer be distinguished at all, and for which idea our understanding has absolutely no concept, i.e., can find no way in which to represent such a thing and its way of existing.[63]

But why must reason demand the assumption that something exists "necessarily" for us to be able to recognize that human cognition, in which possibility and actuality are distinguished, deals only with objects of appearance and not with objects in themselves?

Perhaps the answer to this question is obvious. Kant is able to limit the claims that he makes concerning cognition to the sensible appearance of objects because in the Transcendental Aesthetic he has already presupposed the limits of the cognitive faculties and a realm beyond their grasp that would offer itself for cognition only to an intuitive intellect. This idea of a being with an intuitive intellect has been shown to function as a regulative principle for the teleological examination of nature; yet, in discussing the possible-actual distinction in cognition, Kant is pursuing not the systematic unity of the empirical laws of nature, but the underlying assumptions of the analysis of finite cognition. The "original ground" offered by reason's ideas in this case is not that of an infinite intellect for whom possibility and actuality would not be distinguished; rather, Kant writes that although we are led to think of that which "outstrips [*über-steigt*]"[64] our cognitive faculties, and this outstripping announces our inability to know things in themselves, we must limit our cognitive claims to that which conforms to the dualism of sensibility and understanding. To do so, Kant writes, we must take as our "maxim [*Maxime*]" that "we should think all objects [*Objekte*] in accordance with the subjective conditions for the exercise of our faculties necessarily pertaining to our (i.e., human) nature."[65] This is to say that we need to use a conception of our cognitive faculties to direct how we think about all objects and so avoid pursuing the illusions of metaphysics. Such a conception of our human cognitive faculties does not offer "constitutive principles" that distinguish objects as they are in themselves; rather, the conception of the subject, what Kant describes as "the subjective conditions for the exercise of our faculties," offers a regulative principle that directs our thought of objects and is "appropriate from the human point of view."[66] Kant is here raising a third area of regulative inquiry, which would appear to be tied to the psychological idea. A conception of our finite faculties must be presupposed in order to direct our inquiry into objects, and yet, in the Paralogisms chapter of the first *Critique,* Kant has argued that we can have no knowledge of the subject as it exists in itself. Could it be that the idea of the subject that is beyond our cognitive reach regulates Kant's epistemological inquiries?

VI. Conclusion: The Regulative Pursuit of the Boundary of Phenomena and Noumena

In §76 of the third *Critique,* Kant does not explain the precise functioning of a regulative principle (*Prinzip*) emanating from the psychological idea; however, he has clearly stated that reason's regulative principles do not merely complement the accomplishments of the understanding, but actually afford the examination of our faculties. While the idea of God, reason's ideal, regulates the teleological pursuit of empirical laws of nature, and the cosmological idea regulates the pursuits of both mechanism and freedom, it would appear that the idea of the thinking subject in some way regulates the account of finite cognition.

Such a regulative dependence is not fully explained in this enigmatic section of the *Critique of Judgment,* yet it appears that Kant has highlighted the dualism of sensibility and understanding, and the resulting distinction between possibility and actuality in human cognition, in a manner that directs us to question how it is that they have come to be so distinguished. This is not to question the accomplishments of the Transcendental Analytic; rather, it is to explore how it is that the realm of possible experience has been demarcated such that Kant could explicate human cognition as a function of it. Thus, what remains to be investigated is how human cognition has been limited to the realm of the sensible prior to the critique of metaphysics that it ultimately permits, such that the possible-actual distinction can be deemed basic to all human cognition. Could there be a regulative principle hovering unannounced in the account of finite cognition, with its dualism of sensibility and understanding and the corresponding distinction of possibility and actuality?

While in the *Prolegomena* Kant cryptically describes reason as "setting the boundary to the field of experience through something that is otherwise unknown to it,"[67] in the *Critique of Judgment* this boundary setting is connected to the regulative use of the principles (*Prinzipien*) of reason. Yet the questions with which this chapter began, and with which Kant closes the *Prolegomena,* remain: How can reason be seen to set the bounds for the investigation of finite cognition? And how, if it does, can the universality of the principles (*Grundsätze*) of the understanding be maintained, granted that a regulatively pursued principle (*Prinzip*) is found to underlie their designation?

THREE

The Designation of the Region of Experience in the Critique of Pure Reason

I. In Pursuit of the Kantian Conception of Experience

In the wide-ranging First Introduction to the *Critique of Judgment,* Kant reiterates the general conclusion of the *Critique of Pure Reason,* explaining that "the whole of nature [*die gesamte Natur*] as the totality of all objects of experience constitutes a system in accordance with transcendental laws, namely those that the understanding itself gives *a priori.*"[1] While nature, within the critical project, has come to be understood as the totality of all objects of possible experience, this does not mean that nature will only permit an investigation of these universal laws, for while nature, following from its critical definition, is limited to that which can be subsumed under the *a priori* concepts of the understanding, what can be thus subsumed offers itself for further examination within the critical system. The *Critique of Judgment* can be understood to address precisely such a task. Reflective judgment distinguishes a further way, beyond the mechanism of categorical analysis, that nature can be examined. By pursuing nature's systematic coherence regulatively, we are able to explain how teleological progress is possible within the limits of possible experience, which is to say, the territory within which the categorical analysis of objects has been distinguished. Teleology does not contradict mechanism because, as Kant explains in the antinomy of teleological judgment, teleology pursues its inquiry beyond the territory of mechanistic explanation. Only because finite cognition has been explained as dependent upon the sensible subsumption of particulars under transcendental laws can teleology be distinguished from mechanism, for only thus is finite particularity understood to extend beyond mechanistic analysis.

But why does Kant begin his investigation of cognition in the *Critique of Pure Reason* with the presupposition that cognition depends upon both sensibility and understanding? This question is often answered in a manner that betrays its historicist assumptions. Kant, we know, was answering both rationalism and skepticism, both Leibniz and Hume, in his critical work. He was attempting to save objectivity without, in so doing, making unjustified metaphysical claims. Thus, Kant marks off metaphysical inquiry prior to his systemization of thought, pursuing cognition only in that realm which offers empirical representations. The Copernican turn that produces the dual realms of phenomena and noumena is thus understood as a response to skepticism that does not embrace dogmatism. Philosophy will not only pursue its investigation of cognition merely within the region of empirical objects, but also such objects will be investigated in relation to the cognitive faculties that permit their appearances.

Such an interpretation of Kant, in its attempt to limit his accomplishment to a historically determined, epistemological strategy, denying any positive function for the noumenal realm in the designation of the region of objects of experience, makes Kant appear guilty of conflating an epistemological response to particular historical questions with a metaphysical claim about the composition of our faculties. To state the problem in another way: Does a good answer to Leibniz or Hume constitute a good philosophical position? If Kant's philosophical approach can be justified only as an epistemological response to a historical problem, then our return to it would be merely a historical exercise that offers answers to questions that are no longer living philosophical concerns, since we are neither Leibnizians nor Humeans.

For this reason those who claim that Kant's project is limited to or at least founded upon an epistemological accomplishment attempt to explain that Kant's conceptions are epistemologically correct, regardless of their particular historical origins. In this way one could defend Kant's analysis of cognition as a description of our fundamental and, in some sense, self-evident capacities, and so naturalize Kant's epistemology,[2] or one could describe the critical system as offering a justified account of objects as they exist apart from human thought, and so embrace realism in Kant's name.[3] In either case one has deemed Kant's analysis of our cognitive faculties justified in a manner that appeals to neither its historical origins nor its metaphysical presuppositions.[4] But a defense of Kant's account of our cognitive faculties on either naturalistic or realistic grounds is unable to avoid the metacritical challenge. What justifies the conception of experience that underlies both of these approaches? And how can we defend the use of *a priori* concepts of the understanding, derived from such experience, to establish the illusory nature of all metaphysical claims?[5]

To follow the path of such questions is to accept the need for a metacritique, and so to literally pursue what Hamann demanded only rhetorically. To look for the justification of Kant's analysis of the cognitive faculties is to begin the endless pursuit of that which would justify such criteria of justification.[6] Prescribing such an infinite task for those who want to preserve their Enlightenment confidence in reason is the ironic demand of one who has abandoned the Enlightenment project, but what it also signals is the looming partition of reason from the objects that serve as the criteria of its justification. If we are to demand of critical philosophy that it justify the criteria of its examination of cognition, if we want to trace the progression from cognitive objects to the fundamental truth that is expressed in and that allows us to surpass these mere objects, then we have stumbled onto the path of idealism that culminates in Hegel and, in exemplary fashion, his *Phenomenology of Spirit*. For only if we permit the synthetic surpassing of what seems obvious—the "experienced world"—only if we begin with it and yet relinquish its claims on us, can we be led through the dialectical conflicts that await our attempts to justify this experienced world and to a response that approaches the authority that Hamann demands: the Hegelian absolute. To do so is not to produce a metacritique of the critical investigation of the cognition of objects, but to transcend the experienced world of possible objects for which Kant pursues the conditions of possibility. This is not merely to say that what has been overcome is the Kantian conception of experience, but also that reason will have been severed from the realm of empirical objects that the Enlightenment would have it serve.

Such a Hegelian rejoinder responds to a conception of Kant's transcendental philosophy that would have him attempting to separate his epistemological accomplishment from his critique of metaphysics. While it is obvious that this is the order of the first *Critique*, that the investigation of the conditions of the possibility of experience is undertaken prior to the critique of metaphysics, it is not clear that this is the way to understand the transcendental method. Could it be that the elucidation of the conditions that make the experience of objects possible leads us to a justification of the conception of experience with which critical philosophy begins?[7] Such a possibility, which can be understood to accept the limits to the critical approach for which Hamann criticizes Kant—and in so doing subverts Hegel's criticism—will be developed in the next chapter. But here I will begin with an investigation of why it is that the narrowly epistemological reading of critical philosophy must be rejected. Only by explaining from within critical philosophy how the limits of possible experience have been designated, only, that is, by uncovering a more complex relationship between epistemological and metaphysical concerns in the first *Critique,* will we be able to understand that it need not be read as a dogmatic epistemology, blind to its own method. Doing so I will attempt to challenge the claim that critical philosophy "must leave out a reflexive or systematic comprehension of its own enterprise."[8]

II. Objects of Experience in the Analytic of Principles

This chapter began with Kant's claim in the First Introduction to the *Critique of Judgment* that "the whole of nature [*die gesamte Natur*] as the totality of all objects of experience constitutes a system in accordance with transcendental laws, namely those that the understanding itself gives *a priori.*" The *a priori* concepts of the understanding are the conditions of the possibility of objects of experience, and together they form the system of the transcendental laws of nature. This claim is challenged by Hamann's assertion that to examine objects in terms of the categories, separating their conceptual structure from their sensible determination, is to reduce the complexity of lived experience to the structure of Kant's rationalist dualism. To begin an examination of experience with the presupposition that it can be systematized according to the dualism of sensibility and understanding is to continue the metaphysical project of reductive rationality under the guise of avoiding both dogmatism and skepticism. But is this necessarily so? Does the Kantian investigation of synthetic cognition presuppose that its dualistic account offers access to the fundamental structures of human consciousness? Or does Kant avoid such a bloated claim by designating merely the limited realm of experience within which the analysis of cognition can be said to produce objectivity?

If such a conception of Kant's undertaking can be shown to be the case, then the relevant question will not demand, with Hamann, a metacritique that could justify the dualism of sensibility and understanding, an impossible request that can be understood to have found its fitting conclusion in Hegel's absolute. Rather, the question would ask whether the account of cognition that Kant has been able to produce can, in the terms that it engenders, explain the designation of the limited territory within which it begins. How is it, we would then ask, that the boundary of possible experience has been demarcated such that the system of the conditions of the possibility of synthetic cognition within this limited realm have been deduced?

It is worth noting that the above-quoted passage concerning the system of laws that the understanding gives to itself *a priori* continues with the parenthetical claim that these laws are valid "for appearances, namely, insofar as they, combined in one consciousness, are to constitute experience." Kant goes on to explain:

> For that very reason, experience in accordance with general as well as
> particular laws, insofar as it is considered objectively to be possible in
> general, must also constitute (in the idea) a system of possible empirical
> cognitions [*Erkenntnisse*]. For that is required by the unity of nature, in
> accordance with a principle [*Prinzip*] of the thoroughgoing connection
> of everything contained in this totality of all appearances.[9]

The systematic laws that the understanding gives itself depend, Kant writes, on the constitution of experience. Experience must be defined as the realm of "appearances" as they are "combined in one consciousness," as the totality of "possible empirical cognitions," if the conditions of its possibility are to be deduced. Kant has thus explained that the exposition of cognition does not begin with the designation of the dualism of sensibility and understanding: the investigation of the structure of cognition depends upon the specification of the realm of possible experience, and from such a conception the dualism of sensibility and understanding follows.

Nature offers critical philosophy both mechanical and teleological investigations only because it has been taken as corresponding to the system of possible experience, as the totality of objects that can be sensibly represented and subsumed under *a priori* concepts of the understanding.[10] Nature, for Kant, does not refer to the incomprehensible complexity of lived experience, but to the system of all empirical cognition that is deemed "possible experience" within critical philosophy. To conflate "lived experience" with Kant's "possible experience," to interpret critical philosophy merely as empirical realism and not as transcendental idealism, leads to the demand for a metacritique, for a justification of the structural elements that are presupposed in the critical account of cognition.[11] But if the designation of the boundary of possible experience is recognized as one of Kant's fundamental accomplishments, then the metacritical demand dissipates and is replaced by the question of whether the confinement of experience within the realm of appearances can be justified in the conceptual vocabulary of the critical system.

While interpreters have attempted to justify Kant's assumptions concerning the discursive nature of human cognition by claiming that it is an obvious feature of our perceptual lives, such a naturalized defense, even if it could be proven true, in no way explains why experience should be conceived as limited to that which the discursive faculties describe,[12] for why, we could ask, could not our cognitive faculties exceed the discursive? What the above quotation from the 1781 introduction to the first *Critique* points toward is that the explication of the *a priori* concepts of the understanding depends upon the demarcation of the sphere of possible experience; only when experience has been limited to the totality of empirical cognition can the systematic unity of the understanding be so explained.

But how are we to understand such a role for experience, the seemingly unexamined presupposition of the first *Critique*?[13] What needs to be investigated is whether the designation of the region of possible experience could be guided by a regulative principle (*Prinzip*) that does not presuppose the constitutive authority of its rule, but merely directs the striving toward its never-promised completion. But what would such a regulative principle be like, and further, in what sense can the designation of the realm of possible experience be a reflective accomplishment that depends, as do all reflective acts for Kant, on a regulative principle?

Such questions can be best addressed if we return to the problems raised in the enigmatic §76 of the *Critique of Judgment*. As we have seen, in this section

Kant introduces the issue of a regulative use of reason that concerns our ability to designate the region of objects whose possibility can be distinguished from their existence. The modal categories of possibility and actuality offer determinate judgments that correspond to the region of empirical cognition. Could it be that these categories, and in fact the entire categorical elucidation of cognition, depend upon the designation of the region of possible experience, on the limitation of the search for *a priori* synthetic cognition to what can be presented to us as empirical objects? With this question we have returned to that of the *Prolegomena*: How can the boundary of possible experience be distinguished, how can experience be limited to empirical appearances, to spatial representations, such that its examination provides the boundary within which the categories that permit the critique of reason's metaphysical strivings are deduced?[14]

In order to examine the regulative principle at work in the limitation of experience to objects that conform to the possible-actual distinction, it will be necessary to return to the Postulates of Empirical Thought, Kant's examination of the synthetic principles emanating from the modal categories in the second chapter of the Analytic of Principles (*Die Analytik der Grundsätze*) in the *Critique of Pure Reason*. Kant describes the analytic of principles as "solely a canon for the **power of judgment** that teaches it to apply to appearances the concepts of the understanding, which contain the condition for rules *a priori*" (B171/A132). In following the analytic of concepts in the Transcendental Analytic, this division neither introduces nor justifies the understanding's *a priori* concepts; rather, it investigates the empirical manifestations of the *a priori* concepts of the understanding.

In the second chapter of the Analytic of Principles, titled the Synthetic Principles of Pure Understanding, Kant investigates the synthetic judgments that in their dependence on the schematized categories "flow [*herfließen*] *a priori* from pure concepts of the understanding . . . and ground all other cognitions *a priori*" (B175/A136). The *a priori* concepts of the understanding are the source of the principles (*Grundsätze*) that deem that whatever is encountered as an object will abide by these rules.[15] This is to say that when the sensibly given is subsumed under the categories, this schematization of the sensible and the intelligible distinguishes for each of the categories a principle that, while containing the ground of empirical judgment, is not "grounded in higher and more general cognitions" (A148/B188). For Kant, the region of experience is dependent upon the synthetic accomplishments of the categories. Without such synthesis, Kant explains, experience "would not even be cognition but rather a rhapsody of perceptions" (B195/A156). The principles of the pure understanding are thus at the basis of experience as they distinguish the rules for all objects of experience. In this section Kant investigates such principles in their ability to designate the rules of empirical cognition. The Postulates of Empirical Thought examines the modal principles (*Grundsätze*), those that designate possibility, actuality, and necessity. Hence, it is to that chapter that we must turn in order to investigate Kant's discussion of possibility and actuality in §76 of the *Critique of Judgment*, where the modal designation is described as a regulative accomplishment.

If it can be shown that possibility and actuality, as principles (*Grundsätze*) of the pure understanding, owe their designation to a regulative principle (*Prinzip*) that delineates the realm of possible experience within which the *a priori* conditions of objective cognition have been distinguished, then the systematic account of the *a priori* concepts of the understanding will have shown itself to be dependent upon reason's pursuit of the ideas of metaphysics. Proving this will reveal that the relation of understanding and reason in the critical project is both more complicated and more crucial than has typically been maintained. This is because the realm of experience, as that which permits the designation of the faculties of cognition, cannot itself be explained in the limited conceptual vocabulary that it permits.

In order to better conceive of the modal principles of possibility and actuality, we will need to investigate more closely the Postulates of Empirical Thought, the chapter of the first *Critique* in which the modal categories are discussed insofar as they determine the rules of empirical objects. For if we want to maintain, with Kant in §76 of the *Critique of Judgment*, that the differentiation of possibility and actuality depends upon a regulative principle (*Prinzip*), then we must show that a principle (*Grundsatz*) that follows from one of these categories "plays the role of a principle [*Prinzip*]," as Kant writes in the *Critique of Judgment*,[16] but is not precisely a principle (*Prinzip*), as it depends for its designation on a further principle (*Prinzip*), but one that in distinguishing the region of possible experience, in drawing the boundary between the finite and the infinite, avoids metaphysical dogmatism.

What can be noted initially is that Kant refers to both the Analogies of Experience and the Postulates of Empirical Thought, the principles (*Grundsätze*) that follow from the categories of relation and modality, respectively, as regulative principles (*Grundsätze*). Kant does this in the Analogies section of the Analytic of Principles after having completed the examination of the Axioms of Intuition and the Anticipations of Perception, what he refers to in this section as constitutive principles (*Grundsätze*), and prior to the examination of the Postulates. While this terminology is appropriate for my general argument, as I am looking to interpret the examination of finite cognition in terms of possibility and actuality, and thus the principle of modality as distinguishing a regulative accomplishment and hence as dependent upon a principle (*Prinzip*) emerging from reason's metaphysical pursuits, we must proceed tentatively. At this point in the first *Critique*, Kant has not yet offered a thorough account of regulative accomplishment, which he does only in the Antinomies chapter of the Transcendental Dialectic, and then again in the appendix that follows the

Transcendental Dialectic, before more fully addressing the role of such principles in the First Introduction to the *Critique of Judgment*.

Kant labels the Axioms and Anticipations "mathematical principles [*Grundsätze*]" and the Analogies and Postulates "dynamical principles [*Grundsätze*]" in the introductory remarks to the detailed investigation of the four groups of principles. Kant explains that in the "application [*Anwendung*]" of the pure concepts of the understanding to possible experience, "the use of their synthesis is either **mathematical** or **dynamical**" (B199/A160). The mathematical principles concern the intuition of appearances; they offer the principles of the *a priori* conditions of intuition and are thus "unconditionally necessary," which is to say "apodictic" (ibid.), for without their application to possible experience there could be nothing intuited, no perception at all. For this reason, Kant writes that the mathematical principles relate "to appearances with regard to their mere possibility" (A178/B221), and later he explains that such possibility defines appearances in their sensible givenness. The mathematical principles can be called constitutive principles because they explain the production of appearances in terms of "both their intuition and the real in their perception" (ibid.). Such principles offer intuitive certainty, which does not mean that they subvert the understanding that is their source; rather, it means that their judgment does not demand discursive activity but is immediately evident insofar as through them appearances are intuitively constituted.

The dynamical principles, the Analogies and the Postulates, do not dictate how empirical intuition, which is to say perception, comes about; any certainty that such principles offer is mediated by the need to apply these rules to appearances discursively. While the mathematical principles concern the intuition of appearances, the dynamical principles pertain, Kant writes, to the existence (*Dasein*) of appearances (B199/A160). Their application to possible experience determines the confines of objects of experience. In terms of the Analogies, Kant explains, this application provides the unity of experience that arises from the perceptual manifold, the unity that is the condition for the possibility of objects but that is pursued regulatively (A180/B222). The dynamical principles, insofar as they judge the relations of existence, are necessary for there to be objects of experience, and yet, such judgments are not immediately given but must be pursued as discursive achievements within the confines of the heterogeneity of the perceived. They are thus regulative accomplishments, directing further cognition of experience, but they are not constitutive of the intuition of appearances.[17]

While the regulative function of the principles of relation can be understood according to the example of the pursuit of ever-further mechanistic explanation, directed by the idea of a rational cosmology that does not offer itself for cognition, as has been discussed above but which in the first *Critique* is addressed only later in the Antinomies, the regulative function of the postulates is less clear.

And yet to explain a regulative element in the modal principles has been the goal of this project from the start. What is at issue is whether the very designation of the terrain of possible experience, and thus the critical analysis itself, can be understood to depend upon a regulative principle (*Prinzip*) emanating from its own inquiry.

The categories of modality, Kant writes, "have this peculiarity: as a determination of the object they do not augment the concept to which they are ascribed in the least, but rather express [*ausdrücken*] only the relation to the faculty of cognition" (B266/A219). The Postulates, the principles of modality, are the rules that follow from these categories in their empirical use. These principles restrict the other three groups of categories (quantity, quality, and relation) to their empirical use by denying the transcendental use of the categories in the pursuit of what cannot be empirically given. If the categories are not to have a merely logical application, if they are to determine objects of cognition, then they must pertain to what can be empirically given, which is to say that the categories of quantity, quality, and relation must apply to possible experience if they are to distinguish objects and not merely logical relations. The categories of modality, and the principles stemming from them, designate the confines of the possible, actual, and necessary, thus determining the outline of the relation of the conceptually determined object to the cognitive faculties. In so doing, Heidegger writes, Kant has "at the same time delimited being to the being of the objects of experience [*das Sein zugleich einschränkt auf das Sein der Gegenstände der Erfahrung*]."[18]

This is not to say that the Postulates, the modal principles, merely graft a completed conception of objects, as determined by the three prior groups of categories (quantity, quality, and relation), onto the cognitive faculties of the perceiving subject; rather, the modal principles explain the conception of experience upon which the other principles depend.[19] The preceding principles are already assumed to be limited to the realm of possible experience, which is to say to that which accords with the formal conditions of experience, in the examination of empirical objects. In fact, to deny these categories would entail denying the possibility of experience, and thus the appearance of objects, as the Transcendental Deduction has shown. This is why the categories of modality, and more explicitly the Postulates as the principles (*Grundsätze*) emanating from them, appear to offer little to the examination of the conditions of experience. The determinations that they offer are already latent in the prior categories as what they explain, and the judgments of possibility, actuality, and necessity that they determine, have been used in a seemingly unproblematic way up to this point in the analysis of cognition.

The categories of modality thus explain the presuppositions of the other principles. To examine the conditions of the possibility of objects of experience is to limit the investigation of cognition to what can be empirically given. This designation avoids the pursuit of metaphysical cognition, that is to say, cognition beyond the limits of possible experience, through the determination of the modal principles. These principles explain the rules that determine the confines of experience, and hence the region of possible objects. The modal principles add nothing to the completed determination of the object, for they have distinguished what is to count as an object for our cognitive faculties prior to such determination. What should be evident is that such an explanation of the modal principles, the Postulates, subverts the order of the groups of categories. The categories of modality, the fourth group in the table of categories, and the principles emanating from them designate the terrain within which the determination of objects according to the other three groups of principles can be investigated and so, in this sense, can be said to come prior to the other principles.

What is becoming clear is that if we are to find a regulative principle at the foundation of the designation of the duality of finite cognition, and if we are to explain in this way the dependence of the understanding on reason that Kant promises in the *Prolegomena*,[20] then we will have to investigate the structure of the critical project. Could the examination of the conditions of the possibility of objects of experience point beyond itself to the metaphysical presuppositions that dictate the relation of subject and object that is embedded in the first *Critique*? And could the Postulates, in designating principles that offer, as Kant explains, nothing to the constitution of the object, hint at the further investigation that will examine the presuppositions of transcendental philosophy?

The postulate of possibility (*Möglichkeit*) is the first of Kant's modal principles. An object is deemed possible if it conforms to the conditions of experience, but merely in a formal and not in an empirical manner. If a thing can not only be conceptually determined but can "be thought solely under those conditions on which all objects of experience rest" (B271 / A224), which is to say that such a thing could be given as a spatial appearance, then it is deemed a possible object. "[S]pace is a formal *a priori* condition of outer experience" (ibid.) without which objects cannot be empirically given. Outer experience, as a formal condition, is necessary for an object to be deemed possible. If this formal condition is not met, if a thing that is thought cannot be spatially given, then even if its concept is not internally contradictory it cannot be deemed an object of possible experience. It is a necessary but not sufficient condition of the possibility of a thing that its concept not be contradictory. Thus a thing can be judged an object of possible experience only when its conceptual determination corresponds with the conditions of sensibility, when it can be empirically given and so can have a spatial determination.

The sensible form of space takes precedence over that of time in the judgment of possible experience because, while all thought is temporally determined, only that which is spatially determined can be distinguished as an empirical object.[21] A conceptually determined thing that meets the formal conditions of experience, which is to say it is determined as both temporal *and* spatial, can be deemed a possible object. In the section titled General Comment on the System of Principles, appended at the end of this chapter in the second edition (B288–94), Kant notes, "It is even more remarkable, however, that in order to understand the possibility of things in accordance with the categories and thus to establish the **objective reality** of the latter, we do not merely need intuitions, but always **outer intuitions**" (B291). That we have outer intuitions determines not merely the possibility of those objects being determined, but also, Kant claims, such spatial appearances are essential for distinguishing the categorical structure of experience. This is clear already in the Transcendental Deduction, where in the second edition Kant explains that the representations from which the categories and the unity of apperception are deduced are, in fact, spatial (B137). This is to say that the Deduction begins not from the manifold of merely temporal representations but from the subset of spatial representations within it, those that are both temporal and spatial, which permit the elucidation of the conditions of the possibility of experience.[22]

The postulate of possibility, the modal principle, can thus be understood to distinguish the region of experience as that of spatial appearances. And it is this designation which, as we have seen, permits the deduction of the categories. This is to say that the categories are deduced and the principles that follow from them are elucidated by means of the conception of possible experience that is itself one of these principles, and is in fact in their final group. The principles that emanate from the categories of quantity, quality, and relation, the first three groups, all presuppose the conception of possible experience that is only distinguished by the modal principles that follow them. What is uncovered is an apparent paradox: the Postulates, as offering the conception of possibility that distinguishes the region within which the categories are deduced and from which the principles follow, both designates the region of experience and follows from it. This circularity will be addressed in the following section as we further investigate the designation of the region of possible experience as the starting point of critical inquiry. Before entering into that discussion, however, we will return to the analysis of the modal principles, continuing with the second: actuality (*Wirklichkeit*).

An actual (*wirklich*)[23] object not only meets the formal criteria of experience but is directly perceived as a spatial object, which is to say that the formal possibility is actualized by the sensible intuition, by means of which it can be said to exist. The existence of an object cannot be determined by the concept of the thing (B272/A225), Kant explains, for even if the object meets the formal criteria of experience, its actuality, its determination as existing, cannot be inferred from its possibility. An object can be possible and yet resist direct perception. Such perception is the sensible givenness of the material, which corresponds to the conceptual determination. The actual object thus differs from the possible object only insofar as in the former the object is sensibly given. The actuality of an object marks something more than mere possibility, but what is offered does not denote a furthering of conceptual determination beyond what the possible offers. Kant explains in a footnote at the end of this section:

> **Through the actuality** of a thing I certainly posit more than the possibility, but not **in the thing**; for that can never contain more in actuality than what was contained in its complete possibility. But while possibility was merely a positing of a thing in relation [*Beziehung*] to the understanding (to its empirical use), actuality is at the same time its connection with perception. (A235n / B287n)

What must be remembered is that the modal categories do not add anything to the conceptual determination of the object; they affirm only the relation of the object to the cognitive activity of the perceiving subject. The realm of the actual does not exceed the realm of possible objects. This is because the actual differs from the possible only insofar as the formal conditions of experience that the possible exhibits are, in the actual, sensibly given. The sensible givenness that transforms a possible object into an actual one is the addition of the material to the concept that has already, as a possible object, been judged to correspond to the formal conditions of experience.

While the actuality of an object is dependent upon its sensible givenness, there is, Kant writes, a class of actual objects that are not directly given (A225–26/B273). If an object is not directly perceived but can be judged, according to the Analogies of Experience, as cohering with what is actually perceived, then it too can be judged actual and not merely possible. This is because the Analogies permits the judgment of a thing's determination from its relation to another determination; so, if the latter is sensibly given, then the former, according to the law of its relation, must not only be possible but must be actual, even if it is not directly perceived. The inference of actuality is what Kant, in the third postulate, calls the principle of necessity (*Notwendigkeit*).

Kant writes that the third postulate, following from the modal categories, concerns material necessity and not a purely formal or logical necessity. As we have seen in the examination of actuality, what is actual is what not only conforms to the formal conditions of experience but is also sensibly given. The actual is perceived in a manner that "yields the material for the concept" (A225 / B273). Yet even prior to the perception of the thing, its existence can be cognized if, in accordance with the principle of causal law (the Second Analogy), the thing can be lawfully connected to a perception that is sensibly given. Kant calls such a cognition "comparatively *a priori*" (ibid.), inasmuch as what is possible is transformed into a cognition of what exists without its being sensibly given, as its perception is lawfully promised by means of the causal law, and the state that is promised is necessity. The modal principle of necessity marks off this realm of the "comparatively *a priori*" cognition of the actual by distinguishing the actual, as what is sensibly given, from what coheres with the actual but is not itself perceived. This lawfully promised actual cognition is distinguished from the actual since it follows from the principle of necessity.[24]

What should be clear from this discussion of the Postulates is that while these principles, as Kant explains, offer nothing to the conceptual determination of perceived objects, they do distinguish the limited realm within which the other categories can be applied if they are to determine objects for our cognitive faculties. This is to say, the modal principles explain the types of relations that conjoin conceptually determined objects and our cognitive faculties, and thus limit the use of the categories to the confines of such possible objects. And it is for this reason that Kant writes of the Postulates that they are "restrictions of all categories to merely empirical use" (A219/B266).

We have been searching for an explanation of the path taken by critique. The problem that we have come to recognize is that the categories, and the principles following from them, elucidate the confines of experience only insofar as such experience is designated in advance. The question then concerns how thought can designate in advance what is possible, how it can mark out the limits of its own faculties. It is a question, then, of a certain circularity: How can the conception of experience with which critique begins be anything other than an empirical concept that is itself a product of the investigation that it permits?[25]

III. The Circularity of Experience

In the Transcendental Doctrine of Method, which closes the first *Critique*, Kant returns to the question of the role played by the conception of experience in his account of the principles of the understanding, connecting this initial presupposition to the circular method of his system. Kant explains that when thought investigates the realm of ideas, it can attain no synthetic *a priori* cognition; only the understanding can erect such "secure principles [*sichere Grundsätze*]," but not directly from concepts, rather only when its concepts are taken in relation to "possible experience." Such experience, in the technical sense that Kant here intends, is "entirely contingent [*ganz Zufälliges*]" (A737/B765). If the objects of possible experience are presupposed, then the concepts of the understanding are able to generate principles that are "apodictically certain," but these principles cannot "be cognized *a priori* (directly)" (ibid.).

The principles of pure understanding follow from the unity of the forms of sensibility and the categories of the understanding; these *a priori* elements distinguish the realm of experience which yields to Kant the proof of the principles that are there exemplified. And yet these principles—and this is particularly true of the postulates, the principles related to the modal categories—designate the conception of existence (*Dasein*) that is at work in the Kantian account of experience. Kant explains of such a principle that "it has the special property that it first makes possible its ground of proof, namely experience, and it must always be presupposed in this" (A737/B765).[26] The Kantian principles (*Grundsätze*) follow from the categories of the understanding, which themselves are deduced from the conception of experience; in this way the principles both follow from the initial conception of experience and help to elucidate its confines.[27]

Heidegger, in *What Is a Thing?* (*Die Frage nach dem Ding*), his lecture course from 1935–1936, explains: "the principles of pure understanding are possible through that which they themselves make possible [*Die Grundsätze des reinen Verstandes sind durch dasjenige möglich, was sie selbst ermöglichen*]."[28] Heidegger does not criticize Kant for the circularity of critique; rather, he claims that such circularity points to the manner in which critique can be seen to transform its epistemological beginnings. The principles (*Grundsätze*) do not lay a fixed foundation; "experience," grounded by these principles, is, Heidegger writes, "a circular happening."[29] Kantian experience both permits the analysis of these principles and is defined by them. In this way, Heidegger writes, "what lies within the circle becomes exposed [*was innerhalb des Kreises liegt, eröffnet wird*]."[30] What is exposed, in Heidegger's account of Kant's project, is that which lies between the subject and the thing, a complex entanglement that surpasses the attempt to designate its ground. The circularity of critique directs Heidegger beyond Kant's cognitive claims, leading him to interpret the human being "as he who always already leaps beyond things."[31]

While Heidegger in *What Is a Thing?* elucidates the circular method that allows Kant to point beyond epistemological constraints, he does not here investigate the initial designation of the region of possible experience that permits Kant such analysis, limiting his inquiry to what follows from the circular undertaking that begins with this presupposition.[32] Rather than following Heidegger beyond critique to "the between—between us and the thing [*das Zwischen— zwischen uns und dem Ding*],"[33] my inquiry will be directed toward the fundamental designation of possible experience that permits Kant his analysis, and will investigate what such a designation and the metaphysical presuppositions it entails tell us about the Kantian method.

With this discussion of the circularity of Kantian critique we are brought back to the questions with which we began our investigation of the Analytic of Principles. In §76 of the *Critique of Judgment*, Kant deems only that which permits the possible-actual distinction to be an object for our finite cognition, and he describes such a limitation as one of the examples of the regulative uses of reason. Thus we have approached the postulates in order to investigate whether Kant's examination of these principles (*Grundsätze*) can explain how the differentiation of possibility and actuality might be tied to reason's metaphysical pursuits. This inquiry began with the dual purpose of justifying the criteria through which Kant examines cognition (the metacritical demand) and explaining how Kant is able to mark the boundary of possible experience such that the conditions of its possibility can be distinguished; while we are no nearer to the first, that is, to a response to the demand for a metacritique, the second appears to be coming into focus. The postulates explain the rules that direct the conceptual examination of empirical objects, and yet we have not explained what presuppositions are hidden in such rules, in this choice of empirical objects as the field of philosophical inquiry. Such an inquiry into the metaphysical presuppositions of the examination of cognition in the first *Critique* will not offer the metacritique that Hamann rhetorically demanded, for any such metaphysical principle (*Prinzip*) that can explain the designation of the limitations of experience will not be constitutive but merely regulative; however, if we can uncover a regulative principle that is implicated in the critical examination of objects of experience, then we will have found in Kant's transcendental method a much more complex structure than has typically been distinguished.

This mode of inquiry certainly appears foreign to the linear development of the first *Critique*. Yet it should not be forgotten, however accustomed we have become to the progression of the book, that the Transcendental Aesthetic is a startling, epoch-changing, and yet utterly unjustified beginning point. This opening onto the critical examination of cognition provides the passage to a conception of experience that subverts both skepticism and dogmatism, but does so by means of an "experiment [*Versuch*]" (Bxviii) that dictates the sensible confines of not merely the examination of cognition but philosophical investigation more generally.[34] This is not to raise the possibility either of a further non-temporal and non-spatial form of sensibility, nor of a non-sensible intuition; rather, it is to question whether the account of cognition that follows from this dualistic conception of sensibility—and the manner in which it is developed throughout the Transcendental Logic—begins to address its own presuppositions in the Postulates.

Although the preceding discussion has interpreted the conception of objects of possible experience for which the first *Critique* has pursued the conditions of possibility, we have not yet begun to investigate the justification of this starting point. What must now be examined are the metaphysical presuppositions of the Kantian analysis of cognition: What view of subjects in relation to objects is embedded in the critical accomplishment? If we address this question while reverting to neither the rationalist dream of an ultimate foundation nor the skeptical resignation to its failure, we can investigate the dependence of the Kantian examination of cognition on the designation of the boundary of experience, within which the account of cognition proceeds. This is to say, while the Analytic of Principles affords us a conception of the principles (*Grundsätze*) of the empirical determination of the categories, we can still ask about the presuppositions embedded in the designation of experience that permit cognition to be so conceptualized; this is to move, as we shall see, from the questions of Hamann to those of Hegel, from the discourse of metacritique to that of boundaries. Does not the act of designating the boundary of possible experience, which is essential to critical philosophy, imply a step beyond this boundary, a passage beyond finite cognition into the realm of the infinite that Kant would have us avoid?

In order to continue this inquiry into the metaphysical presuppositions implicit in Kant's designation of possible experience as the field of critical inquiry, the notoriously ambiguous Refutation of Idealism must be examined. What will become apparent is that the interpretive difficulties in Kant's argument, those surrounding the status of "this persistent thing [*dieses Beharrliche*]" outside us that secures the conception of ourselves as temporal, can lead us to investigate the connection that holds between reason's pursuit of non-sensible metaphysical ideas and the understanding's pursuit of finite cognition. The difficulties surrounding the interpretation of this section cannot be easily overcome; however, its argument, inserted into the second edition of the first *Critique*, immediately following the second postulate of actuality, will be seen to direct us to the Transcendental Dialectic in search of an account of the metaphysical underpinnings of Kant's examination of finite cognition.

IV. The Refutation of Idealism and Its Relation to the Postulates

Kant inserted the Refutation of Idealism into the second edition of the first *Critique* in the middle of the Postulates of Empirical Thought with the claim that it was meant to end the

> scandal of philosophy and universal human reason that the existence of things outside us (from which we after all get the whole matter for our cognitions, even for inner sense) should have to be assumed merely **on faith**, and that if it occurs to anyone to doubt it, we should be unable to answer him with a satisfactory proof. (Bxl, n)

Kant placed the Refutation directly after the discussion of the rules governing the empirical designation of actual objects and prior to that of material necessity, the third postulate. The limited, critical conception of actual objects that the Postulates explains would appear to preclude all claims about objects apart from their subjective appearances. However, the Refutation argues that any attempt to begin philosophical reflection with a conception of the temporal determination of empirical consciousness implies a commitment to "something **persistent** [*etwas **Beharrliches**]*" (B275) apart from the temporal flux of appearances. Thus, while the Refutation begins as an argument against Descartes' claim that we know ourselves as thinking subjects with a certainty greater than that which we can claim for the objects we perceive, its final target is much broader, offering an account of why even Kant's transcendental idealism corresponds to "something **persistent**" apart from the phenomenal realm of appearances. In my explication of this argument, what will become clear is that Kant is here examining the presuppositions of the critical project: What, we must ask, is implied in the Kantian adherence to the temporal nature of consciousness? And how does this argument against a Cartesian conception of self-knowledge claim that *all* attempts to examine human existence, which includes the Kantian as well, are committed to the existence of things apart from their temporal representations?

Kant directs his argument in the Refutation at an idealism, attributed to Descartes, that claims that we cannot be certain that objects exist in space outside of us. Kant calls this idealism *problematic idealism* and distinguishes it from what he refers to as *dogmatic idealism,* which claims to be certain that objects do not exist in space outside of us. The latter, Berkeleyan idealism, Kant argues, has been subverted by the very starting point of the first *Critique,* where in the Transcendental Aesthetic Kant has begun with a conception of space as a form of intuition and a condition of the possibility of the experience of objects (B274). Berkeley's idealistic skepticism concerning spatial objects is directed at a conception of space as existing apart from all human perception. Such a view of space and the objects that exist in it leads to a skeptical conclusion, but it is not a necessary view of either space or objects. If space is conceived as a form of intuition, and if objects are understood as the appearances that correspond to such forms of intuition, then the Copernican revolution undertaken by transcendental philosophy will have avoided the position of the dogmatic idealist; and yet this subjectivist turn would appear to leave open the possibility that objects do not actually exist in themselves and that the Kantian accomplishment, in explaining objects as phenomena, forbids any claim about actual things that would correspond to the appearances that we perceive. The question then is: Can Kant argue from the account of the conditions of the possibility of objects of experience that something persistent apart from these appearances exists?

Kant begins the argument of the Refutation by claiming, "I am conscious of my existence as determined in time." This, Kant writes, is the Cartesian position, but it is also the contention implicit in critical philosophy (B275); to deny this would be to embrace a skepticism more radical than that of problematic idealism.[35] Time determination necessitates something permanent according to which its passage can be measured. This persistent thing must be something apart from the determination of time; and it must be a permanent thing that is not within us, which is to say that it is not itself a part of the temporal procession of consciousness. Kant is not referring to a representation of a thing (B275, Bxl, n), but to the need to connect our perception to something distinct from all subjective representation in order to explain temporal determination, and thus also the consciousness of our existence in time. In order to conceive of oneself as temporal, one must presuppose something persistent in relation to which temporal self-awareness, which is to say the awareness of oneself as the unified consciousness of the temporal flux of representations, is possible.

Kant concludes the argument of the Refutation with the claim that "the consciousness of my own existence [*das Bewußtsein meines eigenen Daseins*] is at the same time an immediate consciousness of the existence [*Daseins*] of other things outside me" (B276).[36] Any conception of oneself as temporally constituted depends upon a relation to a permanent thing through which the self can be designated as temporal. This persistent thing, a "**thing** outside me [*Ding ausser mir*]," is distinguished by Kant from the "mere **representation** of a thing outside me" as the precondition of temporal self-determination (B275). But what could Kant mean by the existence of a thing outside me, which is not a representation and is also not, as he adds in the second preface, an intuition (Bxxxix), upon which temporal self-awareness depends? In what sense could a thing be outside me if it is not to be considered a representation constituted by the sensible forms of space and time?

Kant has introduced the argument of the Refutation as one directed at Cartesian idealism, or the skepticism that follows from Descartes' method. I will begin by examining this argument merely insofar as it stands as a refutation of such a skeptical position. Such an analysis will lead to a broader discussion of the role that the Refutation plays within transcendental idealism. This is to say that we will begin our investigation of what such a persistent thing that guarantees temporal self-awareness could be without assuming that such self-awareness refers to the Kantian conception of inner sense and the empirical apperception it affords. Clearly, the argument in the Refutation contra Cartesian idealism does not depend on the explicit conclusions of the Transcendental Aesthetic, unlike both its argument against Berkeleyan idealism and the first edition's discussion of idealism in the Fourth Paralogism.[37] And yet it is an open question whether the Refutation might also apply to the temporal claims of transcendental idealism. Setting aside this question in order to examine whether the Refutation can be understood as a limited argument *only* against Cartesian idealism, we must at least initially be careful not to interpret Kant's terminology in the Refutation as referring to the technical vocabulary of transcendental idealism, for in the critical system this persistent thing, the "**thing** outside me" that is distinguished from the "mere **representation** of a thing outside me," seems, at least at first glance, a contradiction. How can that which is not a representation be "outside me" when *outside* is a spatial term that applies, for Kant, only to appearances as representations?

If we are interpreting the Refutation in such a manner, directed only against Cartesian idealism and bereft of the structure of the critical system, then we can say that the persistent thing with which Kant concludes is but the realist conception of a realm of things existing apart from us. This is to say that what Kant has argued for in the Refutation is that the consciousness "of my existence as determined in time" (B275) of Cartesian idealism depends on the existence of a persistent thing that is not dependent on my perception of it. In this sense the Refutation appears to pose no interpretive problem. The persistence would be that of our everyday conception of objects, which leads us to reject the idealist assumption that our inner consciousness—the Cartesian "I think"—is more certain than the existence of objects apart from us. As Kant writes, "the game that idealism plays has with greater justice been turned against it" (B276). This is to say that outer experience is deemed "immediate [*unmittelbar*]" and the temporal determination of inner experience is what is now relegated to the mediated or indirect element (B277).

And yet interpreting the Refutation in this way makes it appear as if Kant inadvertently produced an argument that refuted his own idealism, for Kant begins the argument against Cartesian skeptical idealism with the premise that "I am conscious of my existence as determined in time [*Ich bin mir meines Daseins als in der Zeit bestimmt bewußt*]" (B275). It is from this premise that he goes on to conclude that there must be something persistent that is not itself a representation in me. So, while this argument is directed against Cartesian idealism, its initial premise, that of being conscious of oneself as determined in time, also addresses Kant's own transcendental idealism, which begins in the Transcendental Aesthetic with our temporal determination, which Kant calls our inner sense.[38] And it is this inner sense which, through the unifying acts of the understanding, and the unity of the I of transcendental apperception, offers us empirical, temporal apperception (B132–35). From this beginning Kant goes on to argue for the developed program of transcendental idealism. Thus, what the Refutation would seem to prove is that even Kant's own transcendental idealism, his Copernican-inspired turn toward the subjective constitution of appearances, necessitates a conception of a thing outside us in a manner apart from all representation. In order to begin where Kant's transcendental idealism does, that is, with the temporal constitution of all of our representations, we must also assume that such a non-representational thing outside us is to be found.[39]

The problem is that in interpreting the Refutation in this way, as an argument directed at Cartesian idealism and as only inadvertently addressing transcendental idealism, the realist conclusion that follows contradicts the Kantian position, for Kant's transcendental idealism embraces empirical realism only insofar as such objects are for us representations.[40] To demand that there be something persistent apart from the representational manifold, as the Refutation does, would appear to deny a fundamental tenet of Kant's idealism by raising the need for some sort of direct access to the very objects that are, for him, beyond our reach.[41]

If we wish to interpret Kant's refutation of problematic idealism while not at the same time inadvertently refuting his own transcendental idealism, then we will need to interpret the Refutation from within Kant's critical system.[42] The question then concerns what such a persistent thing that is not a representation could be both within the conceptual vocabulary of transcendental idealism and as an argument against the problematic or Cartesian idealist who does not embrace the Kantian system. What is clear is that in the Refutation Kant is not reiterating the First Analogy and its designation of the principle of substance as necessary to explain the "persistence [*Beharrlichkeit*]" (B224/A182) that affords temporal change within the realm of appearances.[43] In the First Analogy such persistence is explained by means of the category of substance through which both simultaneity and succession, and thus all time determination, can be distinguished. The Refutation not only uses a form of the same term, referring to the "something **persistent** [*etwas **Beharrliches***]," but connects such persistence to time determination as well.[44] And yet Kant is clear that the persistence to which the Refutation refers is not that of an appearance, and the time determination of the Refutation that the persistent thing affords is not that of spatiotemporal objects;[45] rather, this persistent but non-appearing thing is required not for the temporal determination of objects, but for our own temporal consciousness. The persistent thing of the Refutation does not return to the First Analogy and its examination of the condition of all temporal determination; rather, it describes what all philosophical inquiries that accept the temporal determination of perceptual consciousness must claim about the existence of things apart from perceptual experience.

How then can we interpret the Refutation and the persistent thing for which it argues? If Kant is not in any way referring to an empirical object when the Refutation argues for a persistent thing outside of us, then we would seem to be left with things that are in no way empirical, which is to say objects in either the transcendental or the noumenal sense, as the anchor of our temporal self-awareness. Clearly, the interpretive issues are not easily overcome. Kant has described this persistent thing as "an immediate consciousness of the existence of other things outside me [*ein unmittelbares Bewußtsein des Daseins anderer Dinge außer mir*]" (B276), and as "something actual [*etwas Wirkliches*]" (Bxl).[46] But in what sense either the transcendental object or the noumenon can be "outside" us or "actual," given to "consciousness" or in any way conceived as existing, must be addressed if we are to be able to interpret Kant's Refutation of Idealism in a way that is *not* at odds with his transcendental idealism.

While Kant on occasion refers to the transcendental object as a noumenon, he typically distinguishes such non-sensible things.[47] This is evident in the

Phenomena and *Noumena* chapter, with which Kant ends the Analytic of Principles. In this chapter Kant describes the transcendental object (*Objekt*) as the objective correlate of the subjective unity of apperception in a manner similar to the way that he describes the transcendental object (*Gegenstand*) in the first edition's Deduction (A109). It is transcendental subjectivity that offers the logical unity of apperception, and the transcendental object that offers unity to the manifold of sense data. Kant explains that it is by means of this transcendental object (*Objekt*) that "the understanding unites that [manifold] in the concept of an object" (A250). This transcendental object is that to which the understanding refers appearances, but removed from its role in cognition "nothing would remain through which it would be thought" (A251). This object, Kant writes of the transcendental object, "cannot be called the *noumenon*" (A253), for a noumenon would not in this way play a role in cognition; it refers, rather, to the abstraction from our mode of cognition, to an object only insofar as it is *not* an object of our sensible intuition. This is Kant's negative conception of a noumenon, corresponding to the limits of our finite faculties. It can be contrasted with Kant's positive claim, in which the noumenon refers to "an **object [*Objekt*] of a non-sensible intuition**" (B307) of which we know nothing, but which would be known by one who had an intellectual intuition. To pursue knowledge of the positive sense of noumena, of non-sensible objects, is to court the very errors against which the Transcendental Dialectic argues, but in its negative sense the concept of noumena is "merely a **boundary concept** in order to limit the pretension of sensibility, and therefore only of negative use" (A255/B310–11).[48]

This differentiation of transcendental object (either *Objekt* or *Gegenstand*) and noumenon is maintained in the Ideal of Pure Reason chapter of the Transcendental Dialectic, the critique of the possibility of attaining knowledge of God. Kant explains that the "transcendental object [*Objekt*] lying at the ground of appearances . . . remain[s] . . . inscrutable [*unerforschlich*] for us" (A613–14/ B641–42). He writes that "forces of nature that express their existence [*Dasein*] only through certain effects remain inscrutable for us, for we cannot trace them far enough through observation" (A613/B641). The transcendental object remains but the unfathomable unity of appearances; "existence" can be attributed to it only in the sense of the analytic unity of apperception, which can only be inferred from sensibly existing objects, since it cannot be in any manner observed and thus does not offer itself for further inquiry. On the other hand, the ideas of reason, noumena, cannot even be called "inscrutable." While the transcendental object denotes the unity of the appearance, the noumenon—Kant is here discussing the theological idea—marks "the need [*Bedürfnis*] of reason to complete all synthetic unity by means of it" (A614/B642). The noumenon cannot be transcendentally deduced, and so it cannot even be described as "inscrutable" as it is not "given as a thinkable [*denkbarer*] object" (ibid.) that merely lacks further determination. Rather, noumena are extensions of the categories of the understanding beyond all possible experience. They do not offer objects to be thought, but merely the goals of such objects to our thinking (as either illusion or regulative principle). Noumena offer no certainty, even in the inferential manner of the transcendental object.

What should be clear is that the transcendental object cannot be the persistent thing that the Refutation argues is presupposed in our temporal self-awareness. While it raises a conception of an object distinct from the phenomenal realm, such a transcendental object is inferred from this realm of objects and so presupposes not merely temporal self-awareness but objects of experience, and thus more than the Cartesian idealist need accept. Kant makes this clear in a note on the problem of idealism from the late 1780s: "every object signifies something distinct from the representation" and what is so signified is here described as the "transcendental object [*Gegenstand*] of apperception."[49] This leaves the noumenon as a possibility to interpret the Refutation. In their negative sense noumena refer to no objects at all, marking merely the boundary of cognition, and so offering nothing that could be considered either "persistent" or "outside me" in the manner that the Refutation requires. The positive sense of noumena refers to all that is thought through the furthest extension of the categories of the understanding. This idea raises the possibility of an existence apart from the perceiving subject in a purely intellectual fashion. And yet, such a positive role for noumena is beyond our cognitive faculties and plays no constitutive cognitive role. As should be clear from the previous chapter's discussion of the *Critique of Judgment,* the ideas of reason that guide our pursuit of noumena function not constitutively but only regulatively.[50] Such ideas, insofar as they function as regulative principles, direct inquiry where cognition is not possible. They are conceived as guiding points through which further inquiry is permitted without claiming that such ideas of reason have corresponding objects. Such unattainable ideas of reason to which the understanding is drawn offer regulative principles for the development of our finite faculties when their illusory goals are curtailed by critique. Could the persistent thing of the Refutation refer to such an idea of reason, one that is implicitly at work in all analyses of consciousness as temporal, as the permanent something against which all change is distinguished? While developing such a claim will take much effort, and while the solution to the problems raised in the Refutation will be addressed only in my final chapter, at this point it should be noted that such an interpretation of the Refutation does not suffer from the limitations of one that would attribute such permanence to the transcendental object, since it does not demand that the idealism it wishes to refute adheres to the objects of experience with which the critical system begins. Rather, what it needs to assert is that to accept the claim that consciousness is temporal is, implicitly, to be directed by a conception of an object as a persistent thing apart from human thought, a regulative idea that allows us to distinguish the unified temporal flux. In this way, such a regulative idea of reason could be conceived as offering a response to Cartesian idealism while at the same time fitting into the architectonic of transcendental idealism.

Before we move on to investigate the dependence of temporal self-awareness on a regulative principle emanating from such an idea of reason, we must step back and investigate the initial presuppositions of the Refutation. The Refutation begins with the premise concerning temporal self-awareness. It is from this premise that Kant develops his argument that this beginning entails the persistence of something apart from a temporally determined, perceiving subject. What has here been shown is that this inference applies as well to Kant's transcendental idealism, which begins with the same presupposition. But is such a temporal presupposition, held by both Kant's notion of Cartesian idealism and Kantian idealism, self-evident? As was noted at the start of this discussion of the Refutation, it clearly is not in this way presuppositionless. Kant himself raises a skeptical challenge to a view of the self as temporally constituted in the first edition's Paralogisms chapter. Kant offers a logically possible alternative to the attempt by rational psychology to infer the identity of the thinking subject. Kant claims that the flux of perception, rather than being the successive appearings of perceptual matter for the I that is conscious of its continuous nature, could be composed of utterly distinct perceptual data. The successive perceptions could, Kant writes, follow one another in the fashion of a ball that when striking another ball passes its force on to this other, and thus the apparent unity of consciousness could mask a chain of disparate elements related only as causes and effects (A363–64n). If perceptual experience could be the product of such a process, if the I of unified perceptual experience could not be inferred from the experience of succession, then the presupposition of the post-Cartesian skeptic's position would be shown to be ill-conceived. Consciousness of oneself in time would not be able to justify confidence in the existence of this unified I, and therefore would not necessitate the non-phenomenal persistence of something that the Refutation has inferred from it.[51]

In the Refutation, Kant was clearly aware of a more radically skeptical way to challenge the existence of things apart from the subject as a perceiving consciousness. Not only had he raised such a possibility in the first edition's Third Paralogism,[52] but he had also partaken of the skeptical method of equipollence in the Transcendental Dialectic, in the Antinomy of Pure Reason, and so it would be difficult to claim that in the Refutation Kant overlooked the ways in which his answer to Cartesian idealist skepticism cannot answer more radically skeptical positions. But how can we understand Kant's confidence in having proven the existence of a persistent thing apart from all representation in the Refutation when he has done so only for such a Cartesian presupposition? This is to say that Kant has proven the existence of a persistent thing that stands apart from all perception, but only if we hold that we are conscious of ourselves in time. If we deny the latter, then we need not admit the former.[53]

In this sense, the Refutation fits comfortably in its setting within the Postulates in the Transcendental Analytic. For this chapter, in its entirety, investigates the role of *a priori* concepts in the cognition of empirical objects while bracketing all question of the use of such *a priori* concepts beyond the limits of experience. So too, the Refutation, both as an argument against the method of Cartesian idealism and as an explanation of Kant's own transcendental idealism, addresses idealist skepticism only from the perspective of the consciousness of our existence in time. Kant confirms this point in his introductory remarks to the Refutation when he explains that he will prove that **"inner experience, undoubted by Descartes, is possible only under the presupposition of outer experience"** (B275). "Inner experience" is not a self-evident starting point; rather, its justification as the point of departure in Kant's argument is precisely the fact that Descartes did not doubt it. This question of perspective or orientation in Kant's inquiry should be familiar from the discussion above of the Postulates, where Kant has distinguished the actuality of objects from the perspective of the limitation of objects to spatiotemporal experience and so initiated a circular undertaking. In the Refutation, Kant makes the broader claim that any philosophical inquiry that begins with a commitment to temporal self-awareness, as both Cartesian and transcendental idealism do, must also be committed to the existence of something apart from such temporal consciousness. In this sense, the Refutation reminds us that in beginning transcendental idealism with an investigation of the temporal unity of our thought, in the initial move of the Copernican turn, which is to say prior to the analysis of cognition, we have already marked our dependence on a claim that goes beyond the limits of this inquiry. And what such a presupposition appears to offer is a way to conceive of the role of a regulative principle (*Prinzip*) in the examination of cognition; yet, at this stage, not much more can be said about such a claim.

The pursuit of an account of reason's regulative role in the examination of the presuppositions of the transcendental analysis of cognition is precisely the goal of this book. We have been pursuing the relation of the critique of metaphysics to the examination of finite cognition in the *Critique of Pure Reason*. The question that has led us concerns the dependence of Kant's epistemological accomplishment on a metaphysical presupposition even after the rejection of the possibility of attaining metaphysical knowledge: Must not Kant's epistemology rest on some metaphysical claims concerning, at the least, the conceptions of subject and object on which it depends? The Refutation of Idealism, with its placement within the Postulates in the second edition of the first *Critique*, appears to offer hope for just such an account of the dependence of the Kantian explanation of objectivity on a regulative principle in its reference to a persistent thing that is presupposed in temporal self-consciousness.

That the Refutation, interpreted as such an inference to the metaphysical, should be placed by Kant in the midst of the postulates, directly after and explicitly in reference to his analysis of the comparatively *a priori* actual, is also worthy of note. As was discussed above, in describing the postulate of actuality Kant explains that besides the actual that is given in perception, we can distinguish something as actual when it is designated as such by a law of the understanding. In this way an effect is judged actual when its cause is empirically given: the perception of the cause deems the effect to be actual even if it has not been perceived, and so Kant describes such inferred actuality as "comparatively *a priori*" (A225 / B273). Kant introduces the Refutation by saying that idealism has objected to "these rules for proving existence mediately" (B274). And what he means by this is that Cartesian idealist skepticism begins with a commitment to the idea that objects can be doubted in a way that thought cannot. Kant recognizes that the discussion in the Postulates would not convince the Cartesian idealist, who would not accept the veracity of the causal law on which the inference is based, and so he introduces a further inference that disproves the skeptical conclusion and, at the same time, reminds the reader that transcendental idealism also implies the existence of something beyond the perceptual realm. Thus, while the discussion of actuality in the Postulates distinguishes the mediated actuality of possible objects by means of the understanding's causal law, the Refutation introduces a mediated existence beyond all subjective representation. The latter mediated existence of the Refutation, in stepping beyond the region of possible experience, entails an inference not of the understanding but of reason. Only through the investigation of reason's illusory metaphysical pursuits will we be in a position to address the question of whether such ideas offer the persistent thing that temporal self-awareness demands.

We were led to the Postulates in the search for an explanation of how a regulative principle can be understood to be necessary for the Kantian differentiation of possibility and actuality as promised in §76 of the *Critique of Judgment*. With its placement in the midst of the Postulates in the second edition, the Refutation of Idealism directs this inquiry toward the Transcendental Dialectic in an attempt to justify the criteria through which the conditions of the possibility of objects of experience have been distinguished.

V. Conclusion: The Modal Principles and the Designation of the Region of Experience

How can we develop an account of a positive function for the noumena in the analysis of cognition from Kant's predominately negative critique of metaphysics? This problem is particularly relevant in the case of the Paralogisms chapter: if the rational subject remains elusive, how can this avoid influencing the claims made on behalf of the subjective conditions of experience? Kant writes, "it is never given to us to observe our own mind [*Gemüt*] with any other intuition than that of our inner sense." And thus we "know even ourselves only through inner sense, thus as appearance" (A278/B334). And yet, surely, in the account of the cognitive faculties some sort of knowledge of the mind is being asserted. Kant continues in this passage, in a manner that makes clear his skeptical commitments, by explaining that the source of sensibility, "[i]ts relation to an object . . . lies too deeply hidden for us" (ibid.). What we want, what philosophy has always wanted, is the super-sensible source of appearances, and yet, what is within our reach is an acquaintance with even ourselves merely as phenomenal appearances.

Nevertheless, the critical project has been able to develop a philosophical system that encompasses a wide range of human experience using a conceptual vocabulary that is distinguished by its examination of the limited conception of phenomenal objects. This accomplishment has not refuted the radical skepticism that the antinomies diagnose; rather, it has produced a conceptual structure that stands within the confines of these limitations. In order to excavate the foundations of this structure, we will have to investigate the conception of the subject-object relation that is embedded in Kant's examination of cognition.[54] Thus the Paralogisms chapter, which leaves the question of knowledge of the subject indeterminate yet without contradiction, demands further investigation. What should be clear is that even if its accomplishment is merely that of designating the territory within which we can pursue an examination of cognition, such "boundaries [Grenzen]," as Kant explains, are no mere "limits [Schranken]."[55] The delineation of the territory within which the examination of experience can proceed does not accomplish its task by rejecting all that is beyond human reach, for, as Kant writes and as I have already discussed in chapter 2, this act signifies "setting the boundary to the field of experience through something that is otherwise unknown to it."[56] The designation of the territory within which the non-dogmatic examination of the subjective conditions of experience can proceed is indebted to what is unknown to reason; yet precisely how this is so is the question to which we are brought by the Refutation.

To pursue a response to the question of the persistent thing of the Refutation, a pursuit that examines such a thing apart from subjective consciousness as dependent upon a regulative principle, will have to wait until we have thoroughly investigated the role that a regulative principle in general might play within Kant's analysis of cognition. What should be clear is that the Refutation of Idealism has been able to direct this inquiry beyond the Analytic of Principles and toward the Transcendental Dialectic, with its investigation of the ideas of reason in the pursuit of a regulative principle for the account of cognition in the Transcendental Analytic. This is not to say that the second edition of the first *Critique*, with its Refutation of Idealism, offers a response to the criticism, launched at it in the name of metacritique, to which the original edition was susceptible; rather, the second edition begins to uncover the path that connects the Transcendental Analytic and the Transcendental Dialectic in both editions of the first *Critique,* a path that we must continue to clear through explicit analysis of both the structure of the Kantian conception of experience and the discussion of rational subjectivity in the Paralogisms.

We have begun the work that this task entails if we now recognize not only that the Kantian accomplishment is threatened by a skepticism more radical than that emanating from the Cartesian method, but also that if we want to investigate the importance of the Refutation for the examination of objectivity in the Transcendental Analytic, we will have to investigate the conception of objects with which the critical project has begun, and in so doing search for an answer to the radically skeptical concerns emanating from the Transcendental Dialectic. In the Refutation, Kant has tied his analysis of experience to the existence of something apart from all phenomenal representation, for only in so doing can he deny that what he offers is merely a refined version of idealist skepticism. Kant's Refutation of Idealism explains that critical philosophy must accept the existence of a persistent thing to be viewed in some way as separate from all examination of phenomenal experience. Precisely what such a persistent thing is remains at issue.

Where does this leave us? We must search for a way to understand the modal principles that will allow us to connect them to the regulative pursuit of reason's ideas. In order to examine the conception of persistence that is broached by the Refutation, we will have to pursue a response to the more radical skepticism that, as we move into the Transcendental Dialectic, can be seen to shadow the critical enterprise. But to do so we will have to return to §76 of the *Critique of Judgment* and attempt, at long last, to interpret the dependence of the differentiation of possibility from actuality on a regulative use of reason; only then will reason's pursuits be understood to be relevant for the designation of the subjective conditions of objectivity. Pursuing the persistent thing that the Refutation argues is implied in all self-awareness as governed by a regulative principle is to investigate the dependence of the modal judgments, and hence the designation of the region of experience, on reason's pursuit of that which is beyond its grasp.

FOUR

Transcendental Reflection: Interpreting the Amphiboly via §76 of the Critique of Judgment

I. Transcendental Reflection

Having demonstrated the need for an explanation of the conception of experience with which Kant's analysis begins, we must now pursue such a question within the confines of the *Critique of Pure Reason* if we are to avoid claiming that Kant was initially blind to the presuppositions of the critical enterprise. In §76 of the *Critique of Judgment,* Kant announces the possibility of addressing the critical conception of possible experience, but it is not clear that such an account can be located in the epistemological structure of the first *Critique.* Those who have interpreted the *Critique of Judgment* as initiating great changes in the critical project argue that such a search is pointless.[1] They appear to have support in that the only section that develops the claim that critical epistemology depends upon something beyond its finite limits is the Refutation of Idealism; and the ambiguity of its conclusion seems to raise the possibility that even in 1787, with the inclusion of this section in the second edition of the *Critique of Pure Reason,* and certainly in 1781, with the work's original publication, Kant did not conceive of the regulative dependence of the critical analysis of cognition.

However, concluding the Transcendental Analytic already in the first edition of the *Critique of Pure Reason* is an appendix in which Kant addresses the designation of the terrain of critical experience. In this appendix, titled On the Amphiboly of the Concepts of Reflection, Kant raises what he terms a transcendental reflection (*Reflexion*), or deliberation (*Überlegung*), a reflection back over the completed analysis of cognition, as a necessary counterpoint to this analysis. To interpret this claim, we will begin by returning to §76 of the *Critique of Judgment* and, following Heidegger's suggestions, we will map the discussion of the regulative dependence of the analysis of finite experience back onto the first *Critique.*

Heidegger's late essay "Kant's Thesis about Being"[2] reaffirms Schelling's statement, in reference to §76 of the *Critique of Judgment,* that "[p]erhaps there have never been so many deep thoughts [*tiefe Gedanken*] compressed [*zusammengedrängt*] into so few pages."[3] Unfortunately, in this early work, *Of the I as the Principle of Philosophy; or, On the Unconditioned in Human Knowledge* (*Vom Ich als Princip der Philosophie oder Über das Unbedingte im menschlichen Wissen*), Schelling does not go on to explicate what precisely these "deep thoughts" are; he refers to them in a footnote after the following criticism of Spinoza: "he could never make comprehensible why it is that teleological unity in the finite intelligence can be determined only by the ontological unity in the nonfinite thinking of the absolute substance."[4] By determining the absolute as an object, Spinoza could never explain the connection between the finite, as it aims at the absolute, and the absolute itself. Schelling continues by claiming that Kant recognized this limitation in Spinoza, and then he moves on to the passage concerning the density and profundity of §76 of the third *Critique*.

But Schelling does not further interpret this passage. This is particularly frustrating because, for Schelling, the absolute directs the finite I: "to strive [*streben*] to elicit in the world that which is actuality in the nonfinite, and which is man's highest vocation [*höchste Beruf*]—to turn the unity of aims in the world into mechanism, and to turn mechanism into a unity of aims."[5] For Schelling, to search for a "first principle of philosophy" is to court the death of philosophy; "true philosophy can start only from free actions,"[6] from the action of the I striving to attain the infinite. Free action drives this progression to immanence, from the finite to the infinite, without, for Schelling, the necessity of distinguishing how one could come to conceive of the two sides of the process. This is because, for Schelling, what the *Critique of Judgment* initiates, and what is particularly evident in §76, is that the faculty of understanding that underlies Kant's earlier examination of finite cognition has been surpassed; the *Critique of Judgment* points toward the unity of mechanism and teleology, and hence to the unity of the finite and the infinite, in the speculative philosophical accomplishment of the self positing I. For Schelling, §76 not only argues for the importance of the pursuit of metaphysics for the establishment of regulative principles that direct all areas of critical philosophy, but actually leads to the overcoming of the limits of finite cognition embraced by critical philosophy, and the passage to a speculative philosophy in which human thought is an expression of the absolute.

Does Kant begin the critical project, as Schelling claims, by striving for the "*absolute* agreement [*absolute Zusammenstimmung*] of the absolute I,"[7] or does the account of finite cognition depend in some way upon the regulative use of a principle that not only remains unknown, but also allows for the differentiation of mechanism and teleology, the distinction that, for Schelling, was to be overcome? Furthermore, does not Kant's inclusion of the discussion of possibility and actuality alongside that of moral freedom and teleological judgment in this elusive paragraph point to the dependence of the analysis of finite cognition on this unattainable absolute? An inquiry into the relation of finite cognition to the absolute must be broached if we are to understand Kant's §76 in a manner that neither presupposes the account of finite cognition nor subsumes both it and the absolute under the pursuit of practical freedom. This is to say that critical philosophy must be able to explain how it comes to think of the finite and the absolute such that moral freedom can be contemplated without contradiction.

Heidegger not only agrees with Schelling's general evaluation of §76 of the third *Critique* but also attempts to develop an interpretation of these few pages that would connect them with the central issues of Kant's critical system. Heidegger makes use of Schelling's general judgment of Kant's passage, but his own interest in transcendental reflection is focused more narrowly on connecting this enigmatic conception with the body of Kant's examination of synthetic cognition. In §76, Heidegger recognizes, Kant is investigating the roles of the modal principles, possibility and actuality, in cognition, and this is undertaken in relation to discussions of both freedom and teleological judgment. Heidegger proceeds to connect the discussion of possibility and actuality in §76 to another enigmatic section in the Kantian critical corpus, the discussion of transcendental reflection in the appendix to the Transcendental Analytic of the *Critique of Pure Reason*. This connection will offer a way to examine the need for a regulative principle in Kant's designation of the modal categories of finite cognition. But Heidegger appends a self-deprecating warning: "Because what Schelling says here hits the mark" concerning the profundity of this section, "we must not pretend to think through this §76 adequately."[8]

In "Kant's Thesis about Being," Heidegger investigates the role of the question of being (*Sein*) in the Kantian system. Kant has famously written, "**Being [*Sein*]** is obviously not a real predicate, i.e., a concept of something that could add to the concept of a thing. It is merely the positing of a thing or of certain determinations in themselves" (A598/B626). Kant writes this in the attempt to demonstrate that the ontological proof of the existence of God cannot prove that God actually exists, for the statement that "God is" does not offer anything more than the word *God;* "I add no new predicate as added to the concept of God, but only posit the subject in itself with all its predicates" (A599/B627). For Kant, the being, or existence, of an object does not add anything conceptually to it. While the money that is in my pocket offers me many more consumer choices than the mere thought of the possibility of the money, the fact that I have it, that the money actually exists and is not merely possible, adds nothing to my concept of the object. Its actuality merely concerns my relation to the money and not the concept of the money itself. Both possibility and actuality, as has been explained in the previous chapter's discussion of the Postulates of Empirical Thought, are determinations that follow from the modal categories and concern the relation of the subject to the object that has been determined according to the prior three groups of categories (quantity, quality, and relation). The apparent priority of the categories of quantity, quality, and relation over those of modality is subverted by the role played by the modal categories in marking out the territory within which the other categories are exhibited. The actuality of an object is determined not by its concept but by its being sensibly given; such an actualization adds nothing to the concept of the object. For "objects of pure thinking," such as the soul, the world, or God, where there is no possibility of the sensible givenness of the object, "there is no means whatever for cognizing their existence" (A601/B629), for existence has been limited by Kant to the "unity of experience," to that which can be determined as actual by being given to our senses, and hence posited. Yet this does not preclude the existence of a purely intellectual being; rather, it is the recognition that such a thought "we cannot justify through anything" (ibid.).

In this essay, unlike in his earlier *What Is a Thing?* Heidegger does not end his analysis of Kant's designation of objects with a discussion of the three modal categories that govern existence, or being, insofar as Kant has distinguished existence as what is posited and thus in terms of possibility, actuality, and necessity; rather, Heidegger here investigates how it is that in the Postulates of Empirical Thought and even earlier in the Transcendental Analytic in the table of categories, Kant has been able to distinguish these modalities of thought as the criteria through which being is to be investigated, without asking where the basis of these distinctions lie.[9] If one were to answer, with Kant, that it lies in the nature of human cognition, in our need for sensible representations in order to determine any existence at all, one must still ask how the limits of human cognition can be so distinguished, particularly when the critical project challenges just this sort of naïve realism. If the Kantian investigation of cognition is to avoid the pitfalls of a dogmatic claim about either the nature of the mind or perceptual experience, then it must justify its limitation of the investigation of existence to what is sensibly given prior to the critique of metaphysics that is accomplished according to the criteria that follow from this examination of cognition. Heidegger argues that Kant did not address the question of how the modal judgments can themselves be distinguished until the third *Critique:* "Not until ten years after the *Critique of Pure Reason,* toward the end of his third main work, the *Critique of Judgment* (1790), does Kant touch upon this question, and then quite 'episodically [*episodisch*],' in §76, which bears the heading 'Remark.'"[10] This is not to claim that the designation of the possible-actual distinction is utterly overlooked by Kant in his earlier work. Heidegger's claim is that while Kant did not address the question until the *Critique of Judgment,* the *Critique of Pure Reason* does distinguish a "reflection back [*Rückbesinnung*] over the completed steps of thought,"[11] a further reflective act beyond the thematization of the modal determinations of finite cognition. Such an act does not merely accept "the inevitability of the distinction of possibility and actuality" for the analysis of cognition, but investigates the relation of subject and object implicit in this accomplishment. Heidegger locates this discussion in the account of transcendental reflection in the appendix to the Transcendental Analytic, titled On the Amphiboly of the Concepts of Reflection.

Kant introduces transcendental reflection as "a duty from which no one can escape if he would judge anything about things *a priori*" (A263/B319). Coming at the end of the Transcendental Analytic, which is to say after the *a priori* elements of cognition have been elucidated, this is a rather startling claim. Kant has already examined the elements of all cognition of objects, sensibility and understanding, but now beyond this dualism of faculties and beyond even the bridging act of imagination, he raises a further "duty [*Pflicht*]" that is necessary for *a priori* judgment. Kant begins this section by stating that this discussion will not be concerned with a direct examination of objects; this is to say, transcendental reflection will address neither the *a priori* elements of cognition nor the empirical determinations of such concepts; rather, this examination of what Kant names with the Latin *reflexio*[12] concerns "the state of mind in which we first prepare ourselves to find out the subjective conditions under which we can arrive at concepts" (A260/B316). Thus, Kant does not begin a new inquiry into the mind itself; the critical philosophy denies such direct access into our cognitive faculties. What Kant is after is the ability to distinguish which of the manifold "representations [*Vorstellungen*]" that we encounter are offered as sensible and which as purely intellectual. By avoiding the conflation of representations of sensible intuition and those of the pure understanding, Kant initiates an explanation of what is implied in the very starting point of the first *Critique*. Kant begins his Copernican experiment in metaphysics by searching for the subjective conditions that permit a very limited conception of experience, one that demands both spatial and temporal givenness. And it is in the analysis of the conditions of the possibility of this limited conception of experience that Kant uncovers the *a priori* structure of finite cognition and thus the criteria for the critique of metaphysics.

What we must remember is that the examination of the cognition of objects comes prior to the critique of metaphysics that it makes possible; yet in order to investigate synthetic *a priori* cognition, we must already have parsed our representations such that we can pursue the conditions of the possibility of experience in the realm of what is sensibly given. For Kant, it is essential to distinguish such representations, those that belong to the pure understanding and those that belong to sensible intuition, in order to deny the skepticism that metaphysical inquiries import into the investigation of experience. This offers Kant the basic distinction of the critical project, that between phenomena and noumena, for the parsing of representations that transcendental reflection affords distinguishes "whether" they belong "as *noumena* to the understanding, or as *phenomena* to sensibility" (A269/B325); and this reflective act is needed prior to the critique of metaphysics as it is the foundation upon which the examination of the understanding in its empirical application elucidates the *a priori* concepts that provide such a critique.[13] It is worth noting that this limitation of the field of critical inquiry is a move beyond the initial Copernican experiment (Bxvii). Kant has initiated an inquiry into the subjective conditions of our experience as a way to avoid all discussion of objects as they exist apart from human perception; and yet this turn inward does not necessitate the limitation of what is to count as an object of experience to spatially appearing, empirical objects, for experience could have been defined as including all that can be thought, and it would then have included the non-empirical objects of metaphysical inquiry.

Kant begins a discussion of this designation of the boundary of possible experience only in the appendix to the Transcendental Analytic. Kant's conception of transcendental reflection demonstrates that prior to critical inquiry the field of investigation has already been limited. What this limitation entails is a bracketing of all that will hold such an inquiry back from producing a consistent system, a separating off of noumenal claims until, with the accomplished system, it is able to deduce the illusory status of the claims made in the bracketed metaphysical region. This reflective act permits the use of metaphysical claims as a way not merely to advance the teleological investigation of nature, but, I will argue, to mark out the confines of the bracketed, phenomenal realm.[14]

Transcendental reflection is the act whereby we come to investigate the comparison of representations that underlies all of our judgments. It can be considered a second-order reflection as it returns to the reflective deliberation that we undertake, investigating each deliberative act to see whether the representations that have been ordered find their source in sensible intuition or pure understanding. In order to avoid treating sensible objects as purely intellectual concepts and vice versa, Kant recognizes that we must establish for all representations whether they offer themselves as empirical objects to our cognitive faculties. If not, then such representations need to be distinguished from those which can appear for us and which, as constituting the objects of experience, are entitled phenomena, as opposed to what are offered merely to be thought and are entitled noumena.[15] Kant writes:

> The action [*Handlung*] through which I make the comparison of representations in general with the cognitive power in which they are situated, and through which I distinguish whether they are to be compared to one another as belonging to the pure understanding or to pure intuition, I call **transcendental reflection** [*Überlegung*]. (A261/B317)

This reflective designation of the cognitive faculties to which representations belong allows us to distinguish those representations that allow for sensible deliberation from those that permit only intellectual deliberation (thought with no empirical content), and thus limits the investigation of representations to those that, as sensibly appearing, allow for the differentiation of possibility and actuality. Kant has already made use of this distinction without having offered such an explicit explanation, for only because the investigation of cognition has been limited to what can be sensibly given can the actual, that is to say, what exists, be confined to what has been converted from the possible by its empirical givenness.

What Kant's discussion of transcendental reflection shows is that in order to pursue cognition in the limited phenomenal realm of possible experience, we must already have distinguished those representations that can be sensibly compared from those that can only be intellectually compared; we must distinguish those representations that offer objects that permit the differentiation of possibility and actuality from those whose objects could be conceived as existing without any connection of their actuality to possibility. This is to say that we must distinguish those representations that are merely temporal, those of inner sense, from those that conform to both the temporal and the spatial forms of intuition, those of outer sense, for the representations that offer themselves only to our intellectual powers, the thoughts that have no empirical determination, are still temporal. They are thought, or represented, in a manner that necessitates their temporal ordering, and yet they offer no content that would allow for objective determination.

Kant explains this distinction between appearances of inner and outer sense in the Paralogisms of Pure Reason chapter of the first edition of the *Critique of Pure Reason*. He argues that the analysis of empirical objects, the phenomena of outer sense, offers *a priori* synthetic cognition, while the analysis of inner sense, the investigations of rational psychology, does not (A381). And while the failings of rational psychology are the explicit goal of the Paralogisms of Pure Reason chapter of the Transcendental Dialectic, in both editions, Kant also offers a discussion of the difference between inner and outer sense that is useful for the interpretation of transcendental reflection. The appearances of inner sense, those thoughts or representations that cannot be attributed to objects spatially appearing, are not enduring in the manner of empirical objects; it is the spatiality of objects that offers the substratum or unity in the face of the flux of determinations, and therefore what is merely temporal is by definition mutable, ever changing, and bereft of a determinable object. The soul, like the other ideas of metaphysics, is not determinable as an object; it offers no spatial appearance, but only the logical unity of transcendental subjectivity. Transcendental reflection designates the territory of the analysis of *a priori* synthetic cognition by separating off all representations that have no spatial element, all thoughts that do not offer objects of experience for critical analysis.

By beginning an investigation of cognition with only those representations that are empirically given, Kant has been able to narrow the confines of his philosophical investigation to that which, as sensibly represented, affords both the analysis of the conditions of possible experience and the critique of metaphysics. The explanation of transcendental reflection in an appendix to the Transcendental Analytic is Kant's attempt to distinguish what is presupposed in his philosophical starting point, in the designation of the region of possible experience as that within which philosophical investigation must begin, a beginning that offers wide-ranging accomplishment.[16]

This ability to distinguish the source of our representations and to pursue an investigation of only those that are sensibly given does not raise sensibility as the means of direct access to things in themselves. No such Lockean position is proposed; rather, the pursuit of the examination of cognition in the region of sensible representations allows for the limited investigation of that which conforms to the spatial and temporal forms of sensibility. Such a reflective accomplishment is implicit in both the Transcendental Aesthetic and the examination of the understanding earlier in the Transcendental Analytic.[17] What is sensibly given to our intuition can be conceptually analyzed according to the understanding's categories, while what is given in thought to the pure understanding offers no such sensible givenness, and so permits neither experience nor cognition. Thus, transcendental reflection can be seen to permit the division of our intellectual faculties, separating the empirical use of the categories of the understanding from their transcendent use beyond all possible experience. It both permits the elucidation of the conditions of the possibility of experience and offers a critique of the vain pursuit of metaphysical cognition.[18]

Transcendental reflection is necessary for all *a priori* judgment because without such a parsing of representations experience could not be designated in such a way that its examination could afford an account of synthetic *a priori* cognition. Kant has thus marked out the limits of phenomenal experience. Only those representations that are given through, or can be attributed to, sensible intuition need be compared in order to examine the conditions of the possibility of objects of experience. Experience, for Kant, has been distinguished as confined to those representations that offer, beyond the temporality of thought, a spatial givenness, separating off those that find their source in the pure understanding and that offer no spatial determination. Thus, even prior to the critique of metaphysics, Kant had to be able to designate sensible representations as constitutive of the cognitive realm such that the examination of these objects could yield the conditions of the possibility of experience so conceived.[19]

Such a conception of an orienting reflection that precedes the analysis of transcendental philosophy—a transcendental reflection—directs us to a conception of the Kantian position that stands in opposition to those who claim that

Kant has begun his analysis with an assumption about the character of experience, and so offers a naturalized epistemology that avoids the true challenge of skepticism.[20] The necessity of an initial reflective investigation of the manifold of thought, a running through and dividing of that which offers neither clear divisions nor obvious certainties, places Kant in the tradition of philosophies of reflection that culminates in David Hume's skeptical empiricism. Kant begins his critical philosophy with only the content of his thought, without a conception of the self for whom the temporal flux of thought appears; he begins, that is to say, from a position akin to Hume's view of the mind as conceivable only as a bundle of thoughts.[21] Hume's conception of our philosophical beginnings—and Kant's as well—owes much to the position of Cartesian doubt. If none of our thoughts can be directly deemed to be knowledge, if they do not even offer a criterion to be used in the search for knowledge, then we are forced to address the question of how we can justify our method of philosophizing. Kant attempts to avoid the skeptical limits on philosophy that Descartes initiated and that Hume embraced without resorting to Descartes' metaphysical presuppositions. What needs to be answered is how Kant can justify the transcendental reflection, which limits the field of critical inquiry to that of spatially appearing representations and so affords the construction of the critical system.[22] What metaphysical presuppositions are implied in this orienting act of the critical analysis of cognition?

Kant explains transcendental reflection by distinguishing it from logical reflection, the sort of comparison (*Vergleichung*) implicit in all conceptual thematizations of our perceptual experience; in our originally naïve approach to the manifold of representations, we are realists comparing and contrasting in the attempt to forge cohesive judgments. Such a reflective approach to the perceptual manifold can be seen to be directed by four basic rules, which Kant calls the concepts of reflection. Kant lists the four pairs that underlie all of our empirical judgments as **identity** and **difference**, **agreement** and **opposition**, **inner** and **outer**, and **matter** and **form**. These four sets of concepts are connected by Kant with the four groups of forms of judgment, the logical underpinnings of the table of categories (A262/B318). While the Transcendental Analytic has elucidated the conditions of the possibility of objects of experience, the determinate judgments that constitute such objects are shown to depend upon the prior comparison of representations that provides the setting for determinate accomplishment. Kant explains each of the four pairs in a manner that sheds light on both the dependence of determinate judgment on these types of logical comparisons and, more importantly for the present inquiry, how such pairs exemplify the types of errors into which we can fall if we have not transcendentally reflected and parsed our representations prior to such comparison. Kant calls these errors the *amphibolies* of the concepts of reflection: they are the errors into which we fall if we do not differentiate representations belonging to sensible intuition (those with a spatial component) from those of the pure understanding, which are merely temporal; through these errors we are led to conflate phenomena and noumena in our investigations.

Kant explains that these four pairs of concepts of reflection differ from the categories of the understanding in that "what is exhibited [*dargestellt*] through them is not the object in accordance with what constitutes its concept (magnitude, reality), but rather only the comparison of representations, in all their manifoldness, which precedes the concepts of things" (A269/B325). This "comparison of representations [*Vergleichung der Vorstellungen*]" precedes the determination of objects according to the categories. Logical reflection according to the concepts of reflection precedes "the concepts of things," and the concepts according to which representations are compared distinguish a further reflection, a transcendental reflection, that explains how we avoid the amphiboly of the concepts of reflection. Prior to the accomplishment of objective judgment, we must have already compared the given sensible representations in order to then judge them objectively. The subsumption of what is sensibly given under the *a priori* concepts of the understanding depends upon the pre-categorical comparison of the manifold of representations, and such a comparison must follow the act of transcendental reflection if it is to avoid amphiboly.[23]

The concepts of reflection can thus be understood to explain the types of deliberative approaches that are implied in the determinate judgment that follows from the categories of the understanding.[24] Kant is here explaining that the kind of comparison needed for the accomplishment that precedes determinate judgment according to the *a priori* concepts of the understanding follows four specific pairs of concepts of reflection (*Reflexionsbegriffe*), and it is in these fundamental comparisons that we risk the failure of critical analysis if we have not parsed the representational manifold, dividing the sensible from the intelligible by means of transcendental reflection.

What this appendix offers is an argument for the basic orientation of the critical analysis of experience: phenomena must be distinguished from noumena, for without this distinction we revisit the errors of the tradition. In the appendix to the Transcendental Analytic, Kant finally addresses the initial designation that orients critical philosophy, what he calls *transcendental reflection*. The task of this chapter is to interpret this initial reflective act, which shadows critical accomplishment and which has been, for the most part, ignored by Kant interpreters. By briefly investigating the four pairs of concepts of reflection that Kant explains in the appendix, and their attendant amphibolies, we will be better able to understand the transcendental reflection that Kant claims is necessary in order to avoid such errors, but which, unfortunately, he explains in such a limited fashion.

The first pair of concepts of reflection that Kant addresses is "identity and difference [*Einerleiheit und Verschiedenheit*]," which corresponds with judgments according to the categories of quantity. Kant is here describing how it is that from the manifold of perceived things, judgments of universality and particularity can be differentiated; he explains that to do so we must distinguish noumenal from phenomenal examples. If we examine two objects and discover that they contain the same conceptual determinations,

> [t]hen it is always exactly the same if it counts as an object of pure understanding, not many but only one thing (*numerica identitas*); but if it is appearance, then the issue is not the comparison of concepts, but rather, however identical everything may be in regard to that, the difference of the places of these appearances at the same time is still an adequate ground for the **numerical difference** [*numerischen Verschiedenheit*] of the object (of the senses) itself. Thus, in the case of two drops of water one can completely abstract from all inner difference [*innern Verschiedenheit*] (of quality and quantity), and it is enough that they be intuited in different places at the same time in order for them to be held to be numerically different. (A263–64/B319–20)

If we do not distinguish phenomena from noumena, then we will be tempted to apply the criteria of metaphysical inquiry to the comparison of empirical objects; but in doing so we overlook the particularity of empirical objects that may share the same conceptual determinations but are different precisely because they are intuited in different locations at the same time. Kant describes drops of water that, even if we set aside all question of their "inner difference," which is to say that we assume that the two drops conform to the same conceptual structure, are distinguished because of their different spatial locations. It is just such "numerical difference" that is overlooked by rationalists, like Leibniz, who emphasize only the conceptual structure of empirical objects.

These concepts of reflection both explain the necessity of the comparison of spatial positioning in the attempt to determine empirical concepts and point to the need to reflect transcendentally on our representations, so that we do not attempt to apply the criteria of metaphysical inquiry to the sensible appearances with which we are faced. To do so would be to fall into an amphiboly of a concept of reflection. Leibniz, Kant claims, did precisely this as he "took the appearances for things in themselves, thus for *intelligibilia*, i.e., objects of pure understanding (although on account of the confusion of their representations he labeled them with the name of *phenomena*)" (A264/B320). Kant's critical accomplishment avoids this conflation of phenomena and noumena and so avoids the Leibnizian attempt to explain substances by demeaning the appearance of that which appears.

The second pair of concepts of reflection is "agreement and opposition [*Einstimmung und Widerstreit*]," which corresponds to judgments of quality. Kant explains that as long as we concentrate on noumenal reality, we are forced to claim that there is no such thing as conflict or contradiction between things. We would thus claim that there is always essentially agreement, and what appears to contradict is merely the confused sensible representation of the basic cohesive unity of noumenal reality. But if, through Kant's transcendental reflection, we distinguish the fields of phenomena and noumena, then we are able to contrast the thought of essential noumenal agreement with the possibility of phenomenal reality and its apparent conflicts. What appears need not always agree with all else that appears; Kant describes the possibility of phenomenal contradiction in explaining that "united in the same subject, one [appearance] can partly or wholly destroy the **consequence of the other**" (A265/B321). Kant gives the examples of forces pushing in opposite directions, such that their powers counterbalance each other, and enjoyment that offsets the effect of pain. Both examples emphasize that without transcendental reflection, the metaphysical idea of the unity of all things would lead us, through the amphiboly of the concepts of reflection, to deny the apparent contradictions that abound, distorting phenomenal reality by conflating it with noumenal reality. By distinguishing the phenomenal from the noumenal, such contradictions can be reflectively distinguished without denying the possibility of the ultimate coherence of noumenal reality.

The third pair of concepts of reflection, which Kant calls the "inner and the outer [*das Innere und Äußere*]," corresponds to the categories of relation. What is inner to a noumenal substance is what "has no relation [*Beziehung*] (as far as the existence is concerned) to anything that is different from it" (A265/B321), and so is independent.[25] However, such inner determination can be described merely as that which is thought, offering no outer relations to distinguish its composition. Leibniz took substances to be such noumenal objects and so, for him, substances were bereft of all determination, and so indistinguishable thinking monads (A265–66/B321–22). A phenomenal substance, on the other hand, is determined inwardly only through its relations (*Verhältnisse*), and thus its spatial interactions with other substances. By marking the distinction between the phenomenal and noumenal realms, Kant is able to determine phenomenal objects by means of their outer, spatial, relations, leaving their indeterminate, inner natures to the merely temporal realm of thought. The noumenal is concerned with the inner properties of unrelated objects of pure understanding in thought, and the phenomenal is concerned with spatial objects and their outer relations.

The fourth pair of concepts of reflection is "matter and form [*Materie und Form*]," corresponding to the modal categories. This pair, Kant claims, is the "ground" of all comparisons of representations: all reflective comparisons of empirical representations, all of the comparisons that are required for the conceptual determination of objects, are dependent upon the differentiation of matter and form. Matter "signifies the determinable in general," while form signifies the determination of that matter (A266/B322). In a noumenal investigation of what things are in themselves, "unbounded reality [*unbegrenzte Realität*]" is taken as the matter, while the form is the "limitation" of this reality, insofar as it can be said to differ conceptually from other things (A266–67/B322). First of all, something must be given in order, only then to be distinguished conceptually from others; thus, for objects as noumenally conceived, matter must precede form. The given matter is conceptually distinguished as to its form in relation to others. This is because in an inquiry that takes as its object things in themselves, thought has been taken as referring directly to objects, which is to say that thought distinguishes what the object is in itself, and this object must have its matter given prior to the process of conceptually unraveling its form.

The concepts of matter and form appear to point to the same error as that of the concepts of inner and outer; if matter is said to precede form, as the rationalist claims, then the sensibly given matter is superseded by an analysis of the conceptual form of the given. Spatial representations are judged as being but confused manifestations of that which can be expressed conceptually. And yet, in their relation to the modal categories, the concepts of matter and form go further than the reversal that is at stake in the concepts of inner and outer. Kant here introduces the interrelation of form and matter that is needed for his account of objects of experience. The concepts of form and matter, Kant explains, underlie all other concepts of reflection as they relate to the designation of what is to count as an object for critical inquiry.

In Kant's account of experience, form precedes matter; this is to say that space and time as the *a priori* forms of experience, along with the schematized categories, designate the structure taken by sensibly given matter. What is possible in the transcendental account of experience is that which conforms to such *a priori* form, that whose matter can be given in a way that is determined by just these forms. However, when space and time are taken as "determinations of the things in themselves" (A267/B323), as in the rationalist account, matter is assumed to precede form. Sensibly given matter would thus give way to the conceptually constituted form of the object, whose possibility is distinguished by its reducibility to such an intellectual form. For Kant, such a conception of the object is forever cut off from that which is sensibly given, from both the starting point of and the criteria of justification for its philosophical investigation.

Kant has subverted the accepted order of matter and form: form is conceived as prior to matter insofar as it is the condition of the possibility of phenomenal objects, but such objects can be reduced to neither form nor matter; rather, they are the confluence of both as objects of experience.[26] Transcendental reflection permits such a reconfiguration of the relation of form and matter by limiting critical analysis to those representations that are sensibly given, to those that have a spatial as well as a temporal dimension, and by proceeding to designate the conditions of the possibility of experience according to these spatial appearances. In so doing Kant avoids conceiving of the empirically given as if its matter were something to be surpassed, and as if its possibility concerned its formal determination as a simple essence.

The amphiboly of the concepts of matter and form entails such a rationalist conception, and its avoidance defines critical inquiry. For this reason, Kant describes this fourth pair of concepts as fundamental: the modal categories that it bespeaks designate the terrain of critical inquiry, adding not to the determination of the objects of cognition but to the manner of cognition, to their relation to the cognitive faculties.[27] The avoidance of the amphiboly of the concepts of matter and form thus permits the critical approach that directs the avoidance of the other three amphibolies, which relate to objects so conceived.

These four pairs of concepts of reflection should not be conflated with the categories of the understanding, nor, on the other hand, should they be thought to contradict the account of the categories that the Transcendental Analytic has investigated in such detail; they express, rather, the need to compare representations prior to any determinate judgment, prior to their subsumption under categories. It is according to these four pairs of concepts that the multiplicity of representations must be compared such that empirical concepts can be distinguished. This reflective comparison of our representations provides objects, empirically compared unities, from the raw material of the representational manifold; and yet, the concepts of reflection do not constitute the conditions for the possibility of objects within the critical account of experience. They participate in the generation of the subjective experience of objects, but they cannot address questions concerning the objective correctness of these judgments and are thus open to skeptical concerns. Such a Humean challenge can be seen to be addressed by Kant in the Copernican turn: we have not made any progress in the metaphysical inquiry into what things are in themselves apart from our perception of them, and so we investigate the subjective conditions that make such objects possible. What the appendix to the Transcendental Analytic explains is that the account of the conditions of the possibility of experience that the first *Critique* develops rests upon the subjective judgment of objects, which is explained by means of the concepts of reflection.

What is particularly relevant in the amphibolies section of the appendix for the interpretation of the first *Critique* that I am developing is that Kant's claim is not merely that we must have already compared our representations according to these four pairs of concepts in order to provide an account of the conditions of the possibility of experience. This appendix begins with the explanation of transcendental reflection and the claim that without it *a priori* judgment would not be possible (A263/B319). Without the division of our representations according to their connection to either sensibility or pure understanding, we would fall into the amphibolies, for we would pursue an investigation of all representations, both the sensibly and the intellectually given, both phenomena and noumena, at once. By separating these two types of representations, Kant has marked off a limited region within which to examine the dependence of our experience on the categories of the understanding. The progression from the concepts of reflection to the categories of the understanding must be viewed as an accomplishment that transforms empirical concepts into objects of experience, objects that accord with the *a priori* concepts of the understanding.[28]

The appendix to the Transcendental Analytic forces on the critical philosopher the recognition that the avoidance of both skepticism and dogmatism that the systemization of *a priori* judgment provides is dependent upon the division within the manifold of representations explained by transcendental reflection. Without transcendental reflection we would fall into the amphiboly of the concepts of reflection; we would have either, like Locke, "**sensualized** the concepts of the understanding" or, like Leibniz, "**intellectualized the appearances**" (A271/B327);[29] or else we would risk rejecting such options and embracing the skepticism launched by Hume. If we are to distinguish our judgments of causal relations from mere habits of mind, then we need to differentiate sensible representations from those of the pure understanding, the region of phenomena from that of noumena; and this parsing of our representations must be accomplished prior to the analysis of the conditions of the possibility of the experience of objects, for it distinguishes a limited territory of perceptual judgments within which to pursue the analysis of experience. In the appendix to the Transcendental Analytic, the critical experiment has thus raised its own presuppositions as in need of explanation. To such an end, Kant has distinguished a reflective act prior to critical inquiry, but he has not explained how this orienting act can itself be justified within the conceptual vocabulary of the system that it has produced.

II. Heidegger and Critique

Heidegger's essay "Kant's Thesis about Being" has directed us to Kant's conception of transcendental reflection in the search for the designation of the region of experience within which the Kantian analysis of cognition takes place. While this has led to the search for the manner in which this transcendental reflection can be understood within Kant's conceptual vocabulary, and thus within the method of transcendental inquiry that it bespeaks, Heidegger conceives of it as a reflective move that points beyond critique to that which is more originary and comes prior to the designation of experience. Heidegger both outlines a possible interpretation of the methodology of transcendental philosophy and rejects such an inquiry, pursuing instead an account of that which is covered over in the Kantian construction.

Heidegger interprets Kant's account of transcendental reflection as a reflection on the relation of the knowing subject to the objects known. Transcendental reflection is the mark of the "double role" that thought must be conceived as playing; thought designates both the reflective positing of the existence of objects, and also the "situating" of such positing, a reflection on this reflective designation of being that Kant calls transcendental reflection. Heidegger describes the relation between everyday reflective judging and transcendental reflection as that between the horizon of possibility and the "organon" that permits the examination of the nature of that possibility. He writes:

> Thinking as reflection of reflection means, on the other hand, the process whereby, and also the instrument and organon wherewith, being as glimpsed in the horizon of positedness is interpreted. Thinking as reflection means the horizon, thinking as reflection of reflection means the organon for the interpretation of the being of beings [das Organon der Auslegung des Seins des Seienden].[30]

The reflective interpretation of the reflective positing of being that the appendix to the Transcendental Analytic raises highlights for Heidegger the ambiguity implicit in our thinking. Our capacity to think encompasses both the positing of our empirical lives and the reflective attempt to investigate this positing of being in which being is limited to the realm of sensible appearances.

Heidegger is interested in the act of transcendental reflection, in the need for a second-order reflection to accompany that which distinguishes the "horizon of positedness." He has found in Kant the recognition of the necessity of proceeding beyond the investigation of human possibility, beyond the confines of our ontic involvements, and toward the attempt to embrace the ontological question of the "being of beings" that is covered over not only in what Heidegger, in Being and Time, calls the "everydayness [Alltäglichkeit]"[31] of our being in the world, but also in the history of philosophical attempts to systematize such ontic involvements. Heidegger explains that the attempt to thematize human thinking is complicated by this duality, the ambiguity implicit in thinking.[32]

For Heidegger, Kant's recognition of the need for a further reflection beyond the reflective thematization of our cognitive faculties marks the reduction of the region of experience within which such faculties are distinguished in the Transcendental Analytic. Kant thus begins his philosophical inquiry beyond or, more correctly, prior to the reduction of human experience to the region of empirical experience. Heidegger describes this initial philosophical territory as the "horizon of positedness" in the language of the phenomenological investigation that he develops in Being and Time. For Heidegger, the "point of departure" for philosophy must be the "phenomenal horizon" that distinguishes the extent of our meaningful involvements, an approach that does not presume to view the entities of the world displayed as if they were to be judged by a disinterested observer. Heidegger emphasizes the thinking or positing that itself is prior to the designation of the qualities of entities, prior, that is to say, to "objectivity."[33] To reduce the complexity of our experience to what is "objectively present" not only distorts its meaning within the intentional horizon, but also denies that what we are is primarily our possibility. The horizon of positedness thus designates the possible involvements, the "being possible," that for Heidegger is the most "primordial" encapsulation of human life. This possibility does not refer to what can be sensibly given, what can be actualized as an object for a perceiving subject, but points to that dimension of pre-critical experience within which Kantian empirical experience has been distinguished by the act of transcendental reflection. For Heidegger, sensible objects are not the criterion through which to judge the extent of our possibility, for our worlds are not limited to spatially extended objects; rather than pursuing the conditions of the possibility of objects of experience, Heidegger's *Being and Time*—and the fundamental ontology that it initiates—investigates the structure of our possibility, the structure of that being, *Dasein*, that "is always what it can be and how it is its possibility."[34]

Heidegger's criticism of the Kantian account of objects of experience, launched in *Being and Time (Sein und Zeit)*,[35] is instructive in this regard. Heidegger argues that in his attempt to deduce a native feeling necessary for our orientation, a further *a priori* structure of experience, Kant presupposes the very objects, those that are spatially extended and empirically given, that he then goes on to examine. Heidegger argues that to orient ourselves spatially in a darkened room in which the furnishings have been reversed, as Kant describes in "What Does It Mean to Orient Oneself in Thinking?"[36] requires not only the feeling of the difference between left and right that Kant claims, but also prior experience with the objects, a prior involvement that then allows for our reorientation. Thus, to speak of our spatial orientation in this way does not even begin to address the process of becoming oriented; it offers only an account of reorientation according to a reduced conception of our experience. It overlooks our preliminary involvement, which Heidegger calls our "thrownness [*Geworfenheit*]" into a world of meanings, in which our possibilities are manifest. Heidegger's claim is that the conditions of the possibility of experience are merely the conditions for the types of objects with which Kant begins his investigation. Rather than beginning an inquiry into experience by presupposing a world of spatially extended entities, we should investigate entities as they are encountered within the systems of meaning and involvements that Heidegger, in *Being and Time*, calls "readiness to hand [*Zuhandenheit*]." We must examine our involvements in the world as they are experienced, that is to say, as they present possibilities and meanings within the context of our involvements, rather than analyzing what can be abstracted from our involvements, namely what is present to us, and all others, as objects.[37]

Such an analysis of Kantian critique is further developed in Heidegger's *Kant and the Problem of Metaphysics* (*Kant und das Problem der Metaphysik*), which was published only two years after *Being and Time*.[38] Heidegger's well-known argument in this work maintains that after having begun a discussion of the source of the faculties of sensibility and understanding in his analysis of the objects of experience, Kant "shrank back"[39] from the investigation of the "common root" that he had initiated. Kant says little of this common root, first mentioning it in the first *Critique*'s introduction (included in both editions), where he qualifies it by explaining that the dualism of cognition "may perhaps arise from a common but to us unknown root."[40] Kant briefly returns to such a root of our faculties in the Transcendental Doctrine of Method, where he explains that one of the two stems is now to be called reason. Kant is no longer referring to the faculty of understanding, but to reason in its broad sense, which includes all of the cognitive faculties and so too both understanding and the narrowly construed faculty of reason of the Transcendental Dialectic (A835/B863).[41] While in this second reference to the root of the cognitive faculties Kant removes the qualifying "perhaps,"[42] he appears to have made no effort to investigate what such a source might be. In fact, it is not even clear that such a unified source of our faculties could, in any sense, be known since it could be conceived as a reference to the noumenal realm and to things in themselves as the source of cognition.[43]

Heidegger rejects such an interpretation, deeming the "common root" not only knowable but, in fact, known. Heidegger offers Kant's elusive transcendental imagination as such a unitary source.[44] At the start of the Transcendental Analytic in both editions of the first *Critique*, Kant explains that the *a priori* synthesis of the manifold is the "first origin of our cognition" (A77/B103). The pure manifold must be given prior to all "analysis of our representations" if cognition is to be said to relate to the *a priori* concepts of the understanding. Kant explains that such a synthesis is an effect of the imagination, what he describes as the "indispensable function of the soul [*unentbehrlichen Funktion der Seele*]" (A78/B103). Kant is here not speaking of the empirical imagination, which allows us to compare representations even when they are not given to the senses (B151); he is instead describing a more primordial power that governs "the connection of the manifold *a priori*" (A118). The role of such a power is to provide the form of the synthesis of the manifold prior to any empirical apperception, and so permit the subsumption of such a manifold under the categories by means of the understanding. Kant describes the synthesis that such an imagination provides as "the ground of the possibility of all cognition" (ibid.).

Clearly, such an *a priori* synthesis of the imagination must relate to the understanding, the faculty of *a priori* concepts, if it is to explain the "connection" that governs the manifold. Kant addresses this question most directly in the Schematism chapter, where he explains that the *a priori* concepts of the understanding structure the sensible synthesis of the manifold by means of transcendental schemata.[45] Such temporal rules of the transcendental imagination, corresponding to the *a priori* concepts of the understanding, offer the structure through which the manifold is determined. In permitting us the temporal manifold, the transcendental imagination plays a fundamental role in cognition, bridging the dualism of cognition—sensibility and understanding—by offering the temporal rule corresponding to the *a priori* concepts of the understanding. Kant describes such a transcendental schematism, and the imagination of which it is a product, as "a hidden art in the depths of the human soul" (B180/A141). It is the transcendental imagination as such a "hidden art" that Heidegger connects to the "unknown root" of the cognitive faculties. Such an unknown root, Heidegger explains, is not that of which we simply know nothing: "Rather, it is what pushes against us as something disquieting [*Beunruhigende*] in what is known."[46]

But how independent is this transcendental imagination from the understanding whose *a priori* concepts it temporalizes? Such a question can be addressed if we look at the changes that Kant made to the second edition's Transcendental Deduction. While the Schematism chapter was virtually unchanged in the second edition of the first *Critique,* Kant's fully rewritten Transcendental Deduction subtly alters the presentation of the transcendental imagination, and in particular the way that its role can be conceived in relation to that of the understanding. In the first edition's Transcendental Deduction, Kant explains that the unity of apperception when in relation to the transcendental imagination is itself the faculty of understanding (A119). At first this seems to be at odds with what has been said in the Schematism. The Schematism has explained that the schemata of the transcendental imagination temporalize the categories, but here in the Transcendental Deduction, which is textually prior to the Schematism, it is the transcendental imagination that transforms the analytic I of apperception into the faculty of understanding. What needs to be remembered is the direction of these seemingly opposed analyses. While the Transcendental Deduction argues for the necessity of the *a priori* concepts of the understanding from the subjective I of apperception, the Schematism, coming as it does in the Analytic of Principles (*Grundsätze*), begins with objects of appearance, asking how the already deduced concepts of the understanding can be said to apply to them. Thus, the first edition's Deduction clearly distinguishes the imagination from the understanding, with the former offering the temporal rules associated with the latter's *a priori* concepts, permitting their application to appearances.

However, by the time of the second edition, the *a priori* synthesis that the imagination affords is itself described as "an effect of the understanding" charged with "determining sensibility *a priori*" (B152). So while in both editions this pure synthesis, which permits the subsumption of sensibility under the categories, is described as the "transcendental synthesis of imagination" (A118/B151) and proceeds according to the schemata, in the second edition such a synthesis of imagination is no longer an activity undertaken by the imagination itself, but is instead accomplished by the understanding. Heidegger emphasizes this change, pointing out that in the second edition Kant removed the description of the imagination as one of the three "original sources (capacities or faculties of the soul) which constitute the conditions of the possibility of experience," alongside sense and apperception (A94).[47] In the second edition the transcendental imagination is no longer such an independent source as its function of original synthesis has been annexed to the understanding. Kant, in Heidegger's account, "shrank back" from the account of the transcendental imagination, the "common root" of our cognitive faculties, which offered the subversion of the traditional view of being as what is present to a subject, emphasizing instead the temporal origins of thought. Heidegger's interpretation of Kant's first *Critique* thus argues that the analysis of objectivity launched by Kant's critical project directs us beyond its restricted conception of experience and points toward the transcendental imagination as the temporal source of finite experience, the common root of Kantian dualism; and yet, in the second edition, Kant deemphasized the independence of the imagination, emphasizing instead the role of the faculty of understanding in cognition. What the first edition offers, according to Heidegger, is an "initial sketching-out [*Vorzeichnungen*]" of the role of the transcendental imagination, from which Kant retreated in the second edition.[48] In this way Kant can be said to have given priority in the second edition to the objective rather than the subjective side of the Transcendental Deduction, to the deduction of the objective validity of the categories rather than the investigation of the "powers of cognition [*Erkenntniskräften*]" upon which rests the understanding (Axvi–xvii). Yet it must be noted that even in the first edition where Kant does investigate the subjective side, he explains that "it is the objective deduction that is my primary concern" (Axvii).[49]

In Heidegger's *What Is a Thing?* he goes further in giving Kant credit not only for pointing beyond the objective to the subjective role of imagination, but also for initiating the circular project of critique which permits a subversion of epistemological concerns.[50] Heidegger argues that Kantian experience (*Erfahrung*) is not a thing "present at hand [*vorhanden*]," not the object stripped of our engagement with it and so reduced to its quantifiable elements; it is, rather, as we discussed in the previous chapter, a circular happening that exposes the gap that is to be found in the attempt to examine cognition, a gap that directs us beyond such cognitive analysis.

In "Kant's Thesis about Being," written some twenty-five years after these early interpretations, Heidegger offers an account of Kant's conception of transcendental reflection that recognizes in it a reference to the philosophical reflection that supports the critical analysis of experience, and that initiates this circular undertaking. In this essay, Heidegger explains that in the conception of transcendental reflection Kant has expressed the need in our philosophical questioning to surpass the analysis of experience, and the conception of objects implicit in it, which he had so carefully thematized. Kant recognized the need for an investigation that delves more deeply into the designation of the realm of experience than what is provided in the body of the Transcendental Analytic, offering an examination of what Heidegger calls the "originary character" of being for which representational thought could not possibly form the horizon.[51] In his earlier interpretations of Kantian critique, Heidegger emphasizes, first in *Being and Time,* the limitations of a philosophical analysis that begins its work by examining objects, and then, in *Kant and the Problem of Metaphysics,* the opportunities that such a limited beginning provides, and finally, in *What Is a Thing?* the circular project into which we are initiated by the principles of the understanding. In "Kant's Thesis about Being," he examines the original Kantian reflection on being that underlies the transcendental system's conceptual construction, which Kant calls transcendental reflection. Heidegger has found in the first *Critique* the recognition, on Kant's part, that critical philosophy depends upon a reflection that is prior to the reflective thematization of the positing of being.

Heidegger describes transcendental reflection in the above-quoted passage as the "organon for the interpretation of the being of beings." He has chosen to make use of precisely the term, *organon,* from which Kant distinguishes the accomplishments of the first *Critique.* Kant writes: "An **organon** of pure reason would be the sum total of all those principles [*Prinzipien*] in accordance with which all pure *a priori* cognitions can be acquired and actually brought about" (A11/B24–25). "Organon" refers to the accomplishment that we would hope to produce after the first *Critique* has, as a "discipline [*Disziplin*]," directed us away from metaphysical error, and as a "canon [*Kanon*] of the pure understanding," provided the systemization of *a priori* judgment (A795–96/B823–24). The organon would follow the "propaedeutic [*Propädeutik*]" that is offered in the first *Critique* itself, and distinguish the rational principles (*Prinzipien*) that permit all *a priori* cognition. In this way we could return to the rational underpinnings of the possibility of *a priori* cognition without in so doing surpassing the realm of experience and revisiting the errors of metaphysical dogmatism. But what such a completed organon of thought would be, what principles of reason could offer themselves after the critique of all metaphysical cognition, is left unexplained by Kant. He goes on to write that such an accomplishment "requires a lot, and it is still an open question whether such an amplification of our cognition is possible at all" (A11/B25).

The *Critique of Pure Reason,* as the propaedeutic to the organon of pure reason, investigates pure reason, "its sources and boundaries" (A11/B25), producing in the Transcendental Analytic a "canon" that both directs the empirical use of the understanding and designates the confines of its faculties. There appears to be no access to rational principles (*Prinzipien*): ascertaining this lack of access appears to be one of the accomplishments of the first *Critique;* and yet Kant does raise the possibility of their designation (A795–96/B823–24).

Heidegger uses Kant's term "organon" to describe this second-order reflection as a pursuit beyond the critical canon (A12/B26), one that supersedes the preliminary reflection on empirical experience. Heidegger claims that what needs to be asked, once the conception of transcendental reflection has been distinguished, is:

> What, then, is called being, such that it can be determined by way of representational thinking as positing [*Setzung*] and positedness [*Gesetztheit*]? That is a question that Kant does not ask, just as he does not ask the following ones: What, then, is called being, such that positing can be determined by the structure of form and matter? What, then, is called being, such that in the determination of the positedness of that which is posited, these occur in the twofold form of the subject, on the one hand as sentence-subject in relation to the predicate and on the other hand as ego-subject in relation to the object?[52]

In Heidegger's conception, Kant has developed the philosophical account of being as what is present to a subject, that which conforms to "the structure of form and matter" as elucidated in the Transcendental Analytic, and now this very conception should become questionable. Transcendental reflection is thus understood as forcing us to look at the structure of the reflective investigation of objects, and once this ontic structure is uncovered, the being of the being that has been structurally elucidated should take center stage. Why has the question of what exists—being—been taken to refer to objects standing in opposition to the human subject? Why, that is to say, has the conception of the subject as both the receptor and the agent of the positing of being been assumed when, as Kant has shown in the Transcendental Dialectic, doing so does not offer metaphysical certainty?

For Heidegger, what can be found in the Amphiboly is the opening to the organon that is ambiguously promised in the introduction of the first *Critique* (A11/B24–25). This does not mean that Heidegger is implying that a completed organon of the principles of pure reason can be found, or even produced; rather, the Kantian language of an organon is reconceived by Heidegger. The metaphysical goal of a completed system of principles that is implied in Kant's term "organon" is transformed into the thought that proceeds beyond conceptualization, and in this way marks the passage beyond the critical system. Kant's limited reference in the Amphiboly to the second-order transcendental reflection, which,

Heidegger writes, was "presumably . . . inserted very late, perhaps only after the completion of the *Critique of Pure Reason*,"[53] directs the questioning of the underlying principles of our philosophical approach. Rather than crowning the critical system, as Kant conceived of an organon of pure reason, in Heidegger's account it shows the critical analysis of cognition to have covered over a more primordial reflection. Transcendental reflection directs our gaze to the most basic philosophical questioning in which the designation of being itself proves doubtful, and the question of being thrusts itself to the fore. But if this is so, if the organon to which we are led is neither complete nor able to be completed, then should not the approach to being that has been brought to transcendental reflection become doubtful? Heidegger asks: "[D]oes not what we call 'logic'" also remain ambiguous, according to the view under discussion? "Does not 'logic,' then, as 'organon' and as interpretive horizon of being [*Horizont der Seinsauslegung*] become completely questionable?"[54]

Heidegger's approach to transcendental reflection in his late essay, particularly his interpretation of transcendental reflection's connection to the Postulates of Empirical Thought, emphasizes the limitations of the Transcendental Analytic and the analysis of finite cognition, limitations that would be surpassed in the attempt to conceive the organon of pure reason. Yet Kant turned away from the thought of the organon that would surpass the canon of pure understanding, because the organon could not "serve for expansion" of cognition (A795/B823), for what it offered, and what Kant approached in the Amphiboly, was a reflective questioning that superseded the demand for determinate cognition. Heidegger describes this move beyond critical ontology as "the farthest reaching step that Kant executed in the interpretation of being."[55]

Heidegger proceeds from his analysis of transcendental reflection as the most basic critical reflection to the question concerning being itself that is so ordered and reduced, subverting critical inquiry through the elucidation of its presuppositions. What is assumed is that no coherent account of Kant's method is possible. Heidegger consigns transcendental reflection to the organon of pure reason that would supersede the canon of pure understanding. What has here been proposed is an interpretation that emphasizes the relation of this underlying act of reflection to the critical system that it affords. Transcendental reflection is thus conceived as explaining how critical philosophy determines the boundary within which the analysis of cognition takes place. This designation is itself described by Kant as a reflective act, and yet Kant does not explain how this act, fundamental to the critical enterprise, is justified. If this second-order reflection can be explained within the conceptual system that its use affords, and if such a reflective orienting of thought proves not to contradict the critique of metaphysics launched in the Transcendental Dialectic, then it will offer a way to conceive of the underlying method of transcendental philosophy. Pursuing such an investigation of the method of critique makes use of Heidegger's late interpretation of the importance of transcendental reflection for Kant's conception of being in order to respond to the kind of criticism directed at Kant by Heidegger in his earlier *Being and Time*.[56] Kant begins his analysis of the conditions of the possibility of experience with a conception of the objects whose possibility he then goes on to analyze. As Heidegger argues in *Being and Time*, Kant's account appears not to address this initial assumption, and thus offers merely a reorientation within the domain of the objects that are conceived as given. In *What Is a Thing?* Heidegger broaches the question of the method of critique, while in "Kant's Thesis about Being," in describing the need for a transcendental reflection, a reflection back over the completed steps of critical analysis, Heidegger raises the question of the initial orientation of critical thought. For Heidegger, such a question cannot be properly addressed within the confines of critique: the initial orientation in terms of the subject-object relation cannot be justified, and so Heidegger is directed beyond critique to the thinking from which it has been reduced. But is this necessarily so? Does the need for this initial orienting reflection overwhelm the critical system, or could it be investigated in relation to the circular method that it permits?

Kant's introduction of transcendental reflection in the appendix to the Transcendental Analytic points beyond the objective and the posited, and so offers a way to investigate the method of critical inquiry. This designation of the territory within which the Kantian analysis of cognition—and so the deduction of the categories—has proceeded is itself described by Kant as a reflective act, but he does not explain how this most fundamental accomplishment in the critical enterprise is achieved. Having arrived at Kant's conception of transcendental reflection in the attempt to explain the regulative principle that Kant in §76 of the *Critique of Judgment* claims is relevant for differentiating possibility and actuality, we must now investigate whether transcendental reflection, like other reflective accomplishments in the Kantian system, is dependent for its parsing of representations on a regulative principle. In pursuing the development of the Kantian conception of transcendental reflection, we will be led to the Transcendental Dialectic in search of a regulative principle that could secure the differentiation of phenomenal from noumenal representations, and so the designation of the boundary of possible experience, and do so without subverting the architectonic of critique.

III. Regulating Critique

Kant's transcendental reflection secures *a priori* judgment only by limiting the field in which synthetic cognition is pursued, marking off the excesses of metaphysical inquiry prior to the demonstration of its failure; only by means of the differentiation of sensible representations from those of the pure understanding can the Transcendental Deduction proceed to distinguish the categories and can possibility and actuality be distinguished as the fundamental dualism of cognition. Only for objects that offer themselves to sensible intuition can the actual be distinguished from the possible. While the necessity of such a differentiating act prior to both the elucidation of cognition and the critique of metaphysics should now be apparent, since the field of possible experience must be distinguished in order to provide an account of finite cognition, what is much less obvious is how such an act, and thus the accomplishments that follow from it, can be justified. This query, which in essence takes the method of transcendental analysis itself as its task, will direct this investigation back to the *Critique of Judgment* with the intention of examining transcendental reflection as a mode of reflection that must depend for its accomplishments, as do all acts of reflection, on a regulative principle emanating from the critique of metaphysics.

In order to investigate transcendental reflection as an accomplishment that underlies the Kantian conception of possible experience, and thus not only the Transcendental Aesthetic but also the Transcendental Analytic, which deduces the categories of the understanding within this territory, we need to return to the First Introduction to the *Critique of Judgment,* where Kant explains: "To reflect [*Reflektieren*] (to consider [*Überlegen*]), however, is to compare and to hold together given representations either with others or with one's faculty of cognition, in relation [*Beziehung*] to a concept thereby made possible."[57] The first form of reflection refers to the comparison of representations distinguished by Kant as essential for teleological inquiry; in such reflection the representations are compared with each other in the pursuit of their systematic, which is to say teleological, unity.[58] The second form of reflection can be said to describe aesthetic judgment in which the representations are compared with the cognitive faculties, producing their free play and permitting the reflective pleasure of this judgment of the beautiful.[59] But this second form of reflection also stands as a description of Kant's earlier account of transcendental reflection, the reflective parsing of the field of representations through the comparison of representations with the cognitive faculties upon which they depend.[60] In both aesthetic reflective judgment of the beautiful and transcendental reflection, the given representation is compared not with other representations but with the cognitive faculties themselves; in the case of aesthetic reflection, what is produced is the heightened feeling of pleasure, while transcendental reflection designates the field of inquiry for the analysis of cognition.

Kant goes on to claim that reflection "requires a principle [*Prinzip*]," a rule through which the particular comparison can be made.[61] As was discussed in chapter 2, this principle is the idea that nature is purposive (*zweckmäßig*). In order to search reflectively for the systematic unity of empirical laws, we must presuppose that nature is systematic. To use such a principle regulatively is to allow it to direct the examination of nature while avoiding all claims concerning what it might be in itself. In the teleological judgment of nature, Kant describes this as the objective purposiveness of nature, a regulative principle necessary to judge reflectively the system of the empirical laws of nature. He distinguishes such objective purposiveness from the subjective purposiveness that is presupposed in the aesthetic reflective judgment of the beautiful in which nature's purposiveness for our contemplation is assumed without the designation of empirical rules governing such systematicity.[62]

But what of our ability to reflect transcendentally, to perform the act necessary for any *a priori* judgment? Does it also require a principle to regulate its accomplishment? Kant writes very little about such an orienting reflection, and it should be noted that it was conceived prior to the elucidation of reflective judgment, with the latter's dependence on regulative principles, in the third *Critique*. Yet, that it would itself need a regulative principle appears to follow not merely from its activity of comparing representations to the cognitive faculties, and so its similarity with aesthetic reflection, but also from the role that it must play in the examination of objectivity. The parsing of the representational manifold into that which is sensible and that which is merely intellectual presupposes the validity of this distinction and thus the designation of the sensible realm as the locus of cognition. However, it would seem that the purposiveness of nature, the regulative principle born of the theological idea that governs both aesthetic and teleological reflective judgment, does not constitute the regulative principle of transcendental reflection. The regulative principle of the purposiveness of nature cannot direct transcendental reflection, for it merely promises that nature is governed by an overarching law, one that offers success in both aesthetic and teleological reflection, while transcendental reflection demands a principle that could itself mark out the realm of possible experience and so distinguish what can be given sensibly from what can be thought but can never itself be given as an object of experience.

In pursuing a regulative principle for transcendental reflection, it is worth remembering that there is a further idea of reason that, along with the theological idea, does not lead to antinomy: the psychological idea.[63] While teleological reflection is regulated by the ideal of reason, it could be that transcendental reflection is directed by the psychological idea—the never-cognizable idea of the subject as the unity of inner sense in opposition to appearances in space—in its pursuit of the realm of possible experience. Not only does the psychological idea broach the issues concerning the designation and differentiation of subject and object that are relevant to the task that Kant sets for transcendental reflection, but finding the psychological idea as the regulative principle that designates the region of possible experience will also explain the trio of examples of reason's regulative use listed in §76 of the *Critique of Judgment*.

To develop the hypothesis that it is a regulative principle following from the psychological idea that directs transcendental reflection, we will have to look at both the Paralogisms of Pure Reason and the second section of the appendix to the Transcendental Dialectic, titled On the Final Aim of the Natural Dialectic of Human Reason.[64] Such a prospect raises the possibility that from within the *Critique of Pure Reason* itself the regulative principle of transcendental reflection can be found. This regulative principle promises transcendental reflection the distinction that it needs, that between spatial appearances and non-spatial thoughts, such that it can mark the boundary of possible experience that permits both the analysis of finite cognition and the critique of metaphysics.

In connecting the elusive §76 of the third *Critique* to the modal categories and through them to transcendental reflection, Heidegger has directed my study back to the first *Critique* in pursuit of an answer to the question concerning how it is that Kant can justify the phenomenal realm within which he begins his inquiry into the conditions of the possibility of objects of experience. The connection of the designation of possibility and actuality to an accomplishment of the critique of metaphysics, offered by Kant in §76 of the *Critique of Judgment*, raises a question that Heidegger does not ask: What sort of thinking, what sort of reflective act, is implied in such an account of the regulative principle that makes possible transcendental reflection, and hence *a priori* judgment?[65] The task that remains is to approach the Transcendental Dialectic in pursuit of a regulative principle for transcendental reflection; doing so will allow us to begin to answer the question that Heidegger raises but leaves unanswered near the end of *Kant and the Problem of Metaphysics*: "is there not also a positive problematic to be found in this characterization of the Dialectic, which appears to be only negative?"[66]

The question then is whether the Transcendental Dialectic can be said to offer the regulative principle for transcendental reflection, the act of designating the region of experience within which the *a priori* elements of cognition can be derived: How is it that Kant can justify the initial limitation of his philosophical investigation of cognition to that which can be empirically given prior to the critique of metaphysics that is launched only later in the Transcendental Dialectic? Kant briefly addresses the question of what constitutes experience in critical philosophy at the end of the Postulates of Empirical Thought. He explains that the region of experience that the Transcendental Analytic investigates is that which conforms to the empirical use of the understanding; if experience were not limited by the *a priori* rules of the understanding to the formal conditions of both sensibility and apperception, then it would not be "comprehensible" (A230/B283). Underlying this designation of experience is neither the certainty that there could not be another conception of experience that was not dependent on empirical givenness, nor the claim that the realm of the possible is limited to that which can be empirically given, and hence actualized. What Kant does claim is that by limiting the conception of experience within which cognitive analysis is pursued in critical philosophy to that of empirical possibility, the examination of *a priori* synthetic cognition can proceed. Kant examines this conception of empirical possibility by broaching the issue of its opposite, a non-empirical sense of possibility; doing so highlights the presuppositions implicit in the use in the critical project of the differentiation of possibility and actuality by offering a further conception of possibility: an "absolute possibility [*absolute Möglichkeit*]" (A232/B285), against which the critical designation can be more clearly exposed.

Kantian empirical possibility is limited to the potentially empirically given, which is to say that the possible meets the "formal conditions of an experience in general" (A220/B267) but not the empirical conditions of such an actual experience. The Kantian possible is thus possible actuality, and precludes any conception of possibility that would be formally severed from empirical actuality. In opposition to such empirical possibility, Kant distinguishes a non-empirical conception of possibility that is utterly severed from actuality, what he calls possible "in every respect," or "absolute possibility" (A232/B285). Kant does this in order to distinguish the underlying criteria of the critical examination of cognition. He is asking why one could not posit a different conception of experience than that of critical philosophy, one that was not limited to the formal conditions of empirical givenness and that would thus span the region of thought unlimited by any criteria of its actualization. Such a conception of possibility, Kant writes, would not depend upon "conditions that are themselves merely possible" (A232/B284). Absolute possibility, unlike empirical possibility, would be essentially possible, inasmuch as the condition of its possibility would be unattainable; hence, its possibility could not be transformed by actualization. The Kantian empirically possible, by contrast, is transformed when the condition with which its concept formally agrees is empirically given and what was possible becomes actual. What is empirically possible is actualized when its condition is empirically given to sensibility, but absolute possibility would not be able to be so transformed; it would be possible without the chance of the condition of its possibility being overturned; it would be "possible in all respects" without the chance of its becoming actual.[67] Such a conception of possibility, Kant writes, "can in no way be of empirical use, rather it belongs solely to reason, which goes beyond all possible empirical use of the understanding" (A232/B285).

In highlighting at the end of the Postulates of Empirical Thought, which is to say in the penultimate chapter of the Transcendental Analytic with only the *Phenomena* and *Noumena* chapter remaining, a rather different conception of possibility than that of critical philosophy, Kant has underlined the dependence of critical philosophy not merely on the possible as distinguished from the actual, but also on a conception of experience delimited by the area of empirically possible objects, for experience has been limited to what meets the formal conditions of empirical givenness. The conception of experience with which Kant begins his examination is thus not conceptually neutral. It presupposes a certain conception of possibility as distinguished from actuality, which is precisely the distinction that Kant, in §76 of the *Critique of Judgment,* appears to raise as dependent on a regulative principle. Kant writes that this conception of absolute possibility, or "possibility in every respect," which would initiate a very different investigation of cognition than what the Transcendental Analytic offers, one that has no connection to the sensibly given, must be left "for further treatment later on" (A232/B285), which is to say in the Transcendental Dialectic. Kant will address a conception of absolute possibility only in the part of the first *Critique* that investigates thought as liberated from the boundary of sensible content, the part which offers his critique of metaphysics.

While Kant can distinguish a sense of possibility beyond that of empirical possibility, the question concerning "whether the possibility of things extends further than experience can reach" (A232/B284) must be put aside in order to continue the examination of empirical objects. The Transcendental Analytic proceeds by investigating the empirically possible things that comprise experience precisely by leaving out of play the question of non-sensible objects; only in the Transcendental Dialectic does Kant address the question of whether such absolute possibility, or conversely absolute actuality, can be known; and he does so from the perspective of and with the conceptual tools derived from the analysis of empirical possibility. Thought can think of objects that could never be sensibly given, which is to say objects that could never spatially appear, and yet this is not in itself a reason to avoid pursuing such metaphysical interests.[68]

Only through an investigation of the Transcendental Dialectic can we come to understand the presupposition that underlies the Transcendental Analytic and its investigation of what is empirically possible, for experience has been limited to a conception of possibility that permits both the examination of cognition and the development of the critical system. Transcendental reflection has been shown to be the reflective act that directs this designation of experience as the region in which those objects are to be found for which the possible-actual distinction holds. The regulative principle that directs transcendental reflection must issue from reason's pursuit of the super-sensible; as in the case of teleological judgment, this dependence avoids metaphysical error but can never be objectively justified since its principle evades determinate cognition.

In turning to the Transcendental Dialectic with the goal of finding a regulative principle (*Prinzip*) for transcendental reflection, the relationship that was promised in the *Prolegomena* between understanding and reason has been mapped out;[69] reason's pursuit of metaphysical ideas, when critiqued, does not quell this natural tendency but comes to make use of such unattainable goals as regulative principles. Such metaphysical seepage into the critical philosophy does not merely direct teleological judgment; it also guides the examination of the constitutive features of cognition. In this sense, the elucidation of the dependence of the understanding on reason does not provide the metacritique that Hamann rhetorically demanded, for reason does not offer a principle that is constitutive of the understanding's unity. What reason does offer the understanding is a regulative principle that directs transcendental reflection in a manner that conforms to the pattern of teleological judgment. Understanding is subordinated to reason, yet reason's accomplishments occur only through its alliance with the understanding. In recognizing a regulative principle at the foundation of the account of finite cognition, my investigation has been able to highlight the complex interrelation of elements that is the often-overlooked hallmark of transcendental philosophy: Only through the investigation of empirical cognition can the critique of metaphysics be pursued in a manner that reformulates its ideas, offering the regulative principle (*Prinzip*) that underlies the accomplishments of the examination of objectivity.

This examination of transcendental reflection has raised a way to explain the designation of the territory within which the critical analysis of cognition takes place. In order to comprehend the account of experience that the *Critique of Pure Reason* offers, it is not sufficient to elucidate the sensible forms and intellectual categories that condition the experience of objects; the designation of the territory within which the cognition of objects of experience is pursued must itself be explained. What is found is the necessity of transcendental reflection.[70] The boundary of possible experience has been distinguished without a return to a dogmatic metaphysics. However, the reflective act necessary for the designation of the territory of experience must also be explained: Upon what does such an accomplishment depend? The answer that has here been developed, through a forward glance at the *Critique of Judgment*, is that transcendental reflection— and hence the examination of *a priori* cognition—is itself dependent upon a regulative principle. Kant's Transcendental Dialectic must now be shown to have provided the underpinning of the account of objectivity, which will explain the relation of understanding and reason that the *Prolegomena* promises. But before undertaking this task, it is important to investigate the distance that has been traveled from the metacritical demands that initiated my study.

IV. From Hamann to Hegel

This book began with the attempt to justify the critical dualism of sensibility and understanding through which Kant distinguishes the conditions of the possibility of experience. Hamann's claim is that the dualism of sensibility and understanding with which Kant examines synthetic cognition limits experience to that which can be explained by such rigid classifications; only that which can be thematized in terms of both sensibility and understanding is deemed experience. The complexity of lived experience is reduced to the components that adhere to such rational and empirical forms, ridding it of all that surpasses these narrow confines.[71] However, Hamann's interest in a metacritique appears to entail the rejection of all critical procedure; in pursuing the unified origin that languishes behind Kant's dualisms, Hamann emphasizes the irreducible nature of cultural experience without an investigation of the criteria through which one could judge the failure of all such reductions. In his rush to reject Kant's examination of experience, and in its place assign an unknowable natural origin to thought, Hamann overlooks the intricacy in Kant's account of the relation between reason's metaphysical interests and the regulative boundary that permits the dualistic account of finite cognition. What must be examined is how we are able to parse our representations such that we can distinguish what offers itself as cognition from what, without the critique of our metaphysical strivings, will lead to illusion. Only after transcendental reflection has limited the field of representations to what is sensibly given can cognition be defined by the dualism of sensibility and understanding, and only then can this reduction be justified in terms of its accomplishments.

This dense tangle of relations and dependencies between reason's ideas and the account of synthetic cognition is what I am attempting to unravel. For Kant, reason offers as a regulative principle the *focus imaginarius* (A644/B672), which permits the reflective examination of the "abyss" of human experience.[72] Of course, this conception of the dependence of the examination of objectivity on reason, this reflective aspect of the examination of determinate judgment, must be further examined in the Transcendental Dialectic in order to furnish a positive function for what is more commonly interpreted as the merely negative critique of metaphysical pretensions. And yet, what can already be seen is that what began as a metacritical inquiry in pursuit of the criteria that underlie Kant's transcendental idealism has now limited itself to the question of the relation of reason to this dualism within Kant's examination of objectivity. Hamann's response to the limits of philosophy, to our inability to enunciate a system of experience as it is felt, or lived, in all of its complexity, is to reject any attempt at such a systemization. But is there not another response beyond such a skeptical position? By pursuing the relation of reason to the examination of objectivity, we will not attempt to subvert such skepticism; rather, we will approach Kant's accomplishment as one that follows from the antinomies, that is to say, from the skeptical recognition of the limits of human reason.[73]

In pursuing the relation of reason to the dualism of sensibility and understanding, we have begun to search for the rational underpinnings of the critical examination of objectivity; and yet to do so is not to revert to the metacritical demand for an ultimate response to skeptical concerns. What can be pursued are the metaphysical presuppositions of the account of objectivity: Does the accomplishment of critique itself fall prey to metaphysical contradiction, or can such an accomplishment provide a theoretical structure that both depends upon and affords an approach to metaphysical issues that avoids the history of illusions and contradictions that otherwise appears unavoidable?

To address the Transcendental Dialectic in this manner is to search for a second opening upon the critical project. The Transcendental Dialectic does not merely follow from the designation of the categories, and so remain within the confines of the territory opened by the Transcendental Aesthetic; rather, the critique of metaphysics will come to be seen as an investigation of the presuppositions embedded in that which the Transcendental Aesthetic, the initial and most obvious opening of the first *Critique,* initiates. In following this inquiry into the critical project, one which Kant in the *Prolegomena* assigned to "experts [*Kenner*]" in the critical undertaking,[74] it will be seen that we are pursuing a response to Hegel's critique of Kant rather than Hamann's. For Hamann, the "hypostatizing" of an empty noumenal realm was the error that directed Kant to the dualistic account of cognition and enforced a purified system at the expense of the density of the culture from which it was torn. This is to say that it is the denial of all that is not reducible to the sensible and intellectual criteria of critical philosophy that is the downfall of the project. But is this so? Does critical philosophy utterly deny all that is not deemed by it to be objective? The answer that I have been developing is that Kant's account of objectivity—and the dualism of sensibility and understanding that follows from it—depends upon the pursuit of metaphysics undertaken in the name of reason. What will be seen is that it is Hegel who recognizes that for Kant the noumenal realm is certainly not empty; but what it offers, Hegel claims, is rejected by Kant in his turning from the infinite that he has distinguished from finite cognition. Hegel's interpretation and criticism of Kant's critical philosophy will help to focus this inquiry on the question to which it has been redirected. Can the importance of the infinite for the examination of finite cognition be seen to have a legitimate role to play in the accomplishments of critical philosophy?

In *Faith and Knowledge (Glauben und Wissen),* Hegel argues that, after distinguishing understanding and reason, with the former having as its subject matter finite cognition and the latter the absolute or unconditioned, Kant chooses the former while denying inquiry into the latter, which had readily been thought. Hegel writes that "in choosing between the two his nature despised [*verachtet*] the necessity of thinking the rational, of thinking an intuitive spontaneity, and decided without reservation for appearance."[75] Not only does Kant choose to investigate finite cognition, which is to say cognition based merely on appearances, rather than the accomplishments of absolute reason, but he also attempts to give an essential account of the structure of finite appearances. Hegel criticizes the confidence with which Kant examines finite cognition and the resulting absolute account of the manner in which objects appear. Hegel's claim is that Kant's "essential" account of finite cognition in the *Critique of Pure Reason* can claim validity only by means of "experience and empirical psychology."[76] Kant has attempted to give an account of the essence of finite cognition, of the "in-itself of cognition," but can only do so by means of a crude empirical psychology that assumes that cognition is "in-itself" the way that it appears. This means that Kant restricts himself to an analysis of the cognition that we actually have, so that this starting point is never questioned. Thus, for Kant, although the ideas of reason can be thought, the pure actuality of an intuitive understanding is rejected in favor of a conception of cognition that takes as its limited terrain appearances, and so the division of possibility and actuality as its distinguishing feature.

This account of finite cognition is paired, Hegel claims, with one of absolute reason as "pure abstract unity."[77] In refusing to pass over into the unity of the pure and the empirical, the unity of absolute reason, Kant has distinguished reason as without content and hence as merely regulative.[78] Hegel describes this as a negative account of the "unconditioned character of reason," since reason is viewed as merely pursuing the goals of finite cognition beyond this region; its failure, which is to say its pursuit of illusions, dictates the need to limit its application.

Hegel argues that even Kant eventually recognized the impossibility of addressing finite cognition apart from the absolute, but that he denied that such a dependence of the finite on the absolute overturned the dualistic division with which he had begun his critical account of finite cognition. Kant was not willing to give up his claim that finite cognition was all that was attainable, even when his own dualistic examination of such cognition directed him to that which must be presupposed by it.[79] One need only look to the transcendental unity of apperception, the underlying principle of the unity for consciousness of disparate determinations, and the transcendental imagination, which unifies the determinations themselves, to see, Hegel claims, the dependence of the narrowly circumscribed empirical psychology on that which surpasses these limitations. The heterogeneity of the sensible and the intelligible forces Kant to posit their unity in something that overcomes such dualism: the transcendental imagination, the undivided absolute, which is, Hegel writes, "the identity of heterogeneous elements of this kind."[80] Such unified determinations are *my* determinations only because attached to each is the I of transcendental apperception, the analytic principle of the unity of empirical consciousness.

Yet, Hegel claims, Kant rejected such thoughts, which clearly exceed his empirical psychology, even as his own "critique of the cognitive faculties [*Erkenntnisvermögen*]"[81] showed the dependence of this conception of finite cognition on that which explains the identity of the heterogeneous elements.

The identity that the transcendental imagination provides is not an empty unity; rather, it is the identity through which the heterogeneous can be experienced as the unity of the sensible and the intellectual. This identity, coupled with the unity of apperception that provides the underlying singularity of the determined manifold, offers the key that unlocks Kant's most basic question: How are synthetic judgments *a priori* possible? Their possibility, Hegel writes, must be explained "through the original absolute identity of the heterogeneous,"[82] which is to say an identity that even Kant's dualistic account of finite cognition shows underlies the cognition that it explains.

Kant, Hegel claims, was not able to admit that the examination of the sensible leads to the unity of the sensible and the super-sensible because he had attempted to limit reason to the regulative role that it performs in reflective judgment and to the "mere 'ought'" of morality. And yet the unity that the transcendental imagination must offer the dualism of sensibility and understanding, the unity that the Schematism chapter explains and that the transcendental unity of apperception both depends upon and affords, would seem to differ from the unconditioned, the absolute for which reason strives. Hegel's answer is that the pairing of a merely abstract unity with a purely negative conception of the critique of metaphysics in the Transcendental Dialectic must surely be rejected once we examine Kant's investigation of the place of the absolute in aesthetic judgment. Hegel argues that in this section the bridging of the sensible and the intellectual is explicitly accomplished in the sphere of beauty, inasmuch as Kant cannot avoid connecting this experience to the idea of an intuitive intellect; finite accomplishment is thus quite directly tied to the metaphysical absolute.

In the Kantian system the unattainable ideal of reason plays the role of the guarantor of reflective judgment concerning beauty, providing regulative certainty for the reflection on that which cannot be determined. Hegel explains that the idea of reason, which can never be sensibly given, secures the aesthetic idea, which can never be thought. Hegel denies this dual failure, and the merely methodological role played by the absolute, asking rhetorically why it is that one should proceed "as if the aesthetic idea did not have its exposition in the idea of reason, and the idea of reason did not have in beauty what Kant called its demonstration, namely the presentation [*Darstellung*] of a concept in intuition."[83] For Kant, the super-sensible remains unknowable in a manner that denies the "absolute identity of the sensible and the super-sensible,"[84] permitting only an empirical beauty and an enforced dualism in cognition. Yet, Hegel claims, in the *Critique of Judgment,* where Kant describes the intuitive intellect as that "for which possibility and actuality are one,"[85] the limitations that Kant has foisted upon both beauty and cognition are superseded. Kant has thought the unity of the sensible and the super-sensible, and hence, inadvertently, surpassed finite dualism. For Hegel, Kant's attempt to retain the dualism of the sensible and the intellectual, even after his inquiry into aesthetic experience has highlighted the dependence of sensible experience on the conception of the intuitive intellect, exemplifies his stubborn turning to the finite from what is super-sensible and infinite.

The non-cognizable theological idea that provides the regulative principle of the purposiveness of nature has been shown to be implied in both teleological and aesthetic judgment; it is an idea that surpasses all finite cognition, proceeding into the metaphysical territory that Kant has explicitly critiqued, where it acts as the unifying element in the reflective judgment of the empirical. And what must be recognized, Hegel adds, is that this intuitive intellect, which stands as the regulating principle of reflective judgment, is not different from the conception of the transcendental imagination that unifies the dualism of sensibility and understanding in the examination of cognition.[86] This is because what the conception of an intuitive intellect expresses is the possibility of the unity of heterogeneous elements, sense and concept: in the case of synthetic cognition this underlying homogeneity is attributed to a faculty that exceeds the limitations implicit in finite cognition, and in aesthetic judgment it is attributed to the ideal of reason, to the power of an infinite intellect. Both express the dependence of the account of our finite faculties on that which exceeds them. The examination of finite cognition depends upon a thought that cannot itself be cognized, and what this indicates is that Kant's fanatical commitment to a dualistic conception of finite cognition is overcome through the very accomplishment that it affords, since it is led to affirm the identity of what it claims is heterogeneous.

The dualism of sensibility and understanding embraced by Kant in the examination of finite cognition, which follows from the underlying critical dualism of understanding and reason, leads to the overturning of this latter dualism, for the understanding's contribution to finite cognition has been shown to depend upon that which Kant deemed to be beyond the reach of empirical cognition, that is, a unifying absolute as the source of the cognition that is then deemed to be thoroughly finite. In reflecting on its cognitive faculties, the Kantian subject distinguishes the transcendental imagination as that which mediates between understanding and sensibility; this unification is not merely a further elucidation of the finite faculties but is, Hegel claims, the overcoming of such dualism, as it is itself "intuitive intellect."[87] The absolute unity of an intuitive intellect is the unity that permits the bridging of sensibility and understanding. This unity, according to Hegel, both precedes Kant's dualism and is that to which an account of finite cognition must proceed. Finite consciousness thus catches sight of the unity that must be present for the very experience that has been explained according to the dualism of sensibility and understanding.

Hegel's critique of Kant's division of the empirical and the absolute elucidates the dependence of this critical dualism on a power beyond that of the cognitive faculties of sensibility and understanding. And yet Hegel does not investigate the question of whether the Kantian examination of finite cognition can be justified. While it is certainly true that for Kant the dualism of sense and concept is only mediated, and experience explained, by means of the homogenizing function of the transcendental imagination, but why must this unifying function be conflated with Kant's critical conception of the thought of the intuitive intellect? Finite cognition has been explained by means of the dualism of sensibility and understanding in relation to the imagination taken as its creative source; this allows us to examine our thought of an intuitive intellect, recognize our inability to cognize such an object, and yet make use of such an idea in reflective judgment. The rush to conflate what Kant holds to be separate is particularly apparent in Hegel's examination of Kantian aesthetic judgment. Kant's account of aesthetic judgment depends upon the ideal of reason as that which explains how such a critique of taste, the critical examination of the experience of beauty, is possible; but does the dependence of the critique of aesthetic judgment on a regulative principle deem the experience of beauty to be one of the intuitive, which is to say divine, intellect itself? The fact that we need to admit that the critique of such experience depends upon an unknowable idea hardly justifies the claim that the absolute is achieved in the experience of beauty.[88]

Hamann's response to the seeming impossibility of explaining the complexity of human reason, which is to say its integral connection in cultural life, is to turn from this opacity and only rhetorically to ask for a metacritique of the criteria according to which Kant examines cognition. The skeptical argument that Hamann launches against the Kantian examination of experience, one that could just as easily be directed at any such attempt and that follows from the certainty that philosophical investigation is forever unfaithful to the complexity of lived experience, leads him to reject all philosophical goals and to embrace the individuality, and thus the isolating silence, of an idiosyncratic faith. Hamann recognizes the limitation of any viewpoint, and unlike the ancient skeptics for whom this recognition offers release from any particular position and freedom from the immoderate commitment that intellectual dogma produces, he claims no virtue for this skeptical combat. In terms of the progression toward self-consciousness in Hegel's *Phenomenology of Spirit*, Hamann appears to embody Hegel's idea of "the beautiful soul [*die schöne Seele*]."[89] Distressed by the failings of the pursuit of truth, Hegel's "beautiful soul" finds herself paralyzed by the fear that anything that she could say would distort and misrepresent what thus remains silent. Unlike Hegel, for whom such a state is the impetus to reconciliation with others and the pursuit of the truth of spirit (*Geist*) in the sociopolitical world,[90] Hamann views such despair as the end point of philosophy and the release from its demands. Hamann's skeptical critique of Enlightenment rationality is animated by a faith that, rather than offering him the freedom of the ancient skeptics, produces the alienation of one for whom language can never approach the truth of human experience.[91]

But must philosophy, if it is to avoid such despair, pass over to the absolute from the Kantian investigation of finite cognition? To answer in the negative does not imply that we should set aside the metacritical demand and pursue the examination of finite cognition on its own, for this is precisely what Hegel claims that Kant has attempted, that he has rejected the absolute even as he goes on to prove the necessity of its achievement.[92] Rather, it is to ask whether, contra Hegel, our examination of finite cognition leads us back not to reason's absolute unity but to the regulative principle that follows from the pursuit of the absolute and that affords us the account of objects in terms of the dualism of sensibility and understanding. Thus, rather than agreeing with Hegel that Kant chooses to investigate finite rather than absolute knowing, what is posited is a circular structure for the transcendental system: the ideas of reason through which we uncover the structure of finite cognition are themselves thought by means of the application of the pure concepts of the understanding beyond possible experience.[93] The regulative principle that follows from the pursuit of metaphysics is thus dependent for its elucidation upon the very concepts that it helps to uncover. Only through the interdependence of understanding and reason are we able to examine both finite cognition and reason's absolute; neither offers itself to thought independently, and neither can be superseded, for both are marked by their dependence on that which makes them possible.

To pursue such a goal is not to search for a position that would subvert the skeptical impetus to critique, but to investigate how a systematic account of the human faculties is possible for a consciousness that recognizes such skeptical limits. The third *Critique* leads to a more probing interpretation of the first *Critique*, but not because the distinction between reflective and determinate judgment has been erased; rather, it is because determinate judgment, the region of synthetic cognition *a priori*, has been shown to depend for its designation on a reflective act, which in the first *Critique* Kant calls transcendental reflection and in an elusive fashion describes as necessary for *a priori* judgment about things (B319 / A263).[94]

Kant's dualism is not a simple pulling back from absolute reason that finds reason's mark at the unifying depths of finitude (in the transcendental imagination), as Hegel claims, for Kant is not pursuing "Locke's goal"[95] of an essential account of finitude. In Hegel's view, Kant has proceeded from the crude psychological (empirical) account of finite cognition to the intuitive intellect (as transcendental imagination) without the necessity of an account of the method that has afforded him the constitution of such finite cognition. Yet without an investigation of how Kant elucidates the *a priori* structures of finite cognition, without some sort of critique of the critical accomplishment, Hegel's account is essentially guilty of an error that is the mirror image of the one for which he criticizes Kant. If Kant recognizes both finite and absolute knowing and chooses the former, then Hegel chooses the latter. Absolute knowing is raised as the truth of finite knowing in a manner that prompts similar metacritical questions concerning the designation of the criteria of its analysis of the absolute.

How can both sides of such an errant coin be avoided? How can thought be investigated without giving preference to either the finite or the infinite, that is, in a manner that can justify the terms of its own systemization? Hamann views such a goal as impossible, as an attempt to tear a particular type of human endeavor from the culture in which it is formed; but can reason be investigated in a manner that avoids Hamann's supposition of its absolutely opaque origin in language (and the resulting silence on all philosophical issues) and at the same time in a manner that rejects the Hegelian claim that Kant has unjustifiably chosen to examine finite rather than infinite knowing? What we have learned is that metacritical concerns relating to Kant's critical accomplishment should prompt us to attempt to interpret critical philosophy in a manner that recognizes the interdependence of finite cognition and the metaphysical pursuit of absolute cognition. By taking seriously the claims made by Kant concerning the need for transcendental reflection, his investigation of finite cognition will be seen to be neither arbitrary nor surpassable; rather, it affords conceptual inquiry into our varied communicative accomplishments while avoiding the blind dependence on unexamined metaphysical presuppositions that characterize narrowly construed epistemological inquiries.

V. Conclusion: Transcendental Reflection and the Method of Critique

To pursue such an alternative path for the investigation of the relation between understanding and reason in Kant's transcendental idealism, and to do so in a way that rejects the demands placed on critical philosophy by both Hamann and Hegel, is the task that I have undertaken. Is there not a way to examine the relation of reason and understanding within Kant's analysis of cognition in a manner that explains how Kant neither overlooks the limitations implicit in any examination of human experience, as Hamann claims, nor recoils from the dependence of the examination of finite cognition on the absolute, as Hegel argues? The above examination of transcendental reflection as the act that designates the realm of possible experience has outlined a way out of this problem; what remains to be examined is the manner in which the psychological idea can be seen to function as the regulative principle (*Prinzip*) that affords critical philosophy the ability to designate the modal categories as determinative of experience. To ask about the regulative underpinnings of the analysis of cognition is thus to ask about the regulative principle (*Prinzip*) of reason that underlies the designation of the principles (*Grundsätze*) of the understanding. The regulative use of reason's ideas concerns not merely the narrow region of metaphysical speculation open to us after the accomplishments in the Transcendental Analytic and the limitations imposed on thought by the Transcendental Dialectic, as Hegel's interpretation maintains; rather, the examination of objectivity will be seen to depend upon a regulative principle that can only be designated as such, and thus saved from the illusions to which it is driven by our metaphysical tendencies, after the critical elucidation of our cognitive faculties.

The paradox that appears to define reason's relation to the understanding does not force us to deny the metaphysical context within which critical epistemology is carried out; rather, what must be recognized is that transcendental philosophy has a paradoxical element at its core, and that such complexity is a basic component of the critical system itself, into which the critical philosopher enters in order to deny both skepticism and dogmatism. Only by beginning the philosophical project with the investigation of phenomenal objects can the criteria be distinguished that permit the thematization of the realm of experience. In order to examine how it is that the metaphysical presuppositions of the phenomenal realm can be explained within the conceptual structure of the critical project, the Transcendental Dialectic must be examined. Only if we are able to distinguish a principle (*Prinzip*) that can regulate transcendental reflection's designation of the region of possible experience will the limitations for which Hegel has castigated Kant be transformed into questions that help to clarify the transcendental approach.

FIVE

The Paralogisms of Pure Reason: In Search of a Regulative Principle for Transcendental Reflection

I. The Faculty of Thinking (Axvii)

In the preface to the first edition of the *Critique of Pure Reason*, in what stands as the opening salvo of critical philosophy, Kant writes that although questions concerning "the faculty of thinking [*das Vermögen zu denken*]"—the mind, or reason, in the broadest and most undifferentiated sense—are important, they are not an essential part of the Transcendental Deduction, nor are they necessary for inquiry into the "faculty we call the understanding, and at the same time for the determination of the rules and boundaries of its use" (Axvi).[1] What is central to the Transcendental Deduction is the demonstration of the objective validity of the categories of the understanding; and while one could also trace these categories and the faculty of understanding that they constitute back to their source, to the "faculty of thinking" itself, from out of which they have been distinguished, this latter task, which Kant describes as subjective, does not belong "essentially" to the Transcendental Deduction.

Kant thus distinguishes two aspects of the Transcendental Deduction: the objective interest in the deduction of the categories of the understanding as the conditions that permit objects of experience, and the subjective interest that attempts to examine the intellectual capacities that provide such objective cognition. While such interests obviously overlap, it is the objective that designates the conditions that permit objectively valid judgments—rather than the subjective, which delves into the "faculties of cognition [*Erkenntnisvermögen*]" (Axvii) on which these conditions rest—that are essential for the Transcendental Deduction. In both the first- and second-edition versions of the Transcendental Deduction, Kant proves that the *a priori* concepts of the understanding are a necessary condition of the experience of objects. And while the first edition's version emphasizes the imagination and the threefold synthesis that offers the subjective source of cognition, as opposed to that of the second edition with its emphasis on the role of the understanding in the production of objectivity,

Kant explains in the first edition's preface that the success, even of the original Deduction, depends not on the emphasis on the psychological or subjective elements of cognition, but on the role of the understanding in cognition, and so on the objective side of the Deduction (Axvii).

The investigation of the understanding insofar as it conditions the possibility of objects advances in the Transcendental Analytic without the more general inquiry into the cognitive structure of rational beings, and thus without a clear explanation of the relation of the faculty of understanding to thinking in general, which is to say to that of reason in its broadest sense, of which it is a part. Kant initially directs an investigation of the dependence of objects of experience on the categories of the understanding, setting aside questions that concern themselves with the understanding as a faculty distinguished within the more general account of the faculty of thinking. Kant writes: "the chief question always remains: 'What and how much can understanding and reason cognize free of all experience?' and not: 'How is the **faculty of thinking** itself possible?'" (Axvii). But does this mean that Kant has begun the critical project by denying the need to investigate the particular mode of thought of the human subject, limiting himself to a conception of the understanding as the locus of the categories which condition the possibility of objects and denying the need to justify this designation of the philosophical terrain by connecting the analysis of the understanding to that of the broader capacities of thought? Or, does this emphasis on the objective and not the subjective side of the Deduction, and so on the categories of the understanding rather than on the relation of the understanding to thought in general, even in the first edition, merely begin the critical project, offering an entry into a discussion of the cognitive faculties that will ultimately proceed beyond the understanding to questions concerning the conception of human thinking from out of which it has been carved? It is obviously the latter question that animates my interpretation of the critical project. This is to say that the limited epistemological inquiry in the Transcendental Analytic, that of not only the objective side of the Transcendental Deduction, but also the subjective side initiated in the first edition, must be understood within the context of Kant's attempt to orient philosophy within thought in general, an orientation that is presupposed in the analysis of the understanding undertaken in the Transcendental Analytic.[2] What must be addressed is how the terrain of empirical objects has been designated as that within which the faculty of the understanding will be deduced. What, we could ask, is thought, what is reason, in the broadest Kantian sense in which it refers to all of our cognitive faculties, such that the understanding could be so distinguished?

Kant explains that the question "How is the faculty of thinking itself possible?" is to be set aside only for a time and will be addressed at a later point. He writes that this question attempts to broach the issue of the conception of thinking from out of which the analysis of the understanding has proceeded. Kant refrains from addressing this question at the start of the critical project because, he writes, to do so would make it appear that "I am taking the liberty in this case of expressing an **opinion**, and that the reader might therefore be free to hold another **opinion**" (Axvii). Kant begins the critical project with an examination of the understanding, without addressing the broader question concerning the relation of the understanding to the faculty of thinking in general, in order to avoid the appearance of a merely contingent pursuit of the more fundamental question concerning the nature of thought itself; and he does so even though such a conception of human thought must be presupposed in the analysis of the understanding, for the understanding is conceived in opposition to those uses of our cognitive faculties unconnected to sensibility and so unable to offer the cognition of objects. The critical examination of thought begins with an examination of the conceptual conditions that permit the experience of objects, with the investigation of the understanding and an emphasis on the objective deduction, setting aside the question of the relation of such a faculty to thinking in general, a question that would appear to be merely hypothetical but is, Kant writes, not so. And yet, how can we say anything about the manner of our thinking, apart from the designation of the understanding, when rational psychology, as the Paralogisms of Pure Reason chapter proves, does not offer us knowledge of the rational subject? In the preface Kant comments in parentheses that he will have another "opportunity" to elucidate why the examination of this founding cause is not merely a hypothesis, but he does not explain how or even where this is to be accomplished (Axvii). In fact, he concludes this paragraph in a manner that retreats from this offer by claiming that the objective side of the deduction retains its strength even if the subjective side remains elusive. But can critical philosophy remain "elusive" when it comes to the topic of the underlying conception of human thinking? Is it not essential to return to the question of the faculty of thinking after the analysis of the understanding, in order to examine the conception of thought upon which the examination of cognition in the Transcendental Analytic has been built?

Without a prior investigation of the structure of synthetic cognition, the attempt to examine human thinking directly, which is to say to examine ourselves as rational beings, leads either to dogmatic epistemological claims concerning the structure of all cognition or, with their rejection, to the acceptance of the opacity of human thought. What must be admitted is that in Kant's transcendental system, the question concerning thought in general has been subordinated to the question concerning synthetic *a priori* cognition. Only with the categories produced by such an investigation can we address ourselves as thinking beings in the Paralogisms chapter, and there in a manner that appears thoroughly negative. But this chapter does not merely reject the investigation of rational psychology. What will be seen is that the metaphysical investigation of the rational subject elucidates the regulative principle that has made possible the analysis of cognition and that is thus presupposed in Kant's investigation. It is the recognition on Kant's part that he cannot directly address what it means to be rational without falling into either metaphysical dogmatism or epistemological skepticism that has directed him to pursue a critique of synthetic cognition prior to an analysis of the metaphysical presuppositions of such an inquiry.

The Transcendental Dialectic is the critique of all attempts to apply the *a priori* concepts of synthetic cognition beyond the boundary of possible experience, beyond the region of thought that concerns the appearances of empirical objects. The most obvious conclusion stemming from this inquiry is the merely negative claim that no such metaphysical knowledge is attainable. And while the non-cognizable ideas of reason are readily understood to fulfill certain positive functions beyond the *Critique of Pure Reason,* offering accomplishments in the fields of morality, beauty, and teleology, such a function would not seem possible in relation to the analysis of cognition itself, where *a priori* laws are distinguished and where there would appear to be no room for regulative dependence.

And yet, if we do not address the underlying conception of thought, and hence the approach to human subjectivity implicit in Kant's critical project, then we are forced to embrace a reading of the first *Critique* that claims for it the uncritical acceptance of its starting point. What would then be argued is that philosophical inquiry begins by investigating spatial appearances, which is to say empirical objects, providing an account of the human understanding from a limited conception of human possibility. But to do so, to claim that Kant has naïvely embraced a philosophical starting point that has been raised as questionable throughout the philosophical tradition, not only appears to avoid the questions that Hume raises about the objects that appear to us to be so real, but is also unable to respond to both the anti-Enlightenment voices of Kant's own time and the coming developments in non-Euclidean geometry which challenge the conception of spatiality within which Kantian critique proceeds. If Kant is unable to explain the conception of thought from out of which his analysis grows, then his Copernican revolution in philosophy appears to be but a theoretical subterfuge. Kant would then have merely imported our naïve confidence in the world of appearances into his conception of phenomenal experience.

Such interpretations of critical philosophy, which limit themselves to its epistemological claims, both those stemming from neo-Kantian readings that defend it and those stemming from Hegelian readings that reject it, are the targets of my project. While I have been able to argue that the Transcendental Analytic culminates in the question concerning its underlying conception of experience—in the transcendental reflection that is necessary in order to make any *a priori* judgments and thus to begin the critical inquiry—I still must explain how such a fundamental reflective act can be conceived as having been achieved prior to the construction of the critical edifice. What presuppositions are embedded in Kant's conception of transcendental reflection, in the delimitation of those representations that constitute the field of philosophical inquiry? And further, can such presuppositions be explained by means of a regulative principle emanating from the attempt to attain knowledge of the subject, from, that is to say, the merely analytic unity of apperception with which Kant begins the Transcendental Dialectic in the Paralogisms of Pure Reason chapter?[3]

Kant has explained the unity that transcendental apperception offers as lying at the basis of all concepts, as an *a priori* condition of all conceptual determination.[4] This merely analytic unity of consciousness, this self-consciousness that permits objective cognition but does not offer itself as an object of cognition, also directs the illusory pursuit of metaphysical knowledge of the subject for whom it has secured the possibility of cognition. Could it be that in this attempt to pursue metaphysical knowledge of the rational subject, to develop the founding unity of the analysis of cognition beyond all possible experience, Kant has returned to the question of how it is that the faculty of thinking is itself possible? What this question implies is that the Paralogisms chapter of the Transcendental Dialectic might not merely refute the illusory pursuit of metaphysical knowledge of the rational subject, but actually offer the long-awaited investigation of the faculty of thinking that, as stated above, is promised for another "opportunity" (Axvii). Such issues direct this chapter in the attempt to continue the recovery of the complex relationship between understanding and reason, between epistemology and metaphysics, and thus between the Transcendental Analytic and the Transcendental Dialectic, that is the methodological achievement of Kant's critical system.

The fundamental question of any epistemological inquiry—"Who is the subject of knowledge?"—cannot be addressed directly; rather than rejecting such a skeptical critique of self-knowledge, Kant accepts it and searches for an approach that could examine cognition while avoiding all metaphysical contradiction. And so is born Kant's transcendental method. In turning from the opacity of our thinking to the structure of finite cognition, Kant has not merely rejected all metaphysical knowledge, but has set aside the contentious claims of metaphysical bickering to address our apparent knowledge of the world of spatial appearances. In the "abyss [*Abgrund*]"[5] of reason, Kant has demonstrated a field of *a priori* synthetic cognition, but one that, as it is expressed in both the Transcendental Aesthetic and the Transcendental Analytic, does not justify the presuppositions on which it is built. Attempting to address the metaphysical foundation of Kant's epistemological accomplishment will be seen as the positive task of the Paralogisms chapter of the Transcendental Dialectic. While no metaphysical knowledge concerning the thinking subject is possible, the critique of rational psychology distinguishes the conception of subjectivity which has proven necessary for the analysis of the experience of objects and which, while uncognizable, does not lead to contradiction. What still must be proven is that such a non-contradictory metaphysical conception of the rational subject directs the analysis of the unity of the understanding in a manner akin to that of the regulative use of the theological idea in teleology. The illusory metaphysical idea of a rational subject, to which our thought is directed by a natural disposition, will be shown to explain the presuppositions implicit in the orienting act of transcendental reflection and thus in the analysis of cognition that it affords.

II. Reason and the Unity of the Subject

In the introduction to the Transcendental Dialectic, Kant explains that what he is concerned with in this section of the first *Critique* is transcendental illusion. Such illusion directs us to make use of the categories of the understanding beyond the boundary of possible experience, initiating the pursuit of objects in the metaphysical terrain of what cannot be sensibly given (A296/B352). This pursuit of illusory goals does not follow from a mere error in the application of the categories, an error from which we can simply be redirected; rather, the error follows from principles that direct us to surpass the boundary of possible experience and thus to deny the division in the perceptual manifold that has permitted the analysis of the conditions of the possibility of experience. Kant calls such principles transcendent and contrasts them with the immanent principles that direct the empirical use of the understanding (A296/B353).[6] To uncover the illusory status of such transcendent principles, and to do so in a manner that keeps them from deceiving us, is the stated goal of the Transcendental Dialectic; and yet Kant does not hold out the hope of making these illusions utterly disappear, inasmuch as they are "natural and unavoidable" (A298/B354). We are drawn to this illusory dialectic by the nature of our human reason, and while we can protect ourselves against its deceptive powers "it will not cease to lead our reason on with false hopes, continually propelling it into momentary aberrations that always need to be removed" (A298/B354–55).

Reason (*Vernunft*), as the term is used in the Transcendental Dialectic, is taken in the narrower of Kant's two usages. Reason is the higher faculty of knowledge; it is that to which we are brought after the analysis of the understanding, and the critique of its use is what helps us to avoid illusion. This conception of reason can be distinguished from Kant's reference to reason in the Transcendental Doctrine of Method (A835/B863), where "reason" is the term used to describe all of the cognitive faculties, including understanding, and is thus distinguished from sensibility.[7] As I pursue an examination of reason in the narrower sense in this chapter and, in so doing, explain the relation that holds between reason and understanding in Kant's critical system, what will be seen is that this narrower conception leads to the broader one. Reason is both the higher faculty of knowledge—which is to say further away from the empirical than the understanding, with its dependence on sensible content—but it is also that which in its failure to attain purely rational cognition orders the understanding, and thus the latter falls within its purview. By the end of the first *Critique*, in the Transcendental Doctrine of Method, reason is used in the broader of these two senses, referring to the totality of the cognitive faculties.

But how can the faculty of understanding be conceived as dependent upon that of reason, and thus justify the broader sense of reason? The answer that I have been developing is that reason's investigation of metaphysical thought offers the understanding the principle that regulates its analysis of the conditions of the possibility of experience and thus orients its ontological accomplishments. In the introduction to the Transcendental Dialectic, Kant hints at some such dependence of the faculty of understanding on the pursuits that fall under the heading of reason: "All our cognition starts from the senses, goes from there to the understanding, and ends with reason, beyond which there is nothing higher to be found in us to work on the matter of intuition and bring it under the highest unity of thinking" (A298–99/B355). Kant explains the basic ordering of the first *Critique*, from the account of sensibility to that of understanding and then reason, as the path of cognition, with sensibility marking the beginning and reason the end of this process of bringing "the matter of intuition . . . under the highest unity of thinking." And yet Kant admits to some perplexity when it comes to explaining the "supreme power of cognition [*obersten Erkenntniskraft*]" (A299/B355):[8] How does reason, in its pursuit of non-sensible cognition and specifically its necessary failure at such a task, offer the "material of cognition" anything beyond the merely negative protection from these illusory pursuits? Reason, as has been explained above, is a "**faculty of principles [*Prinzipien*]**" (A299/B356).[9] It encompasses the attempts to attain knowledge of particulars purely conceptually, and thus differs from the efforts of the understanding, which pursues cognition through the application of concepts to what is sensibly given. Whereas the understanding explains the unity of appearances through its *a priori* concepts, reason is the faculty that enables the unity of the rules of the understanding under principles (*Prinzipien*), for it offers, as a *focus imaginarius*, the highest level of conceptual unity to which the categories of the understanding direct us (A302/B359).

Kant explains that reason attempts to reduce the *a priori* concepts of the understanding to a minimum of elements. The demand for conceptual unity made by reason offers not the cognition of objects but the subjective "law of economy for the provision of our understanding" (A306/B362). Since it does not begin its inquiries with objects, reason cannot claim to uncover *a priori* conditions of experience; rather, reason begins by assuming that since the conditioned is given, "then so is the whole series of conditions subordinated one to the other, which is itself unconditioned, also given" (A307–308/B364). Reason begins by assuming the principle that directs its search for the coherence of the understanding. This means that from the start its investigations must prove that it offers something to the understanding, for not only is it shown to fail in its attempt to attain such underlying unity, but whatever it is able to attain is not itself a condition of the possibility of experience. Yet its pursuit follows the path laid out by such *a priori* concepts, developing beyond all possible experience the inquiries marked out by these *a priori* concepts. Since it can offer no objective cognition, its justification will be able to claim only subjective status. This is to say that the syllogistic pursuit of such ideas, the regressive attempt to pursue the subsumption of conditions under universal rules to the unconditioned, will be shown to follow not from the necessities of the object, but from the subjective faculties that have themselves been derived from the experience of objects (A336/B393). It is in the examination of rational psychology that this is most directly addressed. Rational psychology marks the field in which we attempt to transform the logical unity that underlies our subjective faculties into an object of cognition. With the demonstration of the failure of all such attempts, Kant seems to have rejected the possibility of any positive outcome for such psychological inquiries. The question that must be addressed is: Can the syllogistic pursuit of the unconditioned be shown to have objective significance even though its goal proves to be unreachable; or, as Kant writes, "what consequences follow from it for the empirical use of the understanding" (A308–309/B365)?

In pursuit of "the **totality of conditions** to a given conditioned thing" (A322/B379), reason inquires into the various types of inferences that follow from the categories of relation. It is these *a priori* concepts—categorical, hypothetical, and disjunctive judgments—that distinguish the manner in which the condition is related to the conditioned, and thus the way judgments are mediately inferred. These three forms of syllogism mark out paths beyond the understanding's empirical use, describing inferences that are pursued beyond objects that are so conditioned and toward the unconditioned, toward that which would complete the totality of conditions for each inferential path. Each of these chains of regressive inferences pursues a particular type of unconditioned, and while the illusory goals of such inferences offer no objects, that which marks the end of each of these three chains of conditions—the illusory locus of the regress of conditions—Kant terms a *transcendental idea*. In the case of the categorical syllogism, which corresponds to the category of subsistence, it is the psychological idea, the idea of the unified, thinking subject in opposition to which objects exist in space; for the hypothetical syllogism, which corresponds to the category of causality, it is the cosmological idea, the unity of the series of appearances; and for the disjunctive syllogism, which corresponds to the category of community, it is the theological idea, the unity of all objects of thought (A334–35 / B391–92). Each mode of inference is pursued according to the four groups of categories through which the understanding determines empirical objects: quantity, quality, relation, and modality.[10] Thus the three different modes of conditioning that distinguish the patterns of inference in Kant's analysis of experience are here developed in the pursuit of metaphysical knowledge. If the subject of all our representations is to be examined as an object, if the totality of appearances is to be examined as a related whole, and if thought in general is to be examined as a systematic object, then critical philosophy will pursue such tasks in the manner in which the structure of objectivity has been elucidated in the Transcendental Analytic.[11]

Kant argues that the ideas of reason are not arbitrarily chosen since they follow from "the nature of reason itself, and hence they relate necessarily to the entire use of the understanding" (A327 / B384). These ideas follow from the categories of the understanding. The forms of inference announced by the categories of relation refer beyond experience, and their limitation to empirical application in the Transcendental Analytic does not mark the limit of their use (although it does mark the limit of their objective justification). Kant investigates three ideas of reason, following from the three categories of relation. Each of these ideas follows from the use of such categories in pursuit of the unconditioned: the first is the categorical syllogism, which corresponds with the category of inherence and subsistence (that of substance) and allows us to address inquiries into the soul and into what Kant terms rational psychology; the second follows the hypothetical syllogism and so the category of causality, leading to cosmological inquiries; and the third is the disjunctive syllogism, the category of community, and leads to theological inquiries. In accepting the deduction of the *a priori* status of these categories, we have at the same time implicitly initiated the pursuit of the unconditioned to which they refer, a pursuit that offers no objective cognition but can be seen to offer regulative accomplishment. The ideas follow from the nature of reason because reason, in its more limited sense, marks the territory of the use of the *a priori* categories of the understanding beyond its empirical limits. Reason can thus be seen to refer to the use of the understanding; and the limited sense of reason, that of the higher faculty of knowledge, ultimately does not contradict the broader sense, that of all the intellectual faculties, because the latter merely describes the former along with that to which it refers in a single term.[12] We cannot sever Kant's analysis of the understanding from this metaphysical pursuit because the categories lead beyond the area of their accomplishment, beyond the objects that permit their deduction, and toward the region of illusory ideas; and also because the critique of metaphysics that the categories of the understanding permit provides regulative principles that themselves direct the use of the understanding.

While in the introduction to the Transcendental Dialectic, Kant does not explicitly address the orientation of the critical project, and therefore also not the use of the psychological idea for this task, he does discuss in general terms the positive results emanating from the investigation of the transcendental ideas. He writes that these ideas, for which no objects can be cognized, "can still, in a fundamental and unnoticed way, serve the understanding as a canon for its extended [*ausgebreiteten*] and self-consistent [*einhelligen*] use" (A329/B385). At the start of the first *Critique*, Kant explains that the Transcendental Analytic is a "canon" for the empirical use of the understanding and thus for the limits of our application of its *a priori* concepts. If we use these concepts to "synthetically judge, assert, and decide about objects in general with the pure understanding alone" (A63/B88), we have misused this canon by attempting to produce with it an organon that could transcend our finite faculties. The critique of the illusory goal of such an organon Kant locates in the Transcendental Dialectic; and yet, in the introduction to this section, in the second division of the Transcendental Logic, Kant claims that the ideas of reason can themselves, in an unnoticed way, serve the understanding as a canon. Kant explains that such a function will not offer to the understanding objects to cognize beyond the boundary of possible experience, but it will offer guidance to both improve and further the use of the understanding.[13] Yet Kant does not at this stage examine what such guidance would entail. As was discussed above, the theological idea can be conceived as offering the regulative principle that directs teleological judgments and the cosmological idea directs the regulative pursuit of ever-further causal law, both furthering the use of our finite faculties. But how do the ideas of reason offer a canon for the understanding that "improves" its use? By investigating the critique of rational psychology in the Paralogisms chapter, I will address the question of such improvement by raising the regulative principle emanating from it as directing the analysis of the understanding in the Transcendental Analytic. It is such metaphysical interest, when curbed by critique, that offers our finite faculties the "unity of thought" that will be seen to direct the improvement of the use of the understanding. The investigation of rational psychology offers a way to justify the starting point of the *Critique of Pure Reason* through its examination of the subject of the unified faculties to which all appearances relate.

III. Transcendental Apperception and the Thinking Subject

Reason's syllogistic failure to attain metaphysical knowledge is clearly visible in the attempt to determine an object in the field of rational psychology. Not only does this investigation demonstrate one of the trio of transcendental illusions, but also, in its exhibition of the claims that cannot be made on behalf of the soul, self, or subject, it will be seen to direct the investigation to that which can be and already has been claimed for the subject of critical philosophy in the earlier divisions of the first *Critique*. The negative thrust of the Paralogisms chapter will offer a way to conceive of the subject whose faculties have been thematized in the Transcendental Analytic. This does not mean that a conclusive argument for rational psychology can be launched, as such inferences are shown to be utterly inconclusive. They offer neither objective cognition nor definitive rejection of the idea of a rational subject; what they do offer is direction away from the dangers of the claims of both dogmatism and skepticism, a tracing of a map that will allow us to examine the territory of metaphysics and yet remain protected from its illusions. If we can neither ascertain knowledge of the soul nor firmly deny its possibility, then we are left within the ambiguous territory of inconclusive principles that Kant assigns to the regulative use of the ideas of reason; to avoid embracing the errors of either side of this opposition, errors that would follow from either the proclamation or disavowal of all knowledge of the subject (those of dogmatism and skepticism, respectively), we must investigate the conception of subjectivity implicit in the analysis of cognition and interpret such presuppositions as following from the regulative use of the unknowable idea of the rational subject. Doing so will not mark an arbitrary connection, for rational psychology begins from the unity of apperception that offers the logical unity of all synthetic judgments. Kant explains that the "**I think** is thus the sole text of rational psychology, from which it is to develop its entire wisdom" (A343/B401). While the goal of such a pursuit remains unfulfilled, the direction that it takes—developing this underlying unity for which no empirical trace is given—follows from a question provoked by the Transcendental Analytic itself: What conception of subjectivity underlies the critique of reason? That the question itself proves to be inaccessible to our cognitive faculties does not negate its relevance. We will either find a critical answer for it or accept that Kantian critique is blind to its own beginnings.

The Paralogisms chapter demonstrates the errors implicit in the attempt to transform the analytic unity of transcendental apperception into an object of cognition. The pursuit of this idea is the attempt to infer a conception of the self from the transcendental unity of apperception. Kant writes: "Apperception is itself the ground of the possibility of the categories, which for their part represent nothing other than the synthesis of the manifold of intuition, insofar as that manifold has unity in apperception" (A401). The manifold of intuition can be understood to be synthetically unified in the categories only if the categories can be thought as unified in transcendental apperception, the unity of the self that itself offers no synthetic cognition, but is rather the analytic synthesis upon which the account of synthetic knowledge is grounded. The question as to what sort of unity, what sort of subjectivity, is here offered is one that shadows the Transcendental Analytic, since the transcendental unity of apperception, the synthesizing I that accompanies all intuition, neither offers itself as an object of cognition nor explains the designation of the perceptual territory within which the analysis of cognition takes place.

Near the end of the Paralogisms chapter of the second edition of the *Critique of Pure Reason,* Kant explains that the subject that offers unity to the objects of the categories cannot gain a conception of itself by means of the very categories that its unity affords (B422). But what is this subject of the categories that cannot itself be an object of the categories, this transcendental unity of apperception? Kant distinguishes transcendental apperception from empirical apperception. We are conscious of ourselves in inner sense, but this inner perception of ourselves, of our states, of our appearance to ourselves, is ever changing: "it can provide no constant [*stehendes*] or abiding [*bleibendes*] self in this stream of inner appearances" (A107).[14] In a limited way Kant concurs with Hume's conclusion that the self is "nothing but a bundle or collection of different perceptions, which succeed each other with an inconceivable rapidity, and are in a perpetual flux and movement."[15] Our empirical consciousness of ourselves is ever changing, offering no unified object, and yet such an unwieldy self does not end all discussion of apperception for Kant, as it does for Hume; rather, it directs the investigation of the self to that which permits the perceptual unity of empirical, outer experience, for how are we able to perceive the unity of empirical experience if our consciousness offers no unity to the manifold that is perceived? Kant's answer, offered in the Transcendental Deduction in both its first- and second-edition forms, is that not only must the objects of experience be conditioned by *a priori* concepts that precede and permit the conceptual determination of experience, but also consciousness must itself provide unity to the intuited manifold such that the categories can determine objects of experience for the perceiving subject.

Transcendental apperception thus "precedes all experience and makes the latter itself possible" (A107). It grants the unity of human cognition without itself offering any intuitable data or synthetic unity. This is to say that the unity brought to the intuitive manifold is the distinctive feature of transcendental apperception, for it does not offer itself in any other manner. Its unity is a mere logical unity. Our determinate judgment of the objects of experience depends upon a unifying principle through which empirical unities can be conceived within the manifold. The I of transcendental apperception is the correlate of all empirical representation, for without it we would not be conscious of the manifold and so we would be unable to mark its unity and claim it for ourselves. While the temporal form of inner sense is the distinctive mark of all sensible intuition, the unity of apperception underlies both empirical consciousness and the *a priori* concepts of the understanding that permit such determinate judgment. The non-empirical consciousness of ourselves in the I of transcendental apperception "is no intuition at all" but is, Kant writes, an "**intellectual** representation of the self-activity of a thinking subject [*intellektuelle Vorstellung der Selbsttätigkeit eines denkenden Subjekts*]" (B278). This complex phrasing should not be misunderstood. Transcendental apperception does not offer itself as intuition; it is rather the thought or representation of the foundation of the spontaneity of our cognitive faculties, the logical mark of the *a priori* concepts that permit the determination of objects. It is a representation, *eine Vorstellung*, of the pure understanding and not of sensibility. Following the distinction that Kant has drawn in the appendix to the Transcendental Analytic, titled On the Amphiboly of the Concepts of Reflection,[16] it is a representation that must not be conflated with those that offer sensible data. Such intellectual representations must be bracketed so the analysis of cognition can begin with only the sensible manifold and through it produce the critique of that which is merely rational and does not offer empirical content.

Transcendental apperception is thus connected to the transcendental object through the appearances that presuppose the former and refer to the latter. The unity of consciousness that transcendental apperception explains is counterbalanced by the transcendental object. The logical unity of the perceiving subject permits the empirical consciousness of the appearances that themselves refer to an object (*Gegenstand*) that offers no empirical appearance (A108–109). In the Transcendental Deduction, Kant merely marks the position of this nonempirical object; he does not explain why critical philosophy must distinguish a noumenal object that somehow corresponds with phenomenal objects. Such an issue, as we have seen above, is raised in the second edition's Refutation of Idealism, and it can be explained thoroughly only through the unraveling of the regulative underpinnings of the critical analysis of cognition.

Rational psychology encompasses the varied attempts to attain knowledge of the thinking subject, the soul, as it can be conceived as existing apart from all its empirical involvements. Kant's paralogisms demonstrate the errors in the varied attempts to attain such self-knowledge. While the historical context of Kant's paralogisms is important, it must be kept in mind that the paralogisms cannot be construed merely as arguments against past claims in rational psychology. Kant is addressing the kinds of arguments made in rational psychology from the perspective of transcendental philosophy. Rather than attempting to reproduce earlier arguments, Kant shows how his approach offers a way to refute the ill-founded claims of metaphysics. Kant's investigation of rational psychology demonstrates the failings of such inquiries when they are conceived from the perspective of transcendental idealism. In this way they are understood as attempts to transform the logical subject of transcendental apperception into an object of cognition. To do so is to take the form of understanding's judgments, the I that accompanies all empirical determinations, and proceed to employ it transcendentally in a manner that is unrelated to possible experience.

This begins with the I of thought and attempts to pursue it as an object, as the soul of the body that can be perceived by outer sense, without the benefit of any empirical experience. Kant explains that such attempts fail because they take "what exists [*existiert*] merely in thought [*Gedanken*]" (A384), the logical unity of apperception, as an object that itself could exist "outside the thinking subject" (ibid.). The error is that of taking the perceiving subject as an object for itself. The dependence of this science on merely the logical unity of thought distinguishes rational from empirical psychology. This pure science forsakes any particular intuitions of the state of empirical consciousness, the appearances of inner sense, attempting to build itself rationally from the logical necessity of transcendental apperception. Kant argues that all such attempts fail because they must embrace syllogistic errors that concern the form rather than the content of arguments. The failings of rational psychology stem from transcendental paralogisms, errors that are born of erroneous syllogisms that follow from the nature of our human reason and lead inevitably to transcendental illusion.

Kant explains that the "proper goal of rational psychology [*das eigentliche Ziel der rationalen Psychologie*]" (A384) is the soul and the three issues that have historically surrounded its discussion: (1) the communion of body and soul, and thus the role that the soul plays in human life; (2) the soul prior to human life, which relates to the beginning of this communion; and (3) the soul after death, which concerns the end of this communion and the immortality of the soul (ibid.). These questions, which bespeak the rich history of metaphysical inquiry, are the "proper goal of rational psychology," and yet their pursuit has not produced knowledge. Kant explains that such illusory pursuits can be avoided only by means of the analysis of their paralogistic errors. It might thus appear that these questions are the proper goal of rational psychology because they lead to the elucidation of its illusions and the end of its inquiries. However, Kant goes on to explain that questions concerning the communion of body and soul, those relating to a "gap [*Lücke*]" (A395) in our knowledge that we have attempted to fill with paralogistic error, cannot be answered. To attempt to do so is to fall back into the errors of metaphysics, in which the thinking subject is transformed into an object for itself; when that happens, we are guilty of "making thoughts into things and hypostatizing them" (ibid.). But how can we purport to have avoided the errors of past philosophical inquiries when such a gap in our self-knowledge remain unfilled?[17]

Kant would appear to have answered such questions with the accomplishments offered by the Transcendental Analytic, and yet the dualistic epistemology that is there produced does not end all inquiry into "the community between thinking and extended beings" (A393). The critical project has merely converted the question that can be neither dogmatically answered nor skeptically rejected into a more manageable form. Kant explains that the issue that remains is:

"**How is outer intuition**—namely, that of space (the filling of it by shape and motion)—**possible at all in a thinking subject?**" (ibid.). Kant does not offer an explicit answer to this question concerning the underlying metaphysical presupposition of his critical account of cognition. Addressing such a question would essentially investigate how the "gap" in our self-knowledge that cannot be filled, that which leaves our thinking natures hidden even from ourselves, can at least be bridged such that the claims made on behalf of our rational faculties can be said to avoid the illusions into which metaphysical inquiry has historically fallen. But all Kant offers in reply, at least at this point, is that we can only mark such a gap in our knowledge with the transcendental object, to which outer appearances are attributed and which marks the passage beyond the boundary of possible experience (ibid.). What we will see in the following pages is that the critical analysis of rational psychology elucidates the conception of subjectivity that both stands in opposition to the transcendental object and, as an uncognizable and yet irrefutable idea, offers a regulative principle that directs the orientation of critical philosophy within the confines of this limitation of our self-knowledge.

IV. The Critique of Rational Psychology

As we have seen, Kant develops his critique of rational psychology by examining the attempts to transform the subject of thought into an object in accordance with the four groups of categories: quantity, quality, relation, and modality. While Kant does not follow this order, beginning with relation instead of quantity, and in fact with the category of substance, the very category that offers the syllogism that leads to the Paralogisms, he is essentially pursuing the four classes of objective determination in order to investigate the various ways that an object, as defined by critical philosophy, can be determined. Kant is not investigating all of the categories, but only those in each class of categories that "ground the unity of the remaining ones" (A403). In the categories of relation, it is substance that offers the underlying unity that permits the determination of causality and community; for those of quality, it is reality that provides the unity for negation and limitation; for those of quantity, it is the category of unity itself that underlies plurality and totality; and finally, for modality, it is the category of existence that designates the basis from which both possibility and necessity can be determined. These categories direct inquiries in four areas of rational psychology: (1) the thinking subject as substance, as a determinable soul; (2) this subject as simple, as exemplifying unified faculties; (3) this subject as a unity over time, as "numerically identical"; (4) and this subject "in relation to **possible** objects in space" (A344/B402). Through the examination of these four paralogisms, these four errors of inference, we will learn how to protect ourselves from this illicit turning toward metaphysics while investigating how to make use of these inquiries, to which we are naturally drawn in the analysis of our cognitive faculties.[18]

The First Paralogism, substantiality, begins with the claim that the representation that is the "**absolute subject** of our judgments, and hence cannot be used as the determination of another thing, is **substance**" (A348). The paralogism begins from the analytic unity of transcendental apperception, for it is from this point that the inquiries of rational psychology pursue an account of the soul that makes no use of empirical data. While it would seem that the major premise claims precisely what rational psychology has set out to accomplish, that is, to connect transcendental apperception to the soul as substance, this is not the case. What Kant claims in the major premise is that the analytic unity that underlies our judgments and is in that sense the "absolute subject of our judgments," the "I think" that must accompany all our judgments and that cannot be a determination of anything else, is itself a substance but without any sensible determination. As the unity that underlies all empirical judgments, it is only the logical form of the category of substance. It is substance in a most preliminary fashion, and yet, with no sensible content, its claim to substantiality is utterly empty.[19] In stating in this premise that the "I think" of transcendental apperception is itself substance, Kant has set out the project of rational psychology insofar as it attempts to proceed from the logical unity of transcendental apperception to a robust conception of the substantiality of the soul, which is to say the subject that underlies all thought. Thus, while the I of transcendental apperception can be said to be substance, this says nothing further about such underlying unity. All it says is that particular thoughts are determinations, or accidents, of that which, as subject, is the logical substance of their diversity (A349). The conception of substantiality associated with transcendental apperception does not address the questions raised by rational psychology, for we cannot "infer" from it "that I, as a thinking being, **endure** for myself, that naturally **I neither arise** nor **perish**" (ibid.). What the major premise does distinguish is the path that rational psychology pursues. It must fill out this undetermined conception of the substantiality of the "I think" and transform the logical claim made on behalf of transcendental apperception into a determinate judgment, but it must do so without recourse to empirical data concerning this subject's activity. It is, as we know, an impossible task.[20]

While the major premise claims that the absolute subject of our judgments, transcendental apperception, is a logical subject, the minor premise attempts to direct the discussion to the "real [*realen*] subject" that underlies all thought (A350), to the soul, or ourselves as thinking being, inferring the substantiality of the self in itself from that of the merely logical givenness of the transcendental self. Kant writes: "I, as a thinking being, am the **absolute subject** of all my possible judgments, and this representation of myself[21] cannot be used as the predicate of any other thing" (A348). The minor premise begins by claiming that as a thinking being, the empirically constituted *res cogitans* is the absolute subject of all possible judgments. This representation of ourselves as the subject of our judgments offers the unifying substrate of the empirical manifold. A thinking being cannot be, in this sense, a predicate of something else, as it is that in which predicates inhere; thus Kant claims that my thinking nature, my "real" self, is the absolute subject of my judgments. In this minor premise, Kant has moved from the logical I of transcendental apperception, the concern of the major premise, to the essential unity of the thinking self, the soul or the subject in itself.[22]

Kant infers from these premises the conclusion that "I, as thinking being (soul), am **substance**" (A348). If the absolute subject of our judgments, transcendental apperception, is a substance; and if I as a thinking being, which is to say the empirically constituted subject of all thought, am the absolute subject, then the thinking subject of our empirically determined thought is also a substance. And given its empirical nature, as it is the unity of the manifold of thought, the substantiality that it offers would appear to be not of the merely logical variety, but a substantiality that offers determinate cognition of the underlying self of thought, that for which rational psychology has searched in its quest for metaphysical knowledge. However, Kant explains that we are no nearer to the goals of rational psychology than we were before our syllogistic conclusion. We have not provided anything that could transform the logical substance of transcendental apperception into a permanent synthetic cognition of the soul. The First Paralogism has merely attempted to infer the permanence of the soul from the dependence of all *a priori* judgment on transcendental apperception (A349–50). Kant explains that the error has been to pass off the transcendental self "as the cognition of a real subject of inherence [*Inhärenz*]" (A350). The syllogism conflates these two subjects, one of a transcendental variety and one of an empirical variety, under the term "absolute subject" and then infers that what can be said of the transcendental subject can also be said of the empirical, or "real," subject, the subject in itself. Kant describes this conflation as a

> *sophisma figurae dictionis* [sophistry of a figure of speech] in which the major premise makes a merely transcendental use of the category, in regard to its condition, but in which the minor premise and the conclusion, in respect of the soul that is subsumed under this condition, make an empirical use of the same category. (A402–403)

It is a faulty inference inasmuch as it treats radically different claims as if they were the same. The "real" self cannot be claimed to be known as a substance merely because the transcendental subject can be said to be known as such. The transcendental self can be said to be substance because it is a logical necessity as a condition of the possibility of experience; but what proof can be given for the permanence of the "real" self that underlies all thought, when no sensible representation is available to us that could transform the logical I into a cognition of the subject of all thought?

It must be remembered that, for Kant, we are offered to ourselves only as phenomena, as sensible appearances, and not as noumena, that is as we might exist apart from phenomenal appearances. Kant explains in the second edition that the self that is given to us in inner sense is the determinable self, the object of inner intuition, while the thinking subject, the determining self, is forever out of reach (B407). In both versions of the First Paralogism, Kant can be understood to be offering an argument from the perspective of transcendental idealism against Descartes' assumption in the Second Meditation that in marking out the distinction between the subject and the objects that it thinks, we are, while doubting the existence of all objects, able to prove the existence of this subject apart from that which it perceives. Kant accepts the distinction but questions whether the subject as so distinct—for Kant, the transcendental subject—can be conceived as anything apart from the objects for which it offers logical unity. Descartes rejects the possibility of conceiving of knowledge within the realm of appearances, instead pursuing a metaphysical claim about the subject.[23] Kant, however, denies such a metaphysical claim by deeming the thinking subject unknowable except as analytically unifying appearances, and thus by pursuing an analysis of cognition within this realm of appearances.

Kant concludes the First Paralogism in the first edition of the first *Critique* by explaining that this syllogism does not offer any new insight into rational psychology. We can claim that the soul is substance, but the substantial soul in this sense is that of transcendental apperception alone. Its substantiality is only logical and says nothing of the subject as it is in itself apart from the critical apparatus and its limited claims, for the transcendental subject offers no intuition of itself that could distinguish it as an enduring substance and so separate it from the sensible appearances that are given to it. Kant writes: "Therefore one can, to be sure, perceive that this representation [transcendental apperception] continually recurs with every thought, but not that it is a standing [*stehende*] and abiding [*bleibende*] intuition, in which thoughts (as variable [*als wandelbar*]) would change" (A350). And in the second edition's Paralogisms chapter, Kant explains that the task that rational psychology has set for our thinking "perhaps demands more than I will ever encounter anywhere (in it)" (B407).

Before addressing the other three paralogisms as they are developed in the first edition, it is helpful to remain with the second edition for a short while longer. In the second edition, Kant quickly explains each of the four paralogisms before offering a general discussion of the structure of paralogistic arguments, which uses the First Paralogism as its model (B411). In this discussion, the claim that the soul is substance is more easily recognizable as an invalid argument than in the formulation of the first edition, insofar as it transforms the major premise into a form that avoids the ambiguous term *absolute subject,* and yet marks a similar error in reasoning.[24] The major premise states: that which can only be thought as a subject does not exist other than as a subject, and is therefore substance. The major premise refers to the things that we think, which, if they can only be thought as the subjects of judgments, exist only as such and are therefore substances to the extent that they designate that for which predicates can be determined. In the minor premise Kant explains that a thinking being can only be thought as a subject. He concludes by inferring that a thinking being thus exists only as a subject and is substance. The argument reaches the same conclusion as that of the first edition, namely, that the thinking subject is substance, and while it reaches this conclusion by means of different premises, the error is the same: both succumb to the fallacy of a *sophisma figurae dictionis* (A402 and B411). In the first edition, this sophistical term is *absolute subject,* which is taken in different senses in the two premises. In the major premise it refers to transcendental subjectivity, and in the minor premise to the thinking subject in general. The error of such an argument follows from inferring in the conclusion that what can be said of the former applies to the latter, that because the transcendental subject can be said to be substance, so too the subject of all thought is substance. In the second edition, the error does not concern what can be said to be the "absolute subject"; rather, it involves the claim as to "[w]hat cannot be thought otherwise than as subject." In the major premise this refers to that which is thought, while in the minor premise it is the subject as thinking. Both editions illustrate the error of mistakenly deeming the subject that thinks to be a substance, when such a term is distinguished only for the objects that such a thinking subject thinks.

In the discussion of the First Paralogism in both the text and a footnote in the second edition, Kant gives the clearest account of the error implicit in such inferences, elucidating not merely the First Paralogism in both versions but paralogistic arguments in general. Kant explains: "'Thinking [*Denken*]' is taken in an entirely different signification in the two premises" (B411n).[25] In the major premise, "thinking" refers to an object, to that which "can be thought of in every respect, and consequently even as it might be given in intuition" (B411). It thus refers to an object as the subject of a judgment that is determined as a substance. In the minor premise, that which is thought only as a subject concerns the thinking subject, and not the objects that such a subject determines in intuition and thus also not itself as an object of inner sense. The error, like that of the first edition's First Paralogism, is that of an equivocation. Two conceptions of what can only be thought as a subject are conflated. Since the subject that is judged according to the categories is deemed to be a substance, the subject that judges is inferred to be one as well. And yet, the subject that judges, the transcendental subject, cannot be deemed a substance, for not only does it offer no empirical content that could be determined according to this category, but such a subject of thought is, in fact, presupposed in the use of these categories, and it cannot be both the presupposition and the product of the category of substance.[26] Such dependence on ambiguously used terms will be seen to be the cause of error in all of the paralogistic attempts by rational psychology to gain knowledge of the thinking subject.

In the first edition's Second Paralogism, Kant explains that the attempt to determine the simplicity of the soul, and so its immateriality, fails for the same reason that the attempt to determine the substantiality of the soul has been shown to fail. The former, like the latter, attempts to infer something about the subject of thought, in itself, from what can be said of the transcendental self, and does so by means of an argument built around an ambiguous term. The major premise states that a thing whose activity cannot be viewed "as the concurrence of many acting things [*handelnden Dinge*]" is itself simple. This, Kant explains in the second edition, is to claim that that which is one, singular, since it cannot be separated into "a plurality of subjects," can be considered simple (B407). While the major premise in the first edition is phrased in the most general of terms, the Second Paralogism, like the first, depends upon "the formal proposition of apperception" as the basis upon which "rational psychology ventures to extend its cognitions" (A354). The formal unity that transcendental apperception provides empirical thought, insofar as it must be said to accompany all experience, offers merely the subjective condition of such experience. The I of transcendental apperception is logically simple, its unifying activity cannot be attributed to different sources, and yet of this I that is simple one can say nothing other than that it must be presupposed as the condition of the possibility of experience.

From this analytic claim about the simplicity of the transcendental subject, rational psychology would like to infer something about the soul, the thinking I. The minor premise claims that the activity of the soul, the thinking subject, like the transcendental subject, cannot be said to be a combination of a number of different things. This self is a single thing, and its activity cannot be the product of different things. Thus rational psychology concludes that this subject of all thought, the soul, is simple, and the simplicity of the soul deems it to be incorruptible. As with the First Paralogism, this argument is invalid. The attempt to move from a transcendental claim about the subjective conditions of all thought to one that would describe the actual subject of all thought demands a transformation of an analytic claim into a synthetic one; and there is nothing that could justify such a move, nothing that could explain why the manifold of thought is not merely logically unified by a simple subject, but is itself a subject possessing such simplicity. Such a move would put the subject in the role of the object, which is to say in the place of the very objects that it, as the transcendental subject, makes possible (A353–54).

This turning from a transcendental subject to a subject as the unity of all empirical thought explains the error of this paralogism, which, like that of the First Paralogism, is that of building its argument upon an ambiguous term, thus unjustifiably transforming a claim about the logical I of cognition into one concerning the soul, or thinking I. The ambiguous term is "that thing whose action can never be regarded as the concurrence [*Konkurrenz*] of many acting things" (A351) or, as Kant simplifies it in the second edition, "a **singularity** [*ein Singular*] that cannot be resolved [*aufgelöset*] into a plurality of subjects" (B407). In the major premise, this "singularity" of indivisible activity is the transcendental subject, the logical unity that is required for experience; but it is not itself constituted by such experience and thus the claim made concerning it remains an analytic one. One can say of such a thing that it is simple because, as Kant writes, the claim "**I am simple** signifies no more than that this representation **I** encompasses not the least manifoldness within itself, and that it is an absolute (though merely logical) unity" (A355).

In the minor premise, the soul or thinking I is described as such a thing that "can never be regarded as the concurrence of many acting things." The soul refers to the unity of the self, to the thinking I in its totality and not to a mere accumulation of parts. Kant thus concludes, or to be more precise leads the reader to the conclusion, that this soul, which is a thing that is not a "concurrence" of many things, is simple.[27] It should be clear that the manner in which the soul is not such a concurrence of different things is different from the way that the transcendental subject is not such a concurrence. The transcendental subject refers to the logical I of transcendental apperception. It is not a concurrence, or multiplicity, because it is that which brings unity to multiplicity insofar as its logical claim is added to every thought. The minor premise refers not to such a logical claim but to the actual unity of the soul, a unity that purports to surpass that of the logical claim of the transcendental subject insofar as it refers to the actual unity of the soul or thinking I. This "thing" that is not a "concurrence of many acting things" is a different sort of thing from the "thing" of the major premise. And so the conclusion that is said to follow from such different concepts, that is that the soul as such a thing is simple, does not in fact follow. The simplicity of the transcendental subject is not something that the soul or thinking I of the minor premise can be said to share with the transcendental subject, for the simplicity of the transcendental subject refers to its merely analytic claim. The soul or thinking I of the minor premise attempts to go beyond this logical claim for the simplicity of the self to argue that the self that is so unified is itself simple. The syllogism fails to prove this because such a unity of ourselves as thinking subjects demands a synthetic unity rather than the analytic unity of the major premise. Kant explains that the Cartesian attempt to infer the existence of the merely thinking being from the "I think," his *cogito, ergo sum*, fails to move beyond the proposition "I think" (A354–55).[28] It is but a tautology, which is to say that the attempt to transform the I of apperception into the soul as existing in itself can say nothing more than that in every thought the I is implied. Kant writes that "this representation I encompasses not the least manifoldness within itself, and that it is an absolute (though merely logical) unity" (A355). While one may question whether Kant here does justice to Descartes' position, for the judgment of tautology depends upon the manner in which one conceives of the "I think," the analysis clearly expresses Kant's own position, in which the "I think" already refers to transcendental apperception, the analytic unity of the self.[29] To say that the thinking subject is simple, within the Kantian system, says no more than that the transcendental subject is simple, which is but to repeat the analytic unity of the self that Kant uncovers in the Transcendental Deduction. The claim that "**I am simple**," Kant explains in a manner that sums up the Second Paralogism, "must be regarded as an immediate expression of apperception" (ibid.).[30]

The minor premise raises the general problem that rational psychology faces in attempting to transform the manifold of thought into the unity of the soul, for how can we claim knowledge of this synthetic unity? How can the multiplicity of thought be conceived as the unity of the soul? With no way to attain knowledge of the thinking I or subject as simple, rational psychology is unable to prove that the soul, which is to say this thinking subject, is incorruptible. The thinking subject cannot be known to be simple—it could be complex and corruptible—and thus its immortality cannot be assured.[31] Kant thus describes the Second Paralogism as "the Achilles [heel] of all the dialectical inferences of the pure doctrine of the soul" (A351).

In the Third Paralogism, Kant demonstrates the error implicit in the attempt to attain knowledge of the "persistence [*Beharrlichkeit*]" (A366) of the subject through its manifold states, and thus of its personality. In such inquiries, rational psychology transforms a claim legitimately made about the empirical subject into one about the transcendental subject. Unlike the first two paralogisms, where Kant's analysis begins with a claim about the transcendental subject and then attempts to extend this claim to the sort of knowledge that one has of empirical things, Kant here begins with the empirical subject and then attempts to connect the transcendental subject to it. In this paralogism, the external view of the subject as a persisting object, the view "from the standpoint of another" (A362), is illicitly transposed onto the merely logical unity of transcendental apperception.[32] The major premise begins with the claim that "[w]hat is conscious of the numerical identity of itself [*seiner selbst*] in different times" is a person (A361).[33] In the minor premise, Kant states that the soul exhibits just such a consciousness, and thus what is inferred is that the soul is itself a person, which is to say that the identity of which it is conscious can be deemed to be a persisting object. Such an inference is shown by Kant to be mistaken;[34] however, he explains that such a presupposition, that of "the substantiality of the soul" (A365), remains "necessary and sufficient for practical use" (A355–56).

In the major premise, Kant describes the unity or identity of the empirical self. Insofar as I am conscious of myself as unified, as the same subject and so as self-identical through the passage of time, I can call myself "a **person** [eine **Person**]." Such a concept of a "person" thus designates the continuity of the self that deems the variety of temporal experiences to be those of a single subject. While one might infer that Kant is here referring to the I of transcendental subjectivity, the formal self of our synthetic cognition, it should be clear that he is not. The transcendental subject is a purely analytic claim; it offers merely the logical unity that underpins empirical experience and makes possible cognition.[35] Kant is here referring to the self insofar as it is conscious of its own unity through time, which is to say not merely the logical unity that is inferred from experience but the unity of which the self is conscious in experience. Kant makes it clear that the major premise refers to the empirical self in his discussion of the Third Paralogism where he explains that although the identity of the self is something that I find in my own consciousness, and it thus distinguishes me from all that is not me, from this perspective I view myself as an object of outer intuition, and so from the "standpoint of another" (A362). While the temporal nature of my consciousness demonstrates my inner sense, the persistence in time is that of an object that conceives of its continuity in time. Kant writes: "it is this external observer [äußeren Beobachter] who originally considers **me** as in **time**" (ibid.).[36] The identity of the self that Kant here deems a person is that of the unity afforded by the category of substance: it is the self conceiving of itself as an empirical substance, and so as a body among others.[37] From this empirical self-unity, one can infer transcendental subjectivity as the analytic unity of the self, but the "numerical identity" of the major premise proclaims more than the merely logical unity of apperception (A363).

The minor premise claims that the soul, the subject as a thinking being, can be considered just such a thing that "is conscious of the numerical identity of itself" (A361). The syllogism leads to the inference that such a soul is itself a person, and is thus a persisting object. The inference follows from the major premise, and yet the conclusion remains unproven. The soul cannot be known to be a persisting thing, for we are only given to ourselves in inner sense, and there is no objective persistence in what is merely a perceived unity in the temporal flux. Unlike the objects of outer sense, whose spatial persistence can be tracked through their variation in the passing of time, our merely temporal self-awareness can be referred only to the transcendental self that promises unity to the experience of this flux, a formal unity that provides no determination of its own and is thus a merely analytic claim (A362).

The syllogism of the Third Paralogism attempts to prove that the subject, as a thinking thing, is numerically identical, and thus that the soul can be known as a persisting object; however, the syllogism is unable to progress beyond the analytic claim of transcendental subjectivity.[38] While we, as thinking subjects, are given to ourselves in inner sense, we are unable to transform such representations into objective claims.[39] The error of this Paralogism, which leads to the conclusion that an objective claim can be made on behalf of the thinking subject, is the same as that of the earlier Paralogisms: the dependence of the syllogism on an ambiguous term or phrase. In the first edition, the phrase that is used in both the major and the minor premises is "conscious of the numerical identity of itself in different times" (A361).[40] In the major premise, this phrase refers to the empirical identity of the self, the unity that is born in the variety of its temporal experience, which Kant claims offers the persistence of a person. One must be conscious of this unity in order to proclaim the empirical identity of the self that deems it a person. In the minor premise, this middle term—"conscious of the numerical identity of itself in different times" (ibid.)—refers to the analytic unity of the soul. What is so distinguished is the mere logical unity of transcendental apperception, which is inferred from the empirical unity of the subject. To be conscious of the identity of the self in this manner means an awareness of the unity of the self that is distinct from its empirical unity, and yet is inferred from it; and this analytic unity is not the product of adding the I to empirical data in a Cartesian fashion; rather, it requires our "being conscious of their synthesis" (B133). Kant explains in §16 of the second edition's Transcendental Deduction:

> Therefore it is only because I can combine a manifold of given representations **in one consciousness** that it is possible for me to represent the **identity of the consciousness in these representations** itself, i.e., the **analytic** unity of apperception is only possible under the presupposition of some **synthetic** one. (B133–34)[41]

This is to say that transcendental apperception, the logical self or soul distinguished from empirical experience, can only be conceived through an inference from the synthetic unity of empirical experience; and so the "consciousness of the numerical identity of itself" of the syllogism, in the major premise, refers to the empirical subject, while in the minor premise this phrase refers to the logical subject of transcendental apperception that is deduced from this empirical subject of temporal change.

Kant explains that even though the identity of the thinking subject seems certain, and one might be tempted to proclaim its persistence even after the failure of its syllogistic proof, one must not, for the appearance of this identity could be an illusion. One cannot rule out the possibility that the apparent identity of the subject actually veils the discontinuity of a series of substances in which each passes on to the next all past thoughts. Such a chain of substances, which Kant compares to rubber balls hitting and passing on their force to further balls, could produce a substance that is conscious of an unbroken chain of representations, having been passed their cumulative effects, and yet it would not signify that there has been an identical person, a single substance throughout this series (A363–64).[42] Neither the syllogism concerning personality, nor our experience of personal identity, can conclusively prove that the thinking subject is a persistent thing that is identical through time.

The first edition's Fourth Paralogism concerns the attempt to infer knowledge of the thinking subject from the ideality of outer appearances. Rather than directly exemplifying the fallacious transformation of the subject into an object, as do the other paralogisms, it concerns the radical differentiation of subject and object that would appear to provide access to an independent subject. In the manner of the modal principles, it investigates the relation of the subjective faculties to the determined objects, rather than attempting to expand the conceptual determination of the subject. The second edition's version of this paralogism leaves out the explicit critique of Cartesian or skeptical idealism, a discussion that is expanded and inserted into the Transcendental Analytic as the Refutation of Idealism.

Kant begins the first edition's Fourth Paralogism with the following major premise: "That whose existence [*Dasein*] can be inferred only as a cause of given perceptions has only a **doubtful existence** [*Existenz*]" (A366). If an object's existence can be inferred only as the cause of what is given in perception, and can never itself be given in perception, then its existence is uncertain. Kant here, in the major premise, does not explain anything further about that whose existence can only be inferred. By this point in the first *Critique,* it is clear that phenomenal objects can all be perceived. Even when their existence is merely inferred, as in Kant's discussion of the postulate of actuality, where he explains that the existence of an effect can be inferred from its cause when the latter is perceived, what Kant refers to as the determination of existence in a manner that is "comparatively *a priori*" (A225 / B273), such objects *can* still be perceived. But the major premise refers not to such objects whose existence is inferred by means of the causal law, but to that whose existence can *only* be inferred and can never be given in perception. Any such merely inferred existence can be doubted. To say that the existence of that which cannot be directly perceived, that which is only inferred as the cause of the perceived and is not itself the effect of a cause, is doubtful, is to claim that there is no way to be certain of such claims, no way to justify that which does not offer itself as a perceptual object. While in the transcendental system such an unknowable object is described as noumenal, and so beyond our cognitive faculties, the major premise of the Fourth Paralogism does not begin with such a presupposition; in fact, this Paralogism will culminate in a defense of the phenomenal-noumenal distinction as a way to avoid not only the skeptical claims of idealism, but also their metaphysical implications.

The minor premise reads: "Now all outer appearances [*äußere Erscheinungen*] are of this kind: their existence [*Dasein*] cannot be immediately perceived, but can be inferred only as the cause of given perceptions" (A367). Kant here offers the rationalist's claim: we must infer the existence of that which is perceived. Perception itself does not directly proclaim the existence of objects; rather, we proceed through perception to that which is its cause, so inferring the existence of that whose perceptual manifestation did not ensure its existence.

Kant concludes this syllogism by arguing, "Thus the existence of all objects [*Gegenstände*] of outer sense is doubtful" (A367). If the existence of that which can only be inferred is doubtful (major premise), and if the existence of all outer appearances cannot be perceived directly and so can only be inferred (minor premise), then the existence of such outer appearances, which is to say objects, is doubtful. Kant describes this as the proof of the ideality of outer appearances: the existence of that which we perceive is doubtful, and so with Descartes we are left with a self that knows itself in a way that is more certain than its claims about what it perceives.

The conclusion and its implications for our self-knowledge follow from the premises only if the minor premise is understood to refer to all possible objects when it argues that the existence of "outer appearances" is only inferred and so not directly perceived, as an idealist would have it. If all sensible objects can only be known to exist by means of an inference that itself needs to be justified, then the existence of such objects would depend on our ability to offer such a justification. The major premise has denied just such a possibility, embracing the Humean argument that we can never properly understand the workings of causality, and so if the existence of objects depends upon an inference from what is perceived, all claims about such existence will remain dubious. Such a skeptical conclusion is just what the idealist wants: denying any knowledge of the existence of objects and inferring from this that the self, as the locus of such inquiry, is what is known.

But is this necessarily the case? Must the existence of all "outer appearances" be deemed inferred and so doubtful? This is not to ask an empirical question about the truth of the minor premise, and so about the soundness of what would remain a valid argument. Rather, Kant is challenging the validity of the argument, raising his own transcendental idealism in order to show that not only is there a way to conceive of the existence of "outer appearances," those that are deemed doubtful in the minor premise, but also, and more generally, that this demonstrates the fallacious nature of such an argument for rational psychology.[43]

Transcendental idealism has addressed just such a problem, arguing by means of the Copernican turn that perception does offer us direct confirmation of the existence of spatial objects. Kant explains that both skeptical idealism and his own transcendental idealism agree that we cannot gain certainty concerning the reality of "external objects" "from any possible experience" (A369); but the transcendental idealist distinguishes such uncertain "external objects" from objects of perception, about whose existence we can be certain, while the skeptical idealist is led to doubt even those objects that are perceived. Kant explains that such a skeptical idealist begins as a transcendental realist, positing that objects exist apart from human perception. But when she is unable to attain knowledge of such objects, she is led to deny the possibility of attaining knowledge of objects altogether, producing the skeptical position of what Kant later calls "problematic idealism" (ibid.). Such a position implies that the subject as a thinking being is known separately from, and with greater certainty than, the objects whose existence remain in doubt.

By differentiating phenomena and noumena, Kant's transcendental idealism allows us to uncover the error in the syllogism offered by the skeptical idealist. Like the other paralogisms, the fourth errs because of its dependence on an ambiguous term, which leads to a conclusion that has been invalidly inferred from the premises. The ambiguity, in this case, concerns the term "outer [äußer]," which could refer to either that which is outside of our perceptual experience altogether or to that which is a spatially determined object of outer sense, and thus a perceptual object. In the minor premise, "outer" refers to the former, to that which is beyond the limits of possible experience and is merely inferred as the cause of the phenomenal sphere. In the conclusion, "outer" refers to the objects of the outer sense, to appearances, and mistakenly infers that what can be said of what is in some sense noumenally outside of us can also be said of what is phenomenally an object of outer sense.[44] While the ambiguity in the term "outer" and the resulting paralogistic error resemble the form of the other Paralogisms, it must be noted that the ambiguity in this case is between the minor premise and the conclusion, and not between the major and the minor premises, as it is in the other Paralogisms. The ambiguity in the term "outer" allows for what appears to be a valid argument, but it rests on the assumption that what can be said of objects as they exist in themselves, which is to say very little, also distinguishes the limits of our faculties in regard to perceptual experience in general.[45] Skeptical idealism accepts this claim, denying the differentiation of appearances and things in themselves, while Kant's transcendental idealism is built upon this division whose terrain is thematized in the account of transcendental reflection. By distinguishing between phenomena and noumena, following from the two conceptions of the term "outer," Kant's transcendental idealism is able to agree with the denial of knowledge of noumena without proclaiming that the subject is thus conceivable independently of all objects. Kant's transcendental subject is but an analytic claim that offers itself only in relation to the phenomena from whose possible existence it is deduced.

The second edition's Fourth Paralogism begins with the claim that the designation of "thinking being [*denkenden Wesens*]," as distinct from the objects that appear for it, is a merely analytic claim. Such appearances, including that of the perceiving body, are outside of the transcendental subject, but cannot be said to stand in opposition to such a thinking being since they are "distinguished [*unterschieden*]" from this subject only insofar as they are perceived by it (B409). The transcendental subject underlies and makes possible the objects that appear as spatial representations for this thinking self. Kant explains that this account of the thinking subject argues neither for nor against the possibility of its existence apart from spatial objects. I know myself as a thinking being only in relation to such appearances, among which Kant includes our own bodies, so transcendental idealism can say nothing about whether "I could exist merely as a thinking being (without being a human being)" (ibid.).[46]

While the second edition's Fourth Paralogism is not offered in the form of a syllogism, it can be constituted such that it follows the form of the errors of the other Paralogisms.[47] In beginning with an empirical claim in the major premise and then moving to a claim about transcendental subjectivity in the minor premise, it follows most closely the form of the Third Paralogism. The major premise would thus read: That which is distinguished (*unterschieden*) from things outside itself exists apart from them. Then the minor premise would continue: "I distinguish my own existence, that of a thinking being, from other things outside me" (B409). This would lead to the conclusion: I, as a thinking being, exist apart from things outside me.[48] The error here is to conceive of the thinking subject in the manner of an object that can be thought. The major premise refers to the existence of an object that can be "distinguished from things outside it"; this object is a phenomenal one that stands in a spatial relation with other such objects. In the minor premise, what is "distinguished" from things outside it is not a further object that stands in spatial relation with other objects, but the thinking self, the transcendental subject, that offers unity to the variety of thoughts. The transcendental subject is not itself an object in space that can be distinguished in the phenomenal realm from other objects. It is, rather, merely attributed to all such thoughts of objects such that they can be conceived as being my thoughts. The transcendental subject is distinguished from things outside it, but not in the manner of a phenomenal object, and thus not in a manner that offers a synthetic claim about appearances; rather, Kant explains, the transcendental subject is distinguished in a merely analytic way, as a necessity of all objects in order for them to be my thoughts, but this does not in itself add anything to the object, as no new determinate relation has been distinguished (ibid.).

The thinking subject does not distinguish itself from spatial appearances in the way that such appearances do from each other, and so it cannot be said to exist in the manner of spatial appearances. Transcendental idealism avoids such a paralogistic claim because it differentiates between the transcendental subject and the spatial objects to whose appearances it brings unity. The analysis of spatial appearances undertaken in the Transcendental Analytic permits the designation of the transcendental subject as the source of their subjective unity. And this analysis depends upon the designation of the manifold of spatial appearances as the field of critical inquiry, which is to say on the division of the realm of objects from all merely temporal thoughts that are attributed to the subject rather than to objects; and yet this subject, to whom temporal thoughts are attributed, remains elusive. The division on which the analysis of our cognitive faculties rests, that between the thinking subject and the objects it perceives, is one that surpasses these very faculties.

In the second edition, Kant moves the developed argument against Cartesian or problematic idealism to the Refutation of Idealism (B274–79) in the Transcendental Analytic.[49] As was examined above in chapter 3, Kant argues that our temporal self-awareness depends not merely on the spatial matter of appearances but also on something persistent apart from all appearances. Kant develops the argument of the first edition's Fourth Paralogism to include the proposition that all claims for our temporal self-awareness are committed to the existence of some sort of object apart from subjective representations. What such a persistent thing can be said to be will be addressed, finally, in the next chapter. However, the path to a solution should by now be visible: the psychological idea, taken as a regulative principle, will be shown to be that which directs the analysis of phenomenal appearances. Our self-knowledge, except in a merely formal sense, cannot be distinguished from the appearances through which it is demonstrated; and yet, Kantian critique implies the regulative commitment to the idea of the differentiation of the thinking subject and the objects that appear to it, knowledge of which, the Paralogisms chapter proves, is elusive.

While the Fourth Paralogism in both editions denies the possibility of knowledge of the thinking subject apart from the objects that it perceives, such a differentiation of the representational manifold is maintained within the phenomenal field of critical inquiry. Experience in the Transcendental Analytic is limited to that which spatially appears. Representations that are merely temporal, those of inner sense that relate to me only as a thinking being, are set aside so that the critical analysis of cognition can accomplish its task. This division has been shown to be the product of transcendental reflection. Such a parsing of representations, which is undertaken without explicit justification, would appear to follow the division set out in the Paralogisms and is most explicitly demonstrated in both editions of the Fourth Paralogism. Transcendental reflection approaches the manifold of representations directed by the idea of the thinking subject as distinct from the spatial appearances to which it brings unity, an idea that is deemed unknowable in the Fourth Paralogism. And it is not merely the Fourth Paralogism that retains its relevance even after it is shown to be unable to justify its claims, for the conceptions of the soul that are deemed unknowable in the other three paralogisms are also relevant for the division of subject and object that is presupposed in transcendental reflection. The First Paralogism raises the idea of the soul's substantiality, the second its simplicity, and the third its persistence; while none of these conceptions of the soul offer themselves to our cognitive faculties, they are needed for the act of parsing the manifold that transcendental reflection pursues. The subject of thought with which inner representations are associated in the act of transcendental reflection is unified as a substance and conceived as both simple and persisting. The self-unity that these conceptions entail distinguishes the subject from all objects known and so designates the territory thematized in the Fourth Paralogism's discussion of inner and outer.

Near the end of the second edition's Paralogisms chapter, Kant explains the general problem that deems arguments for rational psychology to be paralogistic: "Thus the subject of the categories cannot, by thinking them, obtain a concept of itself as an object [Objekt] of the categories; for in order to think them, it must take its pure self-consciousness, which is just what is to be explained, as its ground" (B422). The transcendental subject cannot use the categories to conceive of itself because it is the ground of such categories, and so such a subject would be attempting to explain itself with that which it explains. And yet, the bedeviling problem for critique is that even after such a limitation is recognized, even after we are convinced of the impossibility of rational psychology, its goals—those of the subject conceived as a substance, simple, persisting, and independent from the objects it perceives—continue to be necessary for the undertaking of the analysis of cognition in the Kantian system. This is because the analysis of the conditions of the possibility of experience, which yields the categories and from which the critique of metaphysics is launched, itself depends on the very idea of a subject as distinct from the objects that it perceives, a unified subject which comes to know itself in opposition to the objects it perceives. This is to say that what is needed in order to undertake Kantian critique is some version of the idea of the soul, the psychological idea that Kant has shown to be unknowable in these paralogisms. The question that remains is: What can be said about this continued commitment to the psychological idea, to that which does not offer itself for our cognition?[50]

V. The Paralogisms and the Orientation of Critique

Kant addresses the most basic orientation of critical inquiry in the final pages of the first edition's Paralogisms chapter without explicitly labeling it a regulative accomplishment that follows from the critique of rational psychology.

However, as we shall see, the issues raised are precisely those that the thinking subject of rational psychology, taken as a regulative principle, can be understood to explain. The question concerns the relation of the critique of metaphysics to the analysis of our finite faculties. The accomplishment of transcendental philosophy has been to show that matter is not utterly distinct from the soul as the object of inner sense. Spatial appearances cannot be known as independent substances but are merely the spatial representations of outer sense that, along with the representations of inner sense, constitute the manifold of thought. While objects of experience are not utterly distinct from the subject that perceives them, as outer representations they are distinguished from representations of inner sense. Kant describes them as those

> whose representations we call external in comparison with those that we ascribe to inner sense, even though they belong as much to the thinking subject as other thoughts do; only they have in themselves this deceptive feature, that since they represent objects in space, they seem to cut themselves loose from the soul, as it were, and hover outside it. (A385)

Representations of outer sense deceive us into thinking that we can know them as existing apart from the manner of their appearance and so as separate from the perceiving subject. In the Paralogisms, Kant has argued that we have no knowledge of what the thinking subject is in itself, and what this means is that claims about the thinking subject cannot be distinguished from those about the objects that appear to it. We are, even to ourselves, but appearances; and yet, while the formal distinction between the subject and the objects it perceives has been rejected, it is just such a distinction, that between the representations of inner and outer sense, that must be maintained for Kant's analysis of experience.

The question that remains after the Kantian rejection of rational psychology concerns the most basic division of critical inquiry: How are inner and outer sense differentiated, and how from the manifold of representations are the constant laws of the understanding, which unify this manifold in experience, distinguished? With the rejection of the possibility of knowledge of the subject as separately existing and the acceptance of the need to inquire into the perceptual manifold in the pursuit of objectivity within this subjective flux, we are left with the problem of how to proceed when the criteria that have guided past epistemological inquiries are forbidden by this starting point. If the first *Critique* is not to be merely a further epistemological project that cannot justify its method, then the criteria used to parse the representational manifold, those that permit the act of transcendental reflection, must be investigated. The most fundamental criterion of the critical analysis of cognition is the designation of possible experience as the region within which this analysis takes place, and thus outer sense as the defining characteristic of possible experience is deemed to be the limited field for the analysis of cognition. Even though the Paralogisms chapter denies the complete division of subject and object, we require just such a division within the representational flux and thus within the phenomenal sphere. Appearances of outer sense, objects, are investigated while those of inner sense, those that are merely subjective, are set aside.

While the critique of rational psychology appears to provide the regulative principle that guides the analysis of cognition, in the Paralogisms chapter Kant announces its continued importance only in the practical sphere. In the second edition, Kant explains that while there can be no rational psychology as a "doctrine [*Doktrin*]" that would expand our self-cognition, there remains the possibility of a "discipline [*Disziplin*]" (B421). For Kant, a "discipline" offers a system of barriers that protect us from reason's natural propensity to pursue transcendent principles. The critique of reason in the Transcendental Dialectic offers such a discipline, a boundary that continues to protect us from such natural illusions. In highlighting the indeterminacy of our claims in rational psychology, Kant explains that the first *Critique* provides a discipline that saves us from both "soulless materialism" and "getting lost wandering about in a spiritualism" (B421). The former would be our error if we assumed that we could be certain that the soul did not exist, the latter if our thoughts of the soul were hypostatized and we assumed that it was accessible to us. In designating this boundary of our finite faculties, the critique of rational psychology

> [r]eminds us to regard this refusal of our reason to give an answer to those curious questions, which reach beyond this life, as reason's hint that we should turn our self-cognition [*Selbsterkenntnis*] away from fruitless and extravagant speculation toward fruitful practical uses, which even if it is always directed only to objects of experience, takes its principles from somewhere higher, and so determines our behavior, as if our vocation [*Bestimmung*] extended infinitely far above experience, and hence above this life. (Ibid.)[51]

The discipline offered by the critique of rational psychology directs us away from metaphysical inquiry and toward practical pursuits. Kant is here referring to the role that the idea of the soul's immortality continues to play in the practical sphere, offering itself as a postulate of the Kantian conception of moral life.[52] But what of the role that the idea of such a subject would appear to play in critical inquiry? Is there only a practical role for the idea of the soul and no theoretical significance to the idea of the subject in opposition to the objects it perceives beyond the merely negative discipline that directs us away from further metaphysical inquiry? This is to ask whether the psychological idea might offer itself as a regulative principle once its cognitive pretensions have been critiqued.

Locating such a regulative role in the critique of rational psychology will help to explain why Kant, as was discussed earlier in this chapter, writes in book 1 of the Transcendental Dialectic that the ideas of reason "serve the understanding as a canon for its extensive and self-consistent use" (A329/B385). A "canon," Kant explains in the Transcendental Doctrine of Method, is "the sum of the *a priori* principles of the correct use of certain cognitive faculties in general" (A796/B824). The Transcendental Analytic is thus the canon for the pure understanding. But what of the ideas of reason? In their speculative use they offer merely illusion and so no cognition, which is to say, no proper doctrine and only a boundary-setting discipline. In the Transcendental Doctrine of Method Kant does recognize a role for a canon of the ideas of reason but limits it to the practical sphere (A797/B825). However, at the start of the Transcendental Dialectic he explains that even though such ideas offer no doctrine they still offer a canon for the use of the understanding's categories. Through such a canon, Kant provocatively explains, the understanding is guided "better and further" in its activities (A329/B385). While such an introductory remark certainly opens the door to the interpretation of a regulative role for the psychological idea, insofar as it offers the initial division of subject and object that is required for the analysis of the understanding, the precise working of such a dependence is not addressed by Kant until the appendix to the Transcendental Dialectic.[53] There, Kant describes the uses of the ideas of reason, after the critique of their cognitive pretensions, as "the hypothetical use of reason [*der hypothetische Gebrauche der Vernunft*]" (A647/B675), and suggestively describes this regulative role for the psychological idea as offering the idea of the unified thinking subject that is required for the analysis of cognition (A683/B711). And in the Transcendental Doctrine of Method, which completes the first *Critique*, Kant returns to the regulative use of the psychological idea, describing the idea of the simple soul as directing the analysis of the powers of the mind (*Gemütskräfte*) (A771–72/B799–800). Such a regulative role for the psychological idea, which will help to explain the analysis of the unified cognitive faculties, will be the subject of the following chapter, developing the canon that is promised at the start of the Transcendental Dialectic and so pairing a theoretical role for the psychological idea with the practical purpose with which the Paralogisms chapter itself ends.

VI. Conclusion:
Rational Psychology and the Analysis of Cognition

While directing us away from the illusory goals of rational psychology, Kant's critique has also distinguished its four approaches as beyond all cognitive determination. What use can be made of such a regulative principle, which directs us into the territory of rational psychology protected from its illusory claims, will be developed in the next chapter. I will investigate the conception of the regulative use of reason that Kant announces in the appendix to the Transcendental Dialectic insofar as it offers, from within the first *Critique* itself, a way to explain the dependence of the analysis of the understanding on a principle emanating from our metaphysical interests. Even though rational psychology offers no determinate cognition, by avoiding its illusory claims we would appear to be able to distinguish the presuppositions of the analysis of the understanding launched by Kant in the Transcendental Analytic. The apparent paradox that this implies will be the issue that directs the following chapter in its investigation of the regulative use of the psychological idea. The question is: How is it that finding a role for a regulative principle implicit in the analysis of the categories of the understanding can avoid toppling the very *a priori* structure that it is meant to support?

SIX

Transcendental Method: The Orientation of Critique

I. Kantian Orientation

In his 1786 essay "What Does It Mean to Orient Oneself in Thinking? [Was heißt: sich im Denken orientieren?]"[1] Kant introduces a conception of orientation that addresses not merely our spatial orientation among material objects but also our speculative orientation in thought. In connecting these two realms of orientation, concerning the sensible and the intelligible, respectively, Kant offers a suggestive way to conceive of the role that the ideas of metaphysics play in designating the region of finite experience. Kant explains that an idea of reason offers a "signpost [*Wegweiser*]" that helps to direct the empirical use of the understanding. Investigating this account of orientation will guide our inquiry to the appendix to the Transcendental Dialectic of the *Critique of Pure Reason* in the search for an account of the orienting role played by the psychological idea after the critique of its cognitive pretensions in the Paralogisms chapter.

Kant's essay marks his entry into the Jacobi-Mendelssohn, or pantheism, controversy,[2] some years after the heated exchange that began as Mendelssohn's attempt to refute Jacobi's claim that Lessing, Mendelssohn's close friend, had at the end of his life embraced Spinozism.[3] For Jacobi, to embrace Spinozism meant to have accepted a pantheism that was essentially a fatalistic atheism.[4] Jacobi, in his 1785 *Concerning the Doctrine of Spinoza in Letters to Moses Mendelssohn* (*Über die Lehre des Spinoza in Briefen an den Herrn Moses Mendelssohn*), contended that Lessing had admitted as much, going so far as to claim that "[t]here is no other philosophy than the philosophy of Spinoza."[5] Jacobi viewed Spinoza as demonstrating a praiseworthy consistency in his rationalist approach, but such consistency led him necessarily to fatalism.[6] Jacobi agreed that Spinoza enunciated the true philosophical position and at the same time he rejected both Spinozism and the philosophical tradition it exemplified. Jacobi was attempting to show that Enlightenment rationalism led necessarily to Spinoza's pantheism, and so to a rejection of the freedom that allows for faith.[7]

Mendelssohn, whose response came in the form of letters to Jacobi and others which were eventually published in *Morning Hours; or, Lectures on the*

Existence of God (*Morgenstunden oder Vorlesungen über das Dasein Gottes*) and *To Lessing's Friends* (*An die Freunde Lessings*), was incredulous.[8] How could Lessing, his close friend, have embraced such a philosophical commitment without his knowledge? This is not to say that Mendelssohn wanted to deny all influence of Spinoza on Lessing; rather, he wanted to deny the charge of full-blown pantheism, and thus atheism, that Jacobi raised in relation to Lessing, and thus by implication not only to Mendelssohn but to the Enlightenment project as a whole.[9] In a letter written to Elise Reimarus, who with her brother acted as intermediaries between Mendelssohn and Jacobi, Mendelssohn stated that any claim about Lessing's Spinozism depended on how Spinozism was conceived.[10] The question for Mendelssohn concerned the role that reason is said to play in human life. If Spinozism is taken to mean an all-encompassing reason that allows room for neither theology nor moral freedom, then Mendelssohn would view such a charge against Lessing as having "misunderstood" not only Lessing's position but Spinoza's as well. In Mendelssohn's early *Dialogues*,[11] through the character of Neophil, he explains that the apparent absurdity of Spinoza's position, the unity of thinking substance that argues against human freedom, is overcome if we distinguish between the world that can be said to have "existed in the divine understanding [*Verstande*]" and the "visible world [*sichtbare Welt*] outside us."[12] Yet, to defend Spinoza in this way, to accept Jacobi's conception of freedom, that is, autonomy from a rule-governed nature, overlooks Spinoza's own conception of the freedom from the emotions that such a naturalistic reason affords.[13] While as an interpretation of Spinoza, Mendelssohn's claim might be questionable, it bespeaks his own attempt to bring together metaphysical speculation and our experience of the "visible world." Without explicitly denying the veracity of the proofs that he had earlier offered for metaphysical truths, Mendelssohn in *Morning Hours* raises the problem of what to do when such metaphysical speculation contradicts our "common understanding [*gemeinen Menschenverstande*]."[14] Mendelssohn's answer is that such common understanding, our "common sense [*Gemeinsinn*]," must restrain our "speculation" and so bring reason back in line with the world of appearances.[15] Mendelssohn does not mean that metaphysical speculation has no role to play, but that if we are to follow it against the path of "common sense," reason must have decisive grounds for choosing speculation over the more evident route.[16] The question is whether Mendelssohn, in embracing common sense, gave away too much, denying the importance of metaphysical speculation for the orientation of our reason in the name of avoiding the charge that the Enlightenment had bequeathed a rationalism that offered only a fatalistic atheism. What is clear is that with his emphasis on common sense, Mendelssohn opened himself to the charge that his position, which is to say his apparent anti-rationalism, was as indefensible as that of the rationalism with which Jacobi charged Lessing.[17]

In "What Does It Mean to Orient Oneself in Thinking?" Kant briefly defends Mendelssohn against the charge that his conception of the orientation of reason by means of common sense demonstrates an anti-rationalist commitment.[18] Kant explains that in emphasizing common sense, Mendelssohn is defending reason against the claims of faith, even as he warns against its speculative excesses.[19] Kant does not say more about how this can be seen in Mendelssohn's work, how his common sense can be defended, but he goes on to introduce his own conception of reason's orientation, describing his task as that of ridding "the common concept of reason [des gemeinen Vernunftbegriffs] of its contradictions, and defending it against its own sophistical attacks on the maxims of healthy reason."[20] Kant defends reason by examining the role that our metaphysical ideas, after their critique, play in the orientation of our thought. In this way, Kant has responded to the pantheism controversy by developing Mendelssohn's defense of reason's orientation, offering a way to conceive of the speculative utility of metaphysics in the orientation of reason that guards against both the skepticism of faith (i.e., Jacobi) and the dogmatism of rationalist metaphysics (i.e., Mendelssohn's earlier position). Kant is able to mark his customary path between skepticism and dogmatism in a way that supports Mendelssohn, the erstwhile dogmatist, by emphasizing his conception of the commonsense orientation, while avoiding discussion of both Mendelssohn's seemingly anti-rationalist conception of common sense and his earlier commitment to metaphysical arguments.[21]

Kant begins this analysis of reason's orientation by discussing directional orientation in space, while describing his goal as that of furthering this notion of spatial orientation in order to examine reason's orientation in thought. Kant explains that we orient ourselves in nature by means of the felt distinction between our left and right sides. Such a feeling explains how that which is conceptually equivalent can also be spatially incongruent. My left and right hands are distinguished in this manner. They are mirror images and so they are incongruent. And yet, this difference is not something external to me, to be thematized conceptually, since it relates to a feeling in me that I cannot define without reference to myself.[22] What such a feeling affords is directional orientation in space, which Kant explains in terms of our orientation within the solar system. Mere conceptual analysis is unable to explain what one knows of the stars in the sky. One can chart the place of given stars, but apart from such conceptual determination the stars offer themselves to us in relations governed by their left-right designations, by, that is to say, the orientation that is defined by the non-conceptualizable feeling of the distinction that one finds within oneself. In order to examine how such directional orientation is distinguishable from all other knowledge, Kant explains that if an astronomer were to find the stars one day reversed, as if they were seen in a mirror, once she distinguished any given star she would overcome this disorientation by noticing the change and reorient-ing herself. Her directional orientation is thus understood to be separable from the knowledge of the stars among which she orients herself.[23]

Kant goes on to explain that we can make use of the same feeling of left-right incongruence in order to orient ourselves within any given space. When entering a familiar but darkened room, we can orient ourselves by means of a single object whose position we remember. From the conception of such an object, for instance the desk on which I have just stubbed my toe, I can orient myself in the room and avoid knocking over the lamp that I know is to the left of the desk. Kant continues by explaining that if the familiar but darkened room that I enter has had its contents reversed, and if the structural layout of the room were congruent, then I would in time be able to reorient myself within it. The point for Kant is that the orientation that my inner, subjective feeling affords me is independent of my knowledge of the objects among which I orient myself, and so I can reorient myself when the objects I encounter do not conform to it.

In the *Prolegomena*, written three years prior to the 1786 essay, Kant makes use of left-right incongruence to explain the limits of categorical explanation and so designate sensibility as a non-conceptual form of experience. While Kant uses the example of left-right incongruence at least five times throughout his writings, and it works to support different stages in his evolving conception of space (from Newtonian absolute space to his critical position),[24] it is surprisingly absent from both editions of the *Critique of Pure Reason*.[25] In this work, Kant uses the example of drops of water, conceptually similar but spatially distinct objects, to argue, contra Leibniz and in a manner similar to the use of incongruence in the *Prolegomena*, that spatiality must be conceived as distinct from conceptual analysis or else we are unable to explain the manner in which we distinguish such otherwise equivalent objects.[26]

In both the example of incongruent counterparts in the *Prolegomena* and that of drops of water in both editions of the first *Critique*, Kant would seem to presuppose a conception of objects and from it explicate the non-conceptual features of such experience. Along with the Heidegger of *Being and Time*, one could criticize Kant for presupposing the field of objects that he then proceeds to examine.[27] Heidegger argues that Kant's analysis of spatial orientation assumes a prior familiarity with the objects among which we orient ourselves, which is to say that we are presumed to have been in the room prior to the lights going out, and in Kant's theory of cognition more generally we distinguish what objects are prior to their analysis. Kant, Heidegger argues, overlooks this presupposition, because he takes perception, and the objects that are so perceived, as self-evident.[28]

Such a challenge to the presuppositions of the Kantian approach has animated this book. I have been tracing the conception of experience through the first *Critique*, arriving in the preceding chapter at the critique of rational psychology and the inability to conclusively claim anything about the subject that both stands opposed to and permits access to objects. We are on the cusp of addressing the role that such failed metaphysical inquiry plays in Kant's epistemological system. What is interesting about Kant's 1786 essay, unlike Kant's other references to left-right orientation, is that in it the orientation of spatial appearances is connected to our speculative orientation in thought. Kant explains that such speculative orientation requires "the maxims of healthy reason [*die Maxime der gesunden Vernunft*]."[29] Our cognitive faculties, he argues, are driven beyond experience in the pursuit of the completion of their syllogistic interests; and yet, as the Transcendental Dialectic of the first *Critique* has shown, such transcendent use of the categories fails. What we are left with, Kant explains, is nothing more than "reason's feeling of its own need [*das Gefühl des der Vernunft eigenen Bedürfnisses*]."[30] What then is to offer us the criteria of "healthy reason [*gesunden Vernunft*]" that would help us avoid all metaphysical error?

The way to avoid error is to disavow judgment in the metaphysical areas of reason's interest; and yet, if such a limit on our use of reason is not plausible, if we are drawn to judge even though the field in which we would judge remains ambiguous, then we must make use of these ideas in ways that avoid proclaiming knowledge and so avoid the errors that Kant demonstrates in the Transcendental Dialectic of the first *Critique*. Such a presupposition of an idea of reason that has proven itself free of contradiction, which Kant in the orientation essay calls a commitment to "a pure rational faith [*Vernunftglaube*]," permits our orientation in thought.[31] Kant describes the process of reason's orientation as cautiously thinking the super-sensible in a way that is "fully in accord [*völlig angemessen*]"[32] with the empirical use of our understanding, for if we did not, then "instead of thinking we would indulge in enthusiasm.[33] We must orient ourselves within the super-sensible, which is to say in relation to the ideas of reason that do not afford us cognition. And this orientation in thought, akin to our orientation in space, allows us to avoid the errors of dogmatism, those of pursuing knowledge of that which stands beyond our finite capacities.

In this essay Kant does not offer much direction as to what is achieved by such orientation. Certainly, there is the negative task of avoiding dogmatic metaphysical claims, which Kant embraces when he warns against speculative "enthusiasm."[34] In terms of the positive role that such metaphysical orientation affords, Kant describes the "need of reason as twofold": theoretical and practical.[35] Kant distinguishes these two uses, describing the theoretical as "conditioned [*bedingt*]," which is to say that the idea of metaphysics must be assumed "if" we are interested in judging, if we are to conceive of the systematic unity of empirical laws, and so view nature as teleological; he describes the practical use of reason as "unconditioned [*unbedingt*]," because in our moral lives "**we must judge**."[36] Kant describes the practical use of such a "need of reason" as "far more important" than the use of conditioned principles in our theoretical orientation.

This is because such a use of reason is not associated with a particular interest that may or may not lead us to judge, in order to find unity in the variety of nature's laws, but instead its use is necessitated because we must judge in the area of our moral concerns and in so doing we implicitly accept the orienting function of reason.[37]

Kant later explains that in order to judge according to the guidance of reason in either the theoretical or the practical domain, we do not need to be explicitly aware of the role that such metaphysical ideas play in our judgment. Such speculative insight is not required for metaphysical direction. The person "who has common but (morally) healthy reason [*der Mensch von gemeiner, doch (moralisch) gesunder Vernunft*] can mark out his path, in both a theoretical and a practical respect."[38] This is not to say that people of such "common" reason conceive of the ideas that are guiding them in this manner; rather, they can pursue the ends that guide such inquiries without conceiving of the role played by these metaphysical interests. Kant explains that it is only the speculative thinker who, through the transcendental project, thematizes the relation of the sensible and the super-sensible, and so conceives of her dependence on metaphysical ideas in her pursuits.[39] Such a speculative thinker orients herself by means of the use of her "rational faith" as a "signpost [*Wegweiser*]" in thought's orientation within "the field of supersensible objects."[40]

In this essay, Kant says little about how thought's speculative orientation takes place, how our commitment to such metaphysical pursuits offers us such a "signpost." Investigating the three ideas of reason examined by Kant in the *Critique of Pure Reason*—the psychological, cosmological, and theological, the three ideas that Kant discusses as regulative principles (*Prinzipien*) in §76 of the *Critique of Judgment*—will offer some help. The cosmological idea offers the regulative principle of both mechanistic analysis, promising the ever-further extension of causal explanation, and transcendental freedom, insofar as such a mechanistic chain cannot be completed, since there exists the possibility of an event that is not mechanistically caused;[41] and the theological idea offers the regulative principle of teleological judgment, directing judgment of the systematic unity of nature's mechanistic laws.[42] This leaves only the psychological idea from the three ideas of reason introduced by Kant in the Transcendental Dialectic of the first *Critique*. Could it be that the idea of the unified subject of all of our experience, that of the soul that is forever out of reach, orients the speculative philosopher in relation to her varied powers (*Kräfte*) and thus permits her the elucidation of the faculties (*Vermögen*) of cognition? In order to address such a possibility, which is to say that our metaphysical interest in rational psychology could function as the signpost that guides the critical examination of experience, we will need to turn to the appendix to the Transcendental Dialectic in the first *Critique*, where Kant describes the varied uses of the ideas of metaphysics after their critique as the "hypothetical use of reason" (A647/B675) and offers his most sustained discussion of the role of the psychological idea after the critique of its cognitive pretensions.

II. The Regulative Use of the Psychological Idea

In the two sections of the appendix to the Transcendental Dialectic, titled On the Regulative Use of the Ideas of Pure Reason (Von dem regulativen Gebrauch der Ideen der reinen Vernunft) and On the Final Aim of the Natural Dialectic of Human Reason (Von der Endabsicht der natürlichen Dialektik der menschlichen Vernunft), Kant explains what he terms "the hypothetical use of reason [*der hypothetische Gebrauche der Vernunft*]" (A647/B675). The ideas that reason has been unable to cognize are to be used as heuristic principles, regulating our progress in the areas of our thought that evade all determinate cognition. The principles that reason affords are regulative rather than constitutive; they do not determine appearances but direct the way that particular appearances are interpreted. The ideas of reason direct us to further explanation of that which cannot be rationally cognized, and thus in these areas that surpass our finite faculties their role is that of "bringing unity into particular cognitions as far as possible and thereby **approximating** the rule to universality" (ibid.). The unity that reason provides for the understanding is that of a *focus imaginarius* (A644/B672), an imaginary point residing beyond the territory of the understanding, where the principles (*Grundsätze*) of the understanding would meet if their development beyond the territory of possible experience afforded cognition. Such a point, Kant explains, which is a "heuristic fiction," provides reason with the goal for its development of the unity of the understanding.[43]

Kant goes on to describe the regulative uses of the "three kinds of transcendental ideas (psychological, cosmological, and theological)" (A671/B699). The critique of metaphysics has ensured that metaphysical ideas are used only as heuristic principles rather than as determinate goals and that their regulated pursuit does not lead to erroneous or inconsistent claims. This not only permits us accomplishments in areas that, without such regulative inquiry, are beyond our faculties, but also guards us against our metaphysical instincts, forcing us to forever continue the process of critique in order to maintain the precarious hold on the principles (*Prinzipien*) which, while affording us regulative use, continue to direct us to their illusory constitutive employment.[44] In the body of the Transcendental Dialectic, this is demonstrated only in the case of cosmology, where the contradictions that arise when we attempt to think of the entirety of the world lead us to make use of this idea as a regulative principle. We pursue ever-further causal connections in our examination of the world in a manner that does not contradict the possibility of transcendental freedom. In the case of cosmology, such a regulative principle, born of the idea that otherwise produces antinomy, does not express anything beyond Kant's examination of mechanism in the Antinomy of Pure Reason chapter of the first *Critique*, in which the possibility of moral freedom is raised alongside this ever-expanding realm of causal analysis.[45] But the psychological and the theological ideas have not had their regulative uses explained in the body of the *Critique of Pure Reason*. After the critique of metaphysics in this work, one could still proclaim adherence to the psychological and theological ideas, for they end not in antinomy but in the ambivalence of their claims. The critique of metaphysics negates the possibility neither of faith in God nor of the immortality of the soul. While knowledge of such metaphysical ideas is out of reach, their thought does not lead to contradiction. And yet, it is not the possibility of continued commitment to these ideas, to faith even after the critique of metaphysics, that the appendix to the Transcendental Dialectic raises; rather, the regulative use of these ideas maintains them merely as hypotheses that direct our examination of perceptual particulars. Such principles regulate our varied attempts to think systematically about our perceptual lives, but they remain hypothetical insofar as they cannot be objectively deduced. They offer, Kant writes, "objective but indeterminate validity [*objective, aber unbestimmte Gültigkeit*]" insofar as they guide possible experience (A663/B691). The ideas of reason remain indeterminate even as they are followed regulatively; they offer no transcendental deduction (A664/B692), and yet they are "objective," serving as rules of possible experience. How this is so, how the "asymptotic" pursuit of the ideas of reason guides possible experience, must be investigated.[46]

Kant explains that the understanding is an object for reason in a manner that resembles the way that sensibility is an object for the understanding (A664/B692). For the understanding to determine connections between the manifold of sensible appearances, it depends upon schemata to mediate between sensible content and intellectual form; so too, for reason to order the understanding there is need of mediation. Kant calls this the "analogue of a schema of sensibility" (A665/B693), offering not the temporalization of the categories, but the ideas in a manner applicable to the *a priori* concepts of the understanding. The schematic use of the ideas of reason does not offer cognition, as does that of the concepts of the understanding; rather, it offers "only a rule or principle of the systematic unity of all use of the understanding" (ibid.). This is to say that it offers only regulative principles.

In explaining the regulative or hypothetical use of the ideas of reason, Kant states: "Reason thus prepares the field for the understanding [*Die Vernunft bereitet also dem Verstande sein Feld*]" (A657/B685) by means of three rules, or "**maxims** of reason" (A666/B695). By examining the three rules, we will be better able to understand the regulative principles through which reason directs the understanding's use. The first is the principle of "**homogeneity** [*Homogenität*]" by which we continually search for the "**sameness of kind** [*Gleichartigkeit*] in the manifold under higher genera" (A657/B685), for unity among difference. The second rule concerns the division of such homogeneity into lower species and so establishes the "**variety** [*Varietät*]" of what is similar. Finally, the third law is the "**affinity** [*Affinität*]" of all concepts: the various species form a continuous progression of change within this homogeneous unity and so offer themselves for empirical cognition. These three rules direct the ever-expanding search for a unified system of explanation. They direct the pursuit of complex unity within the manifold of difference that is perceived. These maxims of the hypothetical use of the ideas of reason closely resemble those of reflective judgment in the Second Introduction to the *Critique of Judgment*. There, Kant explains that the teleological pursuit of the systematic unity of the empirical laws of nature depends upon the presupposition of the principle of the purposiveness of nature. This principle, which offers us the "order of nature," can be expressed in three "propositions [*Sätze*]":[47] first, we must view different species as subordinated under higher genera; second, this unity of species follows principles such that it can be conceived as leading to an ever-higher genus; and third, the great variety of causes must be assumed to "stand under a small number of principles [*Prinzipien*]," and it is their discovery that we pursue.[48]

The similarity between the rules of reason's regulative use and the propositions of teleological judgment is great; both define the manner in which a manifold can be heuristically examined. In order to uncover laws that govern an empirical manifold, laws that distinguish both the diversity of species and their unity under higher genera, we must presuppose the systematic unity that we wish to distinguish. However, it must be noted that in the *Critique of Pure Reason* the ideas of reason offer themselves as regulative goals that direct reason's accomplishment in areas where no determinate cognition is possible, while in the *Critique of Judgment* Kant distinguishes judgment as the faculty that benefits from the use of reason's unknowable principles. In the rejection of the possibility of attaining metaphysical knowledge, reason's principles offer themselves as tools of reflective judgment. Kant distinguishes reflective judgment only in the *Critique of Judgment*. Until the publication of this work, his attempt to draw unity from a manifold of difference was left to reason in its hypothetical use.

Kant's account of the "hypothetical use of reason" in the first *Critique* is certainly not without its difficulties. Kant first describes these principles of "systematic unity" as logical (A648/B676).[49] He explains that if one were to describe them as transcendental, and so deem all of the understanding's cognition as actually derived from them, then such a systematic claim would be "not merely something subjectively and logically necessary, as method, but objectively necessary [*objektivnotwendig*]" (ibid.). The distinction that Kant seems to be drawing is between describing the hypothetical use of reason as needed to bring unity to the understanding as opposed to its being a necessary condition of the objects of experience. Such principles permit no transcendental deduction (A664/B692), since they cannot be deduced from experience; and yet, as Kant goes on to say, such principles of "systematic unity" cannot be merely logical, for they must be "assumed *a priori* as necessary" (A650–51/B678–79).[50] This, Kant explains, is because the systematic unity concerns not merely the cognition that the understanding produces, but the investigation of the understanding itself, which depends upon the idea of the unity of the variety of our "powers [*Kräfte*]" (A651/B679). Here, Kant highlights both the transcendental role of the hypothetical use of reason, which is to say its role in distinguishing our cognitive capacities, and the role that the psychological idea, which follows from the failed pursuits of rational psychology, plays in the analysis of cognition. While it is the latter, the role of the psychological idea, that is the true goal of this chapter, I will remain with the former discussion, that of the transcendental nature of the principles of reason, for a while longer, since it is such an account that allows for the clearest connection of this inquiry to Kant's later analysis of regulative principles in the *Critique of Judgment*. While Kant did not fully develop the account of the hypothetical use of reason in the *Critique of Pure Reason,* and while its activities are attributed to the faculty of judgment in his later works, there is a common inquiry that connects the appendix to the Transcendental Dialectic to the introductions to the *Critique of Judgment:* in all of these, Kant is addressing the uses that can be made of the inquiries into metaphysics in the *Critique of Pure Reason,* inquiries that at first glance might appear only negative.[51]

Kant explains in the *Critique of Judgment* that teleological judgment is able to strive toward the systematic unity of empirical law by presupposing the purposiveness of nature. Only by means of presupposing the principle of the systematic coherence of nature can reflective judgment proceed to ground the possibility of a search for the systematic unity of the empirical laws of nature. This presupposition is nothing but the ideal of reason taken as a regulative principle for reflective judgment.[52] Kant describes the regulative principle that follows from the ideal in the *Critique of Pure Reason* as our acting "**as if** the sum total of all appearances (the world of sense itself) had a single supreme and all-sufficient ground outside its range, namely an independent, original and creative reason" (A672/B700). This ideal of reason, while not presupposing the existence of such an object, transforms it into a regulative principle that directs teleological judgment's pursuit of ever-further systematic unity in the empirical laws of nature. This is to say, the sensible world is viewed "as if the objects themselves had arisen from that original image of all reason" (ibid.), and thus as if it were the product of a divine plan. The hypothetical use of reason's ideal is its use as the regulative principle that is presupposed in teleological judgment. The rules of reason's hypothetical use and the maxims of reflective judgment converge in the accomplishment of teleological judgment.

Yet, is this all that reason's hypothetical use offers? Is it just a prelude to the *Critique of Judgment* and its analysis of reflective judgment, marking merely the passage from mechanism to teleology? What such a position appears to overlook is the regulative principle emanating from the psychological idea. This would be a very difficult conclusion to draw from Kant's text, for he describes the regulative use of all three ideas of reason. In relation to the psychological idea, he writes that we must pursue the unified "fundamental powers [*Grundkräfte*]" of the rational subject as a "hypothetical" goal, "for the benefit of reason [*zu Gunsten der Vernunft*], namely for setting up certain principles for the many rules with which experience may furnish us, and that where it can be done, one must in such a way bring systematic unity into cognition" (A649–50/B677–78). Could the pursuit of the unity of the rational subject with its "fundamental powers" be merely a further teleological accomplishment emanating from the ideal, and hence ostensibly an accomplishment of the *Critique of Judgment*? This does not seem likely, for if the unified subject were itself a teleological accomplishment beyond the region of *a priori* concepts, then it could explain only the attempt to bring unity to the empirical laws that the categories of the understanding afford. It would offer only an empirical psychology dependent upon the idea of systematicity born of the theological idea that, Kant argues in the *Critique of Judgment*, is needed for any such empirical science. It would explain neither the role that the psychological idea plays in such a pursuit nor how such an investigation of our powers provides "the systematic unity of all use of the understanding" (A665/B693), which is to say the unity of not merely empirical concepts, but also the categories, the *a priori* concepts of the faculty (*Vermögen*) of the understanding.

Beyond the teleological pursuit of the systematic unity of nature, the regulative use of the ideas of reason promises the systemization of the understanding itself.[53] Such an ordering of the understanding does not refer to the furthering of mechanistic analysis that the cosmological idea directs,[54] for the understanding, with its categories, is the object of the regulative function that offers the "**touchstone of truth** for its [the understanding's] rules" (A647/B675).[55] What we must do is investigate the regulative principle that emanates from the psychological idea in order to explain how the hypothetical use of reason can be recognized as necessary not merely for causal and teleological investigation, but also for theoretical inquiry into the systematic unity that directs the analysis of the understanding.

In the second section of the appendix to the Transcendental Dialectic, Kant claims that reason continues to direct us to look upon the subject of philosophical inquiry as unified, simple, persistent, and distinct from spatial appearances even though the psychological idea evades cognition (A683/B711). Kant explains that the psychological idea, transformed into a regulative principle, directs us to consider

> all determinations as in one subject, all powers [*Kräfte*], as far as possible, as derived from one unique fundamental power [*einigen Grundkraft*], all change as belonging to the states of one and the same persistent being, and by representing all **appearances** in space as entirely distinct from the actions of **thinking** [*den Handlungen des Denkens*]. (A683/B711)

Kant here directs the regulative use of the four elements of the psychological idea, but he has not directly explained what such a regulative use offers transcendental philosophy.[56] Kant does claim that the hypothetical pursuit of the psychological idea offers a certain advantage: "Now nothing but advantage can arise from such a psychological idea, if only one guards against letting it hold as something more than a mere idea, i.e., if one lets it hold merely relative to the systematic use of reason in respect of the appearances of the soul" (ibid.). If the analysis of the conditions of the possibility of experience offers a conception of the unified faculties of finite thinking, then this unity can only be directed by the psychological idea. The psychological idea distinguishes the conception of subjectivity needed to orient philosophical reflection in its analysis of the conditions of the possibility of experience. In this way, it distinguishes the subject as a unified whole, but also, as the passage explains, opposes it to all spatial appearances, to the phenomenal objects the analysis of which affords Kant, in the Transcendental Analytic, the terrain of possible experience and the elucidation of the faculties of finite cognition.

Kant explains in the second section of the appendix to the Transcendental Dialectic that the regulative use of the psychological idea directs an approach to our inner experience that is guided by the conception of ourselves as persistently existing, simple substances, thinking beings with unified identities (A672/B700). While we can never produce "a systematic unity of all appearances of inner sense" (A682/B710), by beginning our philosophical analysis with the concept of such a unity of empirical thought, we can undertake to examine the faculties of such a subject. The unknowable idea of the subject as it is apart from all that appears to it is used to direct the analysis of the thinking subject thus defined. In this way, critical philosophy is able to designate the boundary of possible experience, and from the variety of our "powers [*Kräfte*]" that appearances exemplify, it can deduce the systematic unity of the "faculty [*Vermögen*]" of the understanding. Such an investigation follows the maxims of the hypothetical use of reason as it pursues first the unity of the understanding, then the divisions that constitute this unity, and finally the affinity of all such differentiated powers. Kant reminds us that this account of the soul's appearance in inner sense is not derived from the idea of a rational subject (ibid.). No such objective determination can avoid the perils of metaphysics; rather, the account of the understanding as the unified faculty of the appearing soul can only be derived from the appearances that constitute experience when directed by the conception of a unified subject (A673/B701).[57]

The critical analysis of experience is therefore a regulative and not a constitutive project.[58] The cognitive faculties of the thinking subject are pursued within the field of appearances, and this investigation is itself directed by the psychological idea. To pursue such a conception of the metaphysical presuppositions of critique is to enter into an investigation of the subject of the reflective project of critical analysis. Kant has begun his analysis of the conditions of the possibility of objects of experience with an implicit adherence to a conception of the relation of objects to the subjects for whom they appear, for the objects constitutive of the experience of this subject are limited to those that spatially appear. The thinking subject, distinguished by the unified faculties of Kantian cognition, thus remains indebted to the regulative principle that permits its analysis.

Reason's failure to attain knowledge of the rational subject in the Paralogisms of Pure Reason chapter of the first *Critique* does not deny the possibility of the regulative pursuit of the unified faculties of such a subject.[59] Reason's hypothetical employment makes use of this idea as a regulative principle that directs the analysis of the faculties of the unified subject. In the pursuit of the systematic unity of the thinking subject, Kant explains the four directions that the idea of the soul offers our inquiries, which follow the paths of the four paralogisms. According to the First Paralogism, reason strives to distinguish "all determinations as in one subject," and so as distinguishing a single substance;[60] following the Second Paralogism, "all powers [*Kräfte*]" are viewed "as derived from one unique fundamental power [*Grundkraft*]" (A682/B710), and so as related to a simple thing; according to the Third Paralogism, the subject is viewed as "unchangeable in itself (identical in personality)" (ibid.), and so as a "persisting being [*beharrlichen Wesens*]" (A683/B711); and, finally, according to the Fourth Paralogism, reason endeavors to distinguish "all **appearances** in space as entirely distinct from the actions of **thinking** [*den Handlungen des Denkens*]" (ibid.). In its hypothetical use, reason claims as a regulative principle precisely those four facets of the psychological idea that lead it into paralogism when they are pursued directly as the characteristics of an object of cognition.

Kant explains that the regulative principle born of reason's psychological idea is that of "a simple independent intelligence" of unified powers that can differentiate between its "actions of thinking" and the objects that it intuits in space. This regulative principle does not afford the cognition of "the soul at all through these assumed predicates" (A683/B711). It avoids such paralogistic reasoning by hypothesizing a unity that, while not offering itself directly to determinate cognition, can be thought without contradiction. This regulative principle directs the explication of the unified faculties of the understanding in its analysis of spatial appearances. While rational psychology fails to attain determinate knowledge of the thinking subject, this idea is the schema of a regulative principle that distinguishes the unified subject from the objects that it perceives. The fourfold schema of the psychological idea provides the regulative principle that directs the examination of spatial appearances by regulating the pursuit of the conditions of the possibility of actual objects, which is to say objects insofar as they can be appearances for a unified subject. While reason is unable to attain knowledge of the thinking subject, in pursuing its task hypothetically it can approach the analysis of cognition with the principle of the self as a simple substance that can distinguish spatial appearances from the merely temporal activity of its thinking, and so offer our finite faculties the possibility of their systemization. Such a principle regulates transcendental reflection, the reflective parsing of the manifold of representations, designating the terrain of the analysis of cognition as that of spatial appearances. Such a regulative principle stemming from the psychological idea, which is to say from speculative inquiry into the soul, is thus implied in the analysis of finite cognition.

Kant states that transcendental reflection is the prerequisite for any *a priori* judgment since it distinguishes the representations of the pure understanding from those that are sensible (A263/B319). It directs the inquiry into objectivity and hence permits the critique of metaphysics. Yet how can such a reflective distinction be made? How can thought be divided prior to all *a priori* judgment according to the very divisions that are justified only through such an analysis? As we investigated above in chapter 2, in §76 of the *Critique of Judgment* Kant connects the regulative use of reason to three different areas of accomplishment without explicitly ascribing the accomplishments to particular ideas of reason. While Kant concludes by describing those areas that are obviously associated with the cosmological and the theological ideas, he begins by claiming that the differentiation of possibility and actuality, which is to say the limitation of the terrain of philosophical analysis to that which, as sensible representation, conforms to the conceptual dualism of possibility and actuality, depends upon a regulative principle. The analysis of the faculties of finite cognition—and thus the transcendental reflection that is their prerequisite—depends upon an accomplishment resulting from the illusory pursuit of metaphysics. While this certainly appears to follow from the psychological idea, from the pursuit of the rational cognition of the subject apart from that which is represented to it, Kant does not explain the precise workings of such a dependence.

Transcendental reflection implies the regulative principle that is only thematized in the appendix to the Transcendental Dialectic in the account of the hypothetical use of reason in relation to the psychological idea. In this sense, transcendental reflection is conceived as dependent upon a regulative principle, and thus as following Kant's analysis, in the later First Introduction to the *Critique of Judgment*, of judgments of reflection as dependent upon regulative principles.[61] Unlike Kant's discussion of the role of the principle of purposiveness in reflective judgments of both beauty and teleology, transcendental reflection requires a regulative principle that directs not the systematic unity of nature but the division of the representational manifold that designates the region of spatial appearances as the limited area of the philosophical investigation of cognition. The psychological idea directs just this sort of division.

In investigating whether the thinking subject can be known apart from the objects of its thought, Kant concludes that we can neither affirm nor deny the knowledge of such a subject. However, it is just such an unknowable idea that can explain the initial presupposition of the critical analysis of cognition. Transcendental reflection readies the manifold of our thought for critical analysis by directing the division of this manifold according to the directives of the uncognizable idea of the rational subject. While the attempt to infer metaphysical knowledge from the analysis of the unified faculties of the subject leads to error, the critique of such metaphysical pretensions points not merely to the dependence of teleological judgment on a principle that follows from the speculative pursuit of metaphysics,[62] but also to the account of the structure of cognition as dependent upon a regulative principle to which we are directed by the transcendental misuse of the *a priori* concepts of the understanding (A296/ B351). This regulative principle is the psychological idea, the unified, rational subject that can distinguish its thought from appearances in space.

The principle (*Prinzip*) that emanates from the psychological idea directs our philosophical reflection to the phenomenal world with the presupposition that spatial appearances can be distinguished in our perceptual experience from that which can be thought but can never appear as an object. It is precisely this principle that is embedded in the accomplishment of transcendental reflection. We come to be able to distinguish the *a priori* rules that guide the understanding by means of the act of transcendental reflection, which must presuppose the distinction between those of our thoughts that refer to spatial objects and those that do not, even though we cannot justify our commitment to distinguishing ourselves as rational subjects from the objects that appear to us. Reason can only hypothetically pursue this principle. Only the psychological idea, taken as the principle of transcendental reflection, can explain how reason's regulative principles afford not merely the extension of mechanistic and teleological inquiry but in fact the analysis of the cognitive faculties of the thinking subject.

What has been shown is that the conceptual analysis of reflective judgment in the *Critique of Judgment* can direct such an analysis of the critical project, deeming such an inquiry to be a regulative accomplishment. The hypothetical use of reason in regard to the psychological idea, rather than producing a paralogism in the attempt to gain knowledge of our thinking natures, must be viewed as a regulative principle that has already been presupposed in the analysis of objects of experience, and such a regulative principle can only be uncovered by means of the said investigation. This regulative principle directs the analysis of the systematic unity of the understanding. It is the presupposed principle that allows us, in conceptualizing the conditions that make possible the objects of experience, to elucidate the systematic unity of the pure concepts of the understanding. In permitting us the analysis of the "systematic unity of the understanding's cognition" (A647/B675), such a regulative principle distinguishes a unified account of the understanding that is neither a rational nor an empirical psychology; rather, it is a regulative pursuit of our unified cognitive faculties that stands at the foundation of Kant's critical inquiry.

III. The Psychological Idea and the Method of Critique

The interpretation of the critical project as dependent upon a regulative principle emanating from the illusory pursuits of metaphysics obviously does not offer a simple foundation for Kant's epistemological analysis. The critique of metaphysics is built upon the understanding's *a priori* concepts, and yet, a regulative principle following from such metaphysical pursuits underlies the accomplishments of transcendental reflection and therefore also the dualism of sensibility and understanding. This dualism is thus not a dogmatically posited structure of Kantian experience, but is rather an achievement dependent upon the hypothetical use of the psychological idea as a regulative principle for the act of transcendental reflection, a reflection that enables the analysis of the cognitive faculties. Reason cannot attain knowledge of such metaphysical ideas, but by avoiding the illusions implicit in such pursuits the regulative principle that directs the analysis of phenomenal experience can be distinguished in the image of the noumenal realm.

In the Transcendental Doctrine of Method, the closing division of the *Critique of Pure Reason*, in the chapter titled the Discipline of Pure Reason, Kant reiterates the general account of the regulative or heuristic use of the ideas of reason and goes on to explain that "[t]hey are merely thought problematically, in order to ground regulative principles [*Prinzipien*] of the systematic use of the understanding in the field of experience in relation to them (as heuristic fictions [*Fiktionen*])" (A771/B799).[63] Kant continues in a manner that corresponds to the interpretation that has here been given concerning the role of the psychological idea by stating that such a regulative principle permits the analysis of the "powers of the mind [*Gemütskräfte*]":

> It is entirely permissible to **think** the soul as simple in order, in accordance with this **idea**, to make a complete and necessary unity of all powers of the mind [*Gemütskräfte*], even though one cannot have insight

into it *in concreto,* into the principle [*Prinzip*] of our judgment of its inner appearances [*inneren Erscheinungen*]. (A771–72/B799–800)[64]

While Kant does not here develop the manner in which the psychological idea can be said to play such a role, his description of the simple soul, the soul of the psychological idea, would appear to be that of a regulative principle for the critical analysis of the subjective faculties, for the unified account of the faculties of finite thinking can be distinguished in relation to this idea of the thinking subject. The idea of a simple subject distinct from objects in space offers the principle of the unity of the subjective powers that permits the judgment of the soul's "inner appearances." Such a judgment is a reflective one that does not permit the cognition of an object but directs inquiry toward an unreachable, regulative principle. The analysis of the understanding offered in the Transcendental Analytic follows such a guide, transforming the varied powers of thinking into the comprehensive unity of the cognitive faculties. But such an account of the finite faculties can be distinguished only in relation to a conception of the simple subject, a metaphysical idea that can itself be transformed into a regulative principle only through the critique of metaphysics that follows from the analysis of the finite faculties. Kant describes such a method as a "perpetual circle [*beständigen Zirkel*]" (B404/A346).[65]

With such an account of the way that the idea of the soul, taken as a regulative principle, directs the analysis of the cognitive faculties, we are able to return to Kant's elusive Refutation of Idealism. That section, added by Kant in the second edition and placed within the analysis of the understanding in the Analytic of Principles of the Transcendental Analytic, can now be interpreted with the help of the role that the regulative function of the psychological idea plays in the Kantian system.

As was seen above in chapter 3, the Refutation of Idealism (B274–79) argues that any attempt to examine consciousness which begins from temporal self-awareness is implicitly committed to a conception of something persistent as distinguished from all subjective representations. Transcendental philosophy, since it begins with the transcendental reflection over the temporal flow of representations, is not exempt from this requirement. In marking the boundary of possible experience as that of the representations constituting empirical objects, Kant has begun his philosophical project with a conception of the relation of a perceiving subject to the objects it perceives. This allows Kant to limit the representational flux to the appearances of objects and to examine only these representations for *a priori* cognition. Implied in this commitment to the appearances of objects is the conception of a unified subject in opposition to objects that are distinct from it. The unknowable idea of the rational subject regulates, or directs, the analysis of cognition. The idea of this subject, distinguished from all objects, forges the schema through which the boundary of possible experience has been distinguished.[66]

This conception of the underlying commitments of Kantian epistemology offers a way to interpret the persistent thing that the Refutation argues is implied in all temporal consciousness. This conception of a persistent thing apart from all temporal self-consciousness is not a claim that Kant limits to the critical enterprise. The Refutation of Idealism has attempted a double task, both denying problematic or Cartesian idealism and at the same time addressing the claim that Kant has produced a further idealism that, like those of the past, is unconnected to a reality beyond its limits. Kant's argument is that all philosophical endeavors that begin from the point of the temporal consciousness of experience, with the experiential unity of temporal succession, are implicitly committed to the existence of something apart from consciousness in relation to which such temporal unity can be distinguished. But this requirement does not necessitate a return to rationalist metaphysics, since what is offered is the regulative use of an unknowable idea as a replacement for such speculative flight. The persistent thing demanded by the temporal consciousness with which critique begins is not an empty noumenal claim; rather, it is the conception of objects, distinguished from the perceiving subject, that the regulative principle, following from the psychological idea, promises.[67] All consciousness of temporal determination depends upon something persistent apart from such temporal flow. One can either embrace an illusory metaphysical claim or accept the regulative function of this non-phenomenal principle. Kant chooses the latter, and so is able to produce the critical system, affording a conception of experience that, while limited to phenomenal claims about the world, must maintain a commitment to the idea of the separate existence of objects and the subjects who perceive them.

IV. "What Is Man?": Transcendental Philosophy as a Physiology of Thinking Nature

Kant can be seen to have further interpreted this dependence of the critical system on a conception of the subject of critique in the *Logic,* where he connects metaphysical inquiry to the pursuit of self-knowledge in a manner that helps to explicate the conception of the subject of critique that underlies the critical enterprise. There, in addition to the three philosophical questions that are asked in the *Critique of Pure Reason* (B833/A805)—"What can I know?" "What ought I to do?" and "What may I hope?"—Kant appends a fourth: "What is man?"[68] Kant explains that the first question relates to "**metaphysics,**" the second to "**morals,**" the third to "**religion,**" and the fourth to "**anthropology,**" and he goes on to say that the first three questions "relate to the last one," and thus that we can understand "all of this as anthropology."[69] The philosopher whose project is conceived as anthropological in this way must be able to distinguish the "sources," "extent," and "profitable use of all knowledge," as well as the "boundaries [*Grenzen*] of reason."[70] The philosophical undertaking thus depends on the elucidation of our finitude, on the accomplishments begun in the *Critique of Pure Reason* insofar as our cognitive faculties are distinguished and the metaphysical interests of reason are curbed. But how, we must ask, is this—the very foundation of Kant's transcendental philosophy—to be conceived as anthropology?

If we return with such a question to Kant's *Anthropology*, where he offers two accounts of anthropology—pragmatic and physiological—it would appear that we are no closer to being able to explain how philosophical inquiry can be said to culminate in anthropology.[71] Pragmatic anthropology, the subject of Kant's *Anthropology*, is the study of what a human being "makes of himself, or can and should make of himself";[72] as an empirical undertaking, it cannot address the way that speculative inquiries might culminate in anthropology. The other option offered by Kant is physiological anthropology, the study of "what **nature** makes of the human being," and so the attempt to offer a theoretical account of what the human being is.[73] While physiological anthropology, insofar as it offers an inquiry into what the human being is as a product of nature, and so *a priori*, might appear to offer just the sort of response that the question "What is man?" needs to produce, and so offer us not only the inquiry that unifies our philosophical pursuits but also the conception of the subject of critique for which we have been searching, Kant dashes all such hopes. He writes that "speculation about this is a pure waste of time,"[74] since one remains but a "spectator [*Zuschauer*]" in the complex workings of nature, and this is even or perhaps most emphatically the case in relation to self-knowledge.[75] But if anthropology offers only pragmatic inquiry, if it offers no science of the thinking subject, then it would seem to challenge the claims of the *Logic*, as it would be able to explain neither that which unites the other three divisions of philosophical inquiry nor how we are able to examine our finite faculties.

What has here been argued is that rational psychology finds its post-critical function in regulating the designation of the terrain of possible experience, and so directing the analysis of the subjective faculties by limiting the scope of this inquiry. Another way to state this is that the post-critical use of the psychological idea designates a regulative answer to the anthropological question "What is man?"—an answer that is guided by the regulative principle emanating from the psychological idea. In the Transcendental Doctrine of Method of the first *Critique*, Kant refers to an immanent physiology that would offer "the metaphysics of thinking nature," which Kant goes on to equate with psychology (A846/B874).[76] This discussion of physiology as post-critical rational psychology differs from Kant's rejection of both a Lockean "**physiology** of the human understanding" (Aix) in the first edition's preface, and a rationalist "physiology of inner sense" in the Paralogisms chapter (B405/A347). Kant, at this late point in the first *Critique*, is using the term "physiology" to refer to neither a metaphysical claim about the soul nor an empirical pursuit that would search for the laws that correspond to the manifold of thought; and he is also not embracing a realist, rational psychology at odds with the critical project, the sort he denies in the description of physiological anthropology in the *Anthropology*.[77] What Kant refers to in the Transcendental Doctrine of Method of the first *Critique* is a critical psychology that makes no use of empirical data whatsoever, but only psychology's "rational cognition" (A846/B875). In the Transcendental Doctrine of Method, Kant gives only a brief account of what such a pursuit would entail. He says that the question such an inquiry answers is: "How can I expect an *a priori* cognition and thus a metaphysics of objects that are given to our senses, thus given *a posteriori*?" (A848/B876). Such a "physiology of the soul" helps to explain how transcendental inquiry can expect to distinguish *a priori* cognition in its reflection on empirical experience. Such philosophical reflection must begin with the conception of an object of both outer and inner sense. We must pursue the critical analysis of cognition from this beginning. The object of outer sense "is accomplished through the mere concept of matter," while that of inner sense depends upon "the concept of a thinking being" (ibid.). Philosophy must start its investigation by presupposing such basic conceptions, beginning with an unfounded confidence in both objects and the thinking subject, and only from there can it offer its analysis of *a priori* cognition. This "rational physiology" of the soul explains the presuppositions of the critical analysis of cognition, for it includes no empirical observation, and its rational component, the psychological idea, offers precisely the division of objects and the thinking subject that critical inquiry demands.[78]

Thus, the term "physiology" can easily mislead, for what rational psychology offers after the critique of its metaphysical interests is a regulative principle that explains the designation of the terrain of critical inquiry by offering a way to conceive of an answer to the question "What is man?" While Kant, in the Architectonic of Pure Reason chapter of the *Critique of Pure Reason*, does not explicitly develop the connection of this rational physiology to the transcendental reflection that has been shown to be the act that parses the representational field, the task here raised for post-critical rational psychology, for what might be described as transcendental psychology, appears to address this, the most basic reflective posture of Kantian critique.[79]

In commenting on the relation of the three philosophical questions to the fourth, the question "What is man?" in Kant's *Logic*, Heidegger, in *Kant and the Problem of Metaphysics*, claims that the essential finitude of *Dasein* shows itself in its metaphysical questioning. Our continued failure to attain the kind of answers we want to the questions of metaphysics brings us to the abyss, to the limits of our knowledge, and to the recognition of ourselves, in the absence of self-knowledge, as finite. Finitude shows itself in the asking of the questions: "[H]uman reason is not finite just because it poses the three questions cited above, but the reverse: it poses these questions because it is finite."[80] For Heidegger, that we ask these unanswerable metaphysical questions marks our finitude,[81] so how from the posing of such questions do we come to recognize the structure of our finite cognition when the question "What is man?" appears to be so thoroughly indeterminate? Such a question has directed this inquiry neither to Heidegger's fundamental ontology nor to Hegel's synthesis of the finite and the absolute, for the manner of our analysis of the finite is precisely the issue; rather, such a question has directed an investigation of the way in which the pursuit of metaphysical ideas, even in its failure, provides us with the regulative principle through which we are able to distinguish the field of experience that permits the Kantian analysis of cognition. Heidegger has shed light on such methodological inquiries in his discussion in *What Is a Thing?* of the circularity of critique, as well as in his later "Kant's Thesis about Being," in which he investigates Kant's notion of transcendental reflection as the act of designating the field of critical inquiry alongside a discussion of the elusive §76 of the *Critique of Judgment*.[82] And yet, Heidegger does not investigate the methodological implications of his analysis of transcendental reflection, emphasizing instead its relation to the ontological source of Kant's cognitive dualism.[83]

What has here been shown is that the analysis of finite cognition depends upon a principle of reason that regulates transcendental reflection on the perceptual manifold. The limited terrain of experience within which the structures of cognition are distinguished is designated by the act that Heidegger in "Kant's Thesis about Being" calls "a reflection back over the completed steps of thought [*eine Rückbesinnung auf die vollzogenen Denkschritte*]."[84] This methodological reflection explains that the epistemology of transcendental philosophy remains tethered to a metaphysical claim. We ask metaphysical questions because we are finite, but the analysis of the structure of our finite thinking depends upon the manner in which we grapple with such unanswerable questions.

Transcendental philosophy thus stands as an accomplishment within the "abyss [*Abgrund*]" of reason.[85] We are able to distinguish the structure of finite cognition only by pursuing an analysis of the human faculties that, as Hegel claims, divides the finite from the infinite. Yet this division is but the starting point of an inquiry that ultimately demands their interconnection. Kant has thus not rejected the infinite in order to pursue the limited terrain of finite thought, as Hegel argues; rather, he has set aside the questions of metaphysics in order to distinguish the conceptual tools that allow him to avoid the illusions of this divine science. And yet, in what should be by this time a familiar refrain, this initial turning from metaphysics, constituted by the act of transcendental reflection, can be justified only by means of the metaphysical critique that it permits.

This examination of the regulative underpinnings of the critical analysis of finite cognition helps to explain why, in the Architectonic of Pure Reason chapter of the Transcendental Doctrine of Method, Kant returns to the discussion of the two stems of cognition and refers to the critical project as beginning from "the point where the general root of our cognitive power [*Erkenntniskraft*] divides and branches out into two stems, one of which is **reason**" (A835/B863). The unnamed stem presumably remains sensibility, and the other is now reason rather than understanding, as Kant had earlier written in the introduction.[86] Kant explains that by "reason," he is referring to "the entire higher faculty of cognition," rather than to the more narrowly circumscribed faculty of metaphysical speculation investigated in the Transcendental Dialectic. Reason in this broader sense thus includes not only its narrower usage but also the faculty of understanding. While Kant had earlier described the two stems of human cognition as sensibility and understanding, in the Transcendental Doctrine of Method that follows the detailed accomplishments of the first *Critique*, he is emphasizing that the second stem, the rational in contrast to the empirical, now can be said to include not only the understanding but also the faculty of metaphysical inference, reason in its narrower sense. Kant's cognitive dualism can now be said to require not merely the understanding and its concepts but reason and its principles, which join with sensibility in cognition. While the understanding is investigated as a separate faculty in the Transcendental Analytic, the order of explanation followed by the first *Critique* need not stop us from discerning that in the completed conceptual system of transcendental philosophy, the inquiries pursued in the name of reason, as the narrowly defined highest of our cognitive faculties, are themselves needed for the prior analysis of the understanding. Understanding falls within the territory that reason has cultivated;[87] however, the examination of the faculty of reason proceeds only with the accomplishments of the analysis of the understanding. Such a relation demonstrates what Kant describes as the "perpetual circle" (B404/A346)[88] of its approach. And in this circle it is "the entire higher faculty of cognition," the involvement of both understanding and reason, that can be opposed to sensibility as the second stem of cognition.[89]

Kant introduces this conception of circularity in terms of the transcendental subject. Any attempt to say something more about such subjectivity, to add a predicate to what is otherwise merely a logical unity, is forced to make use of such subjectivity in its attempt "to judge anything about it" (B404/A346). We are implicated in this circularity when we examine the transcendental subject; rather than denying his dependence on a circular method, Kant embraces it, and not just in terms of the investigation of the transcendental subject.[90] In the Transcendental Doctrine of Method that ends the first *Critique*, Kant explains

that while the speculative use of pure reason does not offer us "synthetic judgment from concepts," and so does not offer *Prinzipien*, it does offer *Grundsätze*
when taken in relation to the sensibly given; and each of these principles, which
are related to the *a priori* concepts of the understanding, exemplifies "the special property [*die besondere Eigenschaft*] that it first makes possible its ground of
proof, namely experience" (A737/B765).[91] Such principles distinguish the realm
of experience—for example the modal principle of possibility, which designates
the region of this inquiry—but at the same time it is experience that allows us to
deduce the *a priori* validity of the category that is the source of such a principle.
The principles (*Grundsätze*) are thus presupposed in that which offers their proof;
and so we are drawn into the circular method of the critical system. But how
are these principles (*Grundsätze*), and the *a priori* concepts of the understanding
from which they follow, accomplishments of the speculative use of reason? Kant
does not say, but what has here been proposed is that it is reason's speculative
pursuit of the psychological idea that offers the regulative principle that directs
the designation of the realm of experience within which the *a priori* concepts
of the understanding can be deduced. The circularity of critique is not merely
a narrowly circumscribed description of either the analysis of transcendental
subjectivity or the *a priori* concepts of the understanding, but is more generally
the method of Kant's undertaking—describing the designation of the realm of
experience by means of the regulative principle emanating from the psychological
idea—a designation which permits both the analysis of cognition and the critique
of metaphysics.[92]

The critical system cannot answer the metacritical demand for an objective
justification of the criteria with which it begins its analysis. Kant accepts the
radically skeptical notion that our conceptual vocabulary is forever limited to our
subjective viewpoint, limited to the criteria of analysis that we have chosen, and
forever lacking the external criteria that would offer it metaphysical certainty.
However, within this "abyss" the circular method of the critical inquiry offers a
conceptually non-contradictory system that provides far-ranging insight into a
wide variety of human concerns.

With such a conception of the regulative role played by the psychological
idea in the designation of the faculty of understanding, we can now understand why Kant, in the appendix to the Transcendental Dialectic, describes the
role played by the post-critical use of the ideas of reason as a *focus imaginarius*
(A644/B672). Kant had first used the term in his 1766 "Dreams of a Spirit-Seer
Elucidated by Dreams of Metaphysics [Träume eines Geistsehers, erläutert
durch Träume der Metaphysik]."[93] In this pre-critical work, Kant explains that if
one takes the light rays that enter the eye and produce images, and trace them
back toward their source, they will intersect at a point that can be described as
the "point of convergence."[94] Kant calls this source the *focus imaginarius*,[95] and

then extends this term to those cases when a person traces out the source of a merely imagined object. Kant describes such a source as a *focus imaginarius* as well, but one whose source is "within me," "inside the brain."[96]

In this pre-critical work, Kant has no criteria to distinguish between the appropriate inference—that the object exists apart from me—and the mistaken assumption that a merely imagined thought has such a source. In describing the clarity of the sensations of our waking lives, Kant concludes that while we are awake, failing to distinguish objects apart from us from figments of the imagination is a sign of madness (*Wahnsinn*),[97] even though in both cases the inference is said to distinguish a *focus imaginarius*. By the time of Kant's first *Critique* each of these inferences comes to have a new title, and the *focus imaginarius* is used in an altogether different fashion. With the critical system, Kant is able to designate the source of the perceived image not as a *focus imaginarius* but as an example of a causal law; and imagined inferences beyond the sensible realm that are not in accord with the causal law, those whose failure to be recognized as such is described as the product of "madness," are called illusions and, in the case of metaphysical flight, transcendental illusions (A295/B352).

In the first *Critique*, this leaves the term *focus imaginarius* to describe the post-critical uses of the ideas of metaphysics. Kant uses the term to describe the ways that the ideas of metaphysics—the soul, the world, and God—can be seen to offer direction while not leading to the illusory pursuit of their objects. Kant explains the *focus imaginarius* in this way as "a point from which the concepts of the understanding do not really proceed, since it lies entirely outside the bounds of possible experience" (A644/B672). The critical system has allowed Kant to distinguish the ways that we are justified in the use of our metaphysical interests, and the *focus imaginarius* is now distinguished as the way that such unattainable metaphysical ideas can be used as regulative principles.[98] In so doing, Kant has transformed the *focus imaginarius* from a product of the imagination and potentially a harbinger of madness into a tool of reason and a product of critique.

But is this correct? Could there be no role for the imagination in the *focus imaginarius* in the first *Critique*, and thus could the threat posed by such a faculty be utterly avoided? Kant does not explicitly connect the role played by the *focus imaginarius* in the first *Critique* to the workings of the imagination, "the faculty for representing an object even **without its presence** in intuition" (B151);[99] however, in the Transcendental Dialectic Kant does connect the imagination to the way that one of the ideas of reason, the cosmological, can be thought. This is Kant's only reference to the imagination in the Transcendental Dialectic, and it comes at the start of the Antinomies chapter. He explains that the unconditioned to which reason strives in its pursuit of the totality of mechanistic causes is contained in the conditioned series *if* one represents such a totality in the imagination (A416/B444).[100] The totality of the series of mechanistic causes is thought by means of the imagination. And it is this totality that offers the cosmological idea as the regulative principle that directs the search for further causes. Such an imagined object leads to the conflicts of the antinomies, and Kant's third antinomy is born of such a use of the imagination; we are directed by the image of the completed series to search for ever-further causes, leaving what seems like no possibility for freedom. The critical system, with its division of the phenomenal and the noumenal realms, saves us from the contradiction to which we are drawn by the cosmological idea. But such a solution, which is to say such a conception of the role that the cosmological idea plays in the critical system, has already appeared in the body of the Transcendental Dialectic, long before Kant introduces the *focus imaginarius* in its appendix.[101]

In this discussion of the *focus imaginarius,* Kant makes no reference to the imagination, this is to say no reference beyond the term itself. The new examples that Kant adds to the list of regulative principles—alongside the cosmological, the psychological, and the theological ideas—make no demand on the imagination. Neither the idea of the soul, nor that of God, can be conceived as objects, and so they remain inferences of reason for which no objects can be determined; but in their cases, unlike that of the cosmological idea, their objects cannot even be imagined. In this way, these two ideas are most fitting of Kant's description of ideas of reason in the *Critique of Judgment.* There, Kant explains that an idea of reason is "a concept to which no intuition (representation of the imagination) can be adequate";[102] neither the psychological nor the theological idea can be represented in the imagination and so they are in this way exemplary ideas of reason, while the cosmological idea, insofar as it can be represented in the imagination, and in this way leads to antinomy, shows itself to be a mixture of the rational and the sensible. In the case of the psychological and the theological ideas, the transcendental illusions that they engender lead not to antinomy, since neither is able to be imagined as an object, and so they do not mark a path for the completion of the series of phenomenal appearances. In these cases, the ideas remain forever abstracted from the realm of objects; the threat that they pose, which the Transcendental Dialectic has dispelled, is one of rational speculation untethered to the realm of objects. Once this threat has been averted, such ideas can be used as regulative principles, a use that Kant explains is "indispensably necessary" (A645/B673). To this end, Kant describes each of the ideas of reason as a *focus imaginarius* when its goal is pursued not constitutively but merely regulatively.

Kant describes the direction given by the *focus imaginarius* as that of a "point" that directs the understanding to the convergence of "all its rules [*aller seiner Regeln*]" (A644/B672). Clearly, Kant is referring to the *a posteriori* concepts, the rules that both the cosmological and the theological ideas direct, but in describing the role of the *focus imaginarius* as directing "all" rules of the understanding, he can be understood to be referring as well to the *a priori* concepts of the understanding, whose analysis the psychological idea has now been shown to address. What is particularly relevant for this inquiry is that Kant goes on to explain that this point is but an "idea" that lies outside "the bounds of possible experience" (ibid.). Such an idea leads to the "deception [*Täuschung*]" that there is such a point toward which the understanding's concepts lead. In order not to be deceived by such an illusion but to continue to be directed by the ideas of reason, Kant compares the *focus imaginarius* to objects that are outside our field of vision but visible in the reflection of a mirror. While the object seen in the mirror appears to stand beyond the plane of the mirror's surface, we can come to recognize the illusion of its appearance. The object only appears to stand beyond the mirror, but it really lies outside our field of vision.[103]

To compare the ideas of reason in their regulative use provided by transcendental philosophy to objects reflected in a mirror, which are otherwise outside our field of vision, is to compare transcendental to optical illusions. Such illusions, unlike logical illusions whose errors can be thoroughly corrected, continue to deceive us even as we come to recognize their distortions. The object whose image the mirror reflects appears to lie beyond the mirror, even though I know that it is but a reflected image that I see in the mirror and that the object whose image I see resides elsewhere. I can correct my sensory perception, teach myself not to be fooled by its illusory appearance, and yet I still perceive it as such.[104] It is in this way that optical illusions are similar to transcendental ones: in both, we continue to be deceived even after we have come to understand the illusion. In optical illusions, it is the imagination that misleads, continuing to offer us such impossible objects; in transcendental illusions, reason continues to be drawn beyond the limits of possible experience. This, Kant explains, is not to conflate optical with transcendental illusions, for in the former our judgment is deceived by the imagination, while in the latter the deception follows from the application beyond their proper limits of concepts born of experience (A295/B352).

In both optical and transcendental illusions, we can learn to avoid accepting these illusory claims. We avoid being deceived by the optical illusion by means of the object. The stick when removed from the water once again appears straight; it offers us the criteria to deem its submerged appearance illusory and so functions for our empirical judgments as the "touchstone [*Probierstein*] for their correctness" (A295/B352). Transcendental illusions offer no such object in relation to which their illusions can be uncovered. The "touchstone of truth" for the use of reason beyond the limits of possible experience is, Kant explains, "the systematic unity of the understanding's cognitions" (A647/B675). But how can such "systematic unity," which is never fully attained, stand as the criterion to judge the uses of reason beyond the limits of possible experience? This problem is particularly difficult since the unity that is to act as the touchstone of our judgment is itself precisely the sort of metaphysical claim that it is meant to help us avoid. Kant offers the metaphor of the mirror's reflective power to address just such a problem. In conceiving of the ideas of reason—the objects of metaphysics that are forever beyond our cognitive reach—as if they were seen outside our field of vision and visible only in the mirror's reflection, we are reminded that the unity which they direct, that of the understanding in its fullest extension, must be taken as elusive. The first *Critique* offers a reflective systemization of the totality of our thought, a mirroring of both what is within our field of vision and what is beyond it. The former are empirical objects, while the latter, which are outside our field of vision, are the ideas of metaphysics; and it is the ideas of metaphysical thought that, in our turning from their direct but illusory pursuit, guide the unified account of the faculties of finite cognition.

The reflective system that transcendental philosophy offers us depends upon the images of objects that are forever outside our field of vision; that which is beyond our finite faculties offers the *focus imaginarius* that directs the conceptual unity of the analysis of all that constitutes our field of vision, and so the varied empirical workings of cognition. Transcendental philosophy is thus marked by both a turning from, and a reflection on, the objects of metaphysics that direct the examination of finite cognition. Such metaphysical ideas must not be taken as objects to be known in themselves, but rather as regulative principles that are distinguished through the reflective accomplishments of the mirror-like capacities of transcendental inquiry. Metaphysics has been purified by critique when we have come to pursue its illusory objects as if they were reflected images that offer our finite faculties, among other things, the goal of their systematic unity.

In the case of the psychological idea, the subject of thought, conceived by means of the unknowable idea of the soul, offers the regulative principle for the act of transcendental reflection; as was shown above, such an act distinguishes the region of experience from all mere metaphysical thought and so allows for the analysis of the faculty of the understanding. The psychological idea helps to explain how Kantian critique directs its inquiry, offering an account of not merely how it is that such an idea of reason is used but how, in fact, Kant distinguishes between what lies "before our eyes" and what "lies far in the background" and so outside our field of vision, when such a distinction cannot be properly justified. This is to say that Kantian critique begins without being able to justify the distinction between the phenomenal objects that are sensibly given to us and the metaphysical ideas toward which we strive; both, in the language of the metaphor, are reflected on the mirror's surface.[105] The regulative role played by the psychological idea permits Kant his transcendental system, offering an answer to the seemingly unanswerable question posed in the *Prolegomena*, concerning the differentiation of phenomena and noumena: "Both are considered together in our reason, and the question arises: how does reason proceed in setting boundaries for the understanding with respect to both fields?"[106]

V. Conclusion:
The Structure of Transcendental Philosophy

The account of transcendental reflection in the appendix to the Transcendental Analytic of the first *Critique* announces the regulative foundation of the entire critical project. The boundary that affords both the account of finite cognition and the critique of metaphysics is distinguished not by the *a priori* necessity of a determinate judgment, but by a reflective judgment that is directed by a regulative principle. The regulative goal that directs transcendental reflection and thus all *a priori* judgment, following from the psychological idea, distinguishes the boundary of possible experience through which conceptual analysis is directed to the limits of ontology. And yet it also must be remembered that the critique of the metaphysical idea of the rational subject that distinguishes this regulative principle is itself dependent upon the analysis of possible experience. The role of such a regulative principle in the analysis of our finite faculties thus demonstrates the circularity of the Kantian enterprise.

Such an orienting of critique explains why, in the Transcendental Aesthetic, Kant begins his analysis of cognition with the presupposition of the priority of outer over inner sense for transcendental philosophy. He writes that "the representations **of outer sense** make up the proper material [*eigentlichen Stoff*] with which we occupy our mind" (B67). But why is the "proper material" of thought that which is spatially determined? Why should we occupy our minds with what is intuited spatially and can be determined as an empirical object, rather than with those thoughts that offer no spatial appearances? The answer should by now be clear: We must occupy ourselves with those thoughts, those representations, that offer outer sense, and not merely the temporal determination of inner sense, because it is the analysis of the limited region of spatial appearances that permits the construction of the system of transcendental philosophy while avoiding both the errors to which our metaphysical dispositions are drawn and the internal inconsistencies that follow from attempts to address merely the temporal constitution of thought.

The regulative principle emanating from the psychological idea demarcates the realm of objects of experience, that of spatial appearances, from within the flux of thought. Such a principle is implied in the analysis of objectivity that discloses both the *a priori* structure of cognition and the limits of conceptual analysis. Thus, it is such a regulative principle that underlies the division of the faculties of understanding and reason, the division born of transcendental reflection over the representational manifold. And it is this division of faculties that limits the examination of cognition to that which offers the confluence of the sensible and the intellectual. The regulative use of reason, after the critique of its metaphysical pretensions, does not pursue an objective principle constitutive of its object; yet the use of such a principle is still, as Kant writes, "objective, but in an indeterminate way (as *principum vagum*)" (A680/B708), since it promotes the understanding's coherent "experiential and determinate use" (B694/A666) without presupposing the determinate metaphysical concept of the unity of the thinking self. The use of such a principle (*Prinzip*) is indeterminate, inasmuch as it affords no cognition. It is not a principle (*Prinzip*) in the full sense of the term, but neither is it a principle in the sense of a *Grundsatz*, of the sort that the categories afford when the sensible is subsumed beneath them;[107] rather, it is a regulative principle (*Prinzip*) that, in directing the analysis of our unified cognitive faculties, orients Kantian critique.

NOTES

Introduction

1. Citations from Kant's *Critique of Pure Reason* (first *Critique*) follow the standard A and B pagination of the first and second editions, respectively, and are placed within the text. References to Kant's other books provide the page number of the translation listed in the bibliography (changes to translations are noted), as well as a bracketed reference to the volume and page number of the *Akademie-Ausgabe* (AA). References to translated works of other authors will give the page number of the translation followed by a bracketed reference to the original edition. If no published translation is cited, the translation is my own.

2. Kant interpreters in the Anglo-American tradition have addressed the self, the subject, or, more typically, the mind of Kantian critique. I will address a number of these interpreters in chapters 1 and 3. Patricia Kitcher and Wayne Waxman exemplify the opposing claims. Kitcher minimizes the claims of the Kantian project, arguing that all Kant offers is an analysis of the phenomenal self (*Kant's Transcendental Psychology*, 22), while Waxman claims that in terms of the subject of critique, Kant has contradicted his professed limits on cognition by introducing a "thing in itself at the center" of his account of cognition (*Kant's Model of the Mind*, 272).

3. Gary Hatfield criticizes Kant for the dependence of his analysis on a conception of experience, arguing that he fails to address his presuppositions: "In taking these starting points as a given, Kant was remarkably oblivious to the charge of begging the question" (*The Natural and the Normative*, 80).

4. Others, including Rüdiger Bubner, Pierre Kerszberg, Pauline Kleingeld, Claude Piché, and Dieter Sturma, have interpreted Kantian critique in terms of such self-referentiality or circularity. I will address these interpreters in chapter 3.

5. Heidegger, *What Is a Thing?* 244 [189].

6. Later in this introduction, I will return to a discussion of Heidegger's analysis of the Kantian transcendental imagination as just such a prior moment.

7. Translation altered.

8. The regulative roles played by the cosmological and the theological ideas (the world and God, respectively) will be investigated in chapter 2. The examination of the regulative role of the psychological idea is the goal of this entire book and will be most directly addressed in chapter 6.

9. Doing so will agree with Karl Ameriks that Kant's lectures on metaphysics demonstrate a continued interest on his part in these arguments, even after he rejected the possibility of knowledge of their objects (Ameriks, "Kant's Lectures on Metaphysics," 25); however, it will offer a way to conceive of such a metaphysical influence on Kant's account of finite cognition without "supplementing Kant's doctrines" by accepting a "modest mentalism" in his name, as Ameriks does (*Kant's Theory of Mind*, 8).

10. Both Pauline Kleingeld and Heinz Heimsoeth investigate the regulative role of the psychological idea, but while Kleingeld writes that it distinguishes "reason's interest in its own unity" (Kleingeld, "Kant on the Unity of Theoretical and Practical Reason,"

318), both maintain that what it offers is merely an account of the empirical subject rather than the transcendental subject that is distinguished in Kant's first *Critique* (Heimsoeth, *Transzendentale Dialektik, Dritter Teil*, 617).

11. Kant goes so far as to argue that our assuming knowledge of the "highest order being" does not grant us the "unity of nature" but "does away with it" (A693/B721, translation altered). If we take the idea of God as a regulative goal for our analysis of nature, then we can progressively pursue such unity in our investigation of nature; but if we instead assume knowledge of such an idea, then we will have disconnected it from the appearances of nature, deeming any apparent unity as merely a "contingent [*zufällig*]" occurrence.

12. See Hamann, "Metacritique of the Purism of Reason."

13. See A672/B700 and A682–83/B710–11.

14. Title translation altered; I have decided to use the traditional English title of this book, *Critique of Judgment* (third *Critique*), rather than the more literal *Critique of the Power of Judgment* that is used in the Cambridge translation. The importance of §76 is emphasized by both Schelling (*Of the I as the Principle of Philosophy*, 127 [vol. 2, 175]) and Heidegger ("Kant's Thesis about Being," 355 [469]).

15. See the First Introduction to the *Critique of Judgment*, where purposiveness is introduced in section v in discussing the principle of all reflective judgment, or what Kant describes as "a peculiar [*eigentümlicher*] concept of the reflective power of judgment" (Kant, *Critique of Judgment*, First Introduction, v, 19 [AA 20, 216], translation altered); see also sections vi and x in the First Introduction, and sections v–viii in the Second Introduction (which was the introduction that was originally published).

16. Kant terms this "the hypothetical use of reason [*der hypothetische Gebrauche der Vernunft*]" (A647/B675).

17. For a naturalizing reading of Kant, see Walsh, "Philosophy and Psychology in Kant's *Critique*," 196; and for an attempt to transform Kant into a realist, see Ameriks, *Kant's Theory of Mind*, 169–70. For discussion of these and other related interpreters, see chapter 3.

18. Heidegger, *What Is a Thing?* 241–42 [187–88].

19. Ibid., 242 [188].

20. A15/B29; see Heidegger, *Kant and the Problem of Metaphysics*, 112 [160]; and Sallis, *Spacings—of Reason and Imagination*, 73–81. For a criticism of Heidegger's association of the transcendental imagination with Kant's source of the dual stems of cognition, that "which may perhaps arise from a common but to us unknown root," see Henrich, *The Unity of Reason*, 19–21. Henrich raises the possibility that such a root is described by Kant as "unknown" not because we have until now failed to conceive of it but because it is by definition beyond our faculties and so relates to the noumenal realm. I will return to this question in chapter 4.

21. Heidegger, *Kant and the Problem of Metaphysics*, §31, 112 [160].

22. Heidegger, *What Is a Thing?* 242 [188].

23. Heidegger, "Kant's Thesis about Being," 337–63 [445–80].

24. Ibid., 361 [478].

25. For Hegel's criticism of Kant's first *Critique*, see Hegel, *Faith and Knowledge*, 90 [vol. 4, 341]. I will address his criticism of Kant in chapter 4.

26. Kant, "What Does It Mean to Orient Oneself in Thinking?" 7–18 [AA 8, 131–47].

27. The pantheism controversy (*Pantheismusstreit*) pitted Friedrich Heinrich Jacobi against Moses Mendelssohn, with the former arguing that Mendelssohn's close friend Lessing was, at the end of his life, a Spinozist. Jacobi's charge was that Lessing had in

this way embraced a pantheism that was essentially a fatalistic atheism. Mendelssohn attempted to defend Lessing against this charge by arguing for the role of common sense in limiting rational speculation, but in so doing he risked embracing the very anti-rationalism that Jacobi promoted and that he wished to reject. In Kant's entrance into this controversy, he briefly defended Mendelssohn's conception of common sense before offering his own account of the role of reason in thinking, one that neither denigrated such a faculty nor praised it in a manner that excluded the possibility of human freedom. See chapter 6 for further discussion of this episode.

28. Andrew Brook, for instance, claims that transcendental apperception offers an awareness of the noumenal self (*Kant and the Mind*, 250–52).

ONE • The Ideas of Reason

1. Kant, *Anthropology from a Pragmatic Point of View*, 231 [AA 7, 119], translation altered. Kant's *Anthropology* was published in 1798, although Kant first lectured on this topic in 1772.

2. Ibid.

3. See A848–49/B876–77, where Kant connects empirical psychology to anthropology.

4. In the *Anthropology*, Kant explains that he will set aside "physiological" anthropology, the study of "what **nature** makes of the human being," in favor of a "pragmatic" anthropology, the study of what a human being "makes of himself, or can and should make of himself" (Kant, *Anthropology*, 231 [AA 7, 119]). (Following the general rule of the Cambridge edition, I have used bold type in the English translation to represent Kant's *Fettdruck*, rather than the italics which are used in a few of the works, including the *Anthropology* and the *Prolegomena*.) In the *Critique of Pure Reason*, Kant disparages such empirical psychology, which he refers to as a "physiology of the human understanding" in reference to Locke (Aix), and its rationalist counterpart, the "physiology of inner sense" (B405/A347), which he opposes in the Paralogisms. I will return to the question of Kant's conception of physiology at the end of this chapter, and then again in chapter 6.

5. The mind is a kind of theatre, where several perceptions successively make their appearance; pass, re-pass, glide away, and mingle in an infinite variety of postures and situations. . . . The comparison of the theatre must not mislead us, they are the successive perceptions only, that constitute the mind; nor have we the most distant notion of the place, where these scenes are represented, or of the materials, of which it is compos'd. (Hume, *A Treatise of Human Nature*, 165)

6. Kant describes his undertaking as an "experiment [*Versuch*]" in the introduction to the second edition of the *Critique of Pure Reason* (Bxvii).

7. For Hume's description of the self as a "bundle," see *A Treatise of Human Nature*, 165. I will return to the skepticism introduced in the first edition's Third Paralogism in chapter 3.

8. Translation altered.

9. Kant writes: "*wir uns gegen uns selbst als leidend verhalten müßten*" (B153). While *leidend* is more typically translated as "suffering," and so the relation to ourselves would be what we suffer or what is borne by us, Kant does not seem to be implying any such hardship. Heiner Klemme explains that what is at issue is passivity; the paradox concerns how we can conceive of ourselves as "at the same time active and passive subjects [*zugleich aktiven und passiven Subjekts*]" (*Kants Philosophie des Subjekts*, 222).

10. Kant explains that the "transcendental unity of apperception" that brings unity to the manifold does so by means of offering an *a priori* identity (A108/B134) that is itself but an analytic, and not a synthetic, unity (B134). Dieter Henrich emphasizes these two passages in "Die Identität des Subjekts in der transzendentalen Deduktion," 52. On the conception of identity that is here manifested, and particularly on its connection to the rules of the understanding, see Henrich, "Identity and Objectivity: An Inquiry into Kant's Transcendental Deduction," in his *The Unity of Reason*, 199–204 (*Identität und Objektivität*, 101–107).

11. See also Kant's First Analogy of Experience (B224–32/A182–89), where he argues that substance as persisting is required of all temporal succession.

12. This might be one of the reasons why in the second edition Kant adds a discussion of the priority of space over time to the end of the Transcendental Aesthetic. Kant describes "the representations of outer sense" as "the proper material [*den eigentlich Stoff*] with which we occupy our mind" (B67). I will return to this emphasis on spatiality.

13. In the *Anthropology*, Kant describes a "paradox" as a "semblance [*Anschein*] of egoism," born of an interest in contradicting what is commonly held (Kant, *Anthropology*, 241 [AA 7, 129]). Kant explains that if this paradox is pursued for reasons other than merely wanting to appear exceptional, then it "arouses [*erweckt*] our mind to pay attention and investigate the matter—and this often leads to discoveries" (ibid.).

14. In the second edition's Transcendental Dialectic, Kant writes: "We cannot **think** any object [*Gegenstand*] except through categories; we cannot **cognize** any object that is thought except through intuitions that correspond to these concepts" (B165; see also B146–47, A50/B74); and in the famous passage in the introduction to the Transcendental Logic, Kant writes: "Thoughts without content are empty, intuitions without concepts are blind" (B75/A51).

15. In *Being and Time*, Heidegger criticizes Kant's account of our spatial orientation by arguing that Kant can only explain how we might orient ourselves in a darkened room where the furnishings have been reversed by means of presupposing a prior knowledge of the objects that are in the room; and in general that Kant is unable to justify the conception of objects with which he begins his analysis (*Being and Time*, §23, 101–102 [109–110]). I will investigate Heidegger's criticism of the Kantian conception of objects in both chapters 4 and 6; Kant's essay "What Does It Mean to Orient Oneself in Thinking?" will be addressed in chapter 6.

16. Wayne Waxman describes this problem concisely:

> [T]he faculty-endowed mind confronts us with what appears to be a quite
> determinate thing in itself right at the center of Kant's supposedly critical
> philosophy: the *source and ground* of our various modes of representation;
> something possessed of a definite constitution; something which acts and
> is affected (by both itself and other things in themselves); and so on. (*Kant's
> Model of the Mind*, 272)

17. Patricia Kitcher denies the distinction between the transcendental I of apperception and the empirical self, arguing, contra Kant's claims, that what he offers is a transcendental psychology as a phenomenal investigation of the underlying thinking self (*Kant's Transcendental Psychology*, 22; see also 140–41, where Kitcher argues against the ideality of time). Andrew Brook argues, contra Kitcher, that we are aware of our noumenal selves in transcendental apperception (*Kant and the Mind*, 250–52), but it is hard to see what is won by such a designation, since Brook recognizes that this awareness implies only "that I am" (ibid., 256; B157) and not in any sense *what* I am.

18. Kant's unusual capitalization of the pronouns *Er* and *Es* is maintained in the translation.

19. Translation altered. Dieter Sturma explains: "Because the 'I think' is included in all of my experienced states [*Weil das 'Ich denke' in allen meinen Erfahrungszuständen enthalten ist*]," I cannot have any concept of it ("Die Paralogismen der reinen Vernunft in der zweiten Auflage," 402); see also Sturma, *Kant über Selbstbewußtsein*, 41). The circularity of critique, and thus of the transcendental system itself, will be an important theme of this entire book; I continue with a discussion of the circularity implicit in the relation of the categories of the understanding to the conception of experience in chapter 3, and a discussion of the circularity of the transcendental system itself in chapter 6.

20. Patricia Kitcher, in "Kant's Real Self," explicitly denies Kant's claim that the subject cannot come to know itself as an object by means of the categories, claiming that "Kant is simply confusing the order of proof with what we might call the order of conceivability" (124). Kitcher recognizes that the unity of apperception must be presupposed in order to deduce the categories, but she claims that the methodological questions related to the order of proof do not imply that the self cannot be thought by means of the categories, for what is proved is that "the only way that we can think at all is through the categories" (ibid., 126). And yet, to deny that Kant has here raised any sort of methodological concern about self-knowledge is to turn Kant into Hume, and so, Allison explains, the "ineliminable" nature of apperception is lost (*Idealism and Freedom*, 66).

21. In chapter 5 I examine the Paralogisms of Pure Reason chapter of the *Critique of Pure Reason*, Kant's arguments against the possibility of a properly rational psychology, and in chapter 6 the uses to which Kant directs such inquiries once we have accepted their limitations.

22. Gottfried Martin asks about this "subject which underlies what is said in the *Critique of Pure Reason*," agreeing that it can be neither the empirical nor the transcendental subject (the former raised by Fries and the latter by neo-Kantians) (*Kant's Metaphysics and Theory of Science*, 177 [207]). Martin offers as his answer the intelligible subject that can be thought but, according to the limits on Kantian knowledge, is unknowable; his answer, as he recognizes, raises "unbridgeable difficulties [*unüberbrückbaren Schwierigkeiten*]" (ibid., 181 [211]). While little can be said of the knowing subject, our commitment to this idea, Martin explains, is born of the "acting subject," and the "intelligible existence of the acting subject is beyond all doubt" (ibid., 181 [212]). Could one agree with Martin that the acting subject has priority, and yet still ask whether there is a properly transcendental way to speak of the Kantian self?

23. Kant distinguishes two general types of metaphysical failure: arguments that attempt to attain knowledge of metaphysical objects are either inherently contradictory, as in the cosmological idea that Kant investigates in the Antinomy of Pure Reason, or inconclusive, as in the psychological and the theological ideas investigated by Kant in the Paralogisms of Pure Reason and the Ideal of Pure Reason, respectively.

24. In the appendix that follows the Transcendental Dialectic in the first *Critique*, Kant describes the theological idea, "the presupposition of a supreme intelligence," as the "**purposive** unity of things [*zweckmäßige Einheit der Dinge*]" (A686–88/B714–16); and in the third *Critique*, Kant introduces "purposiveness" as the regulative principle of reflective judgment in section v of the First Introduction (19 [AA 20, 216]) and in section iv of the Second Introduction (68 [AA 5, 180–81]). See chapter 2 for further discussion of purposiveness. The question of the continuity between the first and third *Critiques* is highly contested. I will argue that while it is true that Kant has further developed both the implications of his system and his terminology in the third *Critique*, there is not any fundamental shift in the

system itself. Interpreters who agree with me in arguing for such continuity include Henry Allison in "Is the *Critique of Judgment* 'Post-Critical'?" (83); Helga Mertens in *Kommentar zur Ersten Einleitung in Kants Kritik der Urteilskraft* (33–46); Bernard Rousset in *La Doctrine Kantienne de l'objectivité* (475–81); Klaus Düsing in *Die Teleologie in Kants Weltbegriff* (38–50); and Michael Friedman in *Kant and the Exact Sciences* (180–83). Interpreters who disagree, who argue that the third *Critique* offers a fundamentally new conception that leads beyond the critical system of the first *Critique*, include Rolf-Peter Horstmann in *Bausteine kritischer Theorie* (127–28); Rudolf Makkreel in "Regulative and Reflective Uses of Purposiveness in Kant" (50–52); and Burkhard Tuschling in both "Intuitiver Verstand, absolute Identität, Idee" (183) and "The System of Transcendental Idealism" (118). I will return to this question and address these and other interpreters in chapter 6.

25. For Kant's account of the role of a regulative principle in mechanism, see A508–15/B536–43, and chapter 2 below.

26. Hegel's claim is that Kant attempted to produce just such an account of appearances bereft of metaphysical input, turning from the realm of metaphysics, the thought of which he "despised [*verachtet*]," to that of appearances (Hegel, *Faith and Knowledge*, 90 [vol. 4, 341]); and yet, Hegel argues, Kant failed at this undertaking and was forced to admit its illicit commitment to just such metaphysical entities. Hegel points to the account of the transcendental unity of apperception as such an instance (ibid., 69 [vol. 4, 327]). I will return to Hegel's interpretation of Kant in chapter 4. The analysis he offers of Kant's intentions, that Kant attempted to examine appearances free of all metaphysical claim, has been greatly influential, both for those who, with him, reject Kant and for those who want to defend Kant in just this way. For such a defense of Kant, one could look back to Hermann Cohen, who reverses the order of the Transcendental Analytic and argues that the categories are dependent upon the principles (*Grundsätze*) of the understanding (*Kants Theorie der Erfahrung*, 345–46). Such principles offer the unity of experience as their highest accomplishment, a conception of experience that is deemed by Cohen to be scientific (ibid., 187). Among current interpreters, one could look to those who continue to defend Kant in a realist manner, although they claim rather less than the authority of Newtonian science for what is described as the "commonsense" spatiotemporal world (e.g., Westphal, *Kant's Transcendental Proof of Realism*, 3). One can also see the Hegelian influence in those who defend Kant's analysis of our faculties as accounts of our self-evident human capacities, regardless of the claims that can be made for the objects that they uncover. Examples of such attempts to naturalize Kant's epistemology include W. H. Walsh, "Philosophy and Psychology in Kant's *Critique*," 196; and Lewis White Beck, "Toward a Meta-Critique of Pure Reason," in his *Essays on Kant and Hume*, 25. I will address both realist and naturalist defenses of Kant in chapter 3.

27. The "principles [*Grundsätze*]" of the understanding both permit us experience and are themselves proven only by means of this conception of experience. Martin Heidegger develops an account of such Kantian circularity in *What Is a Thing?* (241–42 [187–88]). I will address Heidegger's analysis in chapter 3. On the "self-referentiality [*Selbstbezüglichkeit*]" of Kantian critique, see Rüdiger Bubner ("Zur Struktur eines Transzendentalen Arguments," 23–25, and "Kant, Transcendental Arguments and the Problem of Deduction," 462–66); Dieter Sturma ("Die Paralogismen der reinen Vernunft in der zweiten Auflage," 402–403, and *Kant über Selbstbewußtsein*, 41); and Claude Piché ("Self-Referentiality in Kant's Transcendental Philosophy," 264). Pierre Kerszberg refers to such circularity as the paradox of critique (*Critique and Totality*, 87). The role played by such circularity more generally in Kant's system will be addressed in chapter 6.

28. I will return in chapter 6 to Kant's appendix to the Transcendental Dialectic and the account of the post-critical role of the idea of the soul; see especially A682–84/B710–12.

29. Both Hamann and Herder need to be mentioned in relation to the earliest demand for a metacritique (Hamann, "Metacritique of the Purism of Reason"; and Herder, "Eine Metakritik zur Kritik der reinen Vernunft"). I will investigate Hamann's metacritical demands in the pages to come.

30. Hamann wrote his "Metacritique of the Purism of Reason" in 1784, but it was not published until 1800; it was, however, read by both Herder and Jacobi in its unpublished form (see Beiser, *The Fate of Reason*, 38).

31. Hamann, "Metacritique of the Purism of Reason," 522 [vol. 3, 286], translation altered.

32. Ibid., 525 [vol. 3, 289], translation altered.

33. Oswald Bayer explains that Hamann first uses the term "metacritique" in a letter to Herder written on July 7, 1782 (Hamann, *Briefwechsel*, vol. 4, 400), in the context of a discussion of both Kant and Hume (Bayer, *Vernunft ist Sprache*, 207).

34. Hamann, "Metacritique of the Purism of Reason," 522 [vol. 3, 286].

35. Frederick Beiser describes Hamann's undertaking as a return to a faith that is "neither demonstrable nor refutable by" reason (*The Fate of Reason*, 28).

36. Kant, *Prolegomena to Any Future Metaphysics*, §21a, 97 [AA 4, 304].

37. This passage from the first edition's preface to the *Critique of Pure Reason*, concerning the ordering of our philosophical questioning, will be directly addressed in chapter 5. Such a question raises the general theme of Kant's transcendental method: we must first approach cognition, pursuing a methodologically unjustified account of experience, in order to then investigate the presuppositions that permit this analysis.

38. Hamann, "Metacritique of the Purism of Reason," 522 [vol. 3, 286].

39. Bayer explains that Hamann rejects Kant's "chief question," which emphasizes the *a priori* concepts apart from experience, because all concepts are for him linguistic and their roots are to be found in experience (Bayer, *Vernunft ist Sprache*, 314).

40. Heidegger quotes this passage from Hamann (*Briefwechsel*, vol. 5, 177) in his essay "Language" (in *Poetry, Language, Thought*, 191 [13]); the letter was begun on August 6, 1784, with sections written on both the eighth and the tenth. Heidegger sets aside the question of reason and investigates language itself as language: "But we do not ask now what reason may be; here we reflect immediately on language and take as our main clue [*Wink*] the curious statement, 'Language is language'True ("Language," 191 [13]). Hamann has directed him to the abyss of language by means of a "glance, aimed at reason," that "falls into the depths of an abyss." The language of our worlds does not offer itself for rational analysis, as the groundlessness of this abyss opens for us the depth of language, which cannot be captured in the rational structures that are themselves products of this process.

41. Kant, AA 10, 15.

42. See Beiser, *The Fate of Reason*, 24.

43. Kant, *Prolegomena*, §59, 150 (AA 4, 361).

44. Kant explains that "a point is the boundary of the line, yet is nonetheless a *locus* in space" (Kant, *Prolegomena*, §57, 144 [AA 4, 354]).

45. Ibid., §59, 150 [AA 4, 361], translation altered.

46. Interpreters who have addressed this section include Henry Allison (*Kant's Transcendental Idealism* [1983], 7; [2004], 56); Martin Heidegger ("Kant's Thesis about Being," 357–59 [472–75]); Robert Pippin ("Kant on the Spontaneity of the Mind," in his

Idealism as Modernism, 457); and Gerold Prauss (*Kant und das Problem der Dinge an sich*, 82). I will further address these and other interpreters in chapter 4.

47. The term *sensifiziert* is translated by Guyer and Wood as "sensitivized"; by translating it as "sensualized," I have followed both Norman Kemp Smith (London: Macmillan, 1929) and Werner H. Pluhar (Indianapolis: Hackett, 1996).

48. Kant's conception of transcendental reflection will be addressed in chapter 4.

49. Kant, *Prolegomena*, preface, 57 [AA 4, 260].

50. Hume's investigation in *A Treatise of Human Nature* argues that all complex unities are merely associations of simple ideas, dependent upon sense impressions, and joined together through the habitual thought patterns of our experience. Thus, the idea of gold that I have does not refer to a constant meaning or value, since it is forged through a process of association that is never complete. For Hume, the ideas of both gold and souls refer to the general terms that have come to name the conjoined chains of particular sense impressions (see *A Treatise of Human Nature*, 16, for a reference to gold, and 261–62 for soul/self-identity).

51. Kant, *Prolegomena*, §50, 129 [AA 4, 338].

52. While in the *Prolegomena* Kant mentions merely the antinomies in general, in reference to his awakening from dogmatism, in his letter to Garve of September 21, 1798, he refers directly to the third antinomy, that of freedom versus the necessity of nature, although while describing it he mistakenly refers to it as the fourth (Kant, *Correspondence*, 551–52 [AA 12, 257–58]).

53. Kant, *Prolegomena*, preface, 57 [AA 4, 260].

54. See Hamann, "Metacritique of the Purism of Reason," 522 [vol. 3, 286].

55. Kant, *Correspondence*, 551–52 [AA 12, 257–58].

56. Unlike Lewis White Beck, who addresses the contradictory claims made by Kant on behalf of what woke him from his "dogmatic slumber" by claiming that these two reported wake-up calls refer to "very different problems," I find no such radical disparity (Beck, "A Prussian Hume and a Scottish Kant," in his *Essays on Kant and Hume*). Beck points out that the reference to the antinomy in §50 of the *Prolegomena* lacks the autobiographical claim offered in the preface to the same work (the reference to Hume having awakened him from dogmatism)—Kant writes only that the antinomy has the power to "awaken philosophy from its dogmatic slumber" (Kant, *Prolegomena*, §50, 129 [AA 4, 338])—and Beck also argues that these sources sound different alarms. He maintains that the reference in §50 to the antinomies refers to 1769, the preliminary awakening that led to the Inaugural Dissertation (*On the Form and Principles of the Sensible and Intelligible World*) and showed that intelligible objects were not spatial, while the reference to Hume as the cause of Kant's awakening follows a later revision and refers to the full-blown critical project. Even if we accept this distinction, we still must address Kant's letter to Garve of 1798 (Kant, *Correspondence*, 551–52 [AA 12, 257–58]), where the antinomy is again described as having awakened Kant, for this reference to the antinomy is certainly not pre-critical. It is, Beck would appear to be claiming, post-critical, insofar as Kant was by this time complaining in the same letter of declining mental abilities. Could it be, Beck writes, that the return in 1798 to the claim that the antinomy sparked the critical project is "due to a lapse of memory" ("A Prussian Hume and a Scottish Kant," in his *Essays on Kant and Hume*, 119n23), and that it is the expression of one who was losing his critical powers? This appears to be a rather forced conclusion and, it seems to me, an unnecessary one since there need not be only a single catalyst for the critical project. This is not to refute the claim that the antinomy awakened Kant to the Inaugural Dissertation; rather, it is to raise the possibility that Kant referred to the antinomy in the *Prolegomena*, and returned to it in

the letter to Garve in 1798, because the response that it had originally engendered—that is, the distinction between spatial objects and metaphysical thoughts—still held for him.

57. Following Lewis White Beck's lead, I want to see whether a literal response to such rhetorical challenges is possible. See below for further discussion of his important essay "Toward a Meta-Critique of Pure Reason," in his *Essays on Kant and Hume*, 20–37.

58. Kant writes:

> Therefore, the empirical doctrine of the soul can never become anything more than an historical doctrine of nature, and, as such, a natural doctrine of inner sense which is as systematic as possible, that is, a natural description of the soul, but never a science of the soul [*Seelenwissenschaft*], nor even, indeed, an experimental psychological doctrine. (Kant, *Metaphysical Foundations of Natural Science*, 186 [AA 4, 471])

59. In the *Anthropology*, as was explained at the start of this chapter, Kant clearly holds out no hope for a physiology through which we would empirically pursue "knowledge of man [*Kenntnis des Menschen*]" (Kant, *Anthropology*, 231 [AA 7, 119]).

60. See A36/B53, B152–53, B158, and the above discussion of these pages.

61. Beck looks to the physiology of the soul (A846/B874) as a way to explain the "otherwise brutally factual attributes of mind which are presupposed without argument in the *Critique [of Pure Reason]*" ("Toward a Meta-Critique of Pure Reason," in his *Essays on Kant and Hume*, 35). Following François Duchesneau's explanation of the teleological conception of physiology in the eighteenth century ("Kant et la 'physiologie de l'entendement humain,'" 272–73), Beck argues that the physiology of thinking nature could itself be conceived as a teleological accomplishment. Duchesneau raises the foundational role of the physiology of thinking nature, explaining that it helps to direct the analysis of the system of understanding without determining its objective nature (ibid., 275). Yet neither Beck nor Duchesneau offers a way to explain how a teleological accomplishment that unifies mechanistic law is able to explain the prior designation of the cognitive faculties which themselves permit the analysis of mechanistic law. Howard Caygill does not offer a solution to this problem either, but by looking further back to uncover the roots of Kantian physiology in the works of Paracelsus, Telesio, and Campanella, in the sixteenth and early seventeenth centuries, for whom physiology came to be the study of heat as the animating force of matter, its *vis vita*, he is able to draw a suggestive connection to Kant's late *Opus Postumum* with its conception of "caloric [*Wärmestoff*]" (Caygill, "Life and Energy," 22; Kant, *Opus Postumum*, 47 [AA 22, 141]).

TWO • The Boundary of Phenomena and Noumena

1. Kant, *Prolegomena*, §60, 152 [AA 4, 364], translation altered. I have translated *überverdienstlich* as "super-meritorious," following Mary J. Gregor in her translation of the *Critique of Practical Reason*. In this work, Kant explains that he wants educators to avoid giving their "pupils examples of so-called *noble [edler]* (super-meritorious [*überverdienstlicher*]) actions," and to emphasize instead moral duty. In so doing, one can avoid introducing the goal of an "inaccessible perfection [which] produces mere heroes of romance who, while they pride themselves on their feeling for extravagant greatness, release themselves in return from the observance of common and everyday obligation [*Schuldigkeit*]" (Kant, *Critique of Practical Reason*, 263–64 [AA 5, 155]). In our moral life we should avoid attempting to go beyond duty, but in our speculative inquiries there is a role to be played by the metaphysical ideas beyond that of moral duty.

2. Kant, *Prolegomena*, §60, 152 [AA 4, 364].

3. Kant begins this discussion by describing such an investigation as concerned not with "the objective validity of metaphysical judgments, but rather the natural predisposition to such judgments, and therefore [it] lies outside the system of metaphysics, in anthropology" (ibid., 151 [AA 4, 362]). What such an anthropology would be, Kant does not explain, describing such an undertaking as "merely conjectural" (ibid.). I will return to the question of anthropology in chapter 6.

4. Ibid., 152 [AA 4, 364].

5. Ibid.

6. Ibid., §59, 149 [AA 4, 360].

7. Ibid., §60, 153 [AA 4, 364]. How could what appears to be integral to the accomplishments of critique be deemed by Kant to be peripheral, and a task not for all those who want to be critical, but merely for "experts [*Kenner*]" in the accomplished system? Such a question will lead us to the need to distinguish the accomplishments that the investigation of the understanding makes possible from what supports such investigation.

8. Kant writes in §60 of the *Prolegomena* (152–53, AA 4, 364), in his discussion of the influence of reason over the understanding, that "experience, too, [can] be indirectly subject to the legislation of reason."

9. I will return to the cosmological idea and the two areas of regulative accomplishment that follow from it—the mechanistic analysis of nature and practical freedom—later in this chapter.

10. Kant, *Prolegomena*, §60, 152 [AA 4, 364].

11. Schelling, "Of the I as the Principle of Philosophy," 127 [vol. 2, 175]. Schelling's words are reiterated by Heidegger in his essay "Kant's Thesis about Being," 355 [469]; yet neither explicitly explains these profound thoughts. I will address the context of these remarks, in both Schelling and Heidegger, in chapter 4.

12. Kant, *Critique of Judgment*, §76, 271 [AA 5, 401].

13. The same phrasing is at A299/B356.

14. I too will be careful to distinguish the type of principle to which I refer as *Grundsatz* or *Prinzip* for lack of better English translations. To conflate these two terms, as some would have it (see, for instance, Werner Pluhar in his translation of the *Critique of Pure Reason*, 5–6, Avii, n. 7), overlooks Kant's attempt to distinguish the two (A299/B356) and leads to the assumption that the Transcendental Analytic offers a positive discussion of principles of the understanding, while the Transcendental Dialectic offers a merely negative discussion of the attempt to ascertain principles. With their distinction, following Kant's discussion at A299–303/B355–59, and the designation of the principles (*Prinzipien*) that only apply to reason's use, we are led to investigate the sense in which the illusory ideas of reason still offer principles; the answer offered most explicitly in §76 is that they offer regulative principles (*Prinzipien*). On the difference between *Grundsätze* and *Prinzipien*, see Sallis, *The Gathering of Reason* (42); and Heimsoeth, *Transzendentale Dialektik, Erster Teil* (17–18).

15. Kant goes on to write that all universal propositions, even when they "cannot at all furnish synthetic cognition from concepts," can still "be called comparative principles [*komparative Prinzipien*]" (A301/B358, translation altered), which is to say *Grundsätze*.

16. On the difference between *Vernunft* and *Verstand* for Kant, see Hannah Arendt's *The Life of the Mind*, 57–58.

17. Kant, *Prolegomena*, §60, 152 [AA 4, 364].

18. In *Kant and the Dynamics of Reason*, in the chapter titled "The Relation between the 'Understanding' and 'Reason' in the Architectonic of Kant's Philosophy," Gerd

Buchdahl explains that Kant is led beyond the understanding as the conceptual structure of phenomenal cognition to reason in the attempt to complete what is by definition limited and essentially incomplete (170–71, 179). This striving permits teleological accomplishment where no determinate accomplishment is possible. Unfortunately, Buchdahl does not question the limitations that are attributed to phenomenal cognition, which designate it as incomplete and direct reason's striving toward that which would offer it completion. The designation of the bounds of phenomenal experience may itself be a product of the striving of our "metaphysical disposition," in which case the relation of reason and understanding will necessarily be more complex than that of a linear striving for an ever-out-of-reach completion beyond the phenomenal realm.

19. Kant, *Critique of Judgment*, §76, 271–72 [AA 5, 401], translation altered.

20. Ibid., 272 [AA 5, 401], translation altered.

21. In *Kant and the Unity of Reason*, Angelica Nuzzo describes the three areas investigated in §76 as related to the "different thematic fields covered respectively by the three *Critiques*"—understanding, reason, and the power of judgment—as Kant has described them in the "table of the faculties of the *human* mind" (348–49; Kant, *Critique of Judgment*, Second Introduction, 83 [AA 5, 198]). However, Nuzzo does not connect these three thematic fields to Kant's investigation of the three ideas of reason, and so does not interpret these discussions, as Kant introduces them, as examples of the regulative principles that follow from these ideas. Nuzzo limits her interpretation to the claim that the idea of an intuitive understanding in §76 plays the role of a "counter-factual" in relation to each of these areas (*Kant and the Unity of Reason*, 351). Kant is said to have raised the intuitive understanding in order to highlight our human discursive one. Nuzzo explains that only in §77 does Kant offer the intuitive understanding as a "necessary regulative idea" (ibid.), and here only in relation to the purposiveness required for teleological inquiry into nature. In a later article, Nuzzo argues that such a regulative undertaking can be seen already in §76 ("*Kritik der Urteilskraft* §§76–77: Reflective Judgment and the Limits of Transcendental Philosophy," 161–67). Nuzzo describes the "'regulative' validity" (166) of the ideas in the three examples, but does not explicitly tie them to Kant's three ideas of reason. Nuzzo explains the role of the idea of freedom, and that of the purposiveness of teleological judgment, in a manner that corresponds to the cosmological and theological ideas, respectively, but continues to interpret the first example, that of finite cognition, as related not to the psychological idea, but merely to the "counter-factual" idea of an intuitive understanding.

22. Kant, *Prolegomena*, preface, 59 [AA 4, 263], translation altered.

23. Ibid., §60, 153 [AA 4, 364].

24. Ibid. It is worth noting that in the *Prolegomena*, Kant claims that the analytic order of this work follows the synthetic approach of the first *Critique*, marking the *Prolegomena* as a sequel. This would appear to contradict Kant's claim in the first *Critique* that an analytic investigation of the ideas must precede their synthetic analysis. A possible explanation is that since the claim in the first *Critique* concerns metaphysics, in which, it would appear, no synthetic account is possible, all that is possible is an analytic examination of the limits of cognition after the synthetic examination of objective cognition in the Transcendental Analytic. In this sense, the analytic critique of metaphysics would follow the synthetic analysis of cognition.

However, it is not obvious that such a simple solution fits the matter at hand. First, does the synthetic rendering of the account of cognition in the Transcendental Analytic actually precede the critique of metaphysics in the Transcendental Dialectic? This is to ask whether the Transcendental Analytic itself presupposes the accomplishments of the

Transcendental Dialectic, thus making its synthetic account a development from the analytic critique of metaphysics. Second, if we are going to investigate the dependence of the account of cognition on the critique of metaphysics, then should not this examination of metaphysics be viewed as itself a synthetic use of reason's pursuit of the ideas? Such questions are implicit in my investigation of the regulative use of the ideas of reason in §76 of the *Critique of Judgment*. Could the *Critique of Judgment*, in its examination of the role of reason in reflective judgment, offer a synthetic account of the ideas of reason without falling into metaphysical dogmatism?

25. In the Guyer and Wood translation, *reflektierend* is translated as "reflecting" and *bestimmend* as "determining." I have chosen to use "reflective" and "determinative," respectively (following Pluhar in his translation).

26. Kant explains the distinction between reflective and determinative judgment in section v of the First Introduction to the *Critique of Judgment;* I will return to this introduction in the coming pages. On the distinction between these two types of judgments, see Mertens, *Kommentar zur Ersten Einleitung in Kants Kritik der Urteilskraft*, 94–96.

27. For my discussion of the regulative role of reason in aesthetic judgment, see Goldman, "Beauty and Critique: On the Role of Reason in Kant's Aesthetics."

28. Kant also refers to another form of reflection in which representations are compared not with each other but with the "faculty of cognition [*Erkenntnisvermögen*]" (*Critique of Judgment*, First Introduction, v, 15 [AA 20, 211]). Such a further conception of reflection, one not directed toward empirical concept formation, most clearly refers to the aesthetic reflective power of judgment in which "the reflection on a given representation precedes the feeling of pleasure (as the determining ground of the judgment)" (ibid., viii, 27 [AA 224–25]). But it could also refer to the conception of a transcendental reflection (Kant uses both *Reflexion* and *Überlegung*, A260–63/B316–19), which Kant raises in the appendix to the Transcendental Analytic of the first *Critique*, for there Kant introduces an act of reflection through which representations are designated as either sensible or intellectual, with the former designated as the phenomenal realm of inquiry and the latter as the noumenal. Mertens draws this connection in *Kommentar zur Ersten Einleitung in Kants Kritik der Urteilskraft*, 94–95. I will investigate this possibility in chapter 4.

29. Kant, *Critique of Judgment*, First Introduction, v, 15 [AA 20, 211].

30. Ibid.

31. For Kant's discussion of purposiveness in the *Critique of Judgment*, see the third moment of the Analytic of Aesthetic Judgment (§§10–12), where he investigates the *a priori* role that purposiveness plays. See also the First Introduction to the *Critique of Judgment*, where purposiveness is introduced in section v in discussing the principle of all reflective judgment (First Introduction, v, 19 [AA 20, 216]; see also sections vi and x in the First Introduction, and sections iv–viii in the originally published Second Introduction). On the role of purposiveness as the regulative principle of reflective judgment, see Mertens, *Kommentar zur Ersten Einleitung in Kants Kritik der Urteilskraft*, 107–114.

32. In the realm of aesthetic judgment, Kant argues that the principle of purposiveness can also be seen to govern our reflection. When we claim that a particular object is beautiful, and yet we cannot distinguish a law that circumscribes what a beautiful object is, then, Kant argues, hidden in such a reflective judgment there must be the presupposition, and hence the principle (*Prinzip*), that the reflected-upon object offers itself in a purposeful fashion for our reflection. Kant does distinguish the aesthetic power of judgment as directed by such subjective purposiveness from the objective purposiveness of the teleological power of judgment in which the reflective judgment is made about the object or laws rather than our state (Kant, *Critique of Judgment*, First Introduction, xii, 48–49 [AA

20, 249–50]), and yet they are conjoined in that both belong to the reflective power of judgment. Kant writes that "all judgments about the purposiveness of nature, be they aesthetic or teleological, stand under principles *a priori*, and indeed such as belong especially and exclusively to the power of judgment, since they are merely reflective and not determinative judgments" (ibid., x, 41, translation altered [AA 20, 241]). Rudolf Makkreel claims that aesthetic judgments, as constitutive in relation to pleasure and displeasure (ibid., Second Introduction, ix, 82 [AA 5, 196–97]), are therefore not regulative (Makkreel, "Regulative and Reflective Uses of Purposiveness in Kant," 50). He uses this distinction to differentiate the terms "reflective" and "regulative," since teleological judgments are both reflective and regulative while aesthetic judgments are reflective and constitutive rather than regulative. Makkreel emphasizes the distinction between the conception of regulative principles in the first *Critique* and reflective judgment in the third since the latter includes aesthetic judgments that are constitutive rather than regulative. While it is true that Kant does not explicitly call aesthetic judgments regulative, as reflective judgments they still depend upon a principle in order to constitute aesthetic experience (Kant, *Critique of Judgment*, First Introduction, v, 15–16 [AA 20, 211]). The question remains: In what sense does such a principle direct the aesthetic judgment that it constitutes? Makkreel assumes that constitutive and regulative must be at odds, but Kant does not say so; and yet it is true that Kant does not use the term "regulative" to describe the aesthetic power of judgment. This might lead one to agree with Makkreel that there is a relevant distinction between the terms "regulative" and "reflective." However, it does not necessarily follow that they are at odds, as regulative could be a narrower term and reflective a broader one that includes both constitutive and regulative uses of principles of reason. Further investigation of the role of principles in aesthetic judgment is outside the scope of this inquiry. On the relation of the first and third *Critiques,* see below in chapter 6.

33. Kant describes the theological idea, the third of his ideas of reason, as the "ideal of pure reason," distinguishing an ideal as "even further removed from objective reality than the idea" (A568/B596). As such a far-reaching idea, the ideal is thought "not merely in *concreto* but in *individuo*" (ibid.), offering an "individual thing [*Ding*]" that is thought only in the idea. Kant already introduces the regulative principle of nature that follows from the ideal as purposive (*zweckmäßig*) in the *Critique of Pure Reason* (A686–88/B714–16) in the appendix that follows the Transcendental Dialectic. See chapter 6 for further discussion of the relation of reason's regulative use of this principle, raised by Kant in the first *Critique,* and that of reflective judgment, broached by him only in the third *Critique.* On the transcendental ideal, see Béatrice Longuenesse, "The Transcendental Ideal and the Unity of the Critical System," in her *Kant and the Human Standpoint,* 211–35.

34. Kant, *Critique of Judgment,* First Introduction, v, 16n, translation altered [AA 20, 211–12n].

35. Ibid., 18, translation altered [AA 20, 214].

36. Ibid., §76, 274 [AA 5, 404].

37. Ibid., translation altered.

38. Ibid.

39. See ibid., §77, 275 [AA 5, 405].

40. Kant explains the antinomy in the following manner: the thesis is that "all production of material things and their forms must be judged to be possible in terms of merely mechanical laws"; the antithesis is that "some products of material nature cannot be judged to be possible in terms of merely mechanical laws" (ibid., §70, 258–59 [AA 5, 387]).

41. Ibid., §77, 277 [AA 5, 408].

42. Pierre Kerszberg writes that Kant has offered "the long overdue solution of the antinomy of teleological judgment" (*Critique and Totality*, 218); see also Michel Souriau, *Le jugement réfléchissant dans la philosophie critique de Kant*, 114–16; and Nuzzo, *Kant and the Unity of Reason*, 351–53.

43. The teleological investigation of nature depends on the principle of nature as purposive in order to regulate its inquiries, but so too mechanistic analysis depends on a regulative principle. However, the principles differ; in the case of mechanism, Kant explains in the Antinomies of Pure Reason chapter of the first *Critique*, the idea of cosmology—nature as governed by causal laws—regulates not the systematic unity of causal laws, but the designation of causal laws themselves (see A509/B537). I will further address the regulative principle that follows from the cosmological idea in the following section.

44. Kant, *Critique of Judgment*, §76, 274 [AA 5, 404].

45. Ibid., §77, 275 [AA 5, 405].

46. Ibid. In the first *Critique*, Kant describes "intellectual intuition" as "original (*intuitas originarius*)," rather than "derived (*intuitas derivativus*)" (B72). "Intellectual intuition" is another way of describing an "intuitive understanding," "a divine understanding which would not represent given objects, but through whose representation the objects would themselves at the same time be given, or produced" (B145).

47. Kant explains that understanding limits (*einschränkt*) sensibility and in so doing sets bounds (*Grenzen*) for itself. A limit for Kant is a purely negative demarcation, while a boundary is a positive claim, although it can be said to be neither fully within nor without that which is bounded as it designates this relation. See Kant, *Prolegomena*, §59, 150 [AA 4, 361]; and the discussion in chapter 1.

48. The merely negative role of the thing in itself, that which does not offer itself to cognition, can be seen in the Transcendental Aesthetic, where it is raised as that which has no relation to sensibility. On space, see A26–30/B42–45, and on time A32–36/B49–53; and see Martin, *Kant's Metaphysics and Theory of Science*, 166 [194].

49. As will be addressed in the following chapter, the apparent lack of a positive role to be played by the noumenon has led interpreters to conceive of the first *Critique* as a form of naturalism and thus to be either defended as such or rejected as an epistemological dogmatism.

50. Kant, *Critique of Judgment*, §76, 274 [AA 5, 404].

51. Ibid., 273 [AA 5, 403].

52. In this extract, I have kept the Latin *principium*, placing it in italics as Guyer and Wood do for other Latin words, rather than translating it as "principle," as they do in this case, in order to distinguish it from the German *Prinzip*.

53. Both sides of the antinomy of teleological judgment in the third *Critique* (see §70 of the *Critique of Judgment*, where it is set out) can be seen to proceed regulatively. In teleological judgment, the theological idea promises reflective judgment the systematicity it pursues, directing the investigation of nature by means of the regulative use of the idea of the world, in its entirety, as conforming to a purpose. Mechanism makes use of the cosmological idea to direct its expanding determination of experience, without presuming to have completed the regress in the series of conditions.

54. Kant, *Critique of Judgment*, §76, 273 [AA 5, 403–404].

55. Ibid. [AA 5, 404].

56. Ibid., 274 [AA 5, 404].

57. Ibid.

58. Ibid.

59. Kant, *Critique of Practical Reason*, 238–47 [AA 5, 122–34].

60. Onora O'Neill explains that the supreme principle of practical reason is a specific example within the moral sphere of Kant's more general conception of regulative inquiry ("Vindicating Reason," 296).

61. Kant, *Critique of Judgment*, §76, 270 [AA 5, 401].

62. Ibid., 272 [AA 5, 402].

63. Ibid.

64. Ibid., 273 [AA 5, 403].

65. Ibid., translation altered.

66. Ibid.

67. Kant, *Prolegomena*, §59, 150 [AA 4, 361].

THREE • The Designation of the Region of Experience in the *Critique of Pure Reason*

1. Kant, *Critique of Judgment*, First Introduction, iv, 13 [AA 20, 208].

2. Barry Stroud explains that the relevant issue is whether we would set aside the questions posed by "philosophical skepticism" and so "abandon the quest for a general justification of empirical knowledge in favor of a purely naturalistic study of the procedures actually employed by scientists and other knowing subjects" ("The Significance of Scepticism," 277). While Stroud chooses not to set aside the challenge of skepticism, W. H. Walsh defends Kant's system from such a naturalistic perspective. He argues that Kant's critical philosophy is justified in its epistemological presuppositions. Walsh explains that the discursivity of our finite thought is one of the primitive propositions from which Kant builds his philosophical system; and while from a "formal point of view" such propositions are "contingent . . . there is no practical likelihood of our being wrong about them" ("Philosophy and Psychology in Kant's *Critique*," 196). Lewis White Beck describes these foundational claims of Kant's account of finite cognition as "brutally factual yet in some not well-defined sense self-evident; they are factual and not empirical" ("Toward a Meta-Critique of Pure Reason," in his *Essays on Kant and Hume*, 25). Paul Guyer is willing to concede the point but wonders whether "anything other than a verbal victory for the synthetic *a priori* is gained by denying that these premises are empirical" (*Kant and the Claims of Knowledge*, 421). Finally, Richard Rorty has this to say on the naturalizing trend in epistemology: "This cry of 'let's naturalize epistemology!' has become suspiciously popular with analytic philosophy in recent years. I regard it as a reactionary development, a last-ditch attempt to hold on to the atemporal, Kantian, scheme-content distinction in a desperate attempt to avoid Hegel and historicism" ("Transcendental Arguments, Self-Reference, and Pragmatism," 91).

3. One could look back to the Marburg neo-Kantians, such as Hermann Cohen, for a defense of Kant in purely phenomenal terms, tying the principles (*Grundsätze*) of the understanding to a conception of "scientific experience [*wissenschaftlichen Erfahrung*]" (Cohen, *Kants Theorie der Erfahrung*, 187). Kenneth Westphal offers a contemporary version of such realism, arguing for the Kantian faculties from the givenness of the spatiotemporal world, although rather than the scientific truth of this world he argues that we are "cognitively dependent on a commonsense spatiotemporal world" (*Kant's Transcendental Proof of Realism*, 3). What he denies is the phenomenal-noumenal divide, arguing instead that our perceptual experience, which is to say the phenomenal realm, offers access to things in themselves. The latter are not separately existing things of some

sort, but merely further aspects of the same things. Gerold Prauss makes a similar argument in *Kant und das Problem der Dinge an sich* (59–61). Karl Ameriks recognizes that the phenomenal-noumenal divide continues to pose a problem for such realist claims, and yet he explains that if we "modify the orthodox Kantian position" and accept the "theoretically modest view" that the mind conceives of the world as it is in itself, then "we can thereby achieve a comparatively attractive position on personal identity" (*Kant's Theory of Mind*, 169–70). Both Andrew Brook and Paul Abela go further, arguing for this realist position in Kant's name. Brook claims such realism merely for the mind, arguing that, particularly in the second edition, Kant offers a noumenal claim for the self-awareness of transcendental apperception (*Kant and the Mind*, 254–58). Abela goes even further, embracing the realist claim in Kant's name for the correspondence of thought and its object in general (*Kant's Empirical Realism*, 72–73).

4. Gary Hatfield describes these two modes of justification of Kant's project as "the natural and the normative" (the latter is what has here been called realism) in his book of that title. Hatfield writes that a naturalized account of the mind is able to

> describe its processes, mechanisms, or the laws governing its states in a naturalistic vocabulary that excludes terms of epistemic evaluation, such as "true" or "justified" or "valid," from its primitive terms. By contrast, a "normative" vocabulary includes these terms as primitives. To take a normative attitude toward mental states is to treat the applicability of epistemic standards or criteria as essential to their being mental states. (*The Natural and the Normative*, 15)

The "normative" demands such external corroboration for its claims, while the "natural" does not, since it assumes that its self-description is enough. Realism would then be a species of such normative explanation since in it thought is justified by the object that exists apart from its perception.

5. As Walsh points out, Kant addresses the way in which sensibility is distinguished from the understanding as a faculty of *a priori* concepts in the first *Critique* where, contra Leibniz, he raises the need for a non-conceptual spatial sensibility to explain the way that we differentiate conceptually equivalent drops of water (B328/A272; see Walsh, *Kant's Criticism of Metaphysics*, 15; and chapter 4 below for further discussion of this example). Kant argues most directly for this dualism in his various accounts of incongruent counterparts, which, Walsh notes, is "strangely omitted" (*Kant's Criticism of Metaphysics*, 14) from both editions of the first *Critique*. Walsh refers to two of Kant's five published references to incongruent counterparts: the *Prolegomena*, §13, 81–82 (AA 4, 286); and the dissertation, *On the Form and Principles of the Sensible and Intelligible Worlds* (*De Mundi sensibilis atque intelligibilis forma et principiis*), §15, 386–87 [AA 2, 402–403]. The non-conceptual difference between left and right hands points to our ability to distinguish what rationalism conflates; the irreducible difference that the left hand shares with the right hand can be explained only in a non-conceptual manner. This is to say that such spatial orientation escapes all conceptual analysis, and therefore points to the distinction between sensibility and understanding (Walsh, *Kant's Criticism of Metaphysics*, 14–15). Interestingly, among the three references to incongruent counterparts that Walsh omits is Kant's 1786 "What Does It Mean to Orient Oneself in Thinking?" [AA 8, 134–35] in which spatial orientation is connected to orientation in thought in general. I will return in chapter 6 to a discussion of this essay.

These arguments notwithstanding, it is not enough to claim that, for Kant, cognition is indubitably discursive, dependent on the dualism of sensibility and understanding, in order to argue that such cognition should be the focus of philosophical inquiry, for why should we turn from the metaphysical, which surpasses such discursive limits and which Kant admits can be thought, and toward the objects of experience that can be cognized? What justifies this prioritizing of cognition over thought? This is Hegel's challenge to Kant in *Faith and Knowledge,* which will be investigated in chapter 4.

6. Robert Pippin describes such a problem succinctly in his essay "Hegel's Phenomenological Criticism": it is "especially important for a critical epistemology to justify reflectively its own criteria for knowledge of knowledge" (299). This is so, claims Pippin, because there are essentially two possibilities. In the first, Kant must be understood to "beg all of the important questions" "by only 'describing' what he already, in some non-reflective way, takes to be a feature of experience (e.g., causality)" (ibid., 300). Such a reading, which Pippin attributes to the analytic Kant interpreters (especially Strawson and Bennett), begs not only Hume's questions, but also those that have occupied philosophy throughout its history. In the second possibility, if one makes a stronger claim in Kant's name, one that does not make him oblivious to such philosophical questioning, then Kant needs to justify "*how* we know for sure a condition *is* a necessary condition for the possibility of experience without making use of some sense of knowledge that should not be warranted until after our transcendental analysis goes through" (ibid., 299–300).

7. Prauss argues that Kant is unable to offer such a justification (*Erscheinung bei Kant,* 62–63).

8. Pippin, "Hegel's Phenomenological Criticism," 300.

9. Kant, *Critique of Judgment,* First Introduction, iv, 13 [AA 20, 208].

10. In §76 of the *Critique of Judgment,* Kant writes that teleology and mechanism can be distinguished only because human cognition is finite; it depends upon the subsumption of sensible representations under the understanding's *a priori* concepts (§76, 274 [AA 5, 404]). If human cognition were not finite, if we had an intuitive intellect, there would be no distinction between mechanistic and teleological explanation. This is because a mechanistic explanation of causes would itself lead to the systematic explanation of nature, and the ideal that for finite cognition is uncognizable would offer itself for cognition.

11. In a provocative short essay titled "The Concept of Experience and Strawson's Transcendental Deduction," Kim Davies argues that Kant and his interpreters (notably Strawson) exemplify "a forgetfulness of the provenance of the concept of experience inscribed in their work" (203). If our philosophical investigation had begun with a different conception of experience, for instance "the red patches and tickling sensations of the sense-datum theorists" (ibid.), the "concepts of the objective" under which Kantian experience is brought would not be applicable. Davies claims to have attempted a philosophical self-reflection by addressing the underlying conception of experience in critical philosophy that is needed if such a program is not to forget its beginnings. He argues that the claim that the Transcendental Deduction has provided us with a novel philosophical accomplishment exemplifies such forgetfulness, for the categories as the structure of the objectivity of experience are already implied in the conception of experience with which we began our inquiries (ibid.). Yet Davies does not investigate whether such a self-reflection is present in other parts of Kant's critical edifice. Could it be that it is the errors of the interpreters, of Strawson et al., that he has uncovered, rather than the forgetfulness of Kant himself?

12. See note 2 above for a discussion of those who attempt to naturalize Kant's epistemology.

13. Gary Hatfield describes Kantian experience as the sphere of "objectivity or intersubjective validity" (*The Natural and the Normative,* 80). He argues that Kant fails to address his presuppositions: "In taking these starting points as a given, Kant was remarkably

oblivious to the charge of begging the question" (ibid.). In Hatfield's account, such an omission follows from the nature of transcendental arguments that search for the grounds of the possibility of knowledge that is viewed as actual.

14. Kant, *Prolegomena*, §59, 149–50 [AA 4, 360–62].

15. We should remember Kant's distinction between *Grundsätze* and *Prinzipien*, described in the previous chapter. While both sorts of principles permit further cognition without themselves being grounded on something else, *Grundsätze* depend upon sensible content for their cognition while *Prinzipien* do not (see B188/A148, A299–303/B355–59, and above in chapter 2).

16. Kant, *Critique of Judgment*, First Introduction, v, 15 [AA 20, 211].

17. In *Critique and Totality*, Pierre Kerszberg explains the distinction between dynamical or regulative principles and mathematical or constitutive ones: "Because it broaches the heterogeneous, the regulative principle differs from a mathematical principle which organizes the synthesis of the homogeneous, and which is thus constitutive of the manifold" (92).

18. Heidegger, *What Is a Thing?* 240 [186].

19. Manfred Baum explains that the proof of the Analogies depends upon the conception of experience with which it begins (*Deduktion und Beweis in Kants Transzendentalphilosophie*, 199–200; and "Transcendental Proofs in the *Critique of Pure Reason*," 19–20; the English translation is a shorter version of a chapter of the German book).

20. As was discussed in chapter 2, Kant explains that even in the first *Critique* he has not investigated the question of the relation of reason and the understanding, which is to say how experience can be said to be "indirectly subject to the legislation of reason" (Kant, *Prolegomena*, §60, 152–53 [AA 4, 364]). Kant goes on to say that such an inquiry has been directed by the first *Critique* but not explicitly attempted, explaining, "Afterwards it is in each person's discretion, how far he will take his investigation, if he only has been apprised of what may still need to be done" (ibid., 153n [AA 4, 364n]).

21. As both Westphal and Falkenstein point out, the experience of objects depends upon spatiality, and so spatial representations form a "key set" (Westphal, *Kant's Transcendental Proof of Realism*, 19) or "a broad class" (Falkenstein, *Kant's Intuitionism*, 196) within the whole of our temporal representations.

22. In the first edition's Transcendental Deduction, Kant does not explicitly state the requirement that the manifold of representations from which the Deduction proceeds be spatial, and yet he does make clear that the Deduction begins not with all of our representations in general, but with "all representations that can ever belong to our cognition" (A116), this is to say those spatial representations that distinguish the realm of experience and so afford cognition.

23. The category is existence (*Dasein*), while the principle (*Grundsatz*) that follows from it is actuality (*Wirklichkeit*).

24. Kant elucidates the role of the three modal principles by asserting:

> if it [the concept of a thing] is merely connected in the understanding with the formal conditions of experience, its object is called possible; if it is in connection with perception (sensation, as the matter of the senses), and through this determined by means of the understanding, then the object [*Objekt*] is actual; and if it is determined through the connection of perceptions in accordance with concepts, then the object is called necessary. (A234/B286–87)

25. Manfred Baum explains that the question entails whether the designation of possible experience itself depends upon actual experience, on that which is distinguished in an *a posteriori* manner, and so whether actual experience is both the product and the presupposition of critical inquiry. For Baum, this circularity is avoided inasmuch as "Kant asserts the possibility of experience quite independent of any particular actual experience" (*Deduktion und Beweis in Kants Transzendentalphilosophie*, 189; and "Transcendental Proofs in Kant's *Critique of Pure Reason*," 13). For Baum, this original assumption of possible experience is a more general presupposition that allows Kant to investigate the conditions of the possibility of the objects of experience without presupposing what he means to uncover. He does not address the more general presuppositions related to the "possibility of experience."

26. "[E]r die besondere Eigenschaft hat, daß er seinen Beweisgrund, nämlich Erfahrung, selbst zuerst möglich macht und bei dieser immer vorausgesetzt werden muß" (A737/B765). I will return to this passage in chapter 6.

27. Pierre Kerszberg explains that this describes the "paradox" of critique (*Critique and Totality*, 87). Pauline Kleingeld embraces the circularity of critique, attributing such a limitation to the nature of the project itself, since Kant has attempted "a critique of reason by reason" ("Kant on the Unity of Theoretical and Practical Reason," 321). Rüdiger Bubner, Dieter Sturma, and Claude Piché all deem transcendental philosophy, in this way, to be "self-referential" (Bubner, "Zur Struktur eines Transzendentalen Arguments," 15–27; Bubner, "Kant, Transcendental Arguments and the Problem of Deduction," 462–65; Sturma, "Die Paralogismen der reinen Vernunft in der zweiten Auflage," 402–403; Sturma, *Kant über Selbstbewußtsein*, 41; and Piché, "Self-Referentiality in Kant's Transcendental Philosophy," 264). Piché writes:

> This only makes more obvious the tremendous difficulty of the Kantian transcendental argumentation insofar as the transcendental subject comes under the yoke of rules that are, all appropriate transpositions having been made, the same as the ones he imposes on the course of nature. . . . This is the sense in which we can say that the lessons of the Transcendental Analytic are self-referential: they regulate the discourse that brings them to light. (ibid.)

This conception of the structure of transcendental arguments, which claims that their proof depends upon that which they are trying to prove, is in keeping with the current interpretation of the principles. In what follows, I will investigate the subject of critique, and so the Kantian system, in such self-referential terms. For a criticism of Kantian self-referentiality, emphasizing its inability to claim anything about cognition in general, see Richard Rorty's "Transcendental Arguments, Self-Reference, and Pragmatism" (81–83).

28. Heidegger, *What Is a Thing?* 241 [187].

29. "Die Erfahrung ist ein in sich kreisendes Geschehen" (Heidegger, *What Is a Thing?* 242 [188]).

30. Ibid.

31. Ibid., 244 [189].

32. In *Being and Time*, after criticizing Kant for having presupposed the conception of objects that he then analyzes (§23, 101–102 [109–110]), Heidegger goes on to distinguish his conception of the hermeneutic circle (*Zirkel*) of understanding from the circularity of traditional epistemological systems, from systems like Kant's that presuppose a reductive, epistemological conception of objects: "This circle [*Zirkel*] of understanding [*Verstehen*] is not a circle [*Kreis*] in which any random [*beliebige*] kind of knowledge operates, but

it is rather the expression of the existential *fore-structure* of *Dasein* itself (ibid., §32, 143 [153])." The hermeneutic circle (*Zirkel*) avoids an arbitrary conception of objects, expressing rather what Heidegger implies is a fundamental account of the experience of objects. And it is surely Kant whom Heidegger has here in mind when he criticizes a knowledge of objects that replaces "the existential *fore-structure* of *Dasein*."

But even in *Being and Time*, we can see a certain ambivalence on Heidegger's part toward Kant, and toward the analysis of objects that allows Kant to point to the fundamental temporal origins of thought; later in this work, rather than criticizing these epistemological methods, Heidegger appears to argue that it is such an epistemological method that permits us access to the hermeneutic circle. He explains that we "must aim at leaping into this 'circle [*Kreis*]' primordially and completely, so that even at the beginning of our analysis of *Dasein* we make sure that we have a complete view of the circular [*zirkelhafte*] being of *Dasein*" (ibid., §63, 291 [315]). Here, Heidegger uses both terms, *Kreis* and *Zirkel*; the method into which one must leap is a *Kreis* (the term he uses to describe Kant's undertaking), while what this shows of *Dasein* is that it is itself a *Zirkel* (of *Dasein* itself). We must enter the analysis of *Dasein* with a view to the whole, to the "circular [*zirkelhafte*] being of *Dasein*"; and yet, with such a view in mind, we must still find an entry point, a means of beginning our analysis, and such an entrance Heidegger describes in precisely the language that he will come to use for Kantian inquiry: the "circularity [*Kreisgang*]" of the Kantian analysis of objects would appear to permit access to the more fundamental "circle [*Zirkel*]" of the understanding itself. For further discussion of Heidegger and the circularity of Kantian critique, see Goldman, "Kant, Heidegger, and the Circularity of Transcendental Inquiry."

33. Heidegger, *What Is a Thing?* 242 [188].

34. As Kant writes in the preface to the second edition, the Copernican revolution that directs the critical "experiment in metaphysics" concerns the sensible intuition of objects. We must assume that the object "conforms to the constitution of our faculty of intuition" in order to avoid the past failures involved in the pursuit of our metaphysical interests (Bxvii).

35. Kant does raise the possibility of a more radically skeptical position in the first edition's version of the Third Paralogism in the Transcendental Dialectic (A363n). I will address this discussion later in this chapter.

36. Kant also refers to the *Existenz* of such things outside me (B276).

37. I will examine the first edition's Fourth Paralogism within a broader discussion of Kant's Paralogisms in chapter 5.

38. Pierre Lachièze-Rey explains that Kant's Refutation must be seen as directed not merely at Cartesian problematic idealism, but at any "psychological idealism [*idéalisme psychologique*]" (*L'idéalisme Kantien*, 89), by which he means any idealism that does not merely raise questions about the existence of perceived objects, but that "leaves the domain of the real [*quitte le domaine du réel*]" insofar as it "steps back [*s'écarte*]" from empirical phenomena that can be immediately apprehended (ibid.). Lachièze-Rey goes on to say that the Refutation belongs to "the internal dialectic of the system" (ibid., 90) of transcendental philosophy.

39. For such an interpretation of the Refutation, one that claims that it is arguing for a realist account of spatial appearances in the Kantian system, see Rousset, *La Doctrine Kantienne de l'objectivité*, 155–61.

40. For Kant's discussion of the consistency of transcendental idealism and empirical realism, see the Transcendental Aesthetic, A27–28/B43–44 (in relation to space), and A35–36/B52–53 (in relation to time).

41. Eckart Förster makes such a point in "Kant's Refutation of Idealism": "But now it begins to look as though the argument is perhaps too potent to be handled easily by Kant" (294). If the argument is not "integrated into the Kantian system" (ibid., 295), then "it equally seems to refute Kant's own transcendental idealism" (ibid., 294).

42. However, I would not go as far as Henry Allison, who claims that "the Refutation of Idealism is not merely compatible with transcendental idealism, properly construed, it presupposes it" (*Kant's Transcendental Idealism* [2004], 300). This would mean that the refutation of Cartesian, problematic idealism depends upon the acceptance of the Kantian system rather than on the more minimal claim that such an idealist can be said to accept. Is there no way to interpret the Refutation that works both within and without transcendental philosophy?

43. For the First Analogy, see B224–32/A182–89.

44. In the First Analogy, Kant also refers to *das Beharrliche* (B226/A183).

45. Kant is also clear in the second edition's preface that the Refutation is an addition to the book; he explains that it is "the only thing that I can really call a supplement" (Bxxxix).

46. "[O]uter sense is already in itself a relation of intuition to something actual outside me [*etwas Wirkliches außer mir*]" (Bxl).

47. Kant refers to the "transcendental object" of the Deduction as both *Gegenstand* (A109, A358) and *Objekt* (A250, A253, A288/B344, A379, A613–14/B642), seemingly using the phrases interchangeably. While he typically distinguishes the transcendental object from noumena, he does occasionally describe such an object as a noumenon. In the first edition's Paralogisms chapter, Kant describes this non-sensible object "as *noumenon* (or better, as transcendental object [*Gegenstand*])" (A358). Kant also describes the transcendental object (*Objekt*) as a noumenon in the appendix to the Transcendental Analytic (B344/A288), where he explains that "[i]f we want to call this object [*Objekt*] a *noumenon* because the representation of it is nothing sensible, we are free to do so" (A288/B345), and yet unlike the noumena investigated in the Transcendental Dialectic, "we cannot apply any of our concepts of the understanding to it" (ibid.). The transcendental object refers to a non-sensible object so we could call it a noumenon, but it would be so only in a limited sense because noumena, since they allow us to apply our *a priori* concepts to them, permit a further positive rather than a merely negative function. This positive role for noumena will be raised in what follows.

48. In the *Prolegomena* (§30), Kant makes use of the terms "noumena" and "things in themselves" interchangeably; such a connection is also made in the first *Critique* in the first edition's *Phenomena* and *Noumena* chapter, where Kant writes that from the consideration of appearances, as distinct from things in themselves, "arises the concept of a *noumenon*" (A252). He explains that understanding limits itself to the sensibly given, to its empirical and not transcendental use, "by calling things in themselves (things not regarded as appearances) *noumena*" (A256/B312). In the preface to the second edition, Kant also appears to describe things in themselves in a way that corresponds to noumena: "For that which necessarily drives us to go beyond the boundaries of experience and all appearances is the **unconditioned**, which reason necessarily and with every right demands in things in themselves [*Dingen an sich*] for everything that is conditioned" (Bxx). He also describes the "thing in itself" as the true "correlate" of sensible appearances (A30/B45).

49. Kant, *Notes and Fragments*, R 5654, 285 [AA 18, 312]. This is clearly the case for the Kantian system, but such a conception of a transcendental object does not offer a rebuttal to the idealists who do not embrace the critical system.

50. In response to the question of idealism, Kant writes that the things outside of us must be "intellectually presupposed [*intellektuell vorausgesetzt*]" (ibid., R 5653, 281 [AA 18, 306]). Kant explains that this is not a spatial representation "but can be called intellectual intuition, through which we have no cognition of things" (ibid.). While the reference in this note to an intellectual intuition is problematic, Kant appears to be trying to find a vocabulary to describe the role played by such intellectually presupposed things. In this note, from the late 1780s and thus prior to the publication of the *Critique of Judgment,* he does not have the notion of reflective judgment with the regulative role played by ideas of reason that is there developed. In a later reflection from 1790, Kant describes this "persistence [*Beharrlichkeit*]" as in "that which is simultaneous, or in the intelligible, which contains the ground of appearances" (ibid., R 6312, 357 [AA 18, 612]), without further elucidating how the intelligible is conceived.

Luigi Caranti argues that all of these examples of Kant's metaphysical argument against idealism are "clearly incompatible with the limitations that transcendental idealism places on our knowledge" (*Kant and the Scandal of Philosophy,* 160, and see more generally 156–72). He views the first edition's Fourth Paralogism as Kant's most successful argument against skepticism (ibid., 173). See chapter 5 for discussion of this paralogism. Caranti does not investigate the possibility of a regulative relationship between phenomena and noumena.

51. In a further note, Kant begins his argument against idealism by stating that in inner sense "everything is successive, hence nothing can be taken backwards." He goes on to claim that "the ground of the possibility of the latter must lie in the relation of representations to something outside us" (*Notes and Fragments,* R 6312, 357 [AA 18, 612]). Dietmar Hermann Heidemann characterizes this argument as Kant's most successful against idealism, assuming with Kant that inner sense cannot itself be doubted and that its source must be distinct from us (*Kant und das Problem des metaphysichen Idealismus,* 238).

52. It is worth asking why Kant did not include a version of such skeptical concerns in the second edition.

53. While Allison recognizes such a skeptical challenge, he argues that the thought experiment that raises the radically skeptical interpretation of consciousness need not threaten our awareness of ourselves in time since it is launched from a position apart from that of consciousness by a "hypothetical observer" (*Kant's Transcendental Idealism* [1983], 309). Allison argues that the doubts it raises in the realm of metaphysical speculation do not "affect the way in which the self is for itself," for, as Kant writes, "the identity of a person is therefore inevitably to be encountered in my own consciousness" (ibid.). But must the examination of consciousness presuppose this identity? Is the insider's view of a unified consciousness more philosophically justifiable than the skeptical conception of a chain of perception with only the appearance of an identical consciousness (or, for that matter, other denials of this view of consciousness)? Allison seems certain of this, expressing his basic assumption that the investigation of experience must, in some way, follow the Cartesian path. But must it, and must Kant be understood to have assumed, in a similar fashion, the indubitability of the orientation of the critical analysis of experience? Interestingly, Allison removes this discussion of a more radical skepticism than that of the Refutation in the revised edition of *Kant's Transcendental Idealism,* making only a brief reference to the thought experiment in the first edition's Third Paralogism in a later, added chapter on the Paralogisms (ibid. [2004], 345). Myron Gochnauer agrees with my claim, contra Allison, that the Refutation in fact refutes only positions built upon the Cartesian assumption. Gochnauer, however, does not go on to investigate the importance of this assumption for the method of critique ("Kant's Refutation of

Idealism," 205–206). Both Rorty and Heidegger do just that. Rorty criticizes Kantian transcendental arguments on just such a point, arguing that they reject only a specific version of skepticism while claiming "to know in advance the range of the skeptic's imagination" ("Transcendental Arguments, Self-Reference, and Pragmatism," 82). Heidegger argues that the "scandal of philosophy" is not that we have not yet refuted idealism, as Kant claims, but that we continue to look for such proofs, which is to say that we continue to be directed by Cartesian assumptions and the skepticism they entail (*Being and Time*, §43, 190 [205]).

54. John Sallis describes the difficulty for Kant of repairing the ground that the history of metaphysics has destroyed by what Kant describes as its incessant digging of mole tunnels (*Spacings—of Reason and Imagination*, 5–7; and A319/B375–76). See also David Farrell Krell's *Infectious Nietzsche*, where the destabilizing mole tunnels that reason has dug cannot be overcome by the Kantian leveling of the ground of metaphysics. Kant, in Krell's account, is thus a caterpillar and not a mole (*Infectious Nietzsche*, 105–107).

55. See the discussion above, and Kant, *Prolegomena*, §57, 153–54 [AA 4, 354].

56. Kant, *Prolegomena*, §59, 150 [AA 4, 361].

FOUR • Transcendental Reflection

1. As will be shown below, such interpreters of the *Critique of Judgment* range from Schelling ("Of the I as the Principle of Philosophy," 127 [vol. 2, 175]) and Hegel (*Faith and Knowledge*, 86–90 [vol. 4, 339–41]) in the immediate post-Kantian era, to Robert Pippin ("Avoiding German Idealism: Kant, Hegel, and the Reflective Judgment Problem," in his *Idealism as Modernism*, 147–53) and Burkhard Tuschling ("The System of Transcendental Idealism," 118–22) in our own time.

2. Heidegger, "Kant's Thesis about Being," 337–63 [445–80].

3. Schelling, "Of the I as the Principle of Philosophy," 127n [vol. 2, 175n]; and quoted in Heidegger, "Kant's Thesis about Being," 355 [469].

4. Schelling, "Of the I as the Principle of Philosophy," 127n [vol. 2, 175n].

5. Ibid., 127 [vol. 2, 175].

6. Ibid.

7. Ibid., translation altered.

8. Heidegger, "Kant's Thesis about Being," 355 [470].

9. Heidegger writes that Kant distinguishes the modal categories "without its being said, or even asked wherein the basis [*Grund*] for the distinction between being possible [*Möglichsein*] and being actual [*Wirklichsein*] might lie" (ibid., 355 [469]).

10. Ibid.

11. Ibid., 357 [472].

12. Kant begins this appendix by referring to "[d]ie Überlegung (*reflexio*)"; he then goes on to refer to this act as both "*transzendentale Überlegung*" and "*transzendentale Reflexion*." These terms are used interchangeably. See A263/B319 where *Überlegung* and *Reflexion* are used in successive sentences to refer to the same act, which is both "the ground of the possibility of the objective comparison of the representations to each other" (*transzendentale Überlegung*) and necessary if we are to "judge anything about things *a priori*" (*transzendentale Reflexion*). Following Guyer and Wood in their Cambridge translation (1998), both are here translated as "transcendental reflection." In the First Introduction to the *Critique of Judgment*, Kant again uses the verbal forms *reflektieren* and *überlegen* as synonyms in his discussion of reflective judgment (First Introduction, v, 15 [AA 20, 211]). See below for further discussion of these passages concerning transcendental reflection.

13. Allison describes transcendental reflection as "the level of philosophical reflection upon experience" (*Kant's Transcendental Idealism* [1983], 7). In both the original and revised versions of *Kant's Transcendental Idealism*, transcendental reflection is described as the act that distinguishes objects as appearances from things as they are in themselves. He explains that these two ways of considering things exemplify the "two sides of the same act of transcendental reflection" (ibid. [1983], 241; [2004], 56). Graham Bird concurs, explaining that transcendental reflection "is concerned . . . with the distinction between objects of the senses (appearances/phenomena) and objects of understanding or reason (things in themselves/noumena)" (*The Revolutionary Kant*, 540). As does Karin de Boer, who explains that in so doing Kant "designates the phenomenal realm as he restricts the meaning of 'all things'—insofar as it functions as the subject of synthetic a priori judgments—to 'all appearances'" ("Pure Reason's Enlightenment: Transcendental Reflection in Kant's First *Critique*," 65). Robert Pippin emphasizes that in such a designation of the phenomenal realm, transcendental reflection offers a "reflection by a subject on its own sources of knowledge" (*Idealism as Modernism*, 37). He adds that the manner in which we come to conceive of ourselves by means of such reflection "should not be taken to be knowledge about what an experiencer is," and he explains that "Kant is not worried about how a subject could attain knowledge of the subjective structure of experience" (ibid.). And yet, even if Pippin is correct that Kant is not interested in such a methodological question, and §60 of the *Prolegomena* might belie such a claim (see discussion in chapter 2 above), it does not follow that we should not ask how this reflection can itself be deemed critical. While none of these commentators ask such a question, Allison does end the first edition of *Kant's Transcendental Idealism* (1983, 331) by raising the problem posed by the demand for a metacritique, although even he removed such a query from the revised edition (2004).

14. John Sallis explains that the division of phenomena and noumena in the final chapter of the Transcendental Analytic, the chapter that precedes the appendix, describes this division as the "prearticulation" of the first *Critique*:

> Within the metaphoric system this prearticulation is expressed as the division of land from sea, the "unalterable limits" in which the island of truth is "enclosed by nature itself." This division would be one already established before critical reason comes on the scene, a prearticulation that a critical reason could, then, only take over and make directive for itself. (*Spacings— of Reason and Imagination*, 70)

Sallis goes on to describe this prearticulation as born of a "self-articulation, of a certain precritical, presystematic articulation of the field of systematic critique, of a certain opening of reason to itself" (ibid., 71). It is precisely this prearticulation that I am attempting to investigate by means of Kant's conception of transcendental reflection, the act designating the territory within which the understanding, and thus reason, articulates itself and permits the critique of metaphysical illusions. Can such a prearticulation, the "opening of reason to itself," be conceived without transcending the cognitive limits that reason itself has drawn?

15. Prauss describes transcendental reflection as the act through which the objects of experience are won, as "a non-empirical, philosophical theory of this empiricism [*eine nichtempirisch-philosophische Theorie dieser Empirie*]" (*Kant und das Problem der Dinge an sich*, 82).

16. In this way one can, with Alexis Philonenko, describe the Kantian doctrine in its movement as an inverted dialectic, moving not, as in Hegel, from the abstract to the concrete, but from the concrete, in this case the objects of experience, to the abstract

that is the condition of its possibility (Philonenko, "Hegel critique de Kant," in his *Études Kantiennes*, 36).

17. See Prauss, *Erscheinung bei Kant*, 61.

18. While transcendental reflection marks out the division in our representations that affords both the analysis of the understanding and the critique of metaphysics, Kenneth Westphal broadens its project to include "determining what our most basic cognitive capacities are" (*Kant's Transcendental Proof of Realism*, 17). Rather than assigning representations to faculties that are otherwise distinguished, Westphal conflates the act of differentiating representations with that of investigating the faculties themselves. Westphal describes this broadened transcendental reflection as "epistemic reflection"; and while he claims that its task is "providing the inventory of our cognitive capacities on which transcendental reflection, and ultimately transcendental analysis and proof, rely" (ibid.), he goes on to explain that in fact this designation of our "cognitive capacities," this foundation for the kind of transcendental reflection that Kant himself describes, that of differentiating our representations, is itself transcendental reflection. Westphal writes: "To be sure, Kant does not say directly that we learn that our sensibility is passive, and so on, by transcendental reflection, but he has no alternative doctrine about this matter, and he should not have an alternative: almost the whole *Critique* is an exercise in transcendental reflection" (ibid., 49–50).

19. In investigating the "epistemic basis upon which" Kant's Transcendental Deduction depends, Dieter Henrich, in "Kant's Notion of Deduction and the Methodological Background of the First *Critique*," develops an account of reflection that precedes the critical investigation of the Deduction. Henrich builds this account from Kant's *Logic*. In this context, reflection is the "source" from which critical investigation proceeds. It is the spontaneous recognition of the division of our faculties, a reflective knowing that is not undertaken but is rather always under way, and it permits us the varied accomplishments of the tangled web of our cognitive faculties. Henrich connects this account of our natural reflection from Kant's *Logic* to the discussion of *"Überlegen, reflexio"* in the first *Critique*; this, presumably, refers to the appendix to the Transcendental Analytic and Kant's discussion of transcendental reflection, although Henrich does not explicitly cite the section. Henrich adds that in the context of the first *Critique*, "one can hardly grasp its methodological importance" ("Kant's Notion of Deduction," 42). While Kant is short on details concerning transcendental reflection, his brief account announces a conceptual formulation beyond Henrich's discussion of the reflection that underlies critical investigation, for Kant is not here referring to a division of our faculties that occurs without conscious effort, but to the explicit act of transcendental reflection that offers the division of the representational manifold, that between understanding and reason, that is not otherwise given. This is why Kant describes transcendental reflection as a "duty required for *a priori* judgment" (A263/B319). In a manner similar to Henrich, Kirk Pillow interprets transcendental reflection as a passive precondition of critical philosophy (*Sublime Understanding*, 23).

20. See chapter 2 for further discussion of such interpreters of Kant's naturalism.

21. Hume, *A Treatise of Human Nature*, 252. Kant explains that the underlying self, the transcendental unity of apperception, cannot be conceived apart from the predicates that attach to it. While Hume denies in this way that there is a self apart from such thoughts, Kant emphasizes that our thoughts depend upon some such self, but without such thought the self is unknowable. This defines the circularity of the Kantian undertaking, what Kant calls the "perpetual circle [*beständigen Zirkel*]" of the approach (B404/A346; translation altered).

22. Prauss argues that no such justification of Kant's transcendental reflection, the designation of experience, is possible. And so what this reflection designates for Kant is the "fact of experience [*Faktum der Erfahrung*]" for which no argument can be found that offers the principle of its truth (*Erscheinung bei Kant*, 62–63, and, more generally, 58–63). The present inquiry, while accepting Prauss's position, will search for a principle that justifies something other than the truth of the product of this transcendental reflection.

23. Kant describes cognition as awakened by objects

> for how else should the cognitive faculty be awakened into exercise if not through objects [*Gegenstände*] that stimulate our senses and in part produce representations, in part bring the activity of our understanding into motion to compare [*zu vergleichen*] these, to connect them, and thus to work up the raw material of sensible impressions into a cognition of objects that is called experience? (B1)

Béatrice Longuenesse raises this passage as an example of how, for Kant, determinate judgment implies the sort of comparative intellectual activity that is called reflection in his *Logic*. She does so in order to reject the type of interpretation of determinate judgment in the first *Critique* that "deliberately privileges the *determination* of the empirical by the *a priori* (i.e., by the categories and by the mathematical concepts) to the detriment of the *reflective* relation between the intellectual forms and the sensible" (*Kant and the Capacity to Judge*, 112). While Longuenesse writes this in the context of interpreting the principles of reflection, her reference to "the *reflective* relation between intellectual forms and the sensible" concerns the progression from subjective to objective judgments, from the manifold of representations to experience, and not the division of sensible representations from intellectual ones that transcendental reflection demands. In fact, Longuenesse describes her book as "[l]eaving aside transcendental comparison or reflection" in order to concentrate on the investigation of logical reflection in the appendix to the Transcendental Analytic (ibid., 114). In her later *Kant and the Human Standpoint,* she does briefly address transcendental reflection, describing it as our attempt to apply the logical concepts of the discursive understanding to empirical objects (225–26). However, Longuenesse does not investigate this act as one that, in so applying the concepts, designates the field of inquiry.

24. Such an empirical comparison of representations, which precedes determinate judgment according to the categories, would appear to correspond to the distinction that Kant draws in the *Prolegomena* between "judgments of experience [*Erfahrungsurteile*]" and "judgments of perception [*Wahrnehmungsurteile*]." While judgments of experience depend upon pure concepts of the understanding in order to attain objective validity, Kant explains that judgments of perception are only subjectively valid, for they proceed merely according to "the logical connection [*Verknüpfung*] of perceptions in a thinking subject" (Kant, *Prolegomena*, §18, 92 [AA 4, 298]; see also §§19–20). Judgments of experience require *a priori* categories in addition to the logical comparison of sensible representations. In *Kant and the Capacity to Judge*, Béatrice Longuenesse develops such a connection between the terminology of the *Prolegomena* (judgments of perception and experience) and that of the first *Critique* (concepts of reflection, categories) (*Kant and the Capacity to Judge*, 167–97).

25. Kant uses the term *Beziehungen* to describe the sort of inner relations that the noumenal substance would have, while phenomenal substances with their myriad interactions with other substances are described as having *Verhältnisse;* both are translated as relations. This usage follows Kant's general usage of *Beziehungen* to describe relations between either objects and the cognitive faculties or else among the cognitive faculties (see B137 or A119), while *Verhältnisse* concern relations among objects (see B34/A20).

26. Heidegger describes this as the "joining of form and matter" ("Kant's Thesis about Being," 359 [474]). Kant rejects the temporal priority of matter, and the ultimate priority of form, and instead posits being as the confluence of the sensible and the intellectual, of receptivity and spontaneity as they determine possible experience.

27. See A219/B266.

28. Kant concludes this appendix, and so the Transcendental Analytic, with a discussion of the concept of nothing (*Nichts*). This discussion is not easily interpreted, and in its division into four headings it might appear to over-extend Kant's commitment to the architectonic structure of the first *Critique*. Yet, understood in relation to the above interpretation of both transcendental reflection and the concepts of reflection, insofar as the former designates the terrain of objects and the latter their accomplishment, the discussion of the concept of nothing addresses, as a foil to such objectivity, the variety of ways that the object can fail to be so determined. For discussions of this section, see Pierre Kerszberg, "Kant and the Idea of Negation"; and Ernesto Mayz Vallenilla, *Le problème du Néant chez Kant*.

29. Kant writes:

> In a word, Leibniz **intellectualized** [*intellektuierte*] the appearances, just as Locke totally **sensualized** [*sensifiziert*] the concepts of understanding in accordance with his system of noogony (if I am permitted to employ this expression). . . . Instead of seeking two entirely different sources of representation in the understanding and the sensibility, which could judge about things with objective validity **only in conjunction** [*nur in Verknüpfung*], each of these great men holds to only one of them, which in his opinion is immediately related to things in themselves, while the other does nothing but confuse or order the representations of the first. (A271/B327, translation altered)

30. Heidegger, "Kant's Thesis about Being," 361 [478].

31. Heidegger, *Being and Time*, §9, 41 [43–44].

32. Heidegger, "Kant's Thesis about Being," 361 [478].

33. Ibid.

34. Heidegger, *Being and Time*, §31, 134 [143].

35. Ibid., §23, 144 [109–110].

36. Kant, "What Does It Mean to Orient Oneself in Thinking?" 7–18 [AA 8, 131–47]. I will address the conception of orientation raised by Kant in this essay in chapter 6.

37. Heidegger, *Being and Time*, §16, 67–71 [72–76]. A phenomenological investigation, if it is to avoid the legacy of Cartesian dualism, must begin its investigations with what is given, with entities that offer themselves as meaningful, as useful for our purposes, and as offering a developed extension of our bodily involvements in the world. They are, Heidegger writes, our "equipment." Beginning with entities so conceived, which is to say prior to the radical division of our subjectivity from objects of experience, avoids viewing the entities that surround us as artifacts cut off from our personal involvements or, rather, avoids viewing them at precisely that moment in which they do not serve their purpose but are broken and force us to look at them as merely physical things, as artifacts offering themselves equally for analysis to all beings of our cognitive functioning. Such a reduced meaning attributed to the entities that form the web of meanings within which we live Heidegger calls "presence-to-hand [*Vorhandenheit*]."

38. *Being and Time* was published in 1927; *Kant and the Problem of Metaphysics* was first published in 1929.

39. *"Kant ist vor dieser unbekannten Wurzel zurückgewichen"* (Heidegger, *Kant and the Problem of Metaphysics*, §31, 112 [160]).

40. Kant writes: *"die vielleicht aus einer gemeinschaftlichen, aber uns unbekannten Wurzel entspringen"* (A15/B29).

41. In the Transcendental Doctrine of Method, Kant describes his inquiries as beginning "at the point where the general root [*allgemeine Wurzel*] of our cognitive power [*Erkenntniskraft*] divides and branches out into two stems, one of which is reason" (A835/B863). I will return to the question of the renaming of one of the stems, the change from understanding to reason, below in chapter 6.

42. John Sallis points this out in *Spacings—of Reason and Imagination*, 74.

43. Dieter Henrich argues, contra not only Heidegger but also Reinhold, Fichte, Hegel, and Cohen, that the "unknown root" refers to the noumenal realm and so by definition remains unknown because it surpasses our faculties (Henrich, *The Unity of Reason*, 19–20). Rudolf Makkreel agrees with Henrich's claim that the "common root" is unknowable (*Imagination and Interpretation in Kant*, 21). Henrich goes on to raise the possibility that the unknowable root of our faculties is in fact the metaphysical idea of the soul (*The Unity of Reason*, 20–21), the unknowable idea of which offers Kant the regulative pursuit of "the unity of the 'faculties of the mind'" in the appendix to the Transcendental Dialectic (ibid., 26–27). I will address this suggestive remark in chapter 6 when I address the psychological idea in such a regulative function.

44. Heidegger, *Kant and the Problem of Metaphysics*, §31, 112 [160].

45. Heidegger explains that the Schematism elucidates the role played by the transcendental imagination in connecting pure concepts and pure intuition already in the Transcendental Deduction (ibid., §22, 73 [105]).

46. Ibid., §31, 112 [160]. Henrich criticizes this passage, explaining that, for Kant, what is unknown "can disquiet us only as long as we are not certain of its unattainability" (*The Unity of Reason*, 33).

47. Heidegger, *Kant and the Problem of Metaphysics*, §31, 113 [161]. Kant repeats this claim at A115; it too is removed in the second edition.

48. Heidegger, *Kant and the Problem of Metaphysics*, §31, 112–13 [160–61].

49. On the continuity between the two versions of the Transcendental Deduction with their different emphases, see Jennifer Mensch, "Between Sense and Thought," 81–93. See chapter 5 for further analysis of Kant's discussion of the role of the Transcendental Deduction in the first edition's preface.

50. See chapter 3 for a discussion of Heidegger's *What Is a Thing?*

51. Heidegger, "Kant's Thesis about Being," 362 [478].

52. Ibid., 360 [476].

53. Ibid., 357 [472].

54. Ibid., 362 [478–79].

55. Ibid., 357 [472], translation altered. This turning away from the thought of the organon of the critical system should remind us of Heidegger's claim that Kant retreated from the transcendental imagination, the non-conceptual element found in the reflective designation of experience (*Kant and the Problem of Metaphysics*, §31, 112 [160]). In the early comment, Heidegger argues that within critical analysis Kant was forced to admit that which surpassed his conceptual dualism, and yet, he did not pursue this route; in the later "Kant's Thesis about Being," Heidegger has found in the first *Critique* an inquiry into that which permits the analysis of cognition, from whose depths, alas, Kant "shrank back."

56. Heidegger, *Being and Time*, §23, 101–102 [109–110].

57. Kant, *Critique of Judgment*, First Introduction, v, 15 [AA 20, 211].

58. Ibid., vii, 21–24 [AA 20, 219–21]. Rodolph Gasché describes this first form of reflection as that of determinate judgment (*The Idea of Form*, 17–18). He explains that determinate judgment includes a reflective moment, the logical reflection that leads to conceptual determination. This reading of Kant's account of judgment as including both determinative judgment and the "mere [*bloßes*]" faculty of reflective judgment seems appropriate, but in his book's focus on aesthetic and not teleological reflective judgment, Gasché does not add that this form of reflection, in which representations are compared with each other, also refers to the teleological examination of the diversity of causal law (Kant, *Critique of Judgment*, First Introduction, v, 15 [AA 20, 211]).

59. Kant, *Critique of Judgment*, First Introduction, viii, 24–28 [AA 5, 221–26]. In comparing reflective judgments of the beautiful with the immediate pleasure of judgments of sense, Kant explains that the latter do not depend on a comparison of the representation with the faculties of cognition (ibid., 27 [AA 5, 225]).

60. Helga Mertens, in *Kommentar zur Ersten Einleitung in Kants Kritik der Urteilskraft*, draws such a connection (94–95). In what follows I will develop this idea that transcendental reflection, although introduced in the first *Critique*, prior to this systematic analysis of reflection, can be conceived in terms similar to those in the third *Critique*. Karin de Boer notes this "parallel" between Kant's description of reflection in the First Introduction to the third *Critique* and his earlier account of transcendental reflection in the first *Critique*, but she concludes that she "do[es] not think that transcendental reflection constitutes a mode of the faculty of judgment (de Boer, "Pure Reason's Enlightenment," 67n).

61. Kant, *Critique of Judgment*, First Introduction, v, 15 [AA 20, 211]; see the earlier discussion in chapter 2 of the role of regulative principles in reflection.

62. Ibid., xii, 48 [AA 20, 249].

63. As discussed above in chapter 2, *even* in the case of the cosmological antinomies we are afforded a regulative principle. In fact, the solution to the third Antinomy, that of viewing mechanism as a regulative undertaking that permits freedom, is offered already within the body of the first *Critique*. Kant addresses the regulative roles played by the theological and the psychological ideas only in the appendix that follows the Transcendental Dialectic, and there in a rather cursory fashion.

64. See particularly A682–84/B710–12.

65. Heidegger does not ask such a question because, for him, transcendental reflection offers the subversion of the critical continuation of the traditional epistemological stance, marking the way out of critique, and is therefore not in need of transcendental explanation.

66. Heidegger, *Kant and the Problem of Metaphysics*, §45, 172 [245].

67. This conception of "absolute possibility," divorced from any criteria of the empirically actual, can be compared to the conception of the actual that is untarnished by the possible. While the former, as discussed above, is the vast region of thought separated from any criteria of actualization, the latter is the thought of God, an *intellectus archetypus* (Kant, *Critique of Judgment*, §77, 277 [AA 5, 408]; see also the discussion above in chapter 2) for whom all that is thought exists and thus for whom actuality has been separated from possibility.

68. To deny this in Kant's name forces one to conclude that he approached epistemological questions naïvely, oblivious to the philosophical tradition that has continually problematized the object of knowledge.

69. Kant, *Prolegomena*, §60, 152–53 [AA 4, 364].

70. Approaching Kant's account of the conditions of the possibility of experience by means of the analytic of principles rather than the analytic of concepts constitutes a

reversal of the textual order similar to that offered by Hermann Cohen. For Cohen, the analytic of principles offers the source for the deduction of the validity of the categories (*Kants Theorie der Erfahrung*, 345–46). The conception of experience and the categories deduced from it arise from "the highest principle [*dem obersten Grundsatze*]," that of the possibility of experience (ibid., 186–87). Cohen accepts the "scientific" nature of such experience (ibid., 187). What is here being argued is that Kant's conception of experience can be seen to depend on a prior parsing of representations, and so the conception of experience has not merely been presupposed. Such a parsing, that of transcendental reflection, depends upon the critique of metaphysics that the categories it helps to uncover make possible. Thus, what is here offered is an emphasis on the analytic of principles that does *not* claim for itself a foundation in Newtonian science.

71. Hamann, "Metacritique of the Purism of Reason," 522 [vol. 3, 286].

72. Hamann writes in an August 8, 1784, letter to Herder: "I am still waiting for an apocalyptic angel with a key to this abyss [*Abgrund*]" (*Briefwechsel*, vol. 5, 177).

73. This follows quite literally the account that Kant gives of the origin of the critical enterprise in his letter to Christian Garve of September 21, 1798 (Kant, *Correspondence*, 551–52 [AA 12, 257–58]).

74. Kant, *Prolegomena*, §60, 152n [AA 4, 364n].

75. Hegel, *Faith and Knowledge*, 90 [vol. 4, 341]. In what follows I will confine my analysis to Hegel's 1802 *Faith and Knowledge* since it succinctly encapsulates the criticism of Kant that has both greatly influenced the interpretation of his work and offers the challenge to the Kantian system that I am attempting to answer. Clearly, one would need to look beyond this early work of Hegel, and thus beyond his Jena period, to develop a comprehensive reading of his relation to Kant.

76. Ibid., 89 [vol. 4, 341].

77. Ibid., 80 [vol. 4, 335].

78. Ibid.

79. Ibid., 68 [vol. 4, 326].

80. Ibid., 69 [vol. 4, 327].

81. Ibid., 68 [vol. 4, 326].

82. Ibid., 72 [vol. 4, 328].

83. Ibid., 87 [vol. 4, 339], translation altered.

84. Ibid., 87 [vol. 4, 340], translation altered.

85. Ibid., 88 [vol. 4, 340], paraphrasing Kant's *Critique of Judgment*, §76.

86. Hegel, *Faith and Knowledge*, 89 [vol. 4, 341].

87. Ibid.

88. Béatrice Longuenesse accepts Hegel's interpretation of the experienced absolute in Kant's Antinomy of Taste: "If one takes seriously the idea that in aesthetic judgment the feeling of pleasure expressed in the predicate 'beautiful' is universally grounded in the concept of the supersensible . . . it then makes some sense to say that intuiting beauty is consciously intuiting intellectual intuition" (Longuenesse, "Point of View of Man or Knowledge of God," 266; Hegel, *Faith and Knowledge*, 86–88 [vol. 4, 339–40]). And yet, while agreeing with Hegel that Kant's Dialectic of the Aesthetic Power of Judgment and its Antinomy of Taste led further than Kant anticipated, Longuenesse does not follow Hegel toward the experienced absolute; rather, she attempts to turn the examination of the experience of beauty from the Dialectic to the Analytic of the Aesthetic Power of Judgment. For Longuenesse, such a turning back to the analytic avoids the metaphysical unity that Hegel sees in the dialectic, and offers the possibility of the development of the

"point of view of man" (Longuenesse, "Point of View of Man or Knowledge of God," 275) as a way of interpreting Kant's critical philosophy without proclaiming the need for the experience of the intuitive intellect. This turning back to the analytic as a rejection of the Dialectic of Aesthetic Judgment accepts the Hegelian claim that what the Antinomy of Taste does is imbue the experience of beauty with a God-like intuition; this, as I argued above, misinterprets this section, for the rational principle is found to be necessary not for the experience of beauty but for its elucidation and so for a critique of taste. In order to give a systematic account of taste, we must explain it by means of such a regulative principle. To revert to the analytic, as Longuenesse does, without this recognition fails to investigate the presuppositions implicit in the Analytic of Aesthetic Judgment, in, that is to say, the account of beauty that is based in the *sensus communis*. Longuenesse explains that this is the plan for a broader project, with the goal of retreating "once and for all into the Analytic of all three *Critiques*," elucidating the "point of view of man" and "the nature of the ever more complex intertwinings of sensibility and discursivity, passivity and activity, by means of which our access to the world is achieved" (ibid.). This project, diametrically opposed to that which I am developing here, insofar as I am investigating the interconnection of the Analytic and the Dialectic of the first *Critique*, was begun by Longuenesse in *Kant and the Capacity to Judge*, where she explicates the place of the principles of reflection in the production of determinate judgment without investigating the metaphysical presuppositions of this epistemological investigation, without, that is to say, addressing the metaphysical implications of transcendental reflection.

89. John McCumber makes such a connection in *The Company of Words* (15). For Hegel's discussion of "the beautiful soul," see the *Phenomenology of Spirit* (399–407 [vol. 9, 354–61]).

90. Hegel, *Phenomenology of Spirit*, 407–409 [vol. 9, 361–362].

91. McCumber writes that Hamann's "lack of interest in the concrete expression of his thought" (*The Company of Words*, 8) was not limited to his theoretical endeavors, since his philosophical views denied him access to the core of individuality and so also produced a profound social isolation, which McCumber describes as "a failure of dialogue" (ibid., 9). See pages 7–12 of McCumber's book for this analysis of Hamann in relation to Hegel; see also Hegel's 1828 essay on Hamann, "The Writings of Hamann," 47–48 [vol. 16, 179–80].

92. If, following Longuenesse, we attempt to disentangle the analytic from the dialectic in the first *Critique*, assuming this is possible, we would be left with an utterly dogmatic account of experience, and the calls for a metacritique would resound.

93. I will develop such a conception of the circularity that governs the relation of the Analytic and the Dialectic of the first *Critique* in chapter 6.

94. Robert Pippin explains that to investigate the dependence of the analysis of finite cognition on the infinite is to inquire how reason, through its uncognizable ideas, is related to the unity of the understanding that is distinguished in the Transcendental Analytic. Reason, Pippin explains, has "the understanding itself, and its concepts for its object" (*Kant's Theory of Form*, 207). While Pippin is aware of the role of reason in teleology, as is explained in the First Introduction to the *Critique of Judgment*, he explains that he cannot comprehend how a dependence on the ideas of reason could be responsible for the analysis of the understanding. He writes: "all attempts known to me to understand how just these three organizing principles arise from the limitations of the understanding, or even how they actually do help organize appearances in useful ways (particularly the first), have not been particularly successful" (ibid., 211). It should be clear that the current

work is attempting to explain how these regulative principles, and particularly the first one, the psychological, can be understood to function.

95. Hegel, *Faith and Knowledge*, 69 [vol. 4, 326].

FIVE • The Paralogisms of Pure Reason

1. See chapter 1 for discussion of this passage and Hamann's criticism of such a limiting of our goals.

2. I will address the conception of orientation raised by Kant in "What Does It Mean to Orient Oneself in Thinking?" in the following chapter.

3. Heinz Heimsoeth has argued against such limited epistemological readings of critical philosophy. However, without such an investigation of the regulative underpinnings of Kantian critique, he is only able to describe its metaphysical commitments. While he has gone a long way toward uncovering the presuppositions of Kantian epistemology, and the continuity of Kant's critical project with his pre-critical works, he does not reconsider Kant's transcendental method in light of these presuppositions (Heimsoeth, "Metaphysical Motives in the Development of Critical Idealism," 158–99).

4. "The numerical unity of this apperception therefore grounds all concepts *a priori*, just as the manifoldness of space and time grounds the intuitions of sensibility" (A107).

5. We should be reminded of the "abyss" described by Hamann and returned to by Heidegger as the "abyss" of language (see Hamann, *Briefwechsel*, vol. 5, 177; Heidegger, "Language," 191 [12]; and above in chapter 1).

6. Kant here uses the word *Grundsätze* for both the immanent principles of the understanding and the transcendent use of these principles by reason. This would appear to contradict the distinction between *Grundsätze* and *Prinzipien* in Kant's terminology, a distinction that is discussed above in chapter 2. But there is no contradiction, because Kant only distinguishes these terms in the pages following this discussion (A300–301/B356–58). Thus, the transcendent principles (*Grundsätze*) come to be described as *Prinzipien*, while the immanent principles (*Grundsätze*), those that offer themselves as the ground of cognition only with the inclusion of sensible content, come to define the now-limited term *Grundsätze*.

7. John Sallis writes of Kant's two uses of the term "reason": "One ought surely to be provoked by the apparent outrage: the word which names the fundamental matter put at issue in the *Critique of Pure Reason* is left openly ambiguous!" (*The Gathering of Reason*, 44–45).

8. Translation altered.

9. For the same phrasing, see Kant, *Critique of Judgment*, §76, 271 [AA 5, 401].

10. It must be noted that in following the inferences drawn from the categories of relation, the pursuit of the ideas of reason refers to the categories of relation in a double sense, both as the structure of the syllogism pursued and as one of the four ways to attempt to determine an object that would correspond to the chain of inferences.

11. In reference to the architectonic structure that Kant follows in the Transcendental Dialectic, Strawson writes: "This logical framework, in its connexion with the topics of the Dialectic and its elaboration under the guidance of the fourfold division of the categories, is altogether too strained and artificial to be taken seriously, and I shall dispense myself from discussing it further" (*The Bounds of Sense*, 157). While Strawson admits that within this implausible framework, Kant does address important issues concerning analogies between "ordinary and scientific thinking," he rejects Kant's connection of the

dialectic to the analytic, asking, essentially, why metaphysical reasoning should follow just these four paths. This assumes that Kant is attempting to address metaphysical thought in general in the Transcendental Dialectic. In Strawson's investigation of the Paralogisms, he distinguishes these discussions (other than the Fourth Paralogism of the first edition, which he addresses separately) from Kant's project of transcendental idealism, and then he criticizes Kant for neglecting issues that are explained in the Transcendental Analytic (e.g., the "empirical criteria of subject-identity"; ibid., 166). If we separate the critique of metaphysics from Kant's transcendental idealism, the architectonic path that Kant follows into metaphysics certainly does appear arbitrary. Only if we interpret the dialectic as following the conceptual paths that the analytic has uncovered, building a critique of metaphysics from these accomplishments, can its function be seen not merely to be negative in its critique of metaphysical illusion, as Strawson claims (ibid., 155), but also to be positive in addressing the further goals that Strawson recognizes as its plan (including a "proof of the thesis of transcendental idealism"; ibid.) but that he claims it fails to achieve (ibid., 156).

12. This does not mean that there is no confusion surrounding the two uses of *Vernunft*, and we must still be careful to distinguish them. It is just that the two usages do not contradict each other.

13. T. D. Weldon describes "the function of reason treated in the Dialectic" as "doubly reflective" (*Kant's "Critique of Pure Reason,"* 238). While in the Transcendental Analytic thought, or reason in the broader of the two uses, reflects on its structure and limits, in the Transcendental Dialectic thought comes to reflect on this prior reflection, on "its limitations as expounded in the Analytic" (ibid.). Thus, the object of reason, that upon which it reflects, "is the understanding" (ibid.). However, Weldon does not further develop this provocative thought. What, we need to ask, is accomplished in this reflection on the reflective designation of the structure and limits of cognition?

14. Translation altered.

15. Hume, *A Treatise of Human Nature*, 252.

16. See A261/B317, and my discussion of this appendix above in chapter 4.

17. The gaps in our self-knowledge left by the other two areas of rational psychology —the soul prior to life and the soul after life—which concern our immortality, do not appear to play a role in Kant's critical epistemology. But the issue of the soul's immortality returns as a practical postulate of Kantian ethics (Kant, *Critique of Practical Reason*, 238–39 [AA 5, 122–24]). There, Kant argues that we must think of the soul as immortal in order to conceive of the moral perfectibility of human life.

18. I will begin the examination of the Paralogisms chapter with the first edition's detailed discussion of the four paralogisms and supplement it with relevant passages from the condensed version in the second edition. In those cases in which Kant substantially changed the content of a section, as in the Fourth Paralogism, I will directly address the changes.

19. John Sallis, in *The Gathering of Reason*, explains the substantiality of transcendental apperception succinctly:

> On this premise "substance" designates a pure, i.e., unschematized, concept; it has here only a logical and not an objective sense, since categories can have objective validity only through connection with the element of intuition, which is totally lacking in transcendental apperception. Indeed, it can be said quite legitimately that the I is substance. But this amounts simply to mak-

ing a formal distinction between determinations, a distinction which can be made with regard to any and every thing. . . . To say that the I is a substance is thus to say virtually nothing. (82)

20. In her essay "Kant's Paralogisms," Patricia Kitcher interprets the major premise as a claim independent of critical analysis: "I think that Kant regards the major principle as acceptable because it states a commonly accepted definition of 'substance'" (106; see also Kitcher, *Kant's Transcendental Psychology*, 185). Kitcher claims that not only does this conception have roots in Leibniz but it is in fact a tautology and thus is not in need of explanation. Such an interpretation makes it difficult to understand the error to which the pursuit of the substantiality of the soul is brought.

21. Kant writes *Mir selbst*, the "nonstandard" capitalization "suggesting," Guyer and Wood argue in their translation, "that '*Mir*' is a noun rather than a pronoun" (A348, note a). I have, however, refrained from their capitalization of the translation "Myself" which does not, I think, help to clarify the English.

22. Michelle Grier explains, "The 'illusory' nature of the second [minor] premise . . . provides the basis for the paralogistic fallacy" (*Kant's Doctrine of Transcendental Illusion*, 159).

23. Clearly, Descartes reclaims the truth of the objects around us, arguing in both the Third and the Fifth Meditations that God exists and could not be a deceiver, and then in the Sixth Meditation examining the existence of material things; but in beginning with such a complete division between subject and object, and with certainty concerning the former, the "thing that thinks" (Descartes, *Meditations on First Philosophy*, 19), and with doubt about the latter, the only way to protect the truths of the phenomenal world is through a further metaphysical claim. As in Kant's Refutation of Idealism, one could say here that Kant is emphasizing the method of Descartes' undertaking rather than his conclusions.

24. See Ameriks's *Kant's Theory of Mind* (69–71) for a discussion of the superiority of the second edition's First Paralogism over that of the first edition. Claude Piché explains that the category of substance is the "basic concept [*Grundbegriff*]" of transcendental psychology, offering in its "logical sense [*logischen Sinne*]" the subject of all our predicates, and in its "real meaning [*realen Bedeutung*]" persistence through change (*Das Ideal*, 73). For this reason as well as, or perhaps because of, the dependence of the Paralogisms on the syllogistic form of substance as a category of relation, it is apparent why Kant chose substance as the example of the Paralogisms in the second edition.

25. Allison correctly points out that the ambiguity that Kant claims for the term "thought" can really be said to be located in the entire phrase of what "cannot be thought otherwise than as subject" (*Kant's Transcendental Idealism*, 284).

26. Horstmann explains, "that the I cannot be represented as an object in any thinkable sense [*daß das Ich in keinem denkbaren Sinne als Objekt vorgestellt werden kann*]" (*Bausteine kritischer Theorie*, 101).

27. Kant writes only, "Thus etc [*Also etc.*]" (A351), for the conclusion of the syllogism, unlike the other three Paralogisms in the second edition, where he spells out the conclusions to the syllogisms. Likewise, in the minor premise of the Third Paralogism, Kant leads us to his claim while leaving the point unstated, writing, "Now the soul is etc. [*Nun ist die Seele etc.*]" (A361).

28. In the second edition, Kant describes the "I think" as an "empirical proposition" that already contains "the proposition 'I exist'" (B422n). See Descartes' Second Meditation in his *Meditations on First Philosophy*.

29. In "Leibniz and Materialism," Margaret Wilson argues that the Second Paralogism should be understood as directed more at a Leibnizian than at a Cartesian target (in Wilson, *Ideas and Mechanism*, 398–402). In refuting materialist claims about the mind in the "Monadology," Leibniz argues that perception cannot be explained by a mechanistic account of the mind as a machine, concluding that one must look at the simple self, rather than such a compound, in order to conceive of perception (§17, 254). It is such a claim about the simplicity of the soul, or mind, that Kant refutes in the Second Paralogism. The Kantian transcendental subject is a mere logical subject, and is thus empty in regard to the claims that Leibniz's rationalism makes on behalf of the immaterial subject.

30. And apperception, Heimsoeth reminds us, must be regarded as that which is conceived of as abstracted from all "qualities of the subject [*Eigenschaften des Subjekts*]," which is to say all that the metaphysical claim for the simplicity of the soul purports to unite (*Transzendentale Dialektik, Erster Teil*, 120).

31. Even if one could prove that the subject was simple, this would not prove that it—the soul—was immortal. In the second edition, Kant adds a refutation of Mendelssohn's attempt, in his *Phaedo*, to argue that from the soul's simplicity we can infer its immortality. Mendelssohn understood that those like Plato—who in his own *Phaedo* has Socrates argue that since only compound things can be destroyed, the soul as a simple thing cannot (Plato, *Phaedo*, 78b–c)—are vulnerable to the criticism that the soul thus conceived could vanish. Mendelssohn argues that the simple soul is not in this way vulnerable, as it can in no way be diminished and so cannot vanish. In this dialogue, Mendelssohn asks: "Perhaps the soul passes away quickly, disappears in an instant. In and for itself this type of death is possible. But can it be brought about by nature? [*Vielleicht vergehet die Seele plötzlich, verschwindet in einem Nu. An und für sich ist diese Todesart möglich. Kann sie aber von der Natur hervorgebracht werden?*]" (Mendelssohn, *Phädon oder über die Unsterblichkeit der Seele*, in his *Gesammelte Schriften*, vol. 3.1, 70; see also B413–14). Kant points out that the simple soul can undergo no destruction in the manner of objects with external parts, and so as an "extensive magnitude," as an existence, it must exemplify an "internal magnitude." Its "powers [*Kräfte*]," like those of any existence, are distinguished in terms of the variety of their expression as a certain "degree of reality" (B414), a standard that is diminished when such a soul loses its "powers," raising the possibility of its destruction. "For even consciousness has a degree" (ibid.), Kant writes, which is to say that even a minimal claim about this simple soul, while having no external parts, does exemplify a distinction that could be conceived as permitting its destruction. For Kant's account of internal or "intensive magnitudes," see Anticipations of Perception (A166–76/B207–218). The possibility of such an inner destruction, the eventual loss of consciousness, etc., leads Kant to say that Mendelssohn, if he wanted to avoid offering an unintentional proof that the soul is in fact not immortal, should have distinguished a synthetic claim about the subject, which includes its existence and so its finitude, from an analytic one. An analytic claim about the subject of thought, which is to say Kant's transcendental subject, is merely a logical unity that does not include existence, and so has no degree and can be neither diminished nor destroyed (B416–18). And yet, to so limit the claim on behalf of the subject of thought to the analytic claim of transcendental subjectivity makes it impossible to say anything about the existence of this subject.

32. The Kantian conception of the categorical imperative and the moral system it initiates is thus marked by its dependence on the very relations with others that it wishes to legislate. This is no contradiction, and follows Kant's approach in the critical system, which attempts to thematize our commitments rather than radically transform them; see Kant, "What Does It Mean to Orient Oneself in Thinking?" where he reminds us that the person

of "common but (morally) healthy reason," which is to say one without philosophical or speculative insight, already exemplifies a commitment to the moral system that Kant is describing. Such a person, Kant writes, "can mark out his path, in both a theoretical and a practical respect, in a way which is fully in accord with the whole end of his vocation" (Kant, "What Does It Mean to Orient Oneself in Thinking?" 14 [AA 8, 142]).

33. Translation altered.

34. In demonstrating the impossibility of conceiving of a non-empirical, and so non-phenomenal, persistence (*Beharrlichkeit*) of the soul, we should be reminded of the difficulty involved in interpreting the Refutation of Idealism, where Kant raises the need for just such a non-phenomenal, persistent thing.

35. See, for instance, §16 of the second edition's Transcendental Deduction, where Kant distinguishes the analytic unity of transcendental apperception from a synthetic unity (B131–36).

36. Heinz Heimsoeth explains that the "permanence of my self [*Beharrlichkeit meiner Selbst*]" (A363; Heimsoeth, *Transzendentale Dialektik, Erster Teil*, 122) is born of the subject taking itself from the "standpoint [*Standpunkt*]" of an "external observer [*äußeren Beobachter*]" (A362; Heimsoeth, *Transzendentale Dialektik, Erster Teil*, 123). In the time of inner sense, we are not even persistent things for ourselves, but only in the "intersubjective time [*intersubjektive Zeit*]" of external objects is persistence, born of the category of substance, possible.

37. See the First Analogy of Experience for Kant's discussion of the empirical principle (*Grundsatz*) connected with the category of substance (A182–88/B224–32).

38. In the second edition, Kant explains that the identity of the subject

> cannot signify the identity of the person, by which would be understood the consciousness of the identity of its own substance as a thinking being in all changes of state; in order to prove that what would be demanded is not a mere analysis of the proposition "I think," but rather various synthetic judgments grounded on the given intuition. (B408)

39. See B291, where Kant explains that outer intuitions and not merely inner intuitions are needed to "establish the objective reality" of the categories.

40. In the second edition, this is phrased as "the identity of myself in everything manifold of which I am conscious [*der Identität meiner selbst bei allem Mannigfaltigen, dessen ich mir bewußt bin*]" (B408).

41. Translation altered.

42. This discussion was raised in chapter 3 in the examination of the Refutation of Idealism in order to show that Kant had clearly conceived of a skepticism more radical than that which emanates from the Cartesian method prior to his writing the second edition's Refutation.

43. Karl Ameriks raises two ways that Kant can be seen to be challenging the claims of the Fourth Paralogism: the empirical challenge to the soundness of the valid argument and the transcendental challenge to the validity of the argument, concerning the two meanings of the term "outer." Ameriks, however, claims that "it is not clear which of the readings Kant wanted to assign the rational psychologist" (*Kant's Theory of Mind*, 112). It seems to me that priority is given to the latter. Kant's argument does not rest on distinguishing the empirical possibility of an "outer appearance" that indubitably exists, but on the transcendental explanation of the conditions of the possibility of experience conceived as "outer appearances."

44. John Sallis distinguishes the term "outer" as the source of the ambiguity that misdirects the inference of the Fourth Paralogism (*The Gathering of Reason*, 89).

45. Kant makes this point at A373, describing the "ambiguity [*Zweideutigkeit*]" in the term "outside us [*außer uns*]," which transcendental idealism has explained can refer to either things in themselves or appearances. Kant calls the former "external in the transcendental sense [*transzendentalen Sinne*]," while the latter are "**empirically external objects.**" Without such a distinction, Cartesian idealism claims that all that is "outside us" is doubtful, while Kant is able to argue that only things in themselves are doubtful. In the second edition's Refutation of Idealism, where Kant moves this criticism of Cartesian idealism, he adds the claim that even what is "outside" us in a "transcendental sense," what he there describes as "a **thing** outside me [*außer mir*] and not through the mere representation of a thing outside me" (B275), can be known to exist. The criticism of the skeptical idealism in the first edition's Fourth Paralogism is transformed into the second edition's Refutation of Idealism.

46. See Heimsoeth, *Transzendentale Dialektik, Erster Teil*, 169.

47. As noted above, in the second edition Kant offers a single account of the form of all paralogistic error, using the First Paralogism as his model (B410–11). The paralogisms all turn on the ambiguous use of a term, and typically the ambiguous terms are in the major and minor premises. But, in the first edition's Fourth Paralogism the ambiguous terms are in the minor premise and the conclusion, while in the rewritten second edition's Fourth Paralogism the ambiguity can be found in the major and minor premises.

48. C. Thomas Powell offers a version of the second edition's Fourth Paralogism that downplays the role of "existence [*Existenz*]" and the modal category *Dasein*, to which it refers (A344–45/B402–403). Powell formulates the major premise in the following way: "That, the existence of which can be distinguished from that of a given other thing, is different from that thing" ("Kant's Fourth Paralogism," 401). He conceives of the minor premise in the way that I have, but concludes: "Therefore I am different from those things that are outside me" (ibid.). Powell introduces the term "different" (alongside Kant's distinguished, or perhaps differentiated [*unterschieden*]), rejecting Kant's connection of the Fourth Paralogism to the modal categories, and instead emphasizing the Third Paralogism of identity with its discussion of "different times [*verschiedenen Zeiten*]" (A361) and its connection to quantity. Powell describes Kant's use of the modal category of existence as mere "architectonic garnish" (ibid.), but it is hard to explain why Kant would need to return to the territory of the Third Paralogism (in both editions) and to the category of quantity.

49. As Allison points out, Kant has a brief discussion of such problematic idealism at A491–92/B519–20 (*Kant's Transcendental Idealism* [2004], 494).

50. Karl Ameriks, in *Kant's Theory of Mind*, attempts to address the conception of the mind that the *Critique* offers even as it rejects determinate knowledge of the soul. He explains that Kant "takes it as evident that the mind is given to us as an item different from extended matter, and therefore at least in that sense it is a distinct thing" (65). Ameriks recognizes that the commitment to such a conception of the self contradicts "the orthodox Kantian position" (ibid., 169), but he describes it as "supplementing Kant's doctrines" (ibid., 8) while effecting "only a limited weakening of his transcendental idealism" (ibid., 170). Ameriks explains this in terms of the issues surrounding personality in the Third Paralogism. He argues that by modifying Kant's claim that in some way we are in contact with the "matter" of reality, we can arrive at the position that the soul has "some temporally extended nature" (ibid., 169). Ameriks explains that this is to accept

"the immediate sense of time within oneself . . . as valid" (ibid., 170), and thus as offering the unity of our self-identity, a unity that never offers itself theoretically but does offer itself with great force experientially. What is here being investigated is whether Kant's continued commitment to the role of the soul after the rejection of its claims to knowledge can be explained without embracing such realism in Kant's name (see chapter 3, n. 3, for discussion of Ameriks and other realist interpretations of the Kantian system).

51. Translation altered.

52. Kant, *Critique of Practical Reason*, 238–39 [AA 5, 122–24].

53. The way that the ideas of reason can be understood to be a canon for the understanding can be contrasted with Heidegger's interpretation of transcendental reflection as offering, contra Kant's own pronouncements, an organon that, in highlighting the limitations of our logic, supersedes all investigation of cognition (see A795/B823; Heidegger, "Kant's Thesis about Being," 361–62 [478]; and chapter 4 above).

SIX • Transcendental Method

1. Kant, "What Does It Mean to Orient Oneself in Thinking?" 7–18 [AA 8, 131–47].

2. For a detailed discussion of the tortuous path of the *Pantheismusstreit*, as well as its antecedents and its effect on the final years of Mendelssohn's life, see Alexander Altmann's *Moses Mendelssohn: A Biographical Study*, 593–759.

3. Kant originally published the essay in the *Berlinische Monatschrift* (September 25, 1786: 304–329), after being prompted to weigh in publicly on the controversy by a letter dated June 11, 1786, from its editor, Johann Erich Biester (in Kant, *Correspondence*, 255–60, translation altered [AA 10, 453–58]). Biester's interest was not that Kant enter into the acrimonious debate between Mendelssohn and Jacobi over Lessing's legacy, but that Kant defend reason from Jacobi's attacks. While agreeing that Jacobi had been malicious in his treatment of Mendelssohn, Biester, who was clearly not averse to hyperbole, wrote: "But as I said, as far as I am concerned Moses M. and Berlin can stand or fall! It is only *truth* and *reason* that I would not want so visibly threatened [*Nur die Wahrheit u. die Vernunft wünschte ich nicht so sichtbarlich gefährdet*]" (ibid., 257 [AA 10, 455]). See also Mendelssohn's earlier letter to Kant (October 16, 1785, ibid., 231 [AA 10, 413–14]) in which he criticizes the way that both he and Lessing have been treated by Jacobi. But Mendelssohn cannot avoid his own rather personal attack, describing Jacobi's *Concerning the Doctrine of Spinoza in Letters to Moses Mendelssohn* as "an unusual mixture, an almost monstrous birth, with the head of *Goethe*, the body of *Spinoza*, and the feet of *Lavater* [*ein seltenes Gemisch, eine fast monströse Geburt: der Kopf von* Goethe, *der Leib* Spinoza, *u. die Füße* Lavater]" (ibid., 230–32 [AA 10, 414]). It is perhaps not surprising that Biester's philosophical plea rather than Mendelssohn's ad hominem attack prompted Kant to intervene. See Altmann, *Moses Mendelssohn*, 750–52.

4. See below for discussion of this interpretation of Spinoza.

5. Jacobi, *Concerning the Doctrine of Spinoza in Letters to Moses Mendelssohn*, 187 [vol. 1.1, 18].

6. Ibid.

7. Jacobi writes: "If there are only efficient, but no final causes, then the only function that the faculty of thought has in the whole of nature is that of observer" (ibid., 189 [vol. 1.1, 20]). For Jacobi, what was at stake was the intellectual freedom to set aside such mechanistic inquiry, and undertake a "mortal leap [*salto mortale*]" (ibid.).

8. In 1785 Moses Mendelssohn published *Morgenstunden* (*Gesammelte Schriften*, vol. 3.2, 1–175). His *An die Freunde Lessings* was published soon after his death in 1786 (ibid., 177–218).

9. Mendelssohn explains that it was not the charge of Spinozism that bothered him, since there is a "purified Spinozism [*geläuterten Spinozismus*]" that is consistent with religion and morality; rather, it was the claim that Lessing was a "blasphemer [*Gotteslästerer*]" and a "hypocrite [*Heuchler*]" that was offensive (*An die Freunde Lessings*, in *Gesammelte Schriften*, vol. 3.2, 188). Mendelssohn describes Spinoza's pantheism as "refined [*verfeinert*]" (ibid., 136).

10. In the letter to Reimarus, dated August 16, 1783, Mendelssohn writes: "did Lessing take the system [Spinoza's] as Bayle misunderstood it, or as others have better explained it [*hat Lessing das System so genommen, wie es Bayle misverstanden, oder wie andere es besser erklärt haben*]?" (ibid., letter 608, vol. 3, 123). Bayle described Spinoza's pantheism as "the most monstrous hypothesis [*la plus monstrueuse hypothèse*]" (*Dictionnaire historique et critique*, 438). It even surpassed the extravagances of the poets "because at least the poets didn't attribute all of the crimes that are committed and all of the world's deformities to the gods [*car au moins les poètes n'attribuaient point aux dieux tous les crimes qui se commettent et toutes les infirmités du monde*]" (ibid., 439).

11. Mendelssohn, *Dialogues*, in his *Philosophical Writings*, 96–129 [vol. 1, 335–77].

12. Ibid., 102–103 [vol. 1, 344], translation altered.

13. See part iv of Spinoza's *Ethics*, titled "Of Human Bondage; or, The Strength of the Emotions," for a discussion of how we are not our "own masters" when we are under the sway of our emotions (152).

14. Mendelssohn describes the conflict in terms of both "common understanding [*gemeinen Menschenverstande*]" and "healthy understanding [*gesunden Menschenverstande*]" (*Morgenstunden*, in his *Gesammelte Schriften*, 3.2, 80); and when discussing the solution he describes what is at issue as "common sense [*Gemeinsinn*]" (ibid., 81).

15. Ibid., 81–82.

16. Mendelssohn writes:

> Experience has taught me that in most cases right is to be found on the side of common sense, and reason must speak very decisively for speculation, if I should leave common sense and follow it [*Die Erfahrung hat mich gelehrt, daß in den mehresten Fällen, das Recht auf Seiten des Gemeinsinns zu seyn pfleget, und die Vernunft muß sehr entscheidend für die Speculation sprechen, wenn ich jenen verlassen und dieser folgen soll*]. (ibid., 82)

17. Thomas Wizenmann made such a claim in 1786, in his anonymously published *Die Resultate der Jacobischen und Mendelssohnschen Philosophie*, 47. See Beiser, *The Fate of Reason*, 110.

18. Kant, however, praises Wizenmann, whom he refers to as the "acute author of the *Results* [*Resultate*]" (Kant, "What Does It Mean to Orient Oneself in Thinking?" 8 [AA 8, 134]).

19. Ibid.

20. Ibid.

21. Ibid., 7–8 [AA 8, 133–34]. Kant here refers to both *Morgenstunden* ("**common sense** [*Gemeinsinn*]" or "**healthy reason** [*gesunde Vernunft*]") and *An die Freunde Lessings* ("**plain understanding** [*schlichten Menschenverstand*]") as resources for his conception of

orientation. Kant distinguishes these conceptions in Mendelssohn's "last writings" from his earlier emphasis on "the cognition of supersensible objects" (ibid., 7 [AA 8, 133]). For Kant's criticism of Mendelssohn's earlier attempt to offer cognition of the super-sensible, see the Paralogisms chapter in the second edition of the first *Critique* (B413–14); and Mendelssohn, *Phädon oder über die Unsterblichkeit der Seele*, in his *Gesammelte Schriften*, vol. 3.1, 70.

22. Kant writes, "I call this a **feeling** because these two sides outwardly display no designatable difference in intuition [*Ich nenne es ein Gefühl: weil diese zwei Seiten äußerlich in der Anschauung keinen merklichen Unterschied zeigen*]" ("What Does It Mean to Orient Oneself in Thinking?" 8 [AA 8, 135]).

23. Ibid., 8–9 [AA 8, 135].

24. On Kant's pre-critical uses of incongruent counterparts, see Peter Woelert, "Kant's Hands, Spatial Orientation, and the Copernican Turn." For the continuity between Kant's many discussions of incongruent counterparts, see Jill Vance Buroker's *Space and Incongruence: The Origin of Kant's Idealism.* On the privileged role of the body among Kant's varied examples of incongruent counterparts, see Angelica Nuzzo's *Ideal Embodiment,* 21–44.

25. 1768: "Concerning the Ultimate Ground of the Differentiation of Directions in Space [Von dem ersten Grunde des Unterschiedes der Gegenden in Raume]," 367–68 [AA 2, 379–80]; 1770: *On the Form and Principles of the Sensible and Intelligible Worlds (De Mundi sensibilis atque intelligibilis forma et principiis),* §15, 386–87 [AA 2, 402–403]; 1783: *Prolegomena,* §13, 81–82 [AA, 4, 286]; 1786: *Metaphysical Foundations of Natural Science (Metaphysische Anfangsgründe der Naturwissenschaft),* 197–98 [AA 4, 484]; 1786: "What Does It Mean to Orient Oneself in Thinking?" 8–9 [AA 8, 134–35].

26. See A263–64/B319–20.

27. Heidegger, *Being and Time,* §23, 101–102 [109–110]. See chapter 4 for the earlier discussion of Heidegger's criticism of the Kantian conception of orientation.

28. Such a criticism is surprisingly similar to the one that is launched against the dependence of the Kantian notion of objects on a Euclidean conception of space. Graham Nerlich argues that while hands are incongruent counterparts in three-dimensional space, in a fourth dimension their reflected forms are congruent (*The Shape of Space,* 55). Nerlich explains that the shape of space is integral to the analysis of objects in it, and thus any analysis of incongruence "depends on the relation of the filled space to the container space" (ibid., 56).

29. Kant, "What Does It Mean to Orient Oneself in Thinking?" 8 [AA 8, 134].

30. Ibid., 10 [AA 8, 136]. Alexis Philonenko explains that this need of reason offers the "supra-sensible" "analogue of the principle of orientation in space [*analogue du principe d'orientation dans l'espace*]" (Philonenko, Introduction to his French translation of Kant's essay, *Qu'est-ce que s'orienter dans la pensée,* 67). The difference, according to Philonenko, is that orientation in space is constitutive of our experience, while that in thought is regulative (ibid.).

31. Kant, "What Does It Mean to Orient Oneself in Thinking?" 14 [AA 8, 142].

32. Ibid.

33. "[D]enn ohne diese Vorsicht würden wir von einem solchen Begriffe gar keinen Gebrauch machen können, sondern schwärmen, anstatt zu denken" (ibid., 10 [AA 8, 136]).

34. Ibid., 15 [AA 8, 143].

35. Ibid., 12 [AA 8, 139].

36. Ibid.

37. See Elizabeth Rottenberg's *Inheriting the Future: Legacies of Kant, Freud, and Flaubert* (12–13) for a discussion of the "need of reason" in its "unconditioned" practical use.

38. Kant, "What Does It Mean to Orient Oneself in Thinking?" 14 [AA 8, 142].

39. Ibid.

40. Ibid. Kant ends the essay with a general plea that both echoes and deepens the famous one at the start of his 1784 "An Answer to the Question: What Is Enlightenment? [Beantwortung der Frage: Was ist Aufklärung?]" (15–22 [AA 8, 33–42]). While in the earlier essay Kant calls for the "courage to make use of your own understanding" (17 [AA 8, 35]), in the essay written two years later Kant states that while you should "accept what appears to you most worthy of belief," you should not challenge "the prerogative of reason which makes it the highest good on earth, the prerogative of being the final touchstone of truth [*Probierstein der Wahrheit*]" (Kant, "What Does It Mean to Orient Oneself in Thinking?" 18 [AA 8, 146]). This is to say that our free thinking must not challenge the authority of reason. Doing so would lead us to "forfeit [*einbüßen*]" this freedom of thought, setting us on a skeptical path, and would "bring the same misfortune down on the heads of other, innocent parties" (ibid.). Frederick Beiser points out that this should be read not only as a criticism of both Jacobi and Wizenmann, but also as "a timely entreaty given the imminent succession of Frederick Wilhelm II" (*The Fate of Reason*, 118).

41. In the *Critique of Practical Reason*, Kant explains that along with the idea of freedom, morality requires the idea of God as a "postulate of practical reason" (along with that of the soul's immortality); what is postulated is "the exact correspondence [*Übereinstimmung*] of happiness with morality" (240 [AA 5, 125]), and so the possibility that in pursuing our freedom we might also attain our happiness. In "What Does It Mean to Orient Oneself in Thinking?" Kant explains that this assumption helps such a conception of morality to avoid "being taken as a mere ideal" (12 [AA 8, 139]).

42. See chapter 2 for a discussion of both the cosmological and the theological ideas as regulative principles (*Prinzipien*).

43. I will return to the issue of the *focus imaginarius* below.

44. Dieter Henrich, in "Kant's Notion of Deduction," offers a further justification of the regulative use of the ideas of reason that develops Kant's use of the language of legal argument: "The court of reason rules on the basis of the juridical principle that applies in such cases: if a dispute about the rightness of a usage cannot be settled, the usage remains with the possessor: *melior est conditio possendendi* (A777/B805)" (38–39). Unfortunately, he only connects this usage to practical philosophy and not to the critical inquiry itself and the designation of the territory of possible experience. Such a furthering would, I think, be possible within the context of his analysis.

45. See A508–517/B536–45.

46. Béatrice Longuenesse denies that such a role for the ideas of reason is needed. Her claim is that the systematicity of experience is given in the Transcendental Analytic, with the pursuit of this systematic unity already designated in the concepts of reflection investigated by Kant in its appendix (Longuenesse, *Kant and the Human Standpoint*, 233–34; and see chapter 4 for discussion of this appendix). She goes on to ask herself whether her account "gives short shrift to the regulative role of the ideas of pure reason" (ibid., 233) and answers quite clearly: "Well actually, I do think that the Transcendental Analytic, together with its appendix, was sufficient to offer an account of systematicity which does away with the ontological illusion carried by the ideal of pure reason" (ibid.). Longuenesse sees the ideas of reason as important only for the practical use of reason (ibid., 233–35).

47. Kant, *Critique of Judgment*, Second Introduction, v, 71–72 [AA 5, 185].

48. Ibid.

49. Horstmann calls this sentence the last in the appendix "that can be given an unambiguous interpretation [*der ohne Mehrdeutigkeit interpretiert werden kann*]" (*Bausteine kritischer Theorie,* 146; and in an English version titled "Why Must There Be a Transcendental Deduction in Kant's *Critique of Judgment?*" 166).

50. Hermann Cohen writes: "And this logical principle is entirely transcendental [*Und dieses logische Princip ist rein transscendental*]." All experience, he goes on to explain, is "tied [*geknüpft*]" to this principle (*Kants Theorie der Erfahrung,* 553).

51. Interpreters have been strongly divided about the connection between the hypothetical use of reason in the first *Critique* and reflective judgment in the third. Broadly speaking there are two main camps. The first includes those who argue for the transformation of Kant's fundamental project in his later *Critique of Judgment*. Such interpreters hold that there is either a fundamental difference between these two conceptions or, if not, that the earlier version already announces a transformation of Kant's undertaking. The second group of interpreters includes those who argue for the continuity between the two conceptions and the works that contain them.

In the first group, Rolf-Peter Horstmann argues that the hypothetical use of reason raises merely a logical and not a transcendental principle, so distinguishing itself from the transcendental principle of "purposiveness [*Zweckmäßigkeit*]" initiated in Kant's *Critique of Judgment*. While Horstmann is aware that Kant goes on to describe the hypothetical use of reason as establishing a transcendental principle, he questions the "transcendental implications [*transzendentalen Implikationen*]" of such "systematic unity," and so the "objective validity [*objective Gültigkeit*]" that would follow from it (*Bausteine kritischer Theorie,* 127–28; see also 114–15 for his conception of what a transcendental principle would offer). Others, who accept that the appendix to the Transcendental Dialectic of the first *Critique* offers a transcendental and not merely a logical or empirical project, still maintain that it differs from the account of reflective judgment in the third *Critique* insofar as it depends upon reason's metaphysical goals since the universal, even if failed, precedes investigation of the particular, while the later account of teleology in the third *Critique* avoids such a dependence in presupposing merely the suitability of nature for analysis by our finite faculties (see Makkreel, "Regulative and Reflective Uses of Purposiveness in Kant," 50–52). Reinhard Brandt concurs, arguing that the designation of the faculty of judgment in the *Critique of Judgment* symbolizes a break with the metaphysical goals of reason. "In 1788–89 God is overthrown," Brandt writes, because Kant no longer approaches the question of teleology from the perspective of our failed metaphysical inquiry ("The Deductions in the *Critique of Judgment*," 186). In the *Critique of Judgment*, Brandt explains, we proceed with confidence in the "suitability of nature to our cognitive faculties" without reference to the all-encompassing unity of God's design (ibid.). He includes this transformation as one of the "substantial shifts in the overall structure of the Kantian philosophy" (ibid., 187) in the years 1781–1790. Paul Guyer agrees, explaining that in the third *Critique*'s account of the principle of systematicity in reflective judgment,

> Kant does not explicitly retract the first *Critique*'s doctrine of transcendental affinity, and the entire metaphysical picture that it implies . . . [b]ut once he has linked the ideal of systematicity so closely to such fundamental requisites of the possibility of experience itself, an admission like this comes pretty close to the surrender of such a metaphysical model of our relation to reality. ("Reason and Reflective Judgment," 42)

Burkhard Tuschling agrees that the *Critique of Judgment* goes further than the *Critique of Pure Reason* in demonstrating the use of the regulative ideas of metaphysics ("The System of Transcendental Idealism," 118). In the later *Critique of Judgment*, the "intuitive understanding" is distinguished as a power of thinking "preceding and governing the transcendental human faculties and functions" (ibid., 120), without which appearances would not be in accord with causal law (Tuschling, "Intuitiver Verstand, absolute Identität, Idee," 183). In this account, Kant, in the third *Critique*, has directed us beyond the dualisms of his critical philosophy and toward a speculative system. Michel Souriau, in *Le jugement réfléchissant dans la philosophie critique de Kant* (41–45), goes even further, claiming that already in the first *Critique* Kant offers the account of the regulative use of reason that in its similarity with that of reflective judgment in the third *Critique* marks the end of the "dogmatism" of the understanding (ibid., 45).

The second group of interpreters emphasizes the thematic continuity between not only the hypothetical use of reason in the appendix to the Transcendental Dialectic of the first *Critique* and reflective judgment in the third *Critique*, but also the two works themselves. One can look back to Hermann Cohen for such a position (*Kants Theorie der Erfahrung*, 551–55). Others include Henry Allison in "Is the *Critique of Judgment* 'Post-Critical'?" (83) and *Custom and Reason in Hume* (140–49); Helga Mertens in *Kommentar zur Ersten Einleitung in Kants Kritik der Urteilskraft* (33–46); Bernard Rousset in *La Doctrine Kantienne de l'objectivité* (475–81); Klaus Düsing in *Die Teleologie in Kants Weltbegriff* (38–50); Luc Ferry in *Philosophie politique 2* (126–31); Gerd Buchdahl in *Kant and the Dynamics of Reason* (170); Pauline Kleingeld in "Kant on the Unity of Theoretical and Practical Reason" (318–25); and Michael Friedman in *Kant and the Exact Sciences*, 180–83. I will return to these scholars, who are closer to the interpretation I am offering here, in the pages to come.

52. Horstmann assumes that the only principle emanating from reason is the moral principle, explaining that "there is only one transcendental principle of reason, that is, the categorical imperative [*gibt es nur ein einziges transzendentales Prinzip der Vernunft, nämlich den Kategorischen Imperativ*]" (*Bausteine kritischer Theorie*, 156; and the English version, "Why Must There Be a Transcendental Deduction in Kant's *Critique of Judgment*?" 171).

53. Allison argues for the continuity between the account of the hypothetical use of reason in the first *Critique* and that of reflective judgment in the third, but he limits his analysis of the regulative principles to the empirical use of the understanding, explaining that the "coherent employment of the understanding" depends upon such a regulative principle ("Is the *Critique of Judgment* 'Post-Critical'?" 82; and *Custom and Reason in Hume*, 140–43). Allison does not investigate whether such regulative principles have a role to play beyond that of the understanding's empirical use in the designation of its *a priori* features of cognition. In a similar way, Ferry argues for the regulative dependence of determinate judgment as well as the continuity between the first and the third *Critiques* in his *Philosophie politique 2* (126–31), and with Renault in their "D'un retour à Kant" (171). Rousset develops a similar account in *La Doctrine Kantienne de l'objectivité*, explaining that the appendix to the Transcendental Dialectic already marks the break with empiricism ("nous devons rompre avec l'attitude empiriste"; 475) in a manner that does not reject the critical examinations of the categories. Buchdahl calls these "parallel discussion[s]" (*Kant and the Dynamics of Reason*, 170); Düsing explains that in the appendix that concludes the Transcendental Dialectic of the *Critique of Pure Reason* "already the problematic of the *Critique of Judgment* is prefigured [*schon die Problematik der* Kritik der Urteilskraft *vorgebildet ist*]" (*Die Teleologie in Kants Weltbegriff*, 43); and Mertens describes their "close relation

[*enge Beziehung*]" (*Kommentar zur ersten Einleitung in Kants Kritik der Urteilskraft*, 33), and distinguishes Kant's pairing of "hypothetical [*hypothetischem*]" and "apodeictic [*apodik-tischem*]" uses of reason in the first *Critique* as "pointing ahead [*vorausweisen*]" to that of reflective and determinate judgment in the third *Critique* (ibid., 35–36). Friedman states that the later account of reflective judgment in the third *Critique* "in no way goes beyond the methodological regulative maxims already enumerated in the first *Critique*" (*Kant and the Exact Sciences*, 251–52). Rescher, in describing the systematicity of nature, writes, "Kant's position in the two *Critiques* [the first and the third] is in fact wholly uniform in this regard" (*Kant and the Reach of Reason*, 83), while Cohen, already in 1885, describes Kant's various discussions of regulative principles thus: "And in all of these developments the same thought shows itself, only elaborated in an increasingly sharp and clear manner [*Und in allen diesen Entwicklungen zeigt sich derselbe Gedanke, nur schärfer und klarer immer ausgeführt*]" (*Kants Theorie der Erfahrung*, 552). However, these interpreters do not investigate the specific roles played by the different ideas of reason in the earlier account. See below for discussions of the work of Heinz Heimsoeth, Pauline Kleingeld, and Claude Piché, who do investigate the specific, regulative roles of the ideas of reason in the first *Critique*.

54. For Kant's discussion of the regulative use of the cosmological idea in the determination of ever-further mechanistic causes, see A508–567/B536–95.

55. See also A424–25/B452–53. In this passage, which ends the introduction to the Antinomies, Kant explains that transcendental philosophy, unlike mathematics or morality, needs the skeptical method and "permits no touchstone [*Probierstein*] other than its own attempt to bring internal unification [*Vereinigung*] to its assertions." It is only in the appendix to the Transcendental Dialectic that Kant addresses such a touchstone of unification.

56. Unlike most interpreters of this section, Kleingeld, in "Kant on the Unity of Theoretical and Practical Reason," does address the regulative use of the psychological idea. She argues that this principle directs "reason's interest in its own unity" (318). The goal of such self-unity leads us to view all mental powers as manifestations of a single power and so view theoretical and practical reason as in this way united. While Kleingeld recognizes the importance of the regulative pursuit of the psychological idea, explaining that Kant's interest in the self-unity of reason "go[es] to the heart of his transcendental philosophical project as a critique of reason by reason" (ibid., 321), her analysis is hampered by her view that the regulative use of reason guides the pursuit of systematic unity merely in our "empirical knowledge" (ibid., 325). If this were so, then the psychological idea would offer itself merely as a further teleological pursuit, relegating itself to a place far from the "heart" of transcendental philosophy. Heimsoeth offers a similar account of an empirical project that follows from the hypothetical pursuit of the psychological idea, describing the role of the soul as the "goal [*Zielpunkt*] of empirical psychology" (*Transzendentale Dialektik, Dritter Teil*, 617). Michelle Grier agrees that "the idea of the soul grounds empirical investigations in psychology" (*Kant's Doctrine of Transcendental Illusion*, 265). For an account of the regulative role of the psychological idea that claims more than its empirical importance, see Piché's *Das Ideal* (73–74). I will address this account in a later note.

57. The regulative use of the psychological idea for the designation of the starting point of critical inquiry thus concerns the first of what Kant refers to as the trio of issues that have historically surrounded discussions of rational psychology. Critical inquiry depends upon the regulative adherence to the response to the metaphysical inquiry into the "communion of body and soul, and thus the role that the soul plays in human life"

(A384), while rejecting all inquiry into questions concerning both the soul prior to human life and the soul after death (immortality).

58. Westphal offers an opposing view, arguing that the unity, or "affinity of the sensory manifold," is a "material (and mind independent) condition for self-conscious experience" (*Kant's Transcendental Proof of Realism,* 67; see also 91–92).

59. Ameriks argues that Kant did not reject all of his pre-critical metaphysical views, particularly those concerning the soul. To elucidate these pre-critical views, Ameriks looks to Kant's lectures on metaphysics, particularly the Pölitz lectures from the mid-1770s (Ameriks, "Kant's Lectures on Metaphysics," 23–31, and *Kant's Theory of Mind,* preface to the second edition, xiii–xxiii). Ameriks explains that in these lectures, one can see that Kant already had his *"main* negative claim" ("Kant's Lectures on Metaphysics," 26; *Kant's Theory of Mind,* xvii), denying the possibility of an argument for immortality. The positive claims that Kant explicitly makes in these lectures, those for the soul as substance, simple (and thus immaterial), identical, and spontaneous (or free) (Kant, *Lectures on Metaphysics,* 78–81 [AA 28, 265–68]), are ones, Ameriks posits, that could be said to characterize "the general structure of the subject of experience" in his critical system ("Kant's Lectures on Metaphysics," 29; *Kant's Theory of Mind,* xx). While Kant explains his critical commitment to human freedom, the positive role played by the other claims, investigated in relation to rational psychology in the first *Critique,* are not addressed. Ameriks writes that there might be "sympathetic ways to understand these arguments in a theoretical way," but although Kant promised such an account he never provided it ("Kant's Lectures on Metaphysics," 29–30; *Kant's Theory of Mind,* xx–xxi). The investigation of the regulative role played by the idea of the soul, undertaken here, offers the possibility of just such an account of Kant's continued commitment to his earlier metaphysics after his transcendental turn.

60. Piché explains that this "division [*Trennung*]" of substance from all empirical accidents is the "basic concept [*Grundbegriff*]" of transcendental philosophy (*Das Ideal,* 73). Piché writes that this division is "the mere regulative function of the psychological idea [*die bloß regulative Funktion der psychologischen Idee*]" in which the I is designated as in this way substantial (ibid., 73–74).

61. Kant, *Critique of Judgment,* First Introduction, v, 15–16 [AA 20, 211–12].

62. Ferry and Renault describe the "residual role of metaphysics [*rôle résiduel de la métaphysique*]" ("D'un retour à Kant," 171). While this terminology is appropriate for my discussion of the psychological idea and the regulative orientation of critical philosophy, these authors limit their conception of this regulative role to the reflective application of causal law, the regulative component implicit in all determinate judgment, and do not address the orientation of the critical project itself.

63. Translation altered.

64. This passage was discussed in chapter 1 in a preliminary fashion.

65. I will return to Kant's discussion of the "perpetual circle" of his inquiry later in this chapter. The circularity of critique was also discussed in chapter 3.

66. Kant makes this point in a note from 1790–1791. In describing his argument against idealism, he writes: "We are first object of outer sense for ourselves, for otherwise we would not be able to perceive our place in the world and to intuit ourselves in relation to other things" (*Notes and Fragments,* R 6315, 361 [AA 18, 619]). The designation of the realm of spatial objects necessary for cognition requires prioritizing ourselves, our own bodies, as outer appearances. Förster emphasizes this note in his "Kant's Refutation of Idealism," but he raises Kant's conception of our physical selves as objects for ourselves not as a way to conceive of the method of critique more generally, as is here being raised, but as a step beyond critique and toward the "full-fledged idealism of the *Opus*

Postumum" (302; see 299–302). I will leave aside the question of this interpretation of the *Opus Postumum*, but it should be clear that what is here being argued is that the commitment to something beyond the empirical, which the Refutation describes, need not be understood to lead beyond critique. For Förster's interpretation of the *Opus Postumum*, see his *Kant's Final Synthesis: An Essay on the "Opus Postumum."*

67. In this way, the Refutation depends most clearly on the elements of the psychological idea related to the modal categories and so on the Fourth Paralogism. This is not surprising since the Refutation was developed from the first edition's Fourth Paralogism, and so from the argument that the objects outside of us cannot be doubted. See chapter 5 for discussion of the first edition's Fourth Paralogism.

68. Kant, *Logic,* 538 [AA 9, 25].

69. Ibid.

70. Ibid., translation altered.

71. See chapter 1 for a discussion of the conception of anthropology in this work.

72. Kant, *Anthropology,* 231 [AA 7, 119].

73. Ibid.

74. Ibid. Kant explains, in a passage also quoted in chapter 1:

> He who ponders natural phenomena, for example, what the causes of the faculty of memory [*Erinnerungsvermögen*] rest on, can speculate back and forth (like Descartes) over the traces of impressions remaining in the brain, but in doing so he must admit that in this play of his representations he is a mere spectator [*bloßer Zuschauer*] and must let nature run its course, for he does not know the cranial nerves and fibers, nor does he understand how to put them to use for his purposes. (ibid.)

75. See A371, where Kant explains that the self, the object of inner sense, and the objects of outer sense are for us "nothing but representations."

76. See chapter 1 for discussion of such an immanent physiology.

77. Kant, *Anthropology,* 231 [AA 7, 119].

78. In this passage from the Architectonic of the first *Critique,* Michel Foucault recognizes only a failed rational psychology and not a post-critical physiology that would help to address the fourth question, "What is man?" that in the *Logic* Kant appended to his earlier three questions (Foucault, *Introduction to Kant's "Anthropology,"* 73–76). For this reason, Foucault looked for an answer not in the three *Critiques* but in the *Opus Postumum* (ibid., 76–77).

79. While the term "transcendental psychology" seems fitting for such a regulative account of the thinking subject, explaining in this way the manner in which this account avoids both empirical and rational psychology, it is worth noting that in the first edition of the *Critique of Pure Reason,* Kant uses the term "transcendental psychology [*transcendentalen Psychologie*]" (A397) only in reference to the illusory claims of rational psychology and not to its post-critical development. The phrase is not included in the second edition. In an interpretation close to the spirit of what I am offering here, Gary Hatfield calls transcendental psychology "the psychology of the *knowing* mind, of the mind that makes objectively valid judgments" (*The Natural and the Normative,* 86). On the other hand, Kitcher argues that transcendental psychology concerns the phenomenal, and thus the empirical self ("Kant's Real Self," 126, and *Kant's Transcendental Psychology,* 22).

80. Heidegger, *Kant and the Problem of Metaphysics,* §38, 152 [217].

81. "Whosoever asks: What can I do? betrays thereby a finitude" (ibid., 151 [216]).

82. For discussion of Heidegger's *What Is a Thing?* see chapter 3, and for "Kant's Thesis about Being," see chapter 4.

83. Heidegger, "Kant's Thesis about Being," 360 [476]. Interestingly, in Heidegger's late lecture *On Time and Being* (*Zeit und Sein*), first published in 1969 in *Zur Sache des Denkens*, he criticizes his own earlier *Being and Time* for its attempt "to derive human spatiality from temporality [*Zeitlichkeit*]" (*On Time and Being*, 23 [29]), raising the question of our access to the temporal realm of being.

84. Heidegger, "Kant's Thesis about Being," 357 [472].

85. Heidegger quotes this passage from Hamann (*Briefwechsel*, vol. 5, 177) in his essay "Language," 191 [13]. See chapter 1 for discussion of Hamann's account of the "abyss."

86. [T]here are two stems of human cognition, which may perhaps arise from a common but to us unknown root [*die vielleicht aus einer gemeinschaftlichen, aber uns unbekannten Wurzel entspringen*] namely sensibility and understanding, through the first of which objects are given to us, but through the second of which they are thought. (A15/B29)

See chapter 4 for discussion of Kant's two references to the "root" of the cognitive faculties.

87. See A804/B832.

88. Translation altered.

89. As discussed in chapter 4, Henrich makes the suggestive claim that the root of Kantian cognition might in fact be the psychological idea and so "unknown" to us because it surpasses our finite faculties (*The Unity of Reason*, 20–21, 26–27). While Henrich's designation of the psychological idea as the root of the finite faculties is suggestive, he does not address Kant's later reference to such a root of cognition, where beyond sensibility the second stem is now called reason and not understanding (A833/B863), and thus the psychological idea and the regulative uses it affords would be not the root but a growth from one of the stems. And so we can return to the question of such a "common" or "general root." With Heidegger, one could still look to the transcendental imagination as such a root, but now Kant, with the help of reason and the regulative role afforded by the psychological idea, can be said to have thematized the manner in which we are able to point to this "blind though indispensable function of the soul" (A78/B103).

90. This circularity can be contrasted with the "vicious circle [*fehlerhafter Zirkel*]" of what Kant calls "perverted reason [*verkehrten Vernunft*] (*perversa ratio*)," which he describes as arising when we assume that we have access to the object of metaphysical speculation, which is to say one "presupposes what really ought to have been proved [*man das voraussetzt, was eigentlich hat bewiesen werden sollen*]" (A693/B721). Kant also uses the term *Zirkel* with such a negative connotation in the *Groundwork of the Metaphysics of Morals*, where he explains that in the inference from freedom to autonomy, and then to the moral law, he has not introduced "a hidden circle [*ein geheimer Zirkel*]" in his reasoning (99 [AA 4, 453]).

91. Kant's discussion of the "special property" of critique is addressed above in chapter 3.

92. See chapter 3 for a discussion of other interpreters of the circularity of Kantian critique.

93. Kant, "Dreams of a Spirit-Seer," 332–33 [AA 2, 344–45]. On the use of the *focus imaginarius* in this work, see Nuzzo, *Ideal Embodiment*, 85–86.

94. Kant, "Dreams of a Spirit-Seer," 331 [AA 2, 344].

95. Ibid., 332 [AA 2, 345].

96. Ibid., 333 [AA 2, 345].

97. Ibid. [AA 2, 346]. Kant goes on to discuss the limits of our understanding in ways that foreshadow his critical position. He explains that we are "completely ignorant" concerning the question of the soul's immortality, a question that animates our ghost stories. About such questions, Kant explains, we can "have all sorts of opinions . . . but no longer knowledge" (ibid., 338 [AA 2, 351]). On Kant's inability to distinguish belief in spirits from such metaphysical claims until his later "logic of illusions" in the first *Critique*, see Monique David-Ménard, *La Folie dans la raison pure*, 128–29.

98. Nuzzo explains that Kant, in the *Critique of Pure Reason*, offers a use of the *focus imaginarius* that "stands between the former two" uses in the "Dreams of a Spirit-Seer" essay (Nuzzo, *Ideal Embodiment*, 86), that is to say, between a causal inference and a mad flight.

99. The empirical imagination that in the "Dreams" essay threatens madness can be distinguished from the transcendental imagination that is described by Kant in the Transcendental Deduction of the first *Critique* as originally productive and so related to the very possibility of images (A118/B151–52). On the distinction between the empirical and the transcendental imagination in this regard, see Sallis, *The Gathering of Reason*, 146–50.

100. Sallis points out that this is Kant's only reference to the imagination in the Transcendental Dialectic (ibid., 153).

101. See A509/B537, where near the conclusion of the Antinomies Kant explains that ever-further causal explanation is governed by a regulative principle born of the idea of "the absolute totality of the series of conditions." In the appendix to the Transcendental Dialectic, while introducing the regulative roles of the psychological and the theological ideas, Kant returns to such an account of the cosmological idea in its regulative role, what in the appendix he terms the "hypothetical use of reason" (A647/B675); for Kant's return in the appendix to the regulative role of the cosmological idea, see A684–85/B712–13.

102. In the *Critique of Judgment*, Kant contrasts ideas of reason, which cannot be represented in the imagination, with aesthetic ideas, which are represented in imagination and lead to thought but do not offer concepts (§49, 192 [AA 5, 314]).

103. As Michelle Grier points out in *Kant's Doctrine of Transcendental Illusion* (37), Kant's use of the metaphor of a mirror to describe the *focus imaginarius* is very similar to Isaac Newton's account of the mirror image of that which is outside our field of vision in his 1704 *Opticks* (bk. 1, pt. 1, axiom 8, 18). Kant, as Arthur Warda describes, had in his library a copy of Newton's *Opticks* in a Latin edition (Warda, *Immanuel Kants Bücher*, 35; the edition of Newton's book in Kant's library was *Optice*, trans. Samuel Clarke [London: Smith and Walford, 1706]). See also Allison, *Custom and Reason in Hume* (141–42), and *Kant's Transcendental Idealism*, 425–30.

104. On Kant's use of the mirror as a metaphor for the role of the ideas of reason, see Kerszberg, *Critique and Totality*, 74–76.

105. Ibid., 75–76.

106. Kant, *Prolegomena*, §59, 149 [AA 4, 360]; see chapter 2 for discussion of this passage.

107. Kant distinguishes *Prinzipien* from *Grundsätze* at A299/B356. See chapter 2 for discussion of this distinction.

BIBLIOGRAPHY

Abela, Paul. *Kant's Empirical Realism.* Oxford: Oxford University Press, 2002.

Alexander, W. M. *J. G. Hamann: Philosophy and Faith.* The Hague: Martinus Nijhoff, 1966.

———. "Johann Georg Hamann: Metacritic of Kant." *Journal of the History of Ideas* 27 (1966): 137–44.

Allison, Henry E. *Custom and Reason in Hume: A Kantian Reading of the First Book of the Treatise.* New York: Oxford University Press, 2008.

———. *Idealism and Freedom: Essays on Kant's Theoretical and Practical Philosophy.* Cambridge: Cambridge University Press, 1996.

———. "Is the *Critique of Judgment* 'Post-Critical'?" In *The Reception of Kant's Critical Philosophy: Fichte, Schelling and Hegel,* ed. Sally Sedgwick, 78–92. Cambridge: Cambridge University Press, 2000.

———. *Kant's Transcendental Idealism: An Interpretation and Defense.* New Haven, CT: Yale University Press, 1983. Rev. ed., New Haven, CT: Yale University Press, 2004.

Altmann, Alexander. *Moses Mendelssohn: A Biographical Study.* Tuscaloosa: University of Alabama Press, 1973.

Ameriks, Karl. "Kant's Lectures on Metaphysics and His Precritical Philosophy of Mind." In *New Essays on the Precritical Kant,* ed. Tom Rockmore, 19–36. Amherst, NY: Prometheus, 2001.

———. *Kant's Theory of Mind: An Analysis of the Paralogisms of Pure Reason,* new ed. Oxford: Oxford University Press, 2000.

Arendt, Hannah. *Lectures on Kant's Political Philosophy.* Chicago: University of Chicago Press, 1982.

———. *The Life of the Mind.* New York: Harcourt, 1981.

Baum, Manfred. *Deduktion und Beweis in Kants Transzendentalphilosophie.* Königstein: Athenäum, 1986.

———. "Transcendental Proofs in the *Critique of Pure Reason.*" In *Transcendental Arguments and Science,* ed. Peter Bieri, Rolf-Peter Horstmann, and Lorenz Krüger, 3-26. Dordrecht, the Netherlands: Reidel, 1979.

Bayer, Oswald. *Vernunft ist Sprache: Hamanns Metakritik Kants.* Stuttgart-Bad Cannstatt: Fromann-Holzboog, 2002.

Bayle, Pierre. *Dictionnaire historique et critique,* new ed. Paris: Desoer, 1820.

Beck, Lewis White. *A Commentary on Kant's "Critique of Practical Reason."* Chicago: University of Chicago Press, 1960.

———. *Early German Philosophy: Kant and His Predecessors.* Cambridge, MA: Belknap, 1969.

———. *Essays on Kant and Hume.* New Haven, CT: Yale University Press, 1978.

Beiser, Frederick C. *The Fate of Reason: German Philosophy from Kant to Fichte.* Cambridge, MA: Harvard University Press, 1987.

Bencivenga, Ermanno. *Kant's Copernican Revolution.* New York: Oxford University Press, 1987.

Bennett, Jonathan. *Kant's Dialectic.* Cambridge: Cambridge University Press, 1974.

Bird, Graham. *Kant's Theory of Knowledge: An Outline of One Central Argument in the "Critique of Pure Reason."* London: Routledge and Kegan Paul, 1962.

——. *The Revolutionary Kant: A Commentary on the "Critique of Pure Reason."* Peru, IL: Open Court, 2006.

Brandt, Reinhard. "'The Deductions in the *Critique of Judgment:* Comments on Hampshire and Horstmann." In *Kant's Transcendental Deductions,* ed. Eckart Förster, 177–90. Stanford, CA: Stanford University Press, 1989.

Brittan, Gordon G. *Kant's Theory of Science.* Princeton, NJ: Princeton University Press, 1978.

Brook, Andrew. *Kant and the Mind.* Cambridge: Cambridge University Press, 1994.

Bubner, Rüdiger. "Kant, Transcendental Arguments and the Problem of Deduction." *Review of Metaphysics* 28.3 (1975): 453–67.

——. "Zur Struktur eines Transzendentalen Arguments." In *Akten des 4. Internationalen Kant Kongresses,* ed. G. Funke and J. Kopper, vol. 1:15–27. New York: de Gruyter, 1974.

Buchdahl, Gerd. *Kant and the Dynamics of Reason: Essays on the Structure of Kant's Philosophy.* Oxford: Blackwell, 1992.

——. *Metaphysics and the Philosophy of Science.* Cambridge, MA: MIT Press, 1969.

Buroker, J. V. *Space and Incongruence: The Origin of Kant's Idealism.* Dordrecht, the Netherlands: Reidel, 1981.

Caranti, Luigi. *Kant and the Scandal of Philosophy: The Kantian Critique of Cartesian Scepticism.* Toronto: University of Toronto Press, 2007.

Caygill, Howard. "Life and Energy." *Theory, Culture, and Society* 24.6 (2007): 19–27.

Cohen, Hermann. *Kants Theorie der Erfahrung.* 3rd ed. Berlin: Bruno Cassirer, 1918.

David-Ménard, Monique. *La Folie dans la raison pure: Kant lecteur de Swedenborg.* Paris: Vrin, 1990.

Davies, Kim. "The Concept of Experience and Strawson's Transcendental Deduction." In *Immanuel Kant: Critical Assessments,* ed. Ruth F. Chadwick and Clive Cazeaux, 201–203. London: Routledge, 1992.

de Boer, Karin. "Pure Reason's Enlightenment: Transcendental Reflection in Kant's First *Critique.*" Kant Yearbook 2 (2010): 53–73.

Descartes, René. *Meditations on First Philosophy,* trans. John Cottingham. Cambridge: Cambridge University Press, 1986.

Duchesneau, F. "Kant et la 'physiologie de l'entendement humain.'" In *Akten des 4. Internationalen Kant Kongresses,* ed. G. Funke and J. Kopper, vol. 2.1:270–76. Berlin: de Gruyter, 1974.

Düsing, Klaus. *Die Teleologie in Kants Weltbegriff.* Bonn: Bouvier, 1968.

Falkenstein, Lorne. *Kant's Intuitionism: A Commentary on the Transcendental Aesthetic.* Toronto: University of Toronto Press, 1995.

Ferry, Luc. *Philosophie politique 2: Le système des philosophies de l'histoire.* Paris: Press Universitaires de France, 1996.

Ferry, Luc, and Alain Renault. "D'un retour à Kant." In their *Système et Critique,* 156–77. Brussels: Ousia, 1990.

Förster, Eckart. *Kant's Final Synthesis: An Essay on the "Opus Postumum."* Cambridge, MA: Harvard University Press, 2002.

——. "Kant's Refutation of Idealism." In *Philosophy: Its History and Historiography,* ed. A. J. Holland, 287–303. Dordrecht, the Netherlands: Reidel, 1985.

Forster, Michael N. *Hegel and Skepticism.* Cambridge, MA: Harvard University Press, 1989.

Foucault, Michel. *Introduction to Kant's "Anthropology,"* trans. Roberto Nigro and Kate Briggs. Los Angeles, CA: Semiotext(e), 2008.

Friedman, Michael. "Causal Laws and the Foundation of Natural Science." In *The Cambridge Companion to Kant*, ed. Paul Guyer, 161–99. Cambridge: Cambridge University Press, 1992.

———. *Kant and the Exact Sciences*. Cambridge, MA: Harvard University Press, 1992.

———. "Regulative and Constitutive." *Southern Journal of Philosophy* 30, Suppl. (1992): 73–102.

Gasché, Rodolph. *The Idea of Form: Rethinking Kant's Aesthetics*. Stanford, CA: Stanford University Press, 2003.

Gochnauer, Myron. "Kant's Refutation of Idealism." *Journal of the History of Philosophy* 12.2 (1974): 195–206.

Goldman, Avery. "Beauty and Critique: On the Role of Reason in Kant's Aesthetics." In *Internationales Jahrbuch für Hermeneutik*, ed. Günter Figal, vol. 3:203–220. Tübingen: Mohr Siebeck, 2004.

———. "Kant, Heidegger, and the Circularity of Transcendental Inquiry." *Epoché* 15.1 (2010): 107–120.

Grier, Michelle. *Kant's Doctrine of Transcendental Illusion*. Cambridge: Cambridge University Press, 2001.

Guyer, Paul. *Kant and the Claims of Knowledge*. Cambridge: Cambridge University Press, 1987.

———. "Reason and Reflective Judgment: Kant and the Significance of Systematicity." *Nous* 24 (1990): 17–43.

Guyer, Paul, and Allen W. Wood. Introduction to the *Critique of Pure Reason*, trans. Guyer and Wood, 1–80. Cambridge: Cambridge University Press, 1998.

Hamann, Johann Georg. *Johann Georg Hamann Briefwechsel*, vol. 4: *1778–1782*, ed. Arthur Henkel. Frankfurt am Main: Insel, 1959.

———. *Johann Georg Hamann Briefwechsel*, vol. 5: *1783–1785*, ed. Arthur Henkel. Frankfurt am Main: Insel, 1965.

———. "Metacritique of the Purism of Reason" [Metakritik über den Purismum der Vernunft. In *Sämtliche Werke*, ed. Joseph Nadler, vol. 3:281–89. Vienna: Joseph Nadler, 1949–], trans. Gwen Griffith Dickson. In her *Johann Georg Hamann's Relational Metacriticism*, 517–34. New York: de Gruyter, 1995.

Hatfield, Gary. "Empirical, Rational and Transcendental Psychology: Psychology as Science and as Philosophy." In *The Cambridge Companion to Kant*, ed. Paul Guyer, 200–227. Cambridge: Cambridge University Press, 1992.

———. *The Natural and the Normative: Theories of Spatial Perception from Kant to Helmholtz*. Cambridge, MA: MIT Press, 1990.

Hegel, G. W. F. *Faith and Knowledge* [Glauben und Wissen. In *Gesammelte Werke*, ed. Hartmut Buchner and Otto Pöggeler, vol. 4. Hamburg: Felix Meiner, 1968], trans. W. Cerf and H. S. Harris. Albany: State University of New York Press, 1977.

———. "The Writings of Hamann" [Hamanns Schriften. In *Gesammelte Werke*, vol. 16, ed. Friedrich Hogemann and Christoph Jamme. Hamburg: Felix Meiner, 2001]. In *Hegel on Hamann*, trans. Lisa Marie Anderson. Evanston, IL: Northwestern University Pres, 2008.

———. *Phenomenology of Spirit* [Phänomenologie des Geistes. In *Gesammelte Werke*, vol. 9, ed. Wolfgang Bonsiepen and Reinhard Heede. Hamburg: Felix Meiner, 1980], trans. A. V. Miller. Oxford: Oxford University Press, 1977.

Heidegger, Martin. *Being and Time* [Sein und Zeit. Tubingen: Max Niemeyer, 1993], trans. Joan Stambaugh. Albany: State University of New York Press, 1996.

————. *Kant and the Problem of Metaphysics* [*Kant und das Problem der Metaphysik*. Frankfurt: Vittorio Klostermann, 1951], 7th ed., trans. Richard Taft. Bloomington: Indiana University Press, 2010.

————. "Kant's Thesis about Being [Kants These über das Sein." In *Wegmarken*, 445–80. Frankfurt: Vittorio Klosterman, 2004], trans. T. Klein and W. Pohl. In *Pathmarks*, ed. William McNeill, 337–63. Cambridge: Cambridge University Press, 1998.

————. "Language [Die Sprache." In *Unterwegs zur Sprache*, 11–33. Pfullingen: Neske, 1965], trans. Albert Hofstadter. In Heidegger, *Poetry, Language, Thought*, 189–210. New York: Harper and Row, 1971.

————. *On Time and Being* ["Zeit und Sein." In *Zur Sache des Denken*. Frankfurt am Main: Vittorio Klostermann, 2007], trans. Joan Stambaugh. New York: Harper and Row, 1972.

————. *What Is a Thing?* [*Die Frage nach dem Ding?* Tübingen: Max Niemeyer, 1987], trans. W. B. Barton Jr. and Vera Deutsch. South Bend, IN: Regnery/Gateway, 1967.

Heidemann, Dietmar Hermann. *Kant und das Problem des metaphysichen Idealismus*. Berlin: de Gruyter, 1998.

Heimsoeth, Heinz. "Metaphysical Motives in the Development of Critical Idealism." In *Kant: Disputed Questions*, ed. Moltke S. Gram, 158–99. Chicago: Quadrangle, 1967.

————. *Transzendentale Dialektik: Ein Kommentar zu Kants Kritik der reinen Vernunft, Erster Teil: Ideenlehre und Paralogismen*. Berlin: de Gruyter, 1966.

————. *Transzendentale Dialektik: Ein Kommentar zu Kants Kritik der reinen Vernunft, Dritter Teil: Das Ideal der reinen Vernunft*. Berlin: de Gruyter, 1969.

Henrich, Dieter. *Identität und Objektivität: Eine Untersuchung über Kants transzendentale Deduktion*. Heidelberg: Carl Winter Universitätsverlag, 1976.

————. "Die Identität des Subjekts in der transzendentalen Deduktion." In *Kant: Analysen—Probleme—Kritik*, ed. Hariolf Oberer and Gerhard Seel, 39–70. Würzburg: Königshausen and Neumann, 1988.

————. "Kant's Notion of Deduction and the Methodological Background of the First *Critique*." In *Kant's Transcendental Deductions*, ed. Eckart Förster, 29–46. Stanford, CA: Stanford University Press, 1989.

————. *The Unity of Reason*, trans. J. Edwards, L. Hunt, M. Kuehn, and G. Zoeller. Cambridge, MA: Harvard University Press, 1994.

————. "Zur theoretische Philosophie Kants." *Philosophische Rundschau* 1 (1953): 124–49.

Herder, Johann Gottfried. "Eine Metakritik zur Kritik der reinen Vernunft." In *Sprachphilosophische Schriften*, ed. Erich Heintel, 181–227. Hamburg: Meiner, 1964.

Horstmann, Rolf-Peter. *Bausteine kritischer Theorie: Arbeiten zu Kant*. Bodenheim: Philo Verlagsgesellschaft, 1997.

————. "Why Must There Be a Transcendental Deduction in Kant's *Critique of Judgment?*" In *Kant's Transcendental Deductions*, ed. Eckart Förster, 157–76. Stanford, CA: Stanford University Press, 1989.

Hughes, Fiona. "The Technic of Nature: What Is Involved in Judging?" In *Kant's Aesthetics*, ed. Herman Parret, 177–91. New York: de Gruyter, 1998.

Hume, David. *A Treatise of Human Nature*, ed. David Fate Norton and Mary J. Norton. Oxford: Oxford University Press, 2000.

Jacobi, Friedrich Heinrich. *Concerning the Doctrine of Spinoza in Letters to Moses Mendelssohn* [*Über die Lehre des Spinoza in Briefen an den Herrn Moses Mendelssohn*. In *Werke*, ed. Klaus Hammacher and Irmgard-Maria Piske, vol. 1.1, 1–146. Hamburg: Meiner, 1998], trans. George di Giovanni. Montreal and Kingston: McGill-Queen's University Press, 1994, 173–251.

Kant, Immanuel. "An Answer to the Question: What Is Enlightenment? [Beantwortung der Frage: Was ist Aufklärung?]." In *Practical Philosophy*, trans. and ed. Mary J. Gregor, 15–22. Cambridge: Cambridge University Press, 1996. [AA 8, 33–42]

———. *Anthropology from a Pragmatic Point of View* [*Anthropologie in pragmatischer Hinsicht*]. In *Anthropology, History, and Education*, trans. Robert Louden, ed. Günter Zöller and Robert B. Louden, 227–429. Cambridge: Cambridge University Press, 2007. [AA 7, 117–334]

———. "Concerning the Ultimate Ground of the Differentiation of Directions in Space [Von dem ersten Grunde des Unterschiedes der Gegenden im Raum]." In *Theoretical Philosophy, 1755–1770*, trans. and ed. David Walford and Ralf Meerbote, 361–72. Cambridge: Cambridge University Press, 1992. [AA 2, 375–84]

———. *Correspondence*, trans. and ed. Arnulf Zweig. Cambridge: Cambridge University Press, 1999. [AA 10–13]

———. *Critique of the Power of Judgment* [*Kritik der Urteilskraft*], trans. Paul Guyer and Eric Matthews, ed. Paul Guyer. Cambridge: Cambridge University Press, 2000. [AA 5, 20]

———. *Critique of Practical Reason* [*Kritik der praktischen Vernunft*]. In *Practical Philosophy*, trans. and ed. Mary J. Gregor, 133–271. Cambridge: Cambridge University Press, 1996. [AA 5]

———. *Critique of Pure Reason* [*Kritik der reinen Vernunft*], trans. and ed. Paul Guyer and Allen W. Wood. Cambridge: Cambridge University Press, 1998. [AA 3, 4]

———. "Dreams of a Spirit-Seer Elucidated by Dreams of Metaphysics [Träume eines Geistsehers, erläutert durch Träume der Metaphysik]." In *Theoretical Philosophy, 1755–1770*, trans. and ed. David Walford and Ralf Meerbote, 302–59. Cambridge: Cambridge University Press, 1992. [AA 2, 315–84]

———. *Groundwork of the Metaphysics of Morals* [*Grundlegung zur Metaphysik der Sitten*]. In *Practical Philosophy*, trans. and ed. Mary J. Gregor, 43–108. Cambridge: Cambridge University Press, 1996. [AA 4, 385–464]

———. *Kants gesammelte Schriften*, Preußischen Akademie der Wissenschaften. Berlin: de Gruyter, 1902–.

———. *Lectures on Logic*, trans. and ed. J. Michael Young. Cambridge: Cambridge University Press, 1992. [AA 16, 24]

———. *Lectures on Metaphysics*, trans. and ed. Karl Ameriks and Steve Naragon. Cambridge: Cambridge University Press, 1997. [AA 28, 29]

———. *Metaphysical Foundations of Natural Science* [*Metaphysiche Anfangsgründe der Naturwissenschaft*], trans. Michael Friedman. In *Theoretical Philosophy after 1781*, ed. Henry Allison and Peter Heath, 181–270. Cambridge: Cambridge University Press, 2002. [AA 4, 465–566]

———. *Notes and Fragments*, trans. Curtis Bowman, Paul Guyer, and Frederick Rauscher, ed. Paul Guyer. Cambridge: Cambridge University Press, 2005. [AA 18]

———. *On the Form and Principles of the Sensible and Intelligible World* [*De Mundi sensibilis atque intelligibilis forma et principiis*]. In *Theoretical Philosophy, 1755–1770*, trans. and ed. David Walford and Ralf Meerbote, 373–416. Cambridge: Cambridge University Press, 1992. [AA 2, 385–419]

———. *Opus Postumum*, trans. Eckart Förster and Michael Rosen, ed. Eckart Förster. Cambridge: Cambridge University Press, 1993. [AA 21, 22]

———. *Prolegomena to Any Future Metaphysics* [*Prolegomena zu einer jeden künftigen Metaphysik*], trans. Gary Hatfield. In *Theoretical Philosophy after 1781*, ed. Henry

Allison and Peter Heath, 29–169. Cambridge: Cambridge University Press, 2002.
[AA 4, 253–384]

———. "What Does It Mean to Orient Oneself in Thinking? [Was heißt: sich im Denken orientieren?]," trans. Allen W. Wood. In *Religion and Rational Theology*, ed. Allen W. Wood and George di Giovanni, 7–18. Cambridge: Cambridge University Press, 2001. [AA 8, 131–47]

Kemp Smith, Norman. *A Commentary to Kant's Critique of Pure Reason*. New York: Macmillan, 1923.

Kerszberg, Pierre. *Critique and Totality*. Albany: State University of New York Press, 1997.

———. "Kant and the Idea of Negation." In *New Essays on the Precritical Kant*, ed. Tom Rockmore, 37–49. New York: Humanity, 2001.

———. *Kant et la Nature: La nature à l'épreuve de la critique*. Paris: Belles Lettres, 1999.

Kitcher, Patricia. "Kant's Paralogisms." In *Immanuel Kant: Critical Assessments*, ed. Ruth F. Chadwick and Clive Cazeaux. London: Routledge, 1992.

———. "Kant's Real Self." In *Self and Nature in Kant's Philosophy*, ed. Allen W. Wood, 113–47. Ithaca, NY: Cornell University Press, 1984.

———. *Kant's Transcendental Psychology*. New York: Oxford University Press, 1990.

Kleingeld, Pauline. "The Conative Character of Reason in Kant's Philosophy." *Journal of the History of Philosophy* 36 (1998): 77–97.

———. "Kant on the Unity of Theoretical and Practical Reason." *Review of Metaphysics* 52 (1998): 311–39.

Klemme, Heiner. *Kants Philosophie des Subjekts*. Hamburg: Meiner, 1996.

Krell, David Farrell. *Infectious Nietzsche*. Bloomington: Indiana University Press, 1996.

Lachièze-Rey, Pierre. *L'idéalisme Kantien*. Paris: Vrin, 1972.

Lebrun, Gérard. *Kant et la Fin de la Métaphysique*. Paris: Colin, 1970.

Leibniz, G. W. "Monadology." In *Leibniz: Discourse on Method/Correspondence with Arnauld/Monadology*, trans. George R. Montgomery. LaSalle, IL: Open Court, 1973.

Longuenesse, Béatrice. *Kant and the Capacity to Judge: Sensibility and Discursivity in the Transcendental Analytic of the Critique of Pure Reason* [*Kant et le pouvoir de juger: Sensibilité et discursivité dans l'Analytique transcendentale de la Critique de la raison pure*. Paris: Presses Universitaires de France, 1993], trans. Charles T. Wolfe. Princeton, NJ: Princeton University Press, 1998.

———. *Kant and the Human Standpoint*. Cambridge: Cambridge University Press, 2005.

———. "Point of View of Man or Knowledge of God: Kant and Hegel on Concept, Judgment and Reason." In *The Reception of Kant's Critical Philosophy: Fichte, Schelling and Hegel*, ed. Sally Sedgwick, 253–82. Cambridge: Cambridge University Press, 2000.

Makkreel, Rudolf A. *Imagination and Interpretation in Kant*. Chicago: University of Chicago Press, 1990.

———. "Regulative and Reflective Uses of Purposiveness in Kant." *Southern Journal of Philosophy* 30, Suppl. (1992): 49–63.

Martin, Gottfried. *Kant's Metaphysics and Theory of Science* [*Ontologie und Wissenschaftstheorie*. Köln: Kölner Universitätsverlag, 1951], trans. P. G. Lucas. Manchester, England: Manchester University Press, 1955.

McCumber, John. *The Company of Words: Hegel, Language and Systematic Philosophy*. Evanston, IL: Northwestern University Press, 1993.

Mendelssohn, Moses. *An die Freunde Lessings*. In *Gesammelte Schriften*, ed. Fritz Bamburger and Leo Strauss, vol. 3.2, 177–218. Stuttgart: Friedrich Fromann, 1972 [Berlin: Akademie, 1932].

————. *Dialogues* [*Gesammelte Schriften*, vol. 1, 335–377]. In *Philosophical Writings*, trans. and ed. Daniel O. Dahlstrom, 96–129. Cambridge, UK: Cambridge University Press, 1997.

————. *Morgenstunden oder Vorlesungen über das Daseyn Gottes.* In *Gesammelte Schriften*, vol. 3.2, 1–175.

————. *Phaedon oder über die Unsterblichkeit der Seele.* In *Gesammelte Schriften*, vol. 3.1, 7–159.

Mensch, Jennifer. "Between Sense and Thought: Synthesis in Kant's Transcendental Deduction." *Epoché* 10.1 (Fall 2005): 81–93.

Mertens, Helga. *Kommentar zur Ersten Einleitung in Kants Kritik der Urteilskraft.* Munich: Johannes Berchmans, 1975.

Neiman, Susan. *The Unity of Reason.* Oxford: Oxford University Press, 1994.

Nerlich, Graham. *The Shape of Space,* 2nd ed. Cambridge: Cambridge University Press, 1994.

Newton, Isaac. *Opticks.* New York: Dover, 1952 (based on the 4th ed., London: William Innys, 1730).

Nuzzo, Angelica. *Ideal Embodiment: Kant's Theory of Sensibility.* Bloomington: Indiana University Press, 2008.

————. *Kant and the Unity of Reason.* West Lafayette, IN: Purdue University Press, 2005.

————. "*Kritik der Urteilskraft* §§76–77: Reflective Judgment and the Limits of Transcendental Philosophy." *Kant Yearbook* 1 (2009): 143–72.

O'Neill, Onora. *Constructions of Reason: Explorations of Kant's Practical Philosophy.* Cambridge: Cambridge University Press, 1989.

————. "Vindicating Reason." In *The Cambridge Companion to Kant,* ed. Paul Guyer, 280–308. Cambridge: Cambridge University Press, 1992.

Philonenko, Alexis. *Études Kantiennes.* Paris: Vrin, 1962.

————. Introduction to *Qu'est-ce que s'orienter dans la pensée* [Was heißt: sich im Denken orientieren?] by Immanuel Kant, trans. Alexis Philonenko. Paris: Vrin, 1978.

Piché, Claude. *Das Ideal: Ein Problem der Kantischen Ideenlehre.* Bonn: Bouvier Verlag Herbert Grundmann, 1984.

————. "Self-Referentiality in Kant's Transcendental Philosophy." In *Proceedings of the Eighth International Kant Congress,* ed. Hoke Robinson, vol. 2.1:259–67. Milwaukee, WI: Marquette University Press, 1995.

Pillow, Kirk. *Sublime Understanding: Aesthetic Reflection in Kant and Hegel.* Cambridge, MA: MIT Press, 2000.

Pippin, Robert B. "Hegel's Phenomenological Criticism." *Man and World* 8.3 (1975): 296–314.

————. *Idealism as Modernism: Hegelian Variations.* Cambridge: Cambridge University Press, 1997.

————. *Kant's Theory of Form.* New Haven, CT: Yale University Press, 1982.

Powell, C. Thomas. "Kant's Fourth Paralogism." *Philosophy and Phenomenological Research* 48.3 (March 1985): 389–414.

Prauss, Gerold. *Erscheinung bei Kant: Ein Problem der "Kritik der reinen Vernunft."* Berlin: de Gruyter, 1971.

————. *Kant und das Problem der Dinge an sich.* Bonn: Bouvier Verlag Herbert Grundmann, 1974.

Rescher, Nicholas. *Kant and the Reach of Reason: Studies in Kant's Theory of Rational Systemization.* Cambridge: Cambridge University Press, 2000.

Robinson, Lewis. "Contributions à l'histoire de l'évolution philosophique." *Revue de Metaphysique et de Morale* 31 (1924): 269–353.

Rorty, Richard. "Transcendental Arguments, Self-Reference, and Pragmatism." In *Transcendental Arguments and Science,* ed. Peter Bieri, Rolf-Peter Horstmann, and Lorenz Krüger, 77–103. Dordrecht, the Netherlands: Reidel, 1979.

Rottenberg, Elizabeth. *Inheriting the Future: Legacies of Kant, Freud, and Flaubert.* Stanford, CA: Stanford University Press, 2005.

Rousset, Bernard. *La Doctrine Kantienne de l'objectivité, l'autonomie comme devoir et devenir.* Paris: Vrin, 1967.

Sallis, John. *The Gathering of Reason,* 2nd ed. Albany: State University of New York Press, 2005.

———. *Spacings—of Reason and Imagination: In Texts of Kant, Fichte, Hegel.* Chicago: University of Chicago Press, 1987.

Schelling, F. W. J. "Of the I as the Principle of Philosophy; or, On the Unconditioned in Human Knowledge [Vom Ich als Princip der Philosophie oder Über das Unbedingte im menschlichen Wissen. In *Werke,* ed. Hartmut Buchner, Jörg Jantzen, Adolph Schurr, and Anna-Maria Scurr-Lorusso, vol. 2. Stuttgart: Fromann-Holzboog, 1980]. In *The Unconditional in Human Knowledge: Four Early Essays 1794–1796,* trans. Fritz Marti, 63–149. Lewisburg, PA: Bucknell University Press, 1980.

Seebohm, Thomas. "Das Widerspruchsprinzip in der Kantischen Logic und der Hegelschen Dialektik." In *Akten des 4. Internationalen Kant Kongresses,* ed. G. Funke and J. Kopper, 862–74. Berlin: de Gruyter, 1974.

Sellars, Wilfrid. "Metaphysics and the Concept of a Person." In his *Essays in Philosophy and Its History,* 214–43. Dordrecht, the Netherlands: Reidel, 1974.

Sherover, Charles. *Heidegger, Kant and Time.* Bloomington: Indiana University Press, 1971.

Smit, Houston. "The Role of Reflection in Kant's *Critique of Pure Reason.*" *Pacific Philosophical Quarterly* 80.2 (1999): 203–23.

Souriau, Michel. *Le jugement réfléchissant dans la philosophie critique de Kant.* Paris: Alcan, 1926.

Spinoza, Baruch. *Ethics,* trans. Samuel Shirley. Indianapolis, IN: Hackett, 1992.

Strawson, Peter. *The Bounds of Sense.* London: Methuen, 1966.

Stroud, Barry. "The Significance of Scepticism." In *Transcendental Arguments and Science,* ed. Peter Bieri, Rolf-Peter Horstmann, and Lorenz Krüger, 277–97. Dordrecht, the Netherlands: Reidel, 1979.

Sturma, Dieter. *Kant über Selbstbewußtsein: Zum Zusammenhang von Erkenntniskritik und Theorie des Selbstbewußtseins.* Zurich: Georg Olms, 1985.

———. "Die Paralogismen der reinen Vernunft in der zweiten Auflage." In *Kritik der reinen Vernunft,* ed. Georg Mohr and Marcus Willaschek, 391–411. Berlin: Akademie, 1998.

Swain, Charles W. "Hamann and the Philosophy of David Hume." *Journal of the History of Philosophy* 5 (1967): 343–51.

Tuschling, Burkhard. "Intuitiver Verstand, absolute Identität, Idee: Thesen zu Hegels früher Rezeption der Kritik der Urteilskraft." In *Hegel und die "Kritik der Urteilskraft,"* ed. Hans-Friederich Fulda and Rolf-Peter Horstmann, 174–88. Stuttgart: Klett-Cotta, 1990.

———. "The System of Transcendental Idealism: Questions Raised and Left Open in the *Kritik der Urteilskraft.*" *Southern Journal of Philosophy* 30, Suppl. (1992): 109–27.

Vallenilla, Ernesto Mayz. *Le problème du Néant chez Kant,* trans. Jeanine Sartor. Paris: L'Harmattan, 2000.

Walsh, W. H. "Kant and Empiricism." In *200 Jahre Kritik der reinen Vernunft,* ed. Joachim Kopper and Wolfgang Marx, 385–420. Hildesheim: Gerstenberg, 1981.

———. "Kant and Metaphysics." *Kant-Studien* 67.3 (1976): 372–84.

———. *Kant's Criticism of Metaphysics.* Edinburgh: Edinburgh University Press, 1975.

———. "Philosophy and Psychology in Kant's *Critique.*" *Kant-Studien* 57 (1966): 186–98.

Warda, Arthur. *Immanuel Kants Bücher.* Berlin: Breslauer, 1922.

Waxman, Wayne. *Kant's Model of the Mind: A New Interpretation.* New York: Oxford University Press, 1991.

Weldon, T. D. *Kant's "Critique of Pure Reason."* Oxford: Clarendon, 1958.

Westphal, Kenneth R. *Kant's Transcendental Proof of Realism.* Cambridge: Cambridge University Press, 2004.

Wilson, Margaret Dauler. *Ideas and Mechanism: Essays on Early Modern Philosophy.* Princeton, NJ: Princeton University Press, 1999.

Winterbourne, A. T. *The Ideal and the Real.* Dordrecht, the Netherlands: Kluwer Academic, 1988.

Wizenmann, Thomas. *Die Resultate der Jacobischen und Mendelssohnschen Philosophie.* Hildesheim: Gerstenberg, 1984.

Woelert, Peter. "Kant's Hands, Spatial Orientation, and the Copernican Turn." *Continental Philosophy Review* 40 (2007): 139–50.

Yovel, Yirmiahu. *Kant and the Philosophy of History.* Princeton, NJ: Princeton University Press, 1980.

INDEX

focus imaginarius, 115, 130, 164, 180–84, 227n43, 233n93, 234n98, 234n103
Förster, Eckart, 207n41, 231n66
Foucault, Michel, 232n78
freedom: of the Ancient skeptics, 120, 121; *Critique of Practical Reason*, 53, 227n41; Pantheism contra, 158, 159, 224; regulative principle of, 50, 52, 231n59; third antinomy, 5, 30, 31, 37, 41–43, 51, 87, 163–65, 182, 189n27, 194n52, 196n9, 197n21, 215n63 (*see also* mechanism); of thought, 227n40
Friedman, Michael, 230n53

Gasché, Rodolph, 215n58
Gochnauer, Myron, 208n53
Grier, Michelle, 220n22, 230n56, 234n103
Guyer, Paul, 200n52, 201n2, 220n52, 228n51

Hamann, Johann Georg, 4, 8, 11, 22–26, 30, 36, 54, 59–61, 72, 73, 114–16, 120, 122, 193n29, 193n35, 193n38, 193n40, 217n91. *See also* metacritique
Hatfield, Gary, 187n3, 202n4, 203n13, 232n79
Hegel, G. W. F.: aesthetic judgment, 216n88; interpretation of Kant, 21, 73, 116–23, 127, 178, 192n26, 228n75; *Phenomenology of Spirit* [*Phänomenologie des Geistes*], 60, 61, 210n16
Heidegger, Martin, 6, 7, 11, 101, 104, 108, 111, 178, 193n40, 209n53; *Being and Time* [*Sein und Zeit*], 161, 190n15, 213n37; circularity, 2, 205n32 (*see also* circle, circular, circularity); *Kant and the Problem of Metaphysics* [*Kant und das Problem der Metaphysik*], 102, 103, 177, 187n6, 188n20, 214n45, 214n55, 233n89; "Kant's Thesis About Being [*Kants These über das Sein*]," 8, 85, 87–89, 99, 100, 106, 107, 196n11, 209n9, 213n26, 215n65, 224n53; *On Time and Being* ["Zeit und Sein"], 233n83; *What is a Thing?* [*Die Frage nach dem Ding*], 6, 66, 71, 192n27
Heidemann, Dietmar Hermann, 208n51

Heimsoeth, Heinz, 187n10, 218n3, 222n36
Henrich, Dieter, 188n20, 190n10, 211n19, 214n43, 214n46, 227n44, 233n89
Herder, Johann Gottfried, 25, 193n29, 193n30, 193n33, 216n72. *See also* metacritique
Horstmann, Rolf-Peter, 220n26, 228n49, 228n51, 229n52
Hume, David: awakening Kant, 29, 30, 194n5; causality, 13, 47, 149; complex ideas, 127, 194n50; self-identity, 14, 135, 189n5, 189n7, 211n21; skepticism, 58, 59, 93, 98, 99

idea. *See* cosmology; ideal, theological idea; psychology
ideal: opposed to real, 27; theological idea, 45–47, 50, 56, 110, 118–20, 167, 168, 199n33, 203n10, 227n41, 227n46, 228n51. *See also* purposiveness [*Zweckmäßigkeit*], regulative principle [*Prinzip*]; theology
imagination, 13, 16, 89, 181–83, 209n53, 234n99, 234n100, 234n102; transcendental, 7, 102–104, 117–21, 124, 187n6, 188n20, 214n45, 214n55, 233n89 (*see also* schematism). See also *focus imaginarius*
immortality, 42, 43, 137, 145, 155, 165, 219n17, 221n31, 227n41, 231n57, 231n59, 234n97
incongruence, 161, 226n28; incongruent counterparts, 161, 202n5, 226n24. See *also* orientation
intellectus archetypus, 50
intellectus ectypus, 49
intuition [*Anschauung*], 65, 75, 222n39; Axioms of, 64; sensible, 17, 29, 90, 92, 93, 109, 118, 130, 134, 135, 137, 142, 181, 182, 190n14, 206n34, 207n46, 218n4, 219n19, 222n38, 226n22; faculty of, 206n34; forms of, 8, 39, 74, 91, 214n45; intellectual (nonsensible), 14, 31, 49, 50, 55, 72, 78, 200n46, 208n50, 216n88, 217n88; spatial (outer), 68, 138, 146; temporal (inner), 15, 83, 141

Jacobi, Friedrich Heinrich, 158–60, 188n27, 193n30, 224n3, 224n7, 227n40

Kerszberg, Pierre, 192n27, 200n42, 204n17, 205n27, 213n28, 234n104
Kitcher, Patricia, 187n2, 190n17, 192n20, 220n20, 239n79
Kleingeld, Pauline, 187n10, 205n27, 230n56
Klemme, Heiner, 189n9
Krell, David Farrell, 209n54

Lachièze-Rey, Pierre, 206n38
Leibniz, G. W., 29, 58, 59, 95, 161, 202n5, 213n29, 221n29
limit [*Schranke*], 30, 41, 50, 56, 59, 66, 70, 117, 118, 127, 132, 162, 174, 221n31, 231n62; as opposed to boundary, 28, 78, 200n47
Longuenesse, Béatrice, 212n23, 216n88, 217n92, 227n46

Makkreel, Rudolf, 192n24, 199n32, 214n43, 228n51
Martin, Gottfried, 191n22
McCumber, John, 217n89, 217n91
mechanism: contra both freedom and teleology, 54; contra freedom, the third antinomy, 5, 30, 40, 51, 52, 56, 57, 165, 192n25, 215n63; contra teleology, the antinomy of teleological judgment, 47–49, 58, 168, 200n43, 200n53, 203n10; Schelling, on the unity of teleology and, 86. *See also* antinomy, cosmological, third; cosmology
Mendelssohn, Moses: immortality of the soul, 221n31; pantheism controversy, 158–60, 188n27, 224n3, 225n8, 225n10, 225n14, 225n16, 225n21
Mensch, Jennifer, 214n49
Mertens, Helga, 198n28, 215n60, 229n51, 229n53
metacritique, 22, 210n13, 217n92; Hamann, 5, 8, 22–26, 54, 59–62, 72, 73, 84, 114, 115, 120, 193n30; Hamann and Herder, 193n29, 193n33

necessity [*Notwendigkeit*], 86, 93, 95, 100, 103, 109, 114, 116, 121, 137, 140, 151, 185; causal, 13; contra freedom, 194n52; postulate of, 53, 54, 64, 66, 69, 70, 73, 88, 138; unconditioned, 51. *See also* actuality [*Wirklichkeit*]; principle [*Grundsatz*]
Nerlich, Graham, 226n28
Newton, Isaac, 161, 192, 216n70, 234n103
noumena, noumenon, 1, 49, 50, 77–79, 89, 90, 99, 141, 207n47, 210n13; boundary between phenomena and, 30, 35, 36, 89, 94, 95, 150, 184, 200n49, 208n50, 210n14; On the Basis of the Distinction of All Objects [*Gegenstände*] as Such into *Phenomena* and *Noumena*, 49, 56, 78, 112, 207n48. *See also* thing in itself [*Ding an sich*], things in themselves [*Dingen an sich*]; transcendental object [*objekt/ Gegenstand*]
Nuzzo, Angelica, 197n21, 226n24, 234n98

O'Neill, Onora, 201n60, 226n30
orientation: of critique, 10, 19, 20, 21, 81, 94, 108, 125, 133, 138, 153; in space, 101, 161, 190n15, 202n5; in thought, 158, 162, 163; "What Does It Mean to Orient Oneself in Thinking? [Was heißt: sich im Denken orientieren?]," 9, 160. *See also* incongruence, incongruent counterparts

phenomena, phenomenon, 1, 12, 27, 50, 56, 74, 90, 91, 99, 141, 150, 151, 206n38, 210n13, 232n74; boundary between noumena and, 30, 35, 36, 59, 89, 94, 95, 150, 184, 200n49, 208n50, 210n14; On the Basis of the Distinction of All Objects [*Gegenstände*] as Such into *Phenomena* and *Noumena*, 49, 56, 78, 112, 207n48
Philonenko, Alexis, 210n16
physiology, 32–34, 175–77, 189n4, 195n59, 195n61, 232n76, 232n78. *See also* psychology; soul; subject
Piché, Claude, 192n27, 205n27, 220n24, 231n60

Pillow, Kirk, 211n19
Pippin, Robert, 203n6, 210n13, 217n94
Powell, C. Thomas, 223n48
Prauss, Gerold, 202n3, 203n7, 210n15, 212n22
principle [*Grundsatz*], 71, 180, 196n14; causal, 69; modal, 2, 64, 68, 70, 204n23 (*see also* actuality [*Wirklichkeit*]; necessity [*Notwendigkeit*]); substantial, 77, 222n37
psychology: empirical, 12, 32, 117, 137, 168, 173, 189n3, 189n4, 230n56; psychological idea, 3–5, 8–11, 19–21, 33, 38, 41–43, 47, 50, 56, 110, 111, 131, 133, 152, 153, 155–58, 163, 164, 167–77, 180, 183–85, 187n8, 187n10, 197n21, 214n43, 230n56, 230n57, 231n62, 232n67, 233n89; rational, 2, 3, 9, 10, 19, 21, 32, 33, 42, 80, 91, 126, 127, 129, 131–34, 136, 137–41, 143, 145, 149, 153–57, 161, 163, 167, 171, 176, 177, 191n21, 219n17, 220n24, 230n57, 231n59, 232n78; as regulative principle, 3–11, 20, 33, 42, 50, 110, 111, 127, 128, 133, 138, 152, 154–58, 168–76, 180, 184–86, 217n94; transcendental, 177, 190n17, 232n79. *See also* soul, regulative principle
purposiveness [*Zweckmäßigkeit*], regulative principle [*Prinzip*], 5, 19, 41, 45, 48, 49, 110, 119, 166, 167, 188n15, 191n24, 197n21, 198n31, 198n32, 228n51. *See also* ideal; reflection, aesthetic; reflection, teleological; theology, regulative principle [*Prinzip*]

reflection, 29, 45, 109, 118, 172, 183, 184, 198n28, 198n32, 211n19, 212n23, 212n24, 215n61, 217n88, 219n13; aesthetic, 109, 110; Amphiboly of the Concepts of Reflection, 28, 85, 89, 106, 107, 136; concepts of, 94–99, 213n28, 227n46; logical, 93, 94, 212n23, 215n58; philosophical, 21, 27, 28, 73, 169, 172, 177–79, 210n13; self-, 203n11; teleological, 45, 46, 110; transcendental, 7–11, 28, 29, 33, 85, 87, 88–94, 96–102, 104–11, 113–15, 121, 122, 124, 127, 129, 150, 152, 153, 155,

171–74, 184, 185, 194n48, 198n28, 209n12, 210n13, 210n15, 211n18, 211n19, 212n22, 213n28, 215n60, 215n65, 216n70, 217n88, 224n53. *See also* purposiveness [*Zweckmäßigkeit*], regulative principle [*Prinzip*]; teleology; theology
refutation: Hume of knowledge, 29; Kant of Mendelssohn, 221n31; Refutation of Idealism (Refutation), 7, 10, 73, 74–79, 80–85, 136, 148, 152, 174, 175, 206n38, 206n39, 207n41, 207n42, 207n45, 208n53, 220n23, 222n34, 222n42, 223n45, 231n66, 232n67
Renault, Alain, 231n62
representation [*Vorstellung*], 7, 10, 15, 27, 42, 44, 45, 47, 53, 55, 75–77, 79, 80, 82, 84, 90, 96, 109, 135, 139, 171, 182, 190n16, 198n28, 200n46, 213n29, 215n59, 223n45; intellectual, 135, 207n47, 208n50; self, 14, 140
Rescher, Nicholas, 230n53
Rorty, Richard, 201n2, 205n27, 209n53
Rottenberg, Elizabeth, 227n37
Rousset, Bernard, 192n24, 206n39, 229n51, 229n53

Sallis, John, 196n14, 209n54, 210n14, 218n7, 219n19, 223n44, 234n100
Schelling, F. W. J., 38, 85–87
schematism, 103; Transcendental Schematism, 103, 118, 214n45. *See also* imagination, transcendental
sensibility [*sinnlichkeit*]: faculty of, 1, 4, 5, 6, 16, 22–24, 26, 30, 36, 41, 50, 53–58, 61, 62, 78, 83, 89, 90, 102, 103, 111, 114–16, 118–21, 126, 129, 130, 136, 161, 165, 173, 179, 200n47, 200n48, 202n5, 211n18, 213n29, 217n88, 233n86, 233n89; pure forms of, 22, 23, 47, 67, 70, 72, 92, 99, 218n4; spatial, 112, 202n5; temporal, 15
soul: function of the, 102–104, 233n89; Hegel's beautiful, 120, 217n89, 223n50, 230n56; object of inner sense, 32, 137, 154; object of rational psychology, 3, 14, 21, 33, 42, 88, 91, 132, 133, 134, 136–47, 153, 155, 165,

181, 182, 195n58, 214n43, 219n17,
220n20, 220n27, 221n29, 221n30,
221n31, 222n34, 230n57; physiology of the, 177, 195n61; regulative
principle, 3, 5, 6, 10, 20, 34, 155,
163, 169–71, 173, 174, 184, 193n28,
231n59; self-identity, 194n50. *See also*
physiology; psychology; subject
Souriau, Michel, 229n51
space: *a priori* form of, 1, 15, 23, 27, 47,
67, 74, 75, 97, 190n12, 206n40, 218n4;
absolute, 161; appearances in, 10, 17,
110, 131, 138, 151, 154, 169, 170, 172,
174, 193n44 (*see also* Newton, Isaac);
orientation in, 160, 162, 226n28,
226n30 (*see also* orientation, in space);
thing in itself in relation to, 200n48.
See also time
Spinoza, Baruch, 98, 158, 159, 224n3
Strawson, Peter, 218n11
Stroud, Barry, 201n2
Sturma, Dieter, 191n19, 192n27
subject: empirical, 145, 147, 188n10;
finite I, 86, 220n28; I of apperception,
2, 9, 15–17, 76, 80, 103, 117, 133–37,
139, 140, 141, 143–47, 190n17,
191n19, 220n19, 220n26, 222n38;
transcendental, 2, 3, 17, 20, 140–46,
151, 152, 179, 188n10, 191n22,
205n27, 221n29, 221n31. *See also*
physiology; psychology; soul

teleology, 18, 19, 35, 40, 43–45, 47–49,
54, 58, 86, 127, 129, 168, 172, 203n10,
217n94, 228n51. *See also* antinomy,
of teleological judgment; reflection,
teleological; theology, regulative principle [*Prinzip*]
theology, 159; regulative principle
[*Prinzip*], 5, 18, 19, 38, 41, 42, 44, 47,
48, 50, 53, 78, 110, 119, 129, 133, 163,
165, 168, 171, 182, 187n8, 191n24,
197n21, 199n33, 200n53, 227n42,
234n101; theological idea, 78, 132,
182, 191n23 (*see also* ideal; noumena,

noumenon). *See also* purposiveness
[*Zweckmäßigkeit*], regulative principle
[*Prinzip*]; reflection, aesthetic; reflection, teleological
thing in itself [*Ding an sich*], things in
themselves [*Dingen an sich*], 1, 6, 13,
50, 56, 92, 95, 97, 102, 150, 187n2,
190n16, 200n48, 201n3, 207n48. *See
also* noumena, noumenon
time, 7, 12, 66, 82, 95, 103, 122, 124, 125,
127, 146, 148, 158, 175, 176, 178, 180,
181, 189n9, 190n12, 194n56, 200n46,
209n1; *a priori* form of, 1, 15, 23, 47,
67, 75, 97, 190n17, 206n40, 218n4;
appearances in, 74, 76, 77, 222n36;
Being and Time, 100–102, 105, 108,
161, 190n15, 205n32, 209n53, 213n31,
213n34, 213n37, 213n38, 214n56,
226n27; consciousness of oneself in,
80, 81, 208n53, 224n50; thing in itself
in relation to, 200n48. *See also* space
transcendental apperception, 141, 144,
145; first edition, 204n22; second
edition, 14, 15, 68, 103, 222n35;
transcendental deduction, 162, 165;
Transcendental Deduction, 2, 66, 109,
124, 125, 135, 136, 145, 147, 203n11,
211n19, 214n45, 234n99
transcendental object [*object/Gegenstand*],
77, 78, 79, 136, 138, 207n47, 207n49
Tuschling, Burkhard, 229n51

Vallenilla, Ernesto Mayz, 213n28

Walsh, W. H., 118n17, 192n26, 201n2,
202n5
Warda, Arthur, 234n103
Waxman, Wayne, 187n2, 190n16
Weldon, T. D., 219n13
Westphal, Kenneth, 201n3, 204n21,
211n18, 231n58
Wilson, Margaret Dauler, 221n29
Wizenmann, Thomas, 225n17, 225n18
Woelert, Peter, 226n24
Wood, Allen, 200n52, 220n21

AVERY GOLDMAN is Associate Professor of Philosophy at DePaul University.